I0644829

HOW MANY ROADS

HOW MANY ROADS

A Life of Bob Dylan

Scott Peeples

REAKTION BOOKS

In memory of Randy, Faith, and Meghan

Published by
REAKTION BOOKS LTD
2–4 Sebastian Street
London EC1V 0HE, UK

www.reaktionbooks.co.uk

First published 2026
Copyright © Scott Peeples 2026

All rights reserved

EU GPSR Authorised Representative
Logos Europe, 9 rue Nicolas Poussin, 17000, La Rochelle, France
email: contact@logoseurope.eu

No part of this publication may be reproduced, stored in a retrieval system or transmitted, in any form or by any means, electronic, mechanical, photocopying, recording or otherwise, without the prior permission of the publishers. No part of this publication may be used or reproduced in any manner for the purpose of training artificial intelligence technologies or systems.

Printed and bound in Great Britain by Bell & Bain, Glasgow

A catalogue record for this book is available from the British Library

ISBN 978 1 83639 259 0

CONTENTS

I've always been just about being an individual, with an individual point of view. If I've been anything, it's probably that, and to let people know that it's possible to do the impossible.

Bob Dylan, 1986[1]

Prologue: Mythmaking

On Christmas Day 2024 James Mangold's film *A Complete Unknown* opened in theaters across the USA. The film had been announced almost five years earlier, but COVID-19, an industry-wide actors' strike, casting changes, and other delays made for a long production cycle—and years of rumor and anticipation. Adding to the hype was the prospect of seeing the popular and charismatic Timothée Chalamet in the role of a young Bob Dylan.

Unlike most biopics, *A Complete Unknown* dramatizes a relatively short period in the subject's life, the four years from Dylan's arrival in New York in 1961 to his epochal Newport 1965 performance. Even with that relatively compressed time frame, the complex events and extensive cast of real-life characters required a lot of streamlining and a little fictionalizing for the sake of the narrative. Most conspicuously Sara Lownds, with whom Dylan was in love throughout 1965 and who would marry him before the year's end, doesn't appear at all, but Sylvie Russo (the renamed Suze Rotolo), who in real life had broken up with Dylan long before he "went electric," hangs on right up to Newport '65 as a romantic rival to Joan Baez.

Early 1960s Greenwich Village is beautifully recreated, but Dylan seems to simply glide through it rather than become part of a community of artists and performers who, in fact, nurtured and influenced him. There's a Folklore Center but no Izzy Young, no Ramblin' Jack Elliott, and while Dave Van Ronk appears briefly his substantial role in Dylan's development is subsumed by Pete Seeger (portrayed with uncanny precision by Edward Norton). The experiences that changed

Dylan, his songwriting, and his performance style are similarly hard to find. There's no cross-country road trip with Paul Clayton and Victor Maymudes (no Maymudes, in fact); no Greenwood, Mississippi voter registration drive; no Ed Sullivan Show walk-out over network censorship; no meeting the Beatles, only a brief mention of the chaotic 1965 English tour . . . Of course to include all those friends and influences, all of those episodes, would overwhelm a two-hour-and-twenty-minute film. To his credit Mangold focuses instead on the music itself, allowing Chalamet and other actors to perform the songs that made us care about Dylan in the first place.

The film also succeeds in capturing what made the Newport performance such a big deal. The filmmakers credit Elijah Wald's book *Dylan Goes Electric!* as their source, and, while most of the facts represented in the film are well established by multiple memoirs and biographies, Wald's analysis of the events surrounding the 1965 Newport Folk Festival gives the film its thematic structure. Wald argues persuasively that Dylan's individualism represented a break from the political folk movement's emphasis on collectivism, represented by Seeger. *A Complete Unknown* dramatizes this thematic conflict by inflating Seeger's personal, direct influence on Dylan—having them meet, symbolically, in Woody Guthrie's hospital room; having Seeger introduce Dylan to his own audience; and later having him deliver a sermon to Dylan at Newport on why he shouldn't do what he's about to do. Seeger thus becomes a composite character embodying folk music tradition, pitted against youthful rock culture, and a father figure at odds with a rebellious son.

A Complete Unknown received mostly favorable reviews and did well at the box office, bringing in over $140 million worldwide. It was nominated for eight Academy Awards, and Chalamet won a Screen Actors Guild award for "Outstanding Performance by a Male Actor in a Leading Role in a Motion Picture" for his performance. Given its success, the film will probably shape the public perception of Dylan for a generation at least. It succeeded largely because it was made by people who know the facts as well as the lore and who know Dylan himself: Jay Cocks, who as a student journalist interviewed Dylan at Kenyon College in 1964, co-wrote the script with Mangold, who shared it with Dylan and received his input and approval. Jeff Rosen, Dylan's manager, co-produced the film.

Because it focuses on Dylan's rise to fame and his transition to electric music, *A Complete Unknown* reinforces the broad public image of Dylan as a figure frozen in that early-to-mid-1960s period, those four or five years towering in significance over the 58 years of recordings and performances that followed. I couldn't help privileging that same period in this book, spending four of my fourteen chapters on those same years, with a fifth devoted to 1966, the year of *Blonde on Blonde* and the calamitous European tour. After all, it was the period when Dylan first disrupted the musical and cultural landscape and when his career, and the world around it, changed most quickly and most radically.

And yet, as I hope this book will show, Dylan was determined not to remain stuck in the 1960s or to allow audiences to get comfortable with that countercultural "voice of a generation" image. The most casual fan would recognize a long list of indelible songs Dylan wrote and recorded after 1966—even in his supposed career slump of the late 1960s and early '70s he delivered "I Shall Be Released," "All Along the Watchtower," "Lay Lady Lay," "If Not for You," and "Knockin' on Heaven's Door," to name a few. Then there are the thousands of live performances in which he has constantly reinvented his setlists, his bands, his voice, his demeanor, and his arrangements. Dylan has acted in, written, and directed films; authored books; and branched out into painting and sculpture. And of course in 2016, half a century after going electric, he received the Nobel Prize in Literature.

It's hard to think of any performer in any genre who has had as long a career as Dylan, much less one that has exhibited such constant change and reinvention. When his record company organized an all-star tribute in 1992, marking his thirty years as a recording artist, it might have been the celebration of an artist whose work was done. But Dylan's career wasn't even at its halfway point. What's more, his mid- to late-period work—primarily as a musician and songwriter but also as an author and visual artist—is no less vital or interesting than the music celebrated in *A Complete Unknown*.

This book is an introduction to Dylan's life and career, to his music, and to the musical environments he responded to and, occasionally, transformed. His refusal to be identified with genres or larger trends stems from Dylan's unrelenting insistence on artistic freedom, which would be compromised if he acknowledged being part of any movement. While Dylan has always been in conversation (literally and musically) with his contemporaries, he genuinely has defied generic expectations throughout his career. He was not just a folk singer who didn't want to be called a folk singer. He *was* different from other performers who accepted that label—he wrote his own material, and his devotion to rock and roll undercut the studious earnestness that limited so many of his contemporaries. Similarly when he was associated with folk-rock he was really playing something more like Chicago blues with postmodern lyrics. And the experimental, fractured narratives and love songs of *Blood on the Tracks* and *Desire* didn't come across quite like those of confessional singer-songwriters, even though he virtually created that category. It's not just that he didn't like labels—the labels never really fit what he was doing.

If Dylan is too original and too mercurial to be labelled, it's not because unique, fully formed songs spontaneously generate in his head. The archive of notebooks, typescripts, and scribbled-on hotel stationery (housed at the Bob Dylan Center in Tulsa, Oklahoma) demonstrates how constantly Dylan worked on and revised his lyrics. Moreover he has repeatedly emphasized how much traditional music he heard and played when he was coming up, but he clearly didn't stop with traditional music and just as clearly never stopped listening, borrowing, and combining.

Throughout the *Rough and Rowdy Ways* tour of the past few years, the first song Dylan would perform from that album each night was "I Contain Multitudes," reciting his Whitmanesque lyrics with surprising emotion—for me it was the selection that was most transformed from disc to stage. Edgar Allan Poe, the Rolling Stones, William Blake, Beethoven, and Chopin are all part of him, he would tell us. Indeed Dylan has spent the past quarter-century crafting new art out of old parts, becoming a true container of multitudes. You can hear that approach on all his twenty-first-century albums, which reassemble past musical traditions in unpredictable ways. But it's been there all along, in Dylan's amalgam of country, blues, folk, rockabilly, pop, rock, and gospel.

The keys to understanding Dylan's art might be a couple of twenty-first-century side projects: the eclectic satellite radio show *Theme Time Radio Hour* and his 2022 book *The Philosophy of Modern Song*. Both point away from Bob Dylan toward the vast body of recorded music that has inspired him. Both provide rich suggestions for further listening, which we all need, while enriching our appreciation for Dylan's ability to fuse these earlier styles, these sounds, and make them his own. His originality springs from his own encyclopedic appreciation, his loving theft of the full range of popular music. What he began doing in the early 1960s is what he has continued to do into the mid-2020s: putting it all together, bringing it all back home.

1

1941–60: Origins

When Bob Dylan performed at New York's Town Hall on April 12, 1963, audience members received a program consisting of a two-page free verse poem, "My Life in a Stolen Moment." Dylan's reputation was growing rapidly, largely on the strength of Peter, Paul and Mary's hit version of "Blowin' in the Wind," but he had not yet released his breakthrough second album, *The Freewheelin' Bob Dylan*, so the world outside Greenwich Village was just beginning to get acquainted with the up-and-coming songwriter. A biographical poem seemed like a perfect introduction. In a voice borrowed from Huck Finn and Woody Guthrie, he tells his audience that he was born in Duluth but grew up in Hibbing, Minnesota:

> You can stand at one end of Hibbing's main drag
> an' see clear past the city limits on the other end
> Hibbing's a good ol' town
> I ran away from it when I was 10, 12, 13, 15, 15½, 17 an' 18
> I been caught an' brought back all but once

The rest of "My Life" is similarly playful. After he "sat in college at the University of Minnesota/ on a phony scholarship that I never had," Dylan traveled the country, passing through Galveston, Texas; the entire West Coast; Gallup, New Mexico; New Orleans and Shreveport, Louisiana; and Madison, Wisconsin before landing on MacDougal Street in the Village. But he soon hit the road again, "thumbed west and took the wrong road to Florida," and then to South Dakota, Cincinnati, Sioux Falls, Kansas, Iowa, and Minnesota before returning to New York, where "I got recorded by Columbia after being wrote up in the Times."

Like *Chronicles, Volume One*, the memoir Dylan would publish four decades later, "My Life in a Stolen Moment" is a captivating, lyrical sketch—captivating largely because so much of it isn't true. Dylan's actual travels up to that point did include the University of Minnesota and Madison, Wisconsin, as well as Chicago and Denver (neither mentioned in "My Life"). But he had not really run away, had not traveled half as widely as he claimed, nor had he "Got jailed for suspicion of armed robbery" or "Got busted for lookin' like I do."[1]

In retrospect, the fabrications of "My Life in a Stolen Moment" seem pretty obvious, and even in 1963 much of the audience would have appreciated the poetic license Dylan was taking. And yet . . . in 1963, if you didn't know Bob Dylan personally, how would you know which details, if any, belonged to the self-created tall-tale figure but not to Dylan's actual lived experience? Those who did spend time with Dylan in those days knew better than to believe everything he told them, especially about his own past. Since arriving in New York he had been spinning easily unraveled yarns about running away, traveling the Southwest, and meeting famous people. Dave Van Ronk, whose stature in the Greenwich Village folk scene earned him the title "Mayor of MacDougal Street," recalled that "when we found out that a lot of his stories were bullshit, that didn't really lower his stock all that much. It was an old showbiz tradition—all performers changed their names and invented stories about themselves. So we kidded him some, but nobody held it against him." But he adds, somewhat sadly, "I don't think Bobby ever understood that. He never really got the fact that nobody cared who you had been before you hit town."[2]

The boyhood that Dylan preferred not to talk or write about was nothing shameful, just not the romantic life of a runaway hobo folk singer. For the most part, his was a typical early-boomer upbringing. The Minnesota origins he invokes in "My Life" were bona fide: born Robert Allen Zimmerman in Duluth on May 24, 1941, he had moved with his family to Hibbing at the age of six. His father, Abram, was stricken with polio in 1946 and lost his job with Standard Oil, prompting the move 75 miles (120 km) northwest, to Minnesota's Iron Range. Hibbing was the hometown of Robert's mother, Beatty, and the home of Abram's two older brothers, who took him on at the appliance store they had recently opened. Abram and Beatty recovered from the setback that had uprooted them and made a good, comfortable life in Hibbing for Robert and his little brother David, who was born around the time of the move.

After living with Beatty's mother upon their arrival in Hibbing, the family moved to their own house at 2425 7th Avenue in 1948, where they stayed throughout Robert's teenage years. Beatty Zimmerman was warm and outgoing, while Abe was reserved and somewhat distant. Robert had a more affectionate relationship with his mother, but his father was indulgent enough that at age sixteen the young man had his own motorcycle *and* his own car—a Ford convertible, no less. The Zimmermans were solidly middle class, but Hibbing itself was the epitome of working-class Minnesota, a small, frigid town that owed its existence to the mining industry and had a history of brutal battles between labor and management. Dylan no doubt learned this history, which he would commemorate with the bleak ballad "North Country Blues," recorded a few months after the Town Hall concert. Voiced by the wife of an unemployed miner, the song describes the despair of a town that was losing jobs to cheap South American labor, their fate sealed by East Coast businessmen. In the last verse the woman recognizes that her sons will leave home as soon as they can.

The boy who would become Bob Dylan certainly saw no future for himself in Hibbing. "Mostly what I did growing up," he later said, "was bide my time."[3] Another resident of the area told early Dylan biographer Anthony Scaduto, "It's astounding that Bob came out of a non-thinking area, and that's exactly what it is—narrow-minded, everyone conforming to the same point of view, the kids expected to think like their parents and be their parents. Not much was expected of you, except to make enough to live on and raise a family and be like everyone else."[4]

The Zimmermans were part of a small Jewish community—perhaps fifty families—in Hibbing.[5] Dylan later recalled that "there weren't too many Jews in Hibbing, Minnesota. Most of them I was related to."[6] His parents were active in the community, Beatty serving as president of their synagogue's Council of Jewish Women chapter and Abe leading the Louis Stein Lodge 793 of B'nai B'rith.[7] Bob celebrated his bar mitzvah in 1954, his parents feting him with a party for four hundred guests, many of them relatives from Duluth.[8] Throughout his teens Robert spent parts of his summers at Herzl Camp, a Jewish summer camp in northern Wisconsin. His generation of American Jews grew up in the shadow not only of the Holocaust but of a long history of American antisemitism. Yet at the same time the war and the Holocaust were a kind of turning point: blatant antisemitism became socially unacceptable among middle-class WASPs, and Judaism was becoming more a part of mainstream American culture.[9] Asked later about growing up Jewish in a small Midwestern town Dylan would recall, "I never felt anything, like, I had to fight my way through schoolyard crowds, you know? As long as I had a guitar, I was happy."[10] Hibbing's population was a mix of religions and national backgrounds, and Jewish families like the Zimmermans were part of the town's multiethnic (if almost entirely white) social fabric.

In *Chronicles* Dylan writes that "If you were born around this time [the early 1940s] or were living and alive, you could feel the old world go and the new one beginning."[11] He is referring to the entire postwar cultural regeneration, but for young Bobby Zimmerman, popular music was not just the soundtrack but the central feature of this new world. Like John Lennon (born 1940), Paul McCartney (1942), and others who led the 1960s musical revolution, Dylan was the right age for the advent of rock and roll. He turned fourteen in 1955, the year Bill Haley and the Comets topped the charts with "Rock Around the Clock," Elvis became an overnight sensation, and Little Richard's "Tutti Frutti" crossed over with white teenagers. In a 2017 interview Dylan elaborated on the impact of early rock and roll:

> Rhythm and blues, country and western, bluegrass and gospel were always there—but it was compartmentalized—it was great but it wasn't dangerous. Rock and roll was a dangerous weapon, chrome plated, it exploded like the speed of light,

> it reflected the times, especially the presence of the atomic bomb which had preceded it by several years. Back then people feared the end of time. The big showdown between capitalism and communism was on the horizon. Rock and roll made you oblivious to the fear, busted down the barriers that race and religion, ideologies put up.[12]

Rock and roll's defiance became part of his personality. Years later Dylan told an interviewer, "When I first heard Elvis's voice I just knew that I wasn't going to work for anybody and nobody was gonna be my boss."[13] That statement testifies both to Dylan's instantaneous determination to become a successful performer and to the influence of Elvis's voice and image, which embodied the swagger and confrontational posture that Dylan would adopt. He was similarly inspired by James Dean, whose portrait of a sensitive but disaffected teenager in *Rebel Without a Cause* appeared the same year. Robert Zimmerman soaked up early rock and the music it was built from—blues, R&B, and country—blasting out of powerful Midwestern and Southern radio stations such as Little Rock's KTHS and Shreveport's KWKH, whose *Louisiana Hayride* show helped launch Elvis's career while also showcasing a wide range of country performers, including another musical rebel and early idol of Dylan's: Hank Williams.

Robert Zimmerman seems to have been drawn especially to flamboyance as a musical and performance style. Elvis is an obvious example; another is Little Richard, who became such a guiding light that in Robert's senior-year high school yearbook the life's ambition printed under his photo was "to join 'Little Richard.'" Robert played piano before picking up guitar and harmonica, so Richard's driving, percussive chords, played while standing—grooving, really—at the keyboard, were a revelation for a young musician who wanted to break from tradition. And Richard's style, like Elvis's, made it clear that no one was going to tell him what to do. Little Richard had performed in drag before becoming a rock and roll star, and his image remained sexually provocative and androgynous at the height of his 1950s fame. Perhaps even more than Elvis, Little Richard gave Robert Zimmerman a sense of what a fearless performer looked and sounded like and the impact such a performer could have. Dylan scholar Michael Gray accurately describes what might be called the "Little Richard effect":

> By the time you're halfway through . . . "Tutti Frutti", your mind has been mangled by this mad, wild, delicious gibberish from a human voice like no other, roaring and blathering above a band cranking along like a fire truck running amok in the night. By the time the record finishes, you have glimpsed the possibility of a whole new universe.[14]

In his acceptance speech at the Rock and Roll Hall of Fame in 1988 Dylan acknowledged, "I don't think I'd have even started without listening to Little Richard."[15]

Dylan would be equally effusive paying tribute to another rock pioneer, Buddy Holly, in his 2017 Nobel lecture: "He was the archetype. Everything I wasn't and wanted to be." In his junior year in high school Robert saw Holly along with Ritchie Valens and the Big Bopper at a concert in Duluth, just a few days before their fatal plane crash. He describes being transfixed by Holly:

> He was powerful and electrifying and had a commanding presence. I was only six feet away. He was mesmerizing. I watched his face, his hands, the way he tapped his foot, his big black glasses, the eyes behind the glasses, the way he held his guitar, the way he stood, his neat suit. Everything about him . . . Something about him seemed permanent, and he filled me with conviction. Then, out of the blue, the most uncanny thing happened. He looked me right straight dead in the eye, and he transmitted something. Something I didn't know what. And it gave me the chills.[16]

Holly was less outrageous than Little Richard, but, as Dylan notes, he performed with intensity, combining the sounds of "country western, rock 'n' roll, and rhythm and blues." And, perhaps more significantly, he wrote many of his own songs. At the same time, Dylan's description of Holly focuses not on what he heard that night but what he saw—face, hands, foot, glasses, eyes, demeanor, clothes. The image mattered, as did the eye contact Dylan believes he made with the ill-fated star.

Robert Zimmerman's desire for that kind of connection or encouragement shows up in a surprising anecdote in *Chronicles, Volume One*. He describes himself "performing in the lobby of the National Guard Armory" in Hibbing, presumably playing and singing with a band, when the wrestler Gorgeous George bursts through the doors with his entourage and, without breaking stride, makes eye contact with young Robert as he plays. "He winked and seemed to mouth the phrase, 'You're making it come alive.'" Maybe it never happened, but the encounter, as described by Dylan, fits perfectly with his attraction to transgressive yet fearless and highly successful men and to his need for validation at that stage of his life. Gorgeous George became one of the most recognizable celebrities of postwar America by assuming the role of a vain, effeminate wrestler whom audiences loved to hate. With long hair dyed blond and permed, he would preen as his valet tossed rose petals at his feet and sprayed perfume around the ring. He clearly didn't mind being booed as he pursued a gimmicky but provocative performance art. Dylan claims that "It was all the recognition and encouragement I would need for years to come."[17]

He might actually have needed a little more encouragement, because Dylan's early endeavors as a performer made for a bumpy ride. At Herzl Camp he became friends with Larry Kegan and Louie Kemp, both of whom shared his devotion to rock and roll. Along with Kegan, a thirteen-year-old Dylan performed on talent night, hammering out Hank Ballard and the Midnighters' racy hit "Annie Had a Baby" on the piano for about four hundred bemused campers.[18] As a teenager Dylan would frequently visit Kemp in Duluth and Kegan in St Paul, where they "would go to parties, bang on the piano, sing doo-wop songs and get thrown out more times than not."[19] But when Kegan was sixteen (and Dylan seventeen) tragedy struck: on a family vacation in Miami Beach, Kegan dove from a retaining wall into the ocean, not realizing how shallow the water was at low tide. He broke his neck and was paralyzed, confined to a wheelchair for the rest of his life. Louie Kemp recalls that after he and Dylan visited Larry in the hospital not long after the accident, "I saw something I'd never seen before, and would never see again—Bobby with tears in his eyes."[20] (Dylan maintained his friendship with both Kegan and Kemp long after achieving stardom. For instance the three of them reunited in Mexico, where Kegan was living, while Dylan was filming *Pat Garrett and Billy the Kid*. He later brought Kegan onstage to sing Chuck Berry's "No Money Down" at a pair of 1981 concerts and in 1992 had Kegan's band, the Mere Mortals, open for him in Minneapolis.[21] Kemp, who published a 2019 memoir focusing on his relationship with Dylan, came along on the 1974 tour with the Band and then was hired to manage the Rolling Thunder Revue tour in 1976.)

Taking his act beyond Herzl Camp, Robert formed or joined a succession of rock and roll bands in Hibbing: the Jokers, the Shadow Blasters, the Golden Chords. At one point he adopted the name Elston Gunn to lead a band called the Rock Boppers. In December 1956 Dylan, Kegan, and another friend, Howie Rutman, paid five dollars to "cut a record" in a mini-studio at a local shop, Bob comping on piano for a medley of current rock and roll hits—Dylan's first record was a 78-rpm acetate.[22]

Meanwhile he was learning that girls found even mediocre rock musicians attractive. He became romantically involved with his classmate Echo Helstrom, a young woman from the wrong side of the tracks who initially thought Robert was a "goody-goody." It turned out that he and Echo had enough in common—a rebellious attitude, a sense of adventure, and a love of rhythm and blues—to stay together for about a year. Echo witnessed many of Bob's performances, including the gig at the National Guard Armory where he may have encountered Gorgeous George. "All the time," she said,

> they just turned up those amplifiers on those guitars and it was so loud. You couldn't hear Bob . . . He was, you know, just out there singing and I was hollering at the other guys to turn down the amplifier because it was messing up everything . . . I guess he was happy. But I was always embarrassed.[23]

At a high school talent show Robert's band played a Little Richard-esque tribute featuring the shouted line "I gotta girl and her name is Echo," but the performance was similarly overdriven and chaotic, eliciting boos from the audience. "It didn't even bother him," Echo reported; "he was . . . a prophet in his own hometown."[24]

In 1959 Robert graduated from Hibbing High and immediately headed for Fargo, North Dakota, where he bussed tables and hustled for work as a piano player. Echo Helstrom had broken up with him, mainly out of impatience with his seeing other girls on weekend trips to the Twin Cities.[25] He got an opportunity with an up-and-coming singer, Fargo native Bobby Vee, who had just released a single and was starting a tour; within a couple of years Vee would become a teen idol with hits such as "Take Good Care of My Baby" and "The Night Has a Thousand Eyes." Robert, who was still using the stage name Elston Gunnn (he added another n!), played piano on a couple of dates with Vee's band but was soon dropped, either because Vee decided he didn't want a piano player at all or because Gunnn's chops were still limited. ("He was pretty hot," Vee later recalled, "in the key of C."[26]) For a few years Dylan exaggerated his stint with the pop star, but in *Chronicles* he offers a more modest assessment: "I talked my way into joining his group on some of his local gigs, one in the basement of a church. I played a few shows with him, but he really didn't need a piano player and, besides, it was hard finding a piano that was in tune in the halls that he played."[27]

Meanwhile Abe and Beatty Zimmerman wanted their son to attend college. Robert was not academically motivated, but he didn't have much choice. He couldn't support himself playing music and wasn't interested in anything else. Enrolling at the University of Minnesota offered a way out of Hibbing, at least, and access to the music and arts scene centered in the off-campus neighborhood of Dinkytown. One indication of his main interest in moving to the Twin Cities is that he changed his stage name around the same time, leaving Elston Gunnn behind and becoming Bob Dillon, or Dylan. His explanations for this particular name have been evasive and sometimes contradictory over the years; in *Chronicles* he provides a playful but oddly reasonable account of experimenting with other names

Robert Zimmerman's yearbook photograph, 1958.

before arriving at the right one. He liked the sound of Robert Allen, or Allyn for the offbeat spelling, and

> Then sometime later, unexpectedly, I'd seen some poems by Dylan Thomas. Dylan and Allyn sounded similar . . . People had always called me either Robert or Bobby, but Bobby Dylan sounded too skittish to me and besides, there already was a Bobby Darin, a Bobby Vee, a Bobby Rydell, a Bobby Neely and a lot of other Bobbys. Bob Dylan sounded better than Bob Allyn. The first time I was asked my name in the Twin Cities, I instinctively and automatically without thinking simply said, "Bob Dylan."[28]

For most of his career Dylan denied that Dylan Thomas had inspired the name, and when asked if he spelled it like the poet, he would reply that it was spelled D-Y-L-A-N, "as in Bob Dylan."[29]

Biographer Howard Sounes speculated that he was drawing on various Dillons, including a founding father of Hibbing, a Green Bay Packers football player named Bobby Dillon, and the *Gunsmoke* character Matt Dillon. Noting that at early performances in Dinkytown the name was in fact spelled "Dillon," David Hajdu sees the shift from Elston Gunn, inspired perhaps by the modern urban detective Peter Gunn, to Bob Dillon (via *Gunsmoke*) was a cultural and musical transition "from the modern city to the Old West," appropriate for a rocker who was about to become a folk singer.[30] In a 1971 interview Dylan would tell his friend Tony Glover that the new name "allowed me to step into the Guthrie role, with more character . . . I had to be free enough to learn the music, free enough to learn technique." Many years later he made a similar appeal to freedom in regard to adopting a new name: "You call yourself what you want to call yourself," Dylan told Ed Bradley on *60 Minutes*. "This is the land of the free."[31]

As a freshman Dylan lived at the Jewish fraternity Sigma Alpha Mu, but he immediately gravitated toward the Dinkytown music scene and played wherever and whenever he could. His success with women continued, especially when he found common ground with them through music. The father of one girlfriend, Ellen Barker, had an extensive collection of folk music; another, Bonnie Jean Beecher, had a nice record collection of her own and first met Dylan when she overheard him discussing blues singers at a coffeehouse in Dinkytown.[32] Beecher encouraged him to practice on the piano at her sorority house, to the displeasure of her housemates: "[M]y friends would come in and they would just go Uurgh! Who is this geek? I wanted him to play the guitar, which he could play well and which I knew would impress them, but he wasn't having any of it. He was saying, Naw, I want to get this—Hwang! Whwaongg! Hahaha! I was mortified but he didn't give a shit."[33]

In *Chronicles* Dylan complains that back in Hibbing he had repeatedly lost musicians to other bands with "connections" that would open doors to better-paying gigs, which inspired his musical self-reliance: "It was beginning to dawn on me that I would have to learn how to play and sing by myself and not depend on a band until the time I could afford to pay and keep one."[34] But surely that new approach also stemmed from his discovery, around the same time, of folk music, which lent itself more easily to solo performance and shifting collaborations. The first wave of rock and roll had begun to subside in the late 1950s. Buddy Holly had died tragically; Elvis was in the Army and would soon be focusing on movies; Jerry Lee Lewis's career was derailed by outrage surrounding his marriage to a thirteen-year-old cousin; Little Richard had temporarily forsaken secular music (as Dylan himself would twenty years later). As cleaner, more polished young singers like Pat Boone and Paul Anka took over the mainstream youth market with formulaic tunes and arrangements, the more hip musicians and fans revived older, seemingly more authentic forms of popular music, including small-group "trad" or "Dixieland" jazz as well as blues, old-time country, ballads, and work songs that were increasingly classified as American folk music.

In a 1978 interview Dylan identified Odetta as the singer who "turned me on to folk singing" when he heard her record playing in a store. From Odetta he moved on to Harry Belafonte and the Kingston Trio, among the most commercially successful "folk" acts of the late 1950s. Belafonte and the Kingstons, as well as the Weavers and Burl Ives, were folk singers in the sense that they performed songs that developed mostly within distinct national or regional cultures, usually passed down from singer to singer rather than copyrighted by specific composers. But for Dylan and other coffeehouse patrons and performers of Dinkytown—and dozens of other college towns and bohemian enclaves—these popular singers were, at best, a gateway to the "real" folk music which became synonymous with an aesthetic of simple, unpretentious performance and a disdain for commercialism. In fact the rejection of well-groomed folk singers with their crisp harmony vocals and polished arrangements became an article of faith among the coffeehouse cognoscenti.

The musical bible of the underground folk music scene was Harry Smith's *Anthology of American Folk Music*, a compilation of recordings from the 1920s and '30s culled from one man's extensive 78-rpm record collection. Somewhat ironically the 84 tracks were not "folk" in the sense of being field recordings but were instead commercial platters, curated and sequenced by the eccentric Mr Smith onto six 33-rpm discs, a new format when the *Anthology* was released in 1952. Here were "See that My Grave Is Kept Clean" by Blind Lemon Jefferson, "Down on Penny's Farm" by the Bentley Boys, "When the Great Ship Went Down" by William and Versey Smith, "The Coo Coo Bird" by Clarence Ashley, "Sugar Baby" by Dock Boggs. Dave Van Ronk would later claim that folk singers like him "could not have existed" without the *Anthology*: "For almost the first time, it gave us a sense of what traditional music in the United States was all about, from the source rather than from second- and thirdhand interpreters . . . after a while we all knew every word of every song, including the ones we hated."[35]

In Minneapolis Dylan soaked up these songs and more, hanging out with other musicians and aficionados. His home base was a coffeehouse called the Ten O'Clock Scholar, which opened in Dinkytown about a year before Dylan's arrival. The owner, David Lee, recalled Dylan walking in and asking if he could play, declaring boldly but innocently, "I want to be a folk singer." Lee's girlfriend, for one, was not impressed with this work-in-progress: "I always used to feel he had adenoid problems and should take them out. He really was driving business away, he sang so badly. He was always off key, way off key and after he'd sing for a while people would leave."[36] Dylan continued to learn onstage: he played at the Purple Onion pizza parlor in St Paul, the Bastille coffeehouse, and at house parties. According to a friend from Dylan's Minneapolis days, "He went to parties mostly because he wanted to make them into Dylan concerts . . . He preferred playing for audiences rather than with groups of people," the latter being more typical of communal-minded amateurs who would gather for "hootenannies."[37]

Dylan was progressing rapidly by playing in front of people as often as possible and by learning from anyone who knew how to play anything he couldn't. He described it as

> a selfish kind of thing. You could see the [guitar players] and if you knew you could do what they were doing, with just a little practice, and you were looking for something else, you could

> just move on. But . . . when you knew that they knew more than you, well, you just had to listen to everybody. It wasn't necessarily a song; it was technique and style, and tricks and all those combinations which go together.[38]

Dylan quickly became part of a folk music community in Dinkytown. He made friends with "Spider" John Koerner, a singer-guitarist with similar tastes who played regularly at the Scholar and other local hangouts. Koerner, who was a couple of years older and had been living in Minneapolis for some time, was a good connection as well as a good musician, and he knew more traditional songs than Dylan. They played together frequently. Other guitar-playing friends included Gretel Hoffman, her husband Dave Whitaker, Dave Ray, and Tony Glover, the latter of whom made some of the first tape recordings of Dylan performing in Minneapolis. Along with folk music, there was plenty of alcohol and marijuana on the scene, and Dylan indulged in these new habits along with his friends.

Up to this point Dylan had experienced nothing like the runaway, bumming-around life that he would later describe in "My Life in a Stolen Moment." But he decided to give it a try in the summer of 1960, when he hitchhiked from Minneapolis to Denver to check out another folk scene. He had no real connections, but he found a friend of a friend, a singer named Walt Conley, who let him crash at his house. Conley was also booking acts for a club called the Satire, and he hired Dylan to open for the up-and-coming Smothers Brothers, who combined comedy with polite folk music. According to Conley, neither the Smothers nor anyone else in Denver really appreciated Dylan's act.[39] But Conley did help Dylan get a gig in nearby Central City at the touristy Gilded Garter Saloon, singing and probably playing piano for noisy patrons who had little interest in folk music.

His Colorado excursion did little to advance his career, but it did provide him with more hard-knocks experience as a performer, and it exposed him to more professional singers. At a prominent Denver folk and blues club called the Exodus Dylan might have heard a young Judy Collins, who performed there frequently, as well as blues singer Josh White and the decidedly commercial folk singer Bob Gibson. He almost certainly met Jesse Fuller, whose songwriting credits include "San Francisco Bay Blues" and "You're No Good," later the lead track on Dylan's debut album. Fuller performed as a one-man band with apparatuses that included a harmonica rack—Dylan would soon have a rack of his own, a gift from his girlfriend Bonnie Beecher. His stint in Denver ended ignominiously, after he stole a bunch of records from Walt Conley and his housemate Dave Hamil, who discovered the theft and called the cops. No charges were pressed, but the humiliation, along with the lack of success or solid footing in the city, were enough to set Dylan's course back to Minnesota.

Soon after Dylan returned to Minneapolis, someone, probably Dave Whitaker, gave him a copy of Woody Guthrie's memoir *Bound for Glory*. Dylan recalled that he "went through it from cover to cover, like a hurricane, totally focused on every word, and the book sang out to me like the radio."[40] Published in 1943, *Bound for Glory* is Guthrie's account of his early life in Oklahoma and travels during the Great Depression. Like Dylan's *Chronicles, Volume One*, *Bound for Glory* is impressionistic and not strictly factual, and therein lies much of its power. As a self-portrait of a hobo troubadour, it offered a vision of a purposeful life making music on one's own terms.

What's more, Guthrie combined the folk aesthetic—simple song structures, tunes passed down and passed around—with original lyrics of his own, by turns playful and inspirational. The songs were rooted in tradition and seemed to come from and belong to "the people," and yet they were unmistakably Woody Guthrie songs. By strict definition, folk songs had no songwriter and no copyright, but here was Guthrie, very much a *writer* . . . of folk songs. Guthrie's landmark recordings from the 1940s were pressed as LPs throughout the 1950s, mostly on the Folkways label; Dylan had access to them through friends in Minneapolis. He immersed himself in these recordings and for a while performed nothing else: "Woody Guthrie tore everything in his path to pieces," he recalled. "For me it was an epiphany."[41] Not unlike so many later Dylan imitators, Dylan adopted not just Guthrie's catalog but his style, his way of talking, and a kind of hoboish downtrodden posture. At times he even pretended he *was* Guthrie and would answer only to the name Woody.[42]

Woody Guthrie, 1943. Photo by Al Aumuller.

In addition to musicians like Koerner and Glover, Dylan got to know self-made music journalists Jon Pankake and Paul Nelson, who founded a folk magazine called *The Little Sandy Review* in 1958 after being floored by Harry Smith's *Anthology*. They took a keen interest in Dylan, who at the time seemed as devoted to "authentic" folk and blues as they were: *The Little Sandy Review* was a staunch defender of traditional music that was neither overtly political nor commercial. Dylan devotes several pages of *Chronicles* to his encounters with Pankake, who was "part of the folk police, if not the chief commissioner, [and] wasn't impressed with any of the new talent." If Dylan was (eventually) put off by Pankake's purism, and the fact that he wasn't a working musician himself, he was drawn to Pankake's "incredible" record collection, "ones you never saw and wouldn't know where to get."[43] Pankake thought Dylan was overly enamored of Guthrie. Pointing to another Guthrie disciple, Ramblin' Jack Elliott, he argued that if Dylan continued in his current vein he would only be an imitator, a kind of second-rate Jack Elliott. Dylan didn't want to hear it at the time, but he admits in *Chronicles* that "Pankake was right. Elliott was far beyond me."[44]

Dylan's response was simply to keep learning and performing traditional music. Other than wine and women he had little interest in anything else. A home recording made not long before Dylan headed to Denver in May 1960 reveals a competent but rudimentary guitarist and singer whose voice sounds much better than the description of him driving business away from the Ten O'Clock Scholar. In fact Dylan's clear, relatively smooth vocal sounds more like the style he later adopted for *Nashville Skyline* and much of *Self Portrait* than the rougher, half-spoken, Guthrie-esque voice of his early Columbia albums. Only fragments of the full recording circulate today, but the 27 songs Dylan recorded at a friend's home that day include a handful of Guthrie compositions along with traditional songs such as "Roving Gambler," "Take This Hammer," and "500 Miles," as well as the blues standard "Nobody Knows You When You're Down and Out," Jimmie Rodgers's "Blue Yodel #8," and John Jacob Niles's "Go 'Way from My Window," which Dylan would later repurpose for "It Ain't Me Babe."[45]

By the end of 1960 Dylan had dropped out of school, his parents having agreed to give him a year to pursue his dream of becoming a professional singer, after which, according to his father, "if we were not satisfied with his progress, he'd go back to school."[46] But of course there was no turning back at this point. Dylan was improving through constant practice and performing, widening his repertoire of traditional songs while deepening his devotion to Guthrie as a model. Despite the support he had found in Dinkytown and a fairly serious relationship with Bonnie Beecher, his restlessness and ambition were directing him eastward. Dylan had traveled very little, aside from his recent Colorado sojourn, but he knew that there was bound to be more opportunity and more to learn in a bigger city, specifically in New York, the cultural capital of the USA, if not the world, by 1960. He was guided by his Woody Guthrie fixation as well. Guthrie was suffering from Huntington's Disease, a progressive brain disorder characterized by uncontrolled jerking motions as well as mental confusion and loss of concentration. Upon learning that his idol was in a psychiatric hospital in northern New Jersey, Dylan vowed to visit him. So in January 1961 he caught a ride to Madison, Wisconsin, the first stop on a journey to Greenwich Village, where he would indeed be "recorded by Columbia after being wrote up in the Times."

2

1961–62: Becoming

One night in January 1961 Jennifer Warren, a sophomore at the University of Wisconsin, was at a house party in Madison. Her friend Paul Brynnis brought in a young stranger who had just arrived in town, a guitarist and singer calling himself Bob Dylan. The singer offered to play some songs, but then he wouldn't stop. As the party broke up it became clear that Dylan had nowhere to stay, and Brynnis didn't have room, so he went home with Warren and her roommates. But their guest wouldn't go to bed.

"He sat on the stove and started singing again . . . All we wanted to do was go to sleep, me especially, and he just went on with song after song. He didn't know anything about the guitar, just picking chord to chord," Warren recalled. Her not-so-welcome houseguest talked about—and imitated—Woody Guthrie throughout the night and declared his intention to visit his hero in a New Jersey hospital. He was also determined to "hit the Village" and make it in New York. Warren, who grew up in Greenwich Village, told one of her roommates that "the poor kid [was] going to be eaten up alive."[1]

Having left Minneapolis just before Christmas, Dylan had spent a few weeks in Chicago, where his only contact was an acquaintance from Denver named Kevin Krown. He seems not to have gotten any more opportunities or attention as a performer in Chicago than he had the previous year in Denver, but, according to Krown, he did write "Song to Woody," his first significant composition, while he was there. Set to the tune of Guthrie's "1913 Massacre," the tribute casts Dylan in his hero's image, a traveling observer of everyday hardship and a link in a long chain of roving troubadours who offer hope in an otherwise uncaring world. The young man who had just hitchhiked 400 miles (645 km) to a city where he didn't know anyone was placing himself in that tradition.

When he left Minnesota in late 1960 Dylan's stated goal was to visit Guthrie in New Jersey, but from Chicago he traveled back in the direction of the Twin Cities. He didn't stay long in Madison, about a week and a half. Then, when a ride to New York presented itself, he reversed course again. Before leaving Madison he attended a concert by Pete Seeger, already a folk music icon as a member of the Weavers and, before that, the Almanac Singers, the group he had founded in the early 1940s with none other than Woody Guthrie.[2]

Dylan and Fred Underhill, one of Warren's roommates, took turns as substitute drivers on the journey from Madison to New York City near the end of January. The primary driver, Dave Berger, joined the ranks of people who were forced to listen to Dylan's singing and were unimpressed: "As we got into New Jersey, I finally told him, 'Shut the fuck up.'"[3] Berger dropped Dylan and Underhill off in Manhattan on a freezing, snowy night, which Dylan memorialized in the sardonic early song "Talkin' New York." The new arrivals made their way to the Village and found an open-mic night at the Café Wha?, later described by Dylan as "a subterranean cavern, liquorless, ill lit, low ceiling, like a wide dining hall with chairs and tables—opened at noon, closed at four in the morning."[4] The owner, Manny Roth, helped the two new arrivals find a place to stay for the night and soon had Dylan performing afternoon sets regularly.[5] It was a considerably warmer reception than the one Dylan described in "Talkin' New York," where he's kicked off the stage of a folk club for sounding like a hillbilly.

Dylan's satire in "Talkin' New York" is directed at the smoother, more commercial-sounding folk music associated with the Weavers, Belafonte, and the Kingston Trio. The hard-core folk performers, for whom sounding like a hillbilly was a mark of authenticity, positioned themselves in opposition to their more polished contemporaries, adopting the raw, off-kilter aesthetic exemplified by the recordings in the Harry Smith anthology and promoted by Dylan's old friends and critics at the *Little Sandy Review*.[6]

Of course Guthrie was the blueprint of the hard-core folk performer. His lyrics were steeped in social realism and protest, his songs rarely ventured beyond three chords, his vocal range was limited, and his half-spoken delivery defied any expectation that he make it pretty. Dylan arrived in New York imitating that delivery, to the annoyance of captive listeners such as Jennifer Warren and Dave Berger. Even as he developed his own style, the Guthrie-esque attitude that informed his voice remained. As a singer as well as a writer Guthrie had already had a profound influence on folk music, and through Dylan his influence would be amplified, extending through folk to pop and rock singing.

Guthrie was undoubtedly the greatest influence, but Dylan had also absorbed some of the phrasing and plainspoken style of blues singers such as Jesse Fuller and performers on the Harry Smith anthology—Clarence Ashley, Jim Jackson, Mississippi John Hurt, and others. Even in the context of this tradition Dylan's voice had an especially harsh, piercing tone. The result was what *Time* magazine would soon describe as sounding "as if it was drifting over the walls of a tuberculosis sanitorium." The novelist Joyce Carol Oates, an admirer, would refer to Dylan's "raw, very young, and seemingly untrained voice, frankly nasal, if sandpaper could sing." Greil Marcus, whose devotion to Dylan has yielded four influential books, at one point compared the sound of his early-career voice to "a cat stuck in barbed wire."[7]

Dylan's voice has been the source of countless arguments between fans and detractors. But it's undeniable that he permanently changed expectations for singers across popular genres. Dylan scholar John Hughes reflects on what the sound of that voice means:

> This is a voice that clearly refuses to please. It does not mimic an interpersonal intimacy—as might Paul Simon, for instance—offering a kind of virtual friendship, the flattering solace of identifying as a beautiful soul, and the enjoyments of a music whose attractions everyone can understand. Rather, the voice is abrasive, and the effect of the singing is interruptive, uncompromising.[8]

Lacking or avoiding warmth or sweetness, it's a voice that pulls the listener's attention to phrasing—clipping or drawing out syllables and words, moving in front of or behind the beat—as a way of conveying emotion.[9] If not exactly imitated (except by parodists) it inspired generations of singers who sought to convey that same confrontational attitude. Rough, seemingly untrained voices with limited range and questionable intonation would stream through rock music from the mid-1960s onward: think Mick Jagger, Jimi Hendrix, Alice Cooper, Iggy Pop, Patti Smith, Shane MacGowan, Kurt Cobain, PJ Harvey, and virtually every punk singer. What it means to have a "good voice" would be a different conversation once singers and listeners caught on to what Dylan was doing.

Dylan was determined to meet his idol and try out his version of the hardcore folk singer's delivery on him. Within days of his arrival in New York he visited Guthrie at Greystone Hospital in northern New Jersey. He also knocked on the door of the Guthrie home in Queens, where, according to Woody's daughter Nora, he made the babysitter nervous but played guitar for them and her two older siblings, Arlo and Joady.[10] He learned that Woody spent Sundays at the home of Sidsel and Bob Gleason in East Orange, which was much closer to Manhattan than Greystone. Along with Ramblin' Jack Elliott and other Guthrie devotees, Dylan became a regular there.

Back in Minneapolis Dave Whitaker, who had given Dylan a copy of *Bound for Glory*, received a card with Woody's picture on it, on which Dylan had written, "I saw Woody! I saw Woody! He likes my stuff."[11] According to the Gleasons and Nora Guthrie, Woody did like Bob (whether or not he liked his stuff) and would often ask for him.[12] Meanwhile the Gleasons provided Dylan, who had no apartment of his own, a haven in his early days in New York. And they had a large collection of records and tapes, always an attraction for Dylan as he expanded his repertoire. According to Sidsel Gleason,

> We had maybe ninety percent of Woody's record collection. Bobby would start in the morning and listen all day to Woody's records. Carter Family, Big Bill Broonzy, everything. He'd listen

> and after a couple of times Bobby would have the words and the chord progressions.[13]

Some of what Dylan had learned by this point can be heard on a tape he made at the Gleasons' in February or March 1961. He sings Jesse Fuller's "San Francisco Bay Blues," the Western standard "Remember Me (When the Candle Lights Are Gleaming)," Guthrie's "Pastures of Plenty," and a handful of traditional songs following Guthrie arrangements, mostly in a somewhat understated (and slightly nervous) version of his Woody voice. Sidsel Gleason claims that she even gave the near penniless Dylan some of Woody's clothes to wear to a gig, a symbolic gesture if ever there was one.

Meanwhile Dylan was learning to navigate the Greenwich Village folk scene. According to Dave Van Ronk, throughout the 1950s New York had lagged behind Chicago, Boston, Los Angeles, and San Francisco in terms of folk performance venues. But things were changing by the time Dylan arrived in 1961. Folklorist Alan Lomax famously called the Village, in its heyday, the place "where people come to get away from America."[14] By about 1960 it was in the midst of what Van Ronk liked to call "The Great Folk Scare," a period when the music's popularity soared. MacDougal Street became its epicenter.

"We used to call that block [of MacDougal] between Bleeker and 3rd Street the Elephant Walk, and it was more like a slow elephant stampede," recalled Van Ronk. "Eventually they put sawhorses up at either end of the block because the crowds were so heavy that cars could not get through."[15] Coffeehouses like the Café Wha? and the Commons were known as "basket houses," for the method by which performers collected their pay from patrons. Other Village hangouts included the Café Bizarre, where Dylan recalled playing "once or twice," the Café Figaro, the Bitter End, and the White Horse Tavern, famous for having been the site of Dylan Thomas's final days of heavy drinking and a venue for the Irish folk group the Clancy Brothers and Tommy Makem, who counted Bob among their fans.[16] Dylan made the rounds, couch-surfing and playing wherever he could.

But Dylan was determined to move up from the basket houses, and the two Village venues that elevated him were Gerde's Folk City and the Gaslight Café. Gerde's, on West 4th Street, was a former Italian restaurant whose owner, Mike Porco, had been persuaded to rebrand as a music venue in 1960, cashing in on the Great Folk Scare. Dylan played open mic nights there and, in April, less than three months after arriving in New York, got a paid gig opening for the great blues singer-guitarist John Lee Hooker. Van Ronk emceed a regular hootenanny night at the Gaslight on MacDougal Street, which drew prominent performers and rising stars; Dylan recalled it as "a dominant presence on the street, more prestige than anyplace else . . . It was a club I wanted to play, needed to."[17] The Gaslight was a dank basement venue that, like many Village performance spaces at the time, did not serve alcohol. But the Kettle of Fish, upstairs from the Gaslight, did, making the two establishments co-dependent. And by mid-1961, Dylan was a regular at the Gaslight/Kettle, having impressed and befriended Van Ronk and joined his network of Village performers.

That network was a shifting cast of characters that included Mark Spoelstra, a skilled twelve-string guitarist who met Dylan within days of his arrival and who performed frequently with him throughout the spring and summer; Fred Neil, who first gave Dylan the stage at the Café Wha? and who would later write Harry Nilsson's hit "Everybody's Talkin'"; Hugh Romney, a performance artist who, in the late 1960s, became Wavy Gravy (and who would marry Dylan's ex-girlfriend from Minneapolis, Bonnie Beecher); Noel Paul Stookey, who would soon become the "Paul" of Peter, Paul and Mary; Tom Paxton, who was writing much of his own material when Dylan's repertoire still consisted of traditional songs and Guthrie compositions; David Cohen, who would later write and perform under the name David Blue; John Cohen, a banjo and guitar player, photographer, and folklorist whose group, the New Lost City Ramblers, had already recorded several albums for Folkways Records; and Paul Clayton, who at thirty was an elder statesman of the scene with over a dozen albums on premier folk labels.

Then there was Van Ronk, an established Village performer who combined the folklorist's respect for tradition with fluid fingerpicking and an expressive voice that was fuller than Dylan's and—like

Dylan's—often sounded much older than its possessor. A big man with a sharp wit, he made a deep impression on the newcomer: "He turned every folk song into a surreal melodrama, a theatrical piece—suspenseful, down to the last minute. Dave got to the bottom of things . . . Every night I felt like I was sitting at the feet of a timeworn monument."[18] That timeworn monument was only 25, five years older than Dylan. Van Ronk and his wife, Terri Thal, took him under their wing, with Thal becoming Dylan's manager, "not that there was any competition for the job," Van Ronk noted.[19]

Dylan's stated motivation for coming to New York may have been to see Woody, but now that he was there he found a scene where he could thrive as he hadn't in Minneapolis, Denver, or Chicago. For one thing he had good luck in finding superior but sympathetic musicians like Spoelstra and Van Ronk. Beyond that, folk music's appeal in New York (and specifically the Village) was growing so rapidly that there were simply more places to perform and more of an audience, even for open-air sessions at Washington Square, hootenannies, and open mic nights. Audiences and other musicians in New York were more tolerant of, even receptive to, Dylan's Guthrie idolatry and abrasive voice. Dylan had found a new home, and he was fascinated by it.

"I dug it all," he said. "The streets and the snows and the starving and the five-flight walkups and sleeping in rooms with ten people. I dug the trains and the shadows, the way I dug ore mines and coal mines. I just jumped right to the bottom of New York."[20] He would sum it up near the end of 1963, as he was becoming famous: "I would not be doing what I'm doing today if I hadn't come to New York . . . I was reborn in New York."[21]

This idea of being reborn in a new setting is of course a cornerstone of American mythology. Being "self-made" does not refer simply to having earned one's own fortune; it also suggests the freedom to start over with a new identity, to make or remake yourself. Dylan, who would a few years later sing the famous line "He not busy being born is busy dying," had been working on his new identity long before coming to New York, but it was in the coffeehouses of Greenwich Village that his new self really started to work for him, artistically and socially.

In those early days Dylan spent a lot of time at the Folklore Center, a bohemian music shop, library, and way station for musicians on MacDougal Street. Izzy Young, who ran the Center, helped Dylan make contacts, exposed him to more folk music, and listened to him sing and talk. According to Young, "He absorbed everything, reading non-stop and always [borrowing] records from the store and listening to them . . . He would play in the store for anyone who was there."[22] Young must have sensed the newcomer's originality and ambition, because he indulged him, took notes on their conversations, and promoted him in the community.

Dylan fabricated a knockabout past life in his sessions with Young, as he did with anyone who asked and as he would in "My Life in a Stolen Moment." As Van Ronk noted, few if any of Dylan's new acquaintances took his tales of Guthrie-esque adventure seriously, but they did wonder why Dylan took this auto-mythologizing to such lengths. The great folk singer Oscar Brand, who had Dylan perform on his radio show in October, saw it as an expression of insecurity:

> Here he was, a kid from Minnesota, and he came here to a climate where a number of people were already quite seasoned. He was afraid he couldn't compete and afraid he wasn't good enough, so he lied, and that made him afraid he would be caught and we would judge him. I don't think many of us really believed he was that Dust Bowl character he pretended to be. Nobody really cared very much one way or another, because everybody was faking something and afraid in our own way. But he didn't know that.[23]

Van Ronk tells a story of Dylan discovering, during a casual conversation in a Village café, that Ramblin' Jack Elliott was born Elliott Adnopoz in Brooklyn. Dylan responded by laughing uncontrollably. "A lot of us had suspected that Bobby was Jewish," Van Ronk recalled, "and after that we had no doubts."[24] And Elliott wasn't just another folk singer. He was "Woody's son," Guthrie's friend and disciple who "got there" before Dylan, as Jon Pankake had pointed out to Bob in Minneapolis. The fact that both Elliott and Dylan left behind middle-class Jewish upbringings, changing their names and reinventing themselves as hobo troubadours, and that Dylan was previously unaware of this further coincidence suggests that he was laughing at both Elliott and himself. Dylan and Elliott had become friends and performed together occasionally, and the younger man must have felt some anxiety of influence: according to Izzy Young, Dylan claimed not to have learned any songs from Elliott, who, he said, "doesn't know that many songs," even as Dylan was (in Young's view) simply "imitating Jack Elliott."[25]

But the artistic benefit of that anxiety—not wanting to be pigeonholed as an imitator of an imitator, "the Son of Jack"—was that it forced Dylan to seek a new direction, to do things that Elliott and other folk singers weren't doing.[26] So even as he soaked up every performance style, every guitar lick, every song he could master, he looked for ways to set himself apart. In *Chronicles* Dylan describes his realization that he could never match the musicianship or innate feel for traditional songs possessed by someone like Mike Seeger, half-brother of Pete and co-founder of the New Lost City Ramblers; so he just might have to write his own songs.[27] In the meantime he found other ways to stand out, developing a Chaplinesque stage presence, playing up his urchin-like appearance, fumbling nervously with harmonicas or tuning pegs, even stumbling around or falling in front of the audience. Eric Von Schmidt, a Boston singer who befriended Dylan that summer, said that "at first it horrified me. And then I started thinking, this is one of the greatest things I've ever seen in my life. You know? He's doing it. He's got all these people totally buffaloed, totally confused, and yet he's doing a great thing."[28]

Dylan was also becoming more adept at harmonica, and not strictly the piercing, staccato sound he got from playing hands-free on the rack. In fact Dylan made his debut studio recording on harmonica, playing on the lead track, "I'll Fly Away," and two other songs on Carolyn Hester's first Columbia Records album. He had met Hester in Cambridge, MA, home to a thriving folk scene that rivalled Greenwich Village. Terri Thal was trying to book him outside New York, so she sent him to Cambridge that summer, without a gig, to check out the scene and connect with Hester and her husband,

Richard Fariña. It took two trips for Dylan to make that connection, but he quickly became friends with the couple and with Von Schmidt. As was often the case, his timing was uncanny: Hester invited him to play on her record, to be recorded in New York early that fall.

On July 29 WRVR, a new radio station devoted to folk music, broadcast a daylong festival at the Riverside Church in Harlem. Dylan was on the bill along with Van Ronk, Jack Elliott, Tom Paxton, John Cohen, and blues legends Reverend Gary Davis and Victoria Spivey. Dylan, who was introduced as hailing from Gallup, New Mexico, performed the traditional songs "Handsome Molly," "Omie Wise," and "Poor Lazarus" and sang duets with Elliott and guitarist Danny Kalb. More significantly, backstage he met a seventeen-year-old woman named Suze Rotolo.

Suze had grown up in New York, a self-described "red diaper baby" in a family devoted to leftist politics. She was working at the New York CORE (Congress of Racial Equality) office when she met Bob, whom she had already seen performing at Gerde's with Mark Spoelstra.

"We started flirting and talking backstage at Riverside Church early in the day and didn't stop until the day was done," she recalled. By the time the day's festivities moved to a nearby house party, "Bob and I were pretty much glued to each other."[29] Four decades later Dylan described his attraction to Suze on that first meeting: "She had a smile that could light up a street full of people and was extremely lively, had a particular type of voluptuousness—a Rodin sculpture come to life. She reminded me of a libertine heroine. She was just my type."[30]

Along with the Van Ronks, Suze Rotolo expanded Bob's frame of reference with her commitment to civil rights and racial justice, as well as her appreciation for a wide variety of art and music. Post-bop and avant-garde jazz were flourishing at clubs like the Village Vanguard, the Village Gate, and the Five Spot Café, and Dylan heard John Coltrane, Charles Mingus, Archie Shepp, and others who were pushing the boundaries of the music.[31] Suze turned Bob on to Bertolt Brecht, and the couple went to see experimental off-Broadway plays. They also frequented art galleries, and with Rotolo's guidance Dylan began to appreciate the Old Masters as well as twentieth-century Modernists like Picasso and Kandinsky.

He was especially drawn to the work of contemporary pop artist Red Grooms, whose colorful multimedia work had not yet achieved mass appeal. But new combinations of the traditional, the popular, and the avant-garde clearly held a strong attraction for Dylan. Grooms used odd juxtapositions of historical figures and modern urban scenery, presented with an appreciation for the absurd. Dylan "loved the way Grooms used laughter as a diabolical weapon. Subconsciously," he recalled, "I was wondering if it were possible to write songs like that."[32]

He wasn't writing songs "like that" yet, but he *was* writing songs in the summer of 1961. His set at the Gaslight in September included a few of his own compositions, all based on Guthrie songs: "Song to Woody," "Man on the Street," and "Talkin' Bear Mountain Picnic Massacre Blues." The latter song was in the familiar talking blues idiom that dates back to the 1920s, popularized by Guthrie in the 1940s ("Talking Fishing Blues," "Talking Hard Work," "Talking Sailor," and others). The spoken lines that follow each pair of rhyming couplets give the impression of off-the-cuff improvisation, wry commentary on the verses' content.

On "Bear Mountain" Dylan uses the form to great effect, retelling a story he had read in the newspaper about a tour boat overwhelmed by picnickers who had been sold counterfeit tickets. Dylan narrates from the perspective of an unwitting ticket holder, giving a comically deadpan account that alternates between exaggeration and understatement. After being crushed in the crowd he reports nonchalantly on the damage, which includes a cracked head, broken arms and legs, blindness, and baldness. For the final punchline he suggests rounding up the greedy promoters responsible for the melee and sending them to Bear Mountain for a picnic.

Dylan performed "Bear Mountain" and other original talking blues songs when he opened for the Greenbriar Boys, a popular bluegrass revival group, on a two-week run at Gerde's in late September. Dylan was already generating considerable buzz, but he was about to get his big break in the form of a *New York Times* review of his set. In fact it was more like a press release disguised as a review.

"A bright new face in folk music is appearing at Gerde's Folk City," it began. "Although only 20 years old, Bob Dylan is one of the most distinctive stylists to play a Manhattan cabaret in months." The writer, Robert Shelton, was something of a fixture in the downtown folk community. He already knew Dylan personally and had even taken him to hear the Clancy Brothers at Town Hall a few months earlier.[33] Aside from mild qualms about occasional "off-target melodrama" and "stylization," Shelton gave Dylan exactly the description he (or any folk singer) craved. If Dylan's voice was "anything but pretty" it was because he was "trying to recapture the rude beauty of a Southern field hand musing in melody on his porch. All the 'husk and bark' are left on his notes and a searing intensity pervades his songs." Shelton's conclusion summoned an audience that wanted to be a little ahead of the curve:

> But if not for every taste, his music-making has the mark of originality and inspiration, all the more noteworthy for his youth. Mr. Dylan is vague about his antecedents and birthplace, but it matters less where he has been than where he is going, and that would seem to be straight up.[34]

Even the "vagueness" about his personal background puts a positive spin on the fact that most of the time Dylan wasn't being vague so much as he was making stuff up.

Shelton's review was published the day before Dylan joined Carolyn Hester in the studio. At an informal rehearsal for the recording in mid-September Dylan had met the man who signed Hester to Columbia and was producing her album: John Hammond, the legendary talent scout already known for signing or otherwise bolstering the careers of Benny Goodman, Count Basie, Billie Holiday, and, quite recently, Aretha Franklin. Hammond invited Dylan to an informal audition and liked him enough to offer a contract, although it was still only a verbal agreement when Hammond and Dylan met again to record Hester's album on September 30.[35] Suddenly Dylan had the *New York Times* proclaiming him the next big thing and the promise of a deal with Columbia Records. This was an extraordinary turn of events. When he came to New York Dylan probably dreamed of recording for Folkways, Vanguard, or Elektra, small but respected folk music labels; he had tried to get their attention (with Izzy Young's help) but got nowhere. And now he had leapfrogged the boutique labels and landed with one of the largest and most powerful record companies in the world.

Just eight months after his arrival in New York Dylan was grabbing the brass ring that everyone in his circle had been reaching for. Izzy Young booked Carnegie Chapter Hall, a fifth-floor performance space that seated about two hundred, for Dylan's first formal concert. Young rented the hall for $75, spent $35 on programs, and sold tickets for $2. He did not turn a profit: Dylan performed for a sparse audience of about fifty. But his performance shows him growing beyond his Guthrie imitation even as he pays tribute to his idol throughout the evening. He plays both Guthrie's "1913 Massacre" and his own "Song to Woody," set to the same melody. Similarly he sings Guthrie's "Talking Merchant Marine" along with his own "Talkin' Bear Mountain Picnic Massacre Blues" and "Talkin' New York." The rest of the fourteen-song set showcases the range of his repertoire. He brings an almost-frantic intensity to African American blues and gospel—"Gospel Plow," Bessie Smith's "Backwater Blues," and Bukka White's "Fixin' to Die"—as well as the hillbilly standard "Freight Train Blues"; he gently croons the British ballad "Young But Daily Growing" and recites a poem about racism and religious intolerance, "Black Cross," popularized by hipster comic Lord Buckley. Despite the disappointingly small audience, the concert was good practice for Dylan, who would spend the next year transitioning from coffeehouses to concert halls. (Recordings of the concert are widely bootlegged, and several songs are included on volume XVIII of the officially released "Bootleg Series" along with other early Dylan tapes.)

Two weeks later Dylan was in the studio recording his first album, under Hammond's direction. From his small cache of original material, "Song to Woody" and "Talkin' New York" made the cut but not "Bear Mountain," nor the decidedly less comic original song he had been performing, "Man on the Street." The rest of the album was a mix of styles similar to his recent concert (he had performed six of the twelve songs at Carnegie Chapter Hall) and similar in range to albums like *Dave Van Ronk Sings Ballads, Blues, and a Spiritual* from 1959, or the album he had played on for Carolyn Hester. Even among new-generation folk albums, it must have sounded fresh and at least a little challenging to its first listeners, not for the material, which was pretty standard, but for Dylan's deliberately unpolished, feverish delivery.

In fact *Bob Dylan* is a very strong debut, demonstrating how much he had absorbed—from Guthrie, from the *Anthology of American Folk Music* and other records, from scuffling and well-established singers—since his conversion to acoustic music just two years earlier. And yet the debut is not as compelling as the albums that would follow it, and the reason is not just the lack of original compositions. As Paul Williams observes in his study of Dylan as performer, this was the first time he couldn't *see* his audience as he sang. "In one sense," Williams writes,

> this inspired him—he seems to put all his energy and everything he's learned into every song. But his uncertainty about what people wanted from him and what he wanted to give them makes the album less personal, less of a coherent whole; trying so hard actually gets in the way of Dylan making the kind of personal connection with his listeners that he was already achieving in his live performances.[36]

Although now very much a Village person, Dylan hadn't left Minnesota completely behind. He had returned for a visit in May 1961 and he did so again in December. He might have imagined the Christmastime trip as a kind of victory lap, now that he had met his hero, conquered the New York folk scene, played Carnegie Hall (albeit a side chapel) and recorded an album for Columbia. He saw old girlfriends Echo Helstrom, now married with a baby, and Bonnie Beecher, as well as musician friends like Tony Glover, who was amazed at Dylan's musical transformation:

> He was playing at some party or something, and he was like a whole different guy. You know the stories about bluesmen who go to the crossroads and sell their soul to the devil, come back, all of a sudden be able to do stuff, Robert Johnson, Tommy Johnson, that whole mythology. It was one of those deals almost . . . it was like, where's this guy been? You know: he's been to the crossroads.[37]

Glover recorded evidence of Dylan's Faustian deal on what has come to be known as the "Minnesota Hotel Tape," actually made in Bonnie Beecher's apartment on December 22. Fueled by a pint of bourbon, Dylan's performance is intense and uninhibited, arguably better than on his professionally produced debut.[38] He plays a lot of blues and performs only four of the songs he had just recorded with Hammond, suggesting that he was already looking ahead from a record that hadn't been released yet.

Upon returning to New York Dylan rented an apartment on West 4th Street, having spent a year crashing with whoever would have him, and Suze Rotolo moved in. "The place was cozy and full of daylight," she remembered. "It faced the back of the building and overlooked an unkempt garden behind the pizza place in the adjacent building. A constant smell of overcooked tomato sauce wafted up through the windows."[39]

While enjoying this bohemian idyll he stayed busy in the run-up to his album's release. On WBAI's "Folksinger's Choice" show he sang and chatted with the host, Cynthia Gooding, who lavished praise on the young singer between songs. Gooding's effusiveness allowed Dylan to come across as a humble, unpretentious folk singer, repeating his tales of hard traveling and working at carnivals while giving credit to whoever wrote or taught him almost every song he performed. Probably at Suze Rotolo's urging, he played a benefit concert for CORE in February along with Van Ronk and Jack Elliott. Around the same time, he landed recording dates as a harmonica player for Harry Belafonte and for blues greats Victoria Spivey and Big Joe Williams. (A photograph from the latter session would appear on the back cover of the 1970 album *New Morning*.)

Bob Dylan was released in mid-March 1962, with its cover portrait of Dylan in a workingman's sheepskin jacket and corduroy cap, clutching the neck of his Gibson J-50 guitar with both hands. The back cover reprinted Shelton's *New York Times* review along with more extensive notes by one Stacey Williams, a pseudonym for the same Robert Shelton. Probably aware that much of the biography Dylan had been providing friends and interviewers was fabricated, "Williams" condenses his subject's origin story, mentioning Duluth and Hibbing but also apocryphal stints in South Dakota and New Mexico. He cites Charlie Chaplin as a major influence, affirming what many early observers noted about Dylan's onstage demeanor. He also picks up on the prevalence of death in the album's setlist, attributing it partly to a serious illness he claimed the singer had experienced a few months earlier (but for which there is no other evidence).

The debut album didn't make the charts, with only a few thousand sales upon its initial release. But in the logic of folk music or any alternative/underground trend, *not* selling a lot of records added to the buzz. As Greil Marcus describes this moment, "Everybody knew Joan Baez and the Kingston Trio; if you knew Bob Dylan, you knew something other people didn't, something that soon enough everybody had to know."[40]

Dylan stayed busy. A month after the album's release, he was back in Columbia's Studio A for the first session of his second album. On April 25 he was part of an awe-inspiring line-up—Dylan and Pete Seeger alongside modern jazz pioneers Cecil Taylor and Archie Shepp—at a benefit concert at the Palm Gardens hall on 52nd Street. And he was trying out new material at Gerde's, including, on April 16, a song that would make him famous and define his early career.

Dylan claimed to have dashed off "Blowin' in the Wind" in ten minutes.[41] In a speech many years later he continued to stress that his breakthrough song was not labored over but was a natural result of the apprenticeship he had served since turning on to folk music:

> If you sang "John Henry" as many times as me—"John Henry was a steel-driving man/ Died with a hammer in his hand/ John Henry said a man ain't nothin' but a man/ Before I let that

> steam drill drive me down/ I'll die with that hammer in my hand"—if you had sung that song as many times as I did, you'd have written "How many roads must a man walk down?" too.[42]

Of course that's not literally true, but it's a truthful insight into his own process, internalizing songs from the canon of folk, blues, and spirituals, using them as blueprints while experimenting with original lyrics. In this case the melody for the verses came from the nineteenth-century African American folk song "No More Auction Block (for Me)," made popular by Paul Robeson in 1947 and by Odetta, whose 1960 version was certainly familiar to Dylan.

The verses of "Blowin' in the Wind" consist entirely of enigmatic questions. None of them refer explicitly to issues of the moment—the construction of the Berlin Wall, the proliferation of atomic weapons, sit-ins or other protests for racial integration and voting rights—but the questions point to a broader failure to achieve peace and justice. And everyone who heard the song could easily relate the abstractions and metaphors, which sound like they were pulled from the Gospels, to the American sins of racial oppression and the expanding military-industrial complex. And therein lies the lyrics' power: the *listener* provides the frame of reference for abstract questions, which can be read as an innocent, idealistic yearning for a better world or frustration with societal complacency and lack of imagination. Similarly answers that are blowing in the wind may be easily grasped, not hidden but right in front of us—or they may be ungraspable, always moving away from our attempts to comprehend.

When asked for comment in *Sing Out!* magazine, Dylan seemed, appropriately, to want it both ways: "Too many of these hip people are telling me where the answer is but oh I won't believe that. I still say it's in the wind and just like a restless piece of paper it's got to come down some time . . . But the only trouble is that no one picks up the answer when it comes down so not too many people get to see and know it . . . and then it flies away." He goes on to describe it as a generational anthem that questions the establishment's values: "I still say some of the biggest criminals are those who turn their heads away when they see wrong and know it's wrong. I'm only 21 years old and I know there's been too many wars . . . You people over 21 should know better . . . cause after all, you're older and smarter."[43]

By the time of those comments—published along with the lyrics in June 1962—the song had become well known among folkies, but Dylan's July recording for Columbia would not be released until the following April. In the meantime his reputation in the folk world was growing rapidly on the strength of "Blowin' in the Wind" and an expanding songbook.

Dylan began copyrighting his songs in January 1962, when Hammond sent him to Lou Levy, an old-school music publisher. Dylan opens *Chronicles* with a memory of a business lunch with Levy at Jack Dempsey's Restaurant at 58th and Broadway, meeting the great boxer himself and then singing into a tape recorder back at Levy's office, surrounded by glossy portraits of crooners and watching Levy "chomping on a big exotic stogie."[44] Dylan's depiction is a tableau of two generations, even two worlds, colliding for a moment to do business. While Dylan would soon rock the New York-centered music establishment—a Tin Pan Alley world where executives ruled over songwriters and artists, treating them as separate talent pools—he would also eventually thrive in it and become friends with the top executives. But in 1962 he was in awe, somewhat naïve, and in need of a more aggressive, commercial-minded manager.

Folk music impresario Albert Grossman had been scouting, even courting, Dylan for some time, quietly helping him since late 1961. Biographer David Hajdu speculates that Grossman may have paid Mike Porco to start booking Dylan at Gerde's and may have done the same to get Robert Shelton's attention.[45] Grossman was already a powerful agent, managing popular singers including Bob Gibson, Odetta, and Peter, Paul and Mary. The latter act was his own creation; he auditioned singers for their look (young, white, well-groomed, bohemian) as well as their sound and convinced Noel Stookey to use Paul, his middle name, because it sounded better between Peter and Mary. Grossman was less a music lover than an investor in musical talent, and he was good enough at his job to see, before most people did, that Dylan was a very good investment. When Terri Thal returned to New York from a scouting expedition to land gigs for Dylan and Van Ronk further north, Dylan sheepishly broke the news that he had signed with Grossman.[46]

Grossman had an unsavory reputation among the folk musicians he *didn't* manage. Van Ronk, who years earlier had auditioned unsuccessfully for Grossman in Chicago at Grossman's club the Gate of Horn (an episode depicted in the film *Inside Llewyn Davis*), said that Grossman "took a sort of perverse pleasure in being utterly unscrupulous. He could be a wonderful companion, though—it wouldn't be until two days after you saw him that you would realize your underwear had been stolen."[47] Pete Seeger's assessment was more terse: "I pitied the people who had to work with him."[48] Suze Rotolo, on the other hand, remembered Grossman affectionately in her memoir, and gave him credit for "present[ing] his musicians as 'artists,' demanding respect for their work from club owners, record companies, and music publishers."[49]

Dylan had also been working with manager Roy Silver, who brought the young songwriter to the attention of a music publisher with an even more Dickensian name than Albert Grossman: Artie Mogull, who worked for M. Witmark & Sons, a subsidiary of Warner Brothers. Mogull offered Dylan a thousand-dollar advance; either Mogull or Grossman, in the process of taking over Dylan's management, bought out the earlier contract with Leeds Music, where Dylan had demoed just a handful of songs, for another thousand dollars. Thanks to a side deal he had made with Witmark, Grossman stood to take a substantial cut of the overall revenue from Dylan's publishing (35 percent to Dylan's 40 percent), which would become a source of contention years later when Dylan realized how much of his earnings were funneled to his manager.[50] But for now having a publisher and a manager looking to sell his songs encouraged Dylan to write more and to record everything he wrote. To secure copyright, he would tape songs for Witmark at a small Midtown studio housed in the Look Building (as in *Look* magazine). Starting with "Blowin' in the Wind" in July 1962, Dylan would lay down 37 demos for Witmark through January of 1964 (released as volume IX of the Bootleg Series in 2010).

One major folk singer not under contract to Grossman—and not because he hadn't tried—was Joan Baez, by 1962 the sincere, youthful face of the movement. Baez first heard Dylan playing with Mark Spoelstra at Gerde's in 1961. "He looked like an urban hillbilly," she later wrote. "Bouncing from foot to foot as he played, he seemed dwarfed by the guitar . . . His cheeks were still softened with an undefined amount of baby fat. But his mouth was a killer: soft, sensuous, childish, nervous, and reticent. He spat out the words to his own songs . . . He was absurd, new, and grubby beyond words."[51]

In November 1962 Baez appeared on the cover of *Time* magazine, the centerpiece of a condescending article on the folk revival. The opening line was "Anything called a hootenanny ought to be shot on sight, but the whole country is having one." A "promising young hobo" named Bob Dylan received a brief mention: "He makes visits to Woody Guthrie's hospital bed, and he delivers his songs in a studied nasal that has just the right clothespin-on-the-nose honesty to appeal to those who most deeply care."[52]

The *Time* article illustrates the relative positions of Baez and Dylan at the end of 1962: she's the story; he's a footnote. Baez was indeed a phenomenon, her crystal-clear, three-octave soprano voice exuding sincerity, accentuated by her unvarnished beauty and simple dress (*Time* actually referred to her as "nubile" while duly noting that she wore no make-up). Her repertoire at this point consisted almost exclusively of traditional songs, as opposed to the topical songs that political folk singers (like Guthrie and Seeger) favored. Her integrity included not being managed by someone like Grossman and not signing with a company like Columbia, choosing instead the more modest, anti-corporate Vanguard Records. But Baez's artistic purity was already starting to look like a dead end—having made a couple of records of beautifully rendered traditional songs with simple arrangements, what could she do now?

Dylan, who had made only one such record, which didn't sell, was unburdened by expectations, and he was working through the question of his own artistic development by writing his own songs, and at a brisk pace. The fact that he was becoming particularly adept at what he would soon refer to as "finger-pointin' songs" is not surprising, considering Suze Rotolo's influence, combined with the legacy of Guthrie and the encouragement of at least some segments of the folk community.

Sing Out!, the magazine founded in 1950 by political activist Irwin Silber and Pete Seeger, supported both traditional song-mining and the development of topical songs; and a new mimeographed publication called *Broadside*, founded by protest singer Agnes "Sis" Cunningham and her husband Gordon Friesen, was devoted exclusively to political folk music. *Broadside*'s contents were predominantly lyric sheets with basic musical notation, and Dylan was there from the beginning, contributing "Talkin' John Birch" to issue number one in February 1962.

One of Dylan's great early satires, the song is voiced by a wide-eyed new convert of the fervidly anti-communist John Birch Society, a figure similar to the hapless narrator of "Bear Mountain Picnic"—an innocent, uneducated everyman bewildered by anything new or foreign. He tries to sniff out Reds everywhere—chimney hole, toilet bowl—but comes up empty. Of course this anti-communist naif is also dangerous, concluding that 90 percent of the books in the library have to be thrown out, along with 98 percent of the people he knows. By the last verse he's run out of people to investigate and realizes that he'll have to investigate himself.

Dylan continued to publish songs in *Broadside* and the more established *Sing Out!* frequently before demoing them with Witmark. *Broadside*'s April issue included "I Will Not Go Down Under the Ground," later retitled "Let Me Die in My Footsteps," an eloquent protest against the paranoia driving people into fallout shelters. "Blowin' in the Wind" was on page 1 in late May, two months before he recorded it and almost a year before the record was pressed. Four more of Dylan's songs appeared in *Broadside* in late 1962, notably "Ballad of Emmett Till" (retitled "The Death of Emmett Till") and "Oxford Town," which would eventually make it onto his second album.

"Emmett Till," about the infamous lynching of a Black fourteen-year-old near Drew, Mississippi, is earnest in its outrage but formulaic as a protest song. "Oxford Town" is a response to *Broadside*'s invitation for songs about the "Battle of Oxford," rioting by a white supremacist mob upon James Meredith's enrollment at the University of Mississippi. Like "Emmett Till" and most of Dylan's early topical songs, it works on its own terms, yet there's nothing really to distinguish it from the steady stream of similar topical songs in *Broadside*.

But there was plenty to distinguish "A Hard Rain's A-Gonna Fall," which proved not only that "Blowin' in the Wind" was no fluke but that Dylan could create far more evocative imagery than that first breakthrough suggested. Like "Blowin' in the Wind," "Hard Rain" is built around a series of questions, in this case borrowed from the Anglo-Scottish ballad "Lord Randall," in which a dialogue between mother and son reveals that the son has been poisoned by his lover. In "Hard Rain," the blue-eyed son's answers do not gradually reveal a murder plot, nor are they indeterminately "blowin' in the wind." Instead they offer a panorama of vivid, mostly disturbing images that could spring from another era (perhaps a crowded Pieter Brueghel or Hieronymus Bosch landscape) or from America in 1962. Some visions draw attention to the human propensity for violence and indifference to suffering—blood dripping from branches, children holding deadly weapons. Other images are more surreal, sharpening the impression of suffering and impending doom of broken tongues and world-drowning waves. With the last verse the son, who by this point has merged with Dylan in most listeners' minds, vows to travel and unflinchingly report back from this landscape of fear and despair.

Commentators often cite French Symbolist poets, particularly Arthur Rimbaud, as touchstones for the imagery in "Hard Rain"; the catalogues and the heroic stance of the singer also suggest Walt Whitman, whose poems, especially "Song of Myself," hover like intelligence-gathering drones over the American landscape. At the same time Dylan's nightmarish imagery, particularly in the refrain—with "hard" repeated four times—sets him apart from the generally optimistic Whitman. By the time the song was officially released the United States had narrowly avoided nuclear conflict during the Cuban Missile Crisis, which unfolded in October 1962, so listeners naturally associated the hard rain with radioactive fallout. But Dylan wrote the song before the Missile Crisis, and in a 1963 interview with Studs Terkel he denied that the "rain" was specifically atomic rain while affirming its wider apocalyptic meaning: "I just mean some sort of end that's just gotta happen."[53]

"Hard Rain" is a song of experience by a man entering adulthood, almost exactly 21 years old. Not surprisingly it's the song that brought Dylan to the attention of established poets like Allen Ginsberg, himself a disciple of Whitman but whose vision revealed a photographic negative of the American dream. With "Hard Rain" Dylan, like Ginsberg, was countering the postwar optimism and vigor represented by the Kennedy administration and the affluent, nearly all-white suburbs. He was indeed giving voice to a counterculture.

3

1962–63: Awakening

As he focused on his songwriting, Dylan played clubs and coffeehouses less frequently than before, although he did travel to Montreal for a gig at the Finjan Club in July, performing a set that balanced originals and traditional songs. In September 1962 he joined Seeger, the New World Singers, and other folk performers on a program sponsored by *Sing Out!* called a "Carnegie Hall Hootenanny" (and it was the big hall this time). The following month he was part of a "Traveling Hootenanny" put on by Izzy Young's Folklore Center at Town Hall, with a line-up that also featured Judy Collins and John Lee Hooker. In late September or early October he played a full set (seventeen songs) for an invited audience at the Gaslight, recorded at Grossman's direction.

The recording was widely circulated on bootlegs and then finally released by Columbia in 2005 (although not the entire performance). On *Live at the Gaslight 1962* Dylan performs "Hard Rain" at a tempo faster than the studio version that would appear the following year; the choruses at the Gaslight become a sing-along, hinting that the song was already well known among folk singers months before it was available on vinyl.

For the Gaslight taping Dylan still leans heavily on traditional songs, performing only five originals, but he sings nothing primarily associated with Woody Guthrie. Instead he performs five tunes by Black blues singers: Blind Lemon Jefferson's "See That My Grave Is Kept Clean," Lead Belly's "Ain't No More Cane," Reverend Gary Davis's "Cocaine," Blind Willie Johnson's "Motherless Children," and

Robert Johnson's "Kindhearted Woman Blues." Robert Johnson's recordings had been obscure and unavailable on vinyl until Columbia released *King of the Delta Blues Singers* in 1961, and John Hammond had given Dylan a copy. He was blown away, as he testifies in *Chronicles*:

> I listened to it repeatedly, cut after cut, one song after another, sitting staring at the record player. Whenever I did, it felt like a ghost had come into the room, a fearsome apparition. The songs were layered with a startling economy of lines. Johnson masked the presence of more than twenty men. I fixated on every song and wondered how Johnson did it . . . I started meditating on the construction of the verses, seeing how different they were from Woody's. Johnson's words made my nerves quiver like piano wires.[1]

Like Guthrie, Johnson offered a model of songwriting and singing that was raw and confrontational. But Johnson and other Black blues performers developed song structures with more space and a style that could quickly flip from plaintive to aggressive. As if acknowledging the African American source for what was already his most popular song, at the Gaslight Dylan performed "No More Auction Block" but not "Blowin' in the Wind."

Two other songs that were part of Dylan's Gaslight set further demonstrate what a powerful and original songwriter he had already become. "The Ballad of Hollis Brown" could pass for a topical song, but unlike "The Death of Emmett Till" or "Oxford Town," the story Dylan tells here is fictional, and there's no lesson or admonishment attached to it. The matter-of-fact brutality of the song reflects Robert Johnson's influence moving in on Guthrie's. Musically based on the murder ballad "Pretty Polly," "Hollis Brown" builds in tension as the consequences of a South Dakota farmer's poverty—babies crying, wife screaming—overwhelm him.

Once seven shotgun shells are introduced (in the seventh verse) it's clear where the plot is headed, but the dread mounts slowly and painfully; we sympathize more and more with Hollis's despair even as each verse ends with clear foreshadowing of the murders he is bound to commit. Pete Seeger had adapted Ecclesiastes 3:1–8 into "Turn! Turn! Turn!" a few years earlier, singing that there is a time to be born and a time to die. "Hollis Brown" might be read as a grim reflection on the same theme. Seven people are dead on Hollis's farm, and somewhere, Dylan tells us, another seven are being born.

The other breakthrough song Dylan performed that night was "Don't Think Twice, It's Alright." The folk arrangement, homespun vocabulary, and low-key delivery almost hide the song's sardonic wit, akin to Cole Porter's breakup song "Just One of Those Things." Dylan presents a mask of indifference, a cool, casual pose, implicitly saying "I don't want you to feel guilty about forcing me to leave you, because it's not a big deal." But that pose doesn't convince the listener or the singer. He blames her for not loving him enough and for expecting too much. "Don't Think Twice" manages to be at once comic, whether we hear the speaker's refrain as sarcastic or unintentionally ironic, and heartbreaking, for the sorrow and regret he reveals without directly expressing.

Dylan wrote "Don't Think Twice" as he was dealing with a temporary separation from Suze Rotolo, who had left to study in Italy. What was originally planned as a summer trip was extended through the end of the year, as Rotolo relished the experience of living abroad and gained more self-confidence. She recalled, "I loved him, and he loved me, but I had doubts about him, his honesty, and the way life would be."[2] Although Bob hadn't been particularly faithful to Suze, he missed her badly. He made another trip back to Minnesota in August, where he made yet another home recording for Tony Glover, introducing a new song, "Tomorrow Is a Long Time," by declaring that he wouldn't go back to New York until "my girl" returned.[3] At that point he didn't know that she was wasn't returning as planned. He went back to New York and, a few months later, recorded his first great love song at Witmark studios. Over two dozen performers, including Judy Collins, Elvis Presley, Harry Belafonte, and Rod Stewart, would cover "Tomorrow Is a Long Time" before Columbia, in late 1971, included a live Dylan recording of the classic on *Bob Dylan's Greatest Hits, Volume II*.

While Columbia seemed to be in no rush to release the follow-up to Dylan's poor-selling debut album, the company recorded Dylan throughout 1962, putting together seven sessions at Studio A, 7th Avenue at West 52nd Street, from April to December for an album whose working title was *Bob Dylan's Blues*. Dylan plugged away at his new songs while John Hammond and Albert Grossman wrestled for control over the recording and over Dylan's future with the company. In October and November a full band—guitar, bass, drums, and piano—were involved, cutting Dylan's first single, "Mixed-Up Confusion" (which received no promotion and failed to chart), as well as a cover of the Elvis Presley hit "That's Alright." This electric detour notwithstanding, Dylan's second album would be unplugged and solo, with the exception of the gentle bass and drums on "Corrina, Corrina." By mid-December it was complete. Meanwhile British television director Philip Saville, who had seen Dylan perform in New York, invited him to appear in a BBC-broadcast play called *Madhouse on Castle Street*, so Dylan flew to London, eager to check out the English folk scene and possibly make his way to Italy and a reunion with Suze.

Bob and Suze's correspondence must have lapsed by mid-December ("Our letters had crossed in the mail," she recalled), because neither of them realized that she was returning to the States just as he was leaving. When Dylan's rehearsals for *Madhouse* didn't go well, Saville rewrote the script, reassigning his speaking part and creating a new singing-only character called Bobby. He sang three traditional folk songs along with the still-unreleased "Blowin' in the Wind." (No copies of the BBC broadcast are known to have survived.) Dylan was almost certainly less interested in *Madhouse* than he was in meeting and listening to London folk musicians. Although hardly famous in England he was known to aficionados who paid attention to publications like *Sing Out!*—in fact when Dylan ran into the folk singer Martin Carthy at the King and Queen Pub Carthy recognized him from that magazine's cover.[4] Carthy served as a guide for Dylan and taught him some British folk tunes in the process. Most significantly Dylan learned "Scarborough Fair" from Carthy and adapted it with his own lyrics as "Girl from the North Country." Carthy also taught him "Lady Franklin's Lament," which provided the melody for "Bob Dylan's Dream."[5]

Dylan was not welcomed as warmly by folk purists. His mixture of various traditional styles and his method of writing songs on the palimpsest of passed-down melodies (implicitly disrespecting time-honored tunes) rankled respected members of the old guard like A. L. "Bert" Lloyd and Ewan MacColl, folklorist/song collectors and founders of the Singers' Club, where Dylan managed to take the stage.[6] MacColl and his wife Peggy Seeger—sister of Mike and half-sister of Pete—shunned this American punk as inauthentic. It didn't help that Dylan was often drunk and rude to his English hosts as he made the rounds of pubs and clubs.[7] He was frequently joined in this pursuit by two American musician friends, Eric Von Schmidt and Richard Fariña. Dylan had already name-checked Von Schmidt as his source for "Baby, Let Me Follow You Down" on his debut album. Fariña and Dylan were acquainted through Fariña's soon-to-be ex-wife Carolyn Hester, and they would eventually spend much more time together in the company of Fariña's future wife, Mimi Baez, and her sister Joan.[8] Under the pseudonym Blind Boy Grunt (which he used on other occasions to get around his contract with Columbia), Dylan played harmonica and sang back-up on an album Fariña and Von Schmidt recorded at a record shop in London that January. A photograph from January 1963 shows Dylan in a trilby hat, laughing and clapping his hands on a cramped stage in London's Troubadour club with Fariña, Von Schmidt, Martin Carthy, and guitarist Ethan Singer; it seems like a representative snapshot of this English excursion.

Having spent about a month in England—with a side-trip to Rome, where he met with Grossman and (fellow Grossman client) Odetta—Dylan returned to New York in mid-January 1963. In the time between her return and his, Suze Rotolo found that she had been cast as the villain by the Village scenesters, "the Barbara Allen to his Sweet William" in her words. But when Dylan returned they "were right back together again, absorbing the changes that had happened to both of us during our separation."[9] She was in for a bumpy ride though, as Dylan's career was just about to take off.

Dylan spent the early months of 1963 doing radio shows, writing and polishing new songs, and then recording them—a few amateur tapings, visits to Witmark, two songs (as Blind Boy Grunt) for a compilation album released by *Broadside* magazine, and finally in late April another session for Columbia. Because Dylan was not yet 21 when he had signed with Columbia, Grossman had room to maneuver for a more favorable contract, which may have delayed the release of the second album. Another legal issue certainly delayed, and changed, *Freewheelin'*: "Talkin' John Birch" had come to the attention of Columbia's lawyers, who feared a libel suit over the song's assertion that the Birchers "all agree with Hitler's views." Dylan objected to its removal, but ultimately the decision was out of his control.[10] And yet he worked the situation to his advantage, recording five new songs, four of which would appear on the reconfigured *Freewheelin'* album. So "John Birch," along with "Let Me Die in My Footsteps," "Ramblin', Gamblin' Willie," and "Rocks and Gravel," all Dylan originals, were replaced by new originals: "Girl from the North Country," "Masters of War," "Talkin' World War III Blues," and "Bob Dylan's Dream." He also got a new producer, probably a result of contract and recording disputes between Hammond and Grossman. Tom Wilson, who as a Black record producer was a rarity at the time, had worked mainly with avant-garde jazz musicians prior to joining the Columbia staff. He had little interest in or respect for folk music at the time, but with Dylan, and then with Simon and Garfunkel, he would soon help usher in the sound of folk-rock.

The trade-out for the four new tracks improved the album. "Talkin' World War III Blues" is equal to "John Birch" as Cold War satire. The lyrics of "Bob Dylan's Dream" could have been written in a pub fifty or two hundred years earlier, somewhat pedestrian but still a lovely tribute to youthful friendships. "Girl from the North Country" is perhaps the best example of Dylan repurposing a traditional song with beautiful results, a fond remembrance of a lost love (Echo Helstrom? Bonnie Beecher? Suze Rotolo, transplanted to "the North Country"?). And "Masters of War," perhaps the ultimate Dylan "finger-pointin' song," would become a cornerstone of his protest canon. Recorded at the height of the Cold War but before U.S.

involvement in Vietnam was deep or public enough to register on the national consciousness, its anti-war message was politically safe, especially as he singles out no one and refers to no specific war. Moreover, since even the outgoing Republican president and five-star general Dwight Eisenhower had denounced the "military-industrial complex" in 1961, Dylan's targeting of the builders of planes and bombs who "hide behind desks" was not all that radical. Lacking the nuance, detail, or inventive imagery of Dylan's better early songs, "Masters of War" nonetheless succeeds as a broad expression of righteous anger. Its vitriol would find specific targets as the USA sent more and more recruits to Vietnam in the second half of the decade.

The mere fact that Dylan had written eleven of the thirteen songs himself (and claimed arranger or co-author credit for the other two) was historic in pop music history. Spanning eight recording sessions over an entire year (unheard of in the early 1960s), *Freewheelin'* was Dylan's first great album, and it essentially redefined "folk music." The term could still signify the preservation of songs passed down through oral tradition, played on a variety of instruments, typically associated with a specific regional or national tradition—but as a pop music genre, "folk" would now be associated primarily with the sound of an acoustic guitar and a sincere, unaffected voice, and it would especially embrace songwriters who sang their own material. *Freewheelin*'s contents combined, sometimes within the same song, the topical and the personal, the imagistic and the polemic. It had love songs, blues, anthems, and satires, and all seemed to reflect the personality of the performer.

It also had a great cover. On the day of the photo shoot neither Bob nor Suze was dressed warmly enough for the cold, snowy weather—particularly not Bob, whose impractical suede jacket Suze identified as an "image choice." So it's unlikely that photographer Don Hunstein had to direct them to huddle close together as they walked down the middle of Jones Street between Bleecker and West 4th, flanked by parked cars and brownstones. With Dylan slightly hunched from the cold, looking at the street and apparently talking at the moment the photograph was taken, the shot seems totally candid. What makes him look like a star is Suze, half a step behind him, both hands wrapped around his arm, smiling at the camera since he won't. She offered her own analysis of the cover art in her memoir:

> [I]t is one of those cultural markers that influenced the look of album covers precisely because of its casual, down-home spontaneity and sensibility. Most album covers were carefully staged and controlled, to terrific effect on the Blue Note jazz album covers, with their snappy graphics and beautiful black-and-white photographs, and to not-so-great effect on the perfectly posed and clean-cut pop and folk albums. Whoever was ultimately responsible for choosing that particular photograph for *The Freewheelin' Bob Dylan* really had an eye for a new look.[11]

Dylan performed frequently in the weeks leading up to the release of *Freewheelin'*. He did a solo concert, recorded but unreleased by Columbia (until 2025), at the 1,500-seat Town Hall on April 12, playing mostly new songs to the largest audience yet for an all-Dylan show. He introduced himself with the program note consisting of the prose poem "My Life in a Stolen Moment" (described in Chapter One). He concluded the performance with another poem, "Last Thoughts on Woody Guthrie." More directly than "Hard Rain" even, "Last Thoughts" evokes Whitman by way of Ginsberg, and, as Paul Williams notes, it's closely tied to Dylan's songwriting as a spoken-word performance: "It's closer to a rhythm than a melody, but it's a musical rhythm, like if someone were playing chords or tapping on a snare drum in the back of your mind while these words roll and flow and stop and get stuck and flow some more through the front part."[12] Moreover Dylan had the chutzpah, before he had sold more than a few thousand records, to close a concert by reciting a poem.

At the end of April Dylan appeared on Studs Terkel's Wax Museum radio show, playing half a dozen original songs and chatting with his fascinated host, who was twice Dylan's age but clearly aware that his guest was an artist to be taken seriously. In early May he played two brief sets on the opening day of a folk festival at Brandeis University (a recording of which would be released officially almost

Tufts University concert poster, 1963.

fifty years later). His biggest opportunity for pre-album-release promotion was a spot on the Ed Sullivan Show on May 12; he had even told friends and family back in Hibbing (on a trip home earlier that year) to be sure to tune in. But Dylan did not appear on the show. He had decided to play "Talkin' John Birch," the song deleted from *Freewheelin'*, knowing that the selection would be controversial. Sure enough, CBS network censors—from the same company who owned Columbia Records—insisted he perform something else. Dylan refused, walking out on the show altogether. In doing so he took a principled stand that was also sure to attract publicity and bolster his reputation as a protest singer and rebel. He continued to perform the song throughout 1963 and '64, and on at least one occasion he introduced it by its title and then added, "and there ain't nothin' wrong with this song."[13]

A few months earlier Dylan had told *Seventeen* magazine that he hated playing in clubs because people drank and talked and didn't listen: "I can't go out after people. If they want what I've got, they always have to come to me with their hands out and they take from me. That's the way I am."[14] Now that he had some credibility and leverage, that stance was beginning to apply to his career generally. Even though he hadn't had a hit single or album, he could afford to walk out on *The Ed Sullivan Show* to assert control over his own career decisions. On one level he was invoking the principle of freedom of speech; but at the same time he was asserting his own self-determination. He had a manager with a keen eye on the bottom line, but Grossman was really no Colonel Tom Parker, who kept tight control over Elvis's image and pushed him toward the cultural mainstream. As much as he enriched himself on the proceeds of Dylan's labor, Grossman, at this pivotal early stage, had the wisdom to let Dylan create his own public persona.

A few weeks before the Sullivan Show non-appearance, Dylan had traveled to Boston to play a Friday–Saturday stand at the Café Yana; on Sunday he joined Eric Von Schmidt and Ramblin' Jack Elliott at a hootenanny at Club 47, which had been Joan Baez's launch pad and was still Cambridge's premier folk club. Baez showed up and then made the scene at an after-party where the music continued. She had not been particularly moved by Dylan at Gerde's when he was just starting to write his own material, but on this night—April 21, 1963—he played a few new songs that made a stronger impression: "With God on Our Side," "Masters of War," "Hard Rain," and "The Death of Emmett Till." In fact Baez was completely won over, and the two made plans to sing together at the Monterey Folk Festival the following month.[15] Headlined by Peter, Paul and Mary, the Weavers, and the New Lost City Ramblers, the Monterey festival was a big opportunity for Dylan, a week after Sullivan and a week before *Freewheelin'*s release. But he struggled to hold the audience's attention until Baez came onstage to join him for "With God on Our Side." She scolded the audience for not giving Dylan more respect before the pair performed their first public duet.

They were an odd couple, to be sure: Baez, making an unannounced appearance before a worshipful audience, a poised, established performer with a crystalline voice, alongside Dylan, whose demeanor and reputation were part street urchin and part *enfant terrible*, with a voice that could not have presented a starker contrast with his new partner's. Dylan had first performed "With God on Our Side" publicly at the Town Hall concert in April, but it was not among the late additions to *Freewheelin'*. He had borrowed the melody, the opening verses' structure, and to some extent the sentiment from a song he had heard in England: Dominic Behan's "The Patriot Game." Behan's song is nuanced: while loyal to the cause of Irish nationalism, the singer questions blind adherence to the IRA's violent tactics. Dylan's song is an all-out assault on the Christian strain of American exceptionalism, which justifies warfare and state-sanctioned violence as doing God's work. He calls attention from the first line to his own Midwestern origins, evoking the patriotic, law-abiding values of the American heartland.

The song's message is delivered ironically—the speaker never directly challenges the ideology he has been fed but only expresses "confusion" over the obvious hypocrisies the song describes. The tension created by that irony epitomized the nascent youth counterculture: the song *counters* what young people have been taught with what they know to be true. It's not a great song for a duet though, given the singular first-person voice, and particularly not a duet with Baez, whose voice is not well suited to the lyrics' plainspoken, Midwestern affect and the irony that Dylan's delivery underscores. But here she was, harmonizing and blessing the arrival of the folk revival's new voice.

It was the beginning of an intense personal and professional relationship. Dylan spent the days following the Monterey festival at Baez's house in the Carmel Highlands. Baez invited him to perform on her tour that fall, in addition to collaborating at the Newport Folk Festival in July. While it would be an oversimplification to say that Baez fell in love with Dylan and Dylan simply took advantage of the situation, she does seem to have put more heart into the relationship than he did. That said, they both benefited. Dylan represented the future of folk music; Baez was young (Dylan's age) and enormously popular but in an artistic rut, already far from the cutting edge. But not anymore. As David Hajdu put it, after Monterey "if folk was heading witherward to Bob Dylan, it was going toward, not away from, Joan Baez."[16] And for Dylan the payoff was obvious: Baez delivered an audience exponentially larger than the one that had bought a few thousand copies of his debut album.

While Baez and Dylan were forging a partnership in Carmel, copies of *Freewheelin'* were being shipped to record stores across the country, and radio stations were playing Peter, Paul and Mary's version of "Blowin' in the Wind" in advance of its official release.[17] Their version was predictably smooth, with gentle acoustic bass-and-guitar accompaniment and precise vocal harmonies, the pop-folk sound that had already scored them two top-ten hits—the first of which, the Pete Seeger-penned "If I Had a Hammer," featured a similarly abstract social consciousness. "Blowin' in the Wind" was more accusatory than "Hammer," pointing not just to the ideals of freedom, justice, and love but the more specific imperative to call a man a man (not "boy"). Their version saturated the airwaves in the summer of 1963, rising to number two on the *Billboard* pop chart and selling over a million copies.

So by the time Dylan appeared at the Newport Folk Festival in July, he was the undisputed Next Big Thing, almost famous and already revered in the folk world. *Freewheelin'* received strong reviews and sold considerably better than *Bob Dylan*, but the real buzz was about his highly original, poetic songwriting, repeatedly praised onstage by Baez and Peter, Paul and Mary. They would all be together at Newport, along with Seeger, who was one of the festival's organizers, and a roster overloaded with present and future folk and blues legends, many of whom were Dylan's friendly rivals: Dave Van Ronk, Phil Ochs, Ramblin' Jack Elliott, Paul Clayton, Judy Collins, the

At the 1963 Newport Folk Festival with Peter, Paul and Mary, Joan Baez, the Freedom Singers, and Pete Seeger. Photo by Rowland Scherman.

New Lost City Ramblers, Jean Ritchie, Mississippi John Hurt, Doc Watson, John Lee Hooker, Sonny Terry, Ian and Sylvia, the Dillards, Theodore Bikel, and John Hammond, Jr., son of the man who had signed Dylan to Columbia.

Attendance topped 50,000 for the weekend, with "workshop" stages scattered across Freebody Park during the day and the entire audience assembled for main-stage evening concerts. Dylan created a sensation, performing solo and with Baez throughout the weekend. He was at once humble and cocky: slouchy, wearing a rumpled work shirt and laughing nervously, but singing confidently, and when he wasn't singing, walking around Newport with a bullwhip. The festival program featured a prose poem by Dylan, a kind of sequel to "My Life in a Stolen Moment." Framed as a letter to his old friend Tony (Dave) Glover, it was really an open letter to the folk music community. Written in Dylan's Guthrie-derived dialect, its main themes are that the times are too complicated for "which side are you on" songs and that Dylan, inspired as he was by traditional folk music, needs to write his own: "Now's a complicated day/ An' all I'm sayin' is'at I gotta make my own statement bout this day."[18]

The first night ended with Dylan leading an all-star chorus of Baez; Seeger; Peter, Paul and Mary; and the Freedom Singers performing "Blowin' in the Wind" and "We Shall Overcome." The other stars of the folk world were literally lined up behind him, as if anointing him their new leader.

Dylan had solidified his commitment to the Civil Rights Movement by performing with Seeger and Bikel at a SNCC (Student Nonviolent Coordinating Committee) voter registration rally in Greenwood, Mississippi, a few weeks before Newport. With a flatbed truck as a backdrop, flanked by Seeger and numerous SNCC volunteers in work clothes, Dylan in that moment seemed to epitomize the white civil rights crusader. And this was no mere photo op: Greenwood was under siege by Klansmen and other white supremacists; Dylan spent the night before the rally in a church loft and had to lie flat in the back of the car on the way to the rally.[19]

He debuted a song that he introduced as being "about Medgar Evers," the NAACP field secretary who had been murdered a month earlier. But "Only a Pawn in Their Game" is not really about Evers but about his killer, or the stereotypical "pawn" that Dylan imagined to be his killer. The song's thesis is that the "poor white" who pulled the trigger "ain't to blame" because he unwittingly does the work of a self-interested power structure, represented by politicians and law enforcement. Dylan conveys a basic truth about the workings of racist ideology and the need to recognize the systemic racism behind individual acts of violence like Evers's murder.[20] But having written the song so soon after the event, he was probably not aware that the killer, Byron De La Beckwith, was a particularly unsympathetic, eager, and self-motivated "pawn," active in the Ku Klux Klan and the White Citizens Council, who would later trade on his status as Evers's not-convicted murderer, even running for lieutenant governor of Mississippi in 1967. While "Pawn" makes a subtle argument for a three-minute song, it still oversimplifies the responsibility in suggesting that De La Beckwith, or other segregationist foot soldiers, were more victims than culprits. Granted, the song isn't arguing that the killer is not legally liable for his actions; but especially in an environment where De La Beckwith was unlikely to be convicted (two

1964 trials resulted in hung juries), the recurring phrase "he ain't to blame" seems misguided.

Dylan performed "Only a Pawn in Their Game" again at the August 28 March on Washington for Jobs and Freedom, which Medgar Evers's widow attended. He also performed "Blowin' in the Wind" and, with Baez, a recently composed anthem that combined utopian optimism with a thirst for revenge, "When the Ship Comes In." Composed in response to a suspicious hotel manager's insulting treatment (aimed at Dylan's appearance), the song's lyrics mainly expand on the title's metaphor for the inevitable day of victory of "our side."[21] But the song also revels in the unspecified enemies' defeat, forecasting a schadenfreude that seems out of place with the inclusive ideals of the march.

According to Baez, Dylan was very reluctant to perform in front of a quarter million protesters at the march, but she persuaded him: "We had to look straight at each other when we were singing. It was just too moving to look out at that sea of faces. We never sang that way, staring straight into each other's eyes. We gave each other strength, and it was very intimate and the most public thing we ever did." Aside from Peter, Paul and Mary (who of course also sang "Blowin' in the Wind"), Dylan and Baez were the only white performers at the Lincoln Memorial. Other singers included Mahalia Jackson, Marian Anderson, Odetta, and the SNCC Freedom Singers—the biracial line-up underscores the alliance between the young, white folkies and the Movement. But it was an uneasy alliance: Dick Gregory, the comedian-activist, probably spoke for many when he later asked, "What was a white boy like Bob Dylan there for?"[22] Dylan may have wondered the same thing, as this performance, in front of a quarter million marchers, was essentially his last direct involvement with organized protest for over a decade.

Dylan spent the late summer and early fall performing as an unannounced guest at Joan Baez concerts—gradually audiences became more receptive—and hanging out with her in Carmel while writing at a frantic pace. When he was on the East Coast, he spent time in Woodstock, New York, at Albert Grossman's house, a couple of hours north of the City. He and Suze Rotolo hadn't broken up, but the relationship was destabilized, to say the least, by his open-secret romance with Baez and his rapidly growing fame. After a solo concert at Carnegie Hall on October 26 Rotolo and Terri Thal helped draw waiting fans away from Dylan's path from the hall to the limo, playing the role of decoys. "I remember being very frightened by the energy of the crowd," she recalled. "They literally charged the limousine, pounding on the roof and slapping at the windows, yelling to get Bob's attention." Rotolo did not like the ever-patient girlfriend role. By now she had moved out of the West 4th Street apartment she had shared with Dylan and moved in with her sister Carla, who conspicuously disliked Bob. For her part Suze "hated being thought of being so-and-so's chick: I did not want to be a string on Bob Dylan's guitar."[23]

Meanwhile Dylan recorded his third album over the course of six sessions—three in August, three in October—at Columbia's Studio A. The track that opens the album and provides its title is a kind of sequel to "Blowin' in the Wind." "The Times They Are A-Changin'" doesn't ask questions; it exhorts and warns the older generation to either get behind the young generation or get out of the way. As generational anthems go, this one is much clearer, calling out the establishment, two categories at a time: writers and critics, senators and congressmen, mothers and fathers. Like "Blowin' in the Wind," it has a deliberate ring of biblical prophecy, culminating in a direct reference to the Gospel of Matthew—"so the last shall be first, and the first last"—at the song's conclusion. With this song Dylan had fully, if temporarily, embraced the role of prophet and spokesman for his generation.

"The Times They Are A-Changin'" is both rousing and somber, a description that fits the rest of the album. Whereas the aptly titled *Freewheelin'* showcased the wide range of Dylan's early songwriting, *Times* features songs of protest and social realism almost exclusively, the exceptions being a pair of breakup songs. The arrangements are stark: just Dylan with acoustic guitar and harmonica—similar to *Freewheelin'*, but without even the single bass-and-drums-backed track. The black-and-off-white cover seems to mirror the stark tone of the music, with a photograph (by Barry Feinstein) of Dylan frowning down at the viewer, eyes half shut and hidden in shadow—it resembles the Depression-era photographs of Dorothea Lange or Walker Evans. The album's original cover even has a lightly textured surface, as if to appear less mass-produced or to blunt any cheerful reflective light.

The Times They Are A-Changin' is a dark masterpiece, consistent in sound and mood as well as quality. In addition to the title song, "With God on Our Side," "The Ballad of Hollis Brown," "Only a Pawn in Their Game," "When the Ship Comes In," and "North Country Blues" (all previously discussed), it features another celebrated "finger-pointin' song," "The Lonesome Death of Hattie Carroll." In February 1963, at a charity ball in Baltimore's Emerson Hotel, William Zantzinger, a wealthy 24-year-old tobacco farmer, got very drunk and began verbally and physically abusing the serving staff. After ordering a drink from Carroll, who was working as a bartender, he beat her with a decorative, metal-tipped cane, calling her a "n—" and a "bitch." Carroll retreated to the kitchen and then collapsed and was taken to a hospital, where she died of a brain hemorrhage hours later. Zantzinger's lawyers got the original murder charge reduced to manslaughter and argued that underlying health conditions were responsible for the 51-year-old Carroll's death. At the trial Zantzinger claimed to have no memory of the incident because of his drinking. He was found guilty but received a mere six-month jail sentence and a $625 fine.[24]

Dylan embellished only a little (and dropped the "t" from Zantzinger's name), but more successfully than in "Only a Pawn," he anatomized the racial disparities, reminiscent of slavery, in which the incident was situated. He was determined to show that Zantzinger's actions were more than a random act of violence and even more determined to show how the justice system itself is implicated. The judge makes a pretense of administering justice—Dylan bears down on the hypocrisy over the course of the final verse—before delivering the six-month sentence. The first three choruses had admonished listeners that now was not the time for tears—instead that time comes with the final verse, which declaims the light sentence that Zantzinger received. The song could hardly be more topical, having been recorded just two months after Zantzinger's trial, and yet, grounded as it is in a specific case, it resonates far beyond it, suggesting ways in which the times have not changed.[25]

The other three are songs of parting. "One Too Many Mornings" and "Boots of Spanish Leather" both reflect the fading of Dylan's relationship with Suze Rotolo; the latter, a beautiful ballad based musically on "Scarborough Fair" (though not quite as blatantly as "Girl from the North Country"), evokes the sense of abandonment Dylan must have felt when Rotolo extended her time in Italy. The album's final track, "Restless Farewell," pairs with the earlier "Bob Dylan's Dream," a song that marks the end of something—not a romantic relationship but a phase of the singer's life, a time spent in a particular place with a particular group of people. It's an appropriate closer, a valedictory to the phase of Dylan's career that *The Times They Are A-Changin'* epitomized.

As with *Freewheelin'*, the *Times* sessions produced several strong tracks that didn't make the cut, a habit of Dylan's that still tantalizes fans and critics who reconstruct "lost albums"; it also provides seemingly countless revelations in the official Bootleg Series initiated in 1991. "Paths of Victory," "Only a Hobo," "Moonshiner," "Seven Curses," "Eternal Circle," and "Suze (The Cough Song)" can all be found on the first Bootleg Series release. Two others, perhaps the two best, were released on 1985's *Biograph* box set: "Percy's Song" and "Lay Down Your Weary Tune." The latter song, replaced at the last minute by "Restless Farewell," was based on a Scottish ballad Dylan heard on an old 78-rpm record.[26] The lyrics are a Transcendentalist hymn, something Ralph Waldo Emerson might have written a hundred years earlier. In each verse the natural world creates music, the morning breeze like a bugle, crashing winds like cymbals, and so on. Lay down your weary tune, the singer tells us; nature is the true source of music. It's an even better song than "Restless Farewell" and would have made a great closer, but perhaps it was too life-affirming to fit the album's dark mood.

Just after *Times* had been completed but well before its release, *Newsweek* magazine published a brief profile of Dylan that exploded his self-mythologizing. Explicating his fans' religious devotion, the uncredited reporter (Dick Schaap) describes Dylan sarcastically:

> He has suffered; he has been hung up, man, without bread, without a chick, with twisted wires growing inside him. His audiences share his pain, and seem jealous because they grew up in conventional homes and conventional schools. The ironic thing is that Bob Dylan, too, grew up in a conventional home, and went to conventional schools. He shrouds his past in contradictions, but he is the elder son of a Hibbing, Minnesota, appliance dealer named Abe Zimmerman, and, as Bobby Zimmerman, he attended Hibbing High School, then briefly the University of Minnesota.

The article goes on to reveal that, in contradiction of Dylan's claims ("I don't know my parents") he had visited his family in Minnesota recently, and Abe and Beatty attended his Carnegie Hall concert in October. The reporter also repeats a "rumor" that Dylan bought "Blowin' in the Wind" from a New Jersey high school student, and points out that the anti-commercial folk singer "has two agents who hover about him, guarding his words and fattening his contracts."[27] Dylan was furious, not only at *Newsweek* but at his family for talking to *Newsweek* and at Grossman for not finding a way to block the publication. More significantly the *Newsweek* debacle initiated a career-long distrust of the press. According to Robert Shelton, whose *New York Times* article had helped launch Dylan's career two years earlier and who spoke with Dylan just after the article appeared, "Dylan turned from an accessible subject into a cagey game-player who toyed with interview questions, who developed the outrageous 'anti-interview,' saying shocking, even deleterious things, things he often didn't believe. He became dubious that even the emerging underground press could understand him."[28]

Dylan articulated this hostility to the press in one of the "11 Outlined Epitaphs" printed on the back cover and insert to *The Times They Are A-Changin'*:

> ah but mine is of another story
> for I do not care t be made an oddball
> bouncing past reporter's pens

co-operatin with questions
aimed at eyes that want t see
"there's nothin here
go back t sleep
or look at the ads
on page 33"

Here Dylan suggests that by "co-operatin" with the commercial press he is a pawn in their game, the end of which is advertising. In doing so he becomes trivialized, fodder for the shallow amusement of consumers:

I don't like to be stuck in print
starin out at cavity minds
who gobble chocolate candy bars
quite content an satisfied
their day complete
at seein' what I eat for breakfast
the kind of clothes I like to wear
an the hobbies that I like t do

Other epitaphs are more oblique, often evoking beat poetry. He once again describes the bleak, small-town life and landscape of Hibbing, his debt to Woody Guthrie, his devotion to "beautiful Sue," his memories of the Van Ronks' apartment, and a catalogue of influences and inspirations that includes Paul Clayton, Edith Piaf, Marlene Dietrich, Allen Ginsberg, Modigliani, Miles Davis, William Blake, Johnny Cash, and Pete Seeger. Moreover the gesture of including a collection of free verse poems instead of traditional liner notes was a sign, as if one were needed, that Dylan's ambitions and his relationship with his audience transcended those of the typical performer.

On Friday, November 22 President Kennedy was killed in Dallas. Fifty-seven years later Dylan would make the assassination the focal point of his epic spoken-word recording, "Murder Most Foul." At the time, though, he expressed his feelings about the assassination in lines of poetry that would later be incorporated into "Chimes of Freedom":

"the colors of Friday were dull/ as cathedral bells were gently burnin/ strikin for the gentle/ strikin for the kind."[29]

Along with millions of other Americans Dylan was glued to the television throughout the weekend; Suze Rotolo remembered watching with him and her sister Carla when Lee Harvey Oswald was shot on Sunday 24th: "Bob barely spoke and would not leave the TV."[30] Dylan also performed a concert in upstate New York just a few days later. He told biographer Anthony Scaduto, "I had to go on stage, I couldn't cancel. I went to the hall and to my amazement the hall was filled. Everybody turned out for the concert. The song I was opening with was 'The Times They Are A-Changin'' and I thought, 'Wow, how can I open with that song? I'll get rocks thrown at me.' . . . But I had to sing it, my whole concert takes off from there."[31]

Dylan's forthcoming album, which featured three songs about murders, became all the more poignant, appropriate to the national mood. Kennedy's death shook Dylan as it did all Americans; it probably also played a role in his pivot away from politics. According to his friend, folk singer Eric Anderson, "He might even have had fears of assassination himself, being the center of attention and saying the kinds of things he was saying."[32]

On December 13, three weeks after Kennedy was shot, Dylan was presented with the Tom Paine Award at a fundraiser hosted by the Emergency Civil Liberties Committee (ECLC), a group that epitomized the left-wing establishment, similar to the ACLU in its mission. Dylan was uncomfortable with the situation, being embraced—implicitly owned—by the old guard, in this case about 1,400 mostly middle-aged, well-dressed men and women.[33] He got drunk and, when it was time to accept the award, gave a rambling speech that insulted his hosts. He began and ended his remarks by aligning himself with students who, months before, had defied the U.S. travel ban to Cuba—"because they're all young and it's took me a long time to get young and now I consider myself young. And I'm proud of it." He spent about half of the short, impromptu speech lamenting the fact that he was in a room full of old people with bald heads. "Old people when their hair grows out, *they* should go out. And I look down to see the people that are governing me and making my rules—and they haven't got any hair on their head—I get very uptight about it." The audience laughed—especially with a group dedicated to defending free speech, a few jokes about bald heads weren't likely to upset anyone. But Dylan's diatribe against the old guard, basically anyone over thirty, was serious and consistent with the theme of "The Times They Are A-Changin'."

He went on to say that he made distinctions about people based not on race but instead on how they dress—casually like himself and other young people, or "respectably" like the old: "I was on the March on Washington up on the platform and I looked around at all the Negroes there and I didn't see any Negroes that looked like none of my friends. My friends don't wear suits. My friends don't have to wear any kind of thing to prove that they're respectable Negroes." (Behind him on the dais sat the writer James Baldwin, an invited speaker, wearing a suit.) He was still on fairly safe ground at that point but seemed determined to drive a wedge between himself and the "respectable" group that wanted to adopt him. So he compared himself to Lee Harvey Oswald: "I got to admit that the man who shot President Kennedy, Lee Oswald, I don't know exactly where—what he thought he was doing, but I got to admit honestly that I, too—I saw some of myself in him." And then the boos began.[34]

Dylan later wrote a prose-poem-as-letter to the ECLC leadership, attempting to explain his remarks and to mend fences but not exactly apologizing for his behavior. He offered to pay the group to make up for the funds they expected to raise from his appearance. About a year later Clark Foreman, the group's leader, tried to accept the offer and asked for $6,000, but the "debt" was never paid.[35]

The ECLC incident received little notice at the time, but it has since become part of Dylan lore, depicted for instance in Todd Haynes's Dylan-inspired film *I'm Not There* as well as Martin Scorsese's documentary *No Direction Home* (but not the more commercially oriented James Mangold film *A Complete Unknown*). As with the *Newsweek* article, it contributed to the tension between Dylan and mainstream culture (even though the ECLC was politically well to the left of mainstream). Indeed the end of 1963 found Dylan in an odd, precarious position: hailed as a genius, far more famous and successful than he had been a year earlier, but exhibiting self-sabotaging tendencies and already facing a media backlash. Meanwhile he was waiting for the release of an album that was more challenging and depressing than *Freewheelin'*, which is to say more challenging and depressing than anything on the pop charts.

Like the closing track to his third album, the ECLC debacle was a "restless farewell" to the politically engaged phase of his career. Dylan told the room full of bald heads that "There's no black and white, left and right to me anymore; there's only up and down and down is very close to the ground. And I'm trying to go up without thinking of anything trivial such as politics." It's significant that Dylan took no stand on any real issue in his drunken speech; he certainly did not in any way defend Oswald. He just said that he saw some of himself in Oswald, suggesting that he knew how Oswald *felt*—presumably alienated and confused, "hung up." And that was the essence of the break Dylan was making with the political left. It no longer mattered that he shared the movement's values—opposition to war, racism, and anti-communist hysteria. His opposition, his rebellion, was directed at *any* kind of doctrine or political position. To be young was a feeling. To be free, not to belong to anyone or any organization, was his cause.

4
1964: Transformation

In February 1964, the month after *The Times They Are A-Changin'* was released, Dylan appeared on two North American television shows. The first was filmed for the Canadian Broadcasting Corporation on February 1, the final installment of a series called *Quest*. He plays a thirty-minute set, three songs each from his last two albums, opening with "The Times They Are A-Changin'" and closing with "Restless Farewell." The stage set is a rural tavern, constructed for the film, populated by solitary men—lumberjacks, apparently—in work clothes. Dylan sings and strums while strolling and sitting among these men, who at various times listen, chuckle (at "Talkin' World War III Blues"), contemplate, smoke, and play cards but never talk or applaud. The set and Dylan's performance has an ersatz folk quality that, in retrospect, seems to undermine its own authenticity: it places Dylan in a rustic environment, a room without a stage, as if he is in fact a latter-day Woody Guthrie who has stumbled into this tavern, but at the same time producer Daryl Duke heightens the show's staginess in having the men pay little attention to the performer (or to each other), suggesting that these "folk" are in fact props. (Dylan would create a similar, even more surreal environment for his *Shadow Kingdom* film in 2021, released for streaming at the height of the COVID-19 pandemic.)

Near the end of February Dylan performed on a very different set, that of Westinghouse's syndicated *The Steve Allen Show*. He sang "The Lonesome Death of Hattie Carroll" (also included in the *Quest* program), but he spent about half of his screen time sitting with

Allen, who seemed unfamiliar with Dylan's music and a little skeptical about his appeal. The former *Tonight Show* host devoted an awkward amount of time to reading quotes from the press about Dylan and then reading from one of the "11 Outlined Epitaphs" on the back cover of *The Times They Are A-Changin'* while the studio piano player provided cocktail-lounge accompaniment; he then asked Dylan to describe and explain "Hattie Carroll" before singing it. Dylan came across as appropriately uncomfortable with the praise, modest about his own writing, but totally confident and focused in his delivery of "Hattie Carroll." This time he had a real audience in the studio—like Allen, formally dressed (the men in coats and ties), in contrast to Dylan, wearing his usual work shirt and jacket, a costume disguised as an anti-costume.

Whether singing to actors playing woodsmen or to a variety show audience, Dylan was "performing authenticity," to borrow Andrea Cossu's phrase, which is not to say he was pretending or betraying some "true" self, merely that he was inhabiting a persona he'd been developing since he began singing Woody Guthrie songs back in Minnesota, a persona that was as legitimate as any public self he might assume. But with hit record albums, television appearances, and concerts attended by thousands of adoring fans, tensions between the unpretentious, anti-establishment folkie and the commercial performing artist would become more pronounced throughout 1964.

Dylan began the year attempting to stay on good terms with the folk music community by writing a six-page open letter (structured as a free verse poem) to *Broadside*, the magazine that had championed him even before his first album was released. Published in the January 20 issue, the letter is humble and confessional, written with the dropped consonants and avoidance of capitalization and apostrophes that marked Dylan's Guthrie "voice," and it must have reassured the editors and readers of what was still a hand-made, non-commercial publication:

> I am now famous by the rules of public famiousity
> it snuck up on me
> an pulverized me

I never knew what was happenin
it is hard for me t walk down the same streets
I did before the same way because now
I truly dont know
who is waitin for my autograph . . .

Dylan describes the guilt he feels over his own success but persistently presents himself as still in the *Broadside* congregation. He professes his love for Pete Seeger and Suze Rotolo while deflecting the idolatry he is now subject to:

an I know I have a long way t go
when the day comes when I can love everything
that breathes the way I love sue then
I will truly be a Jesus Christ ha ha
(but I dont wanna be a Jesus Christ ha ha)

He even praises fellow folk singers Paul Wolfe and Phil Ochs before pledging, "I am with you more'n ever" and wishing "love t everybody in your house."[1]

In the *Broadside* letter Dylan is directly and diplomatically addressing the fact that he is now in a different category, on a different level, from the folk singers who still surround him. At this moment, at least, he wanted (or said he wanted) to still be one of them. But that attempt to have it both ways would be short-lived: perhaps it was impossible to sustain good relations with the scene he was transcending, but soon enough Dylan would shed his compunctions about alienating other folk singers and *Broadside* readers.

In fact the turning point may well have occurred right after the *Broadside* letter, in between the two television broadcasts. A couple of days after the CBC taping Dylan set out on a cross-country trip, leaving from New York in a station wagon along with Victor Maymudes, Paul Clayton, and Pete Karman. They made an odd foursome. Maymudes, whom Suze Rotolo described as "Bob's silent and creepy buddy-bodyguard," did most of the driving.[2] Clayton, who had recorded a series of well-regarded, themed folk albums (whaling songs, lumberjack songs, murder ballads) in the 1950s, brought a large stash of drugs, mostly amphetamines. These would be supplemented with marijuana, which the travelers occasionally had mailed to them at destinations along the way—and which they kept in a jar labeled "marijuana" on the dashboard.[3] Karman, an old friend of Suze Rotolo, later reported that Suze wanted him to come along to "keep an eye on" Dylan, especially since the trip would culminate in a series of shows in California, where they would meet up with Joan Baez.[4] Dylan carried a portable typewriter, working on poetry and material for his next album. He also brought copies of his new album to give away to fans and unsuspecting strangers along the way.

They headed south to Charlottesville, Virginia, and then west through Harlan County, Kentucky, where they delivered donated clothing for miners on strike. They proceeded south along the Blue Ridge Mountains of North Carolina, stopping in Flat Rock to call on the poet Carl Sandburg, who was by then well into his eighties. Showing up unannounced at Sandburg's house, Dylan introduced himself as a fellow poet, and although Sandburg was unfamiliar with his work, he still chatted for about an hour with the young man and his friends and promised to listen to Dylan's and Clayton's albums. According to Maymudes and Karman, Dylan was disappointed that Sandburg hadn't heard of him and had hoped for a longer visit.[5]

Dylan was not "on tour," but he did have a couple of shows lined up, including one at Emory University on February 8, so the quartet made their way to Atlanta next. Then they headed to New Orleans for Mardi Gras. Not surprisingly, the four young men embraced the experience, watching the Comus parade, staying out all night drinking, making friends, meeting fans, and barely dodging fights.[6] Maymudes later recalled the group passing a young man with a guitar on Bourbon Street singing "Don't Think Twice, It's Alright": "Bob told him, 'You sing that very well.' The guitar player looked at Bob and said, 'You . . . you. No, it couldn't be. You aren't Bob Dylan, are you?' Dylan replied, 'No, I'm not,' in a dry, matter-of-fact tone."[7]

Next they made their way to Dallas, where they investigated the scene of Kennedy's assassination in Dealey Plaza, and then on to Denver, where Dylan was booked for a performance on February 15.

A week later in California he was reunited with Baez, who joined him onstage at the Berkeley Community Center. He spent the rest of the month hanging out with her, appearing on *The Steve Allen Show* in Los Angeles, and playing additional concerts in Riverside, San Diego, and Santa Monica.

The excitement surrounding Dylan's performances continued to grow. The singer Maria Muldaur, who was backstage after the Santa Monica show, described the fervor of Dylan's fans, as she and others helped him get from the hall to a waiting car: "I felt like my ribs were gonna be crushed . . . When Elvis did a show in New York, people would press at him and rip his clothes off. It was like that."[8]

If Pete Karman's role on the trip had been to keep Dylan from straying, then it was time to get rid of Pete Karman. Dylan and Maymudes badgered Karman with insults and did their best to make him uncomfortable; he either voluntarily flew home or was sent back east. Karman's spot in the station wagon was filled by Bob Neuwirth, a folk singer and visual artist whose path had crossed Dylan's in New York but who would now become the most prominent member of his entourage. Dylan later described Neuwirth as someone who "could talk to anybody until they felt like all their intelligence was gone. With his tongue, he ripped and slashed and could make anybody uneasy, also could talk his way out of anything. Nobody knew what to make of him." Along with Grossman and Maymudes, Neuwirth helped build a wall around Dylan as his fame increased. "Neuwirth was a bulldog," Dylan would recall. "He didn't provoke me, though, not in any way,"[9] which might mean that Dylan wasn't bothered by Neuwirth's provocations, but more likely, because Neuwirth was *his* henchman, he was rarely on the receiving end of his verbal bullying.

Dylan was also acquiring a long-distance entourage of well-known admirers. Johnny Cash had discovered *Freewheelin'* and was playing it constantly. In March Cash professed his admiration in a letter to *Broadside:* "I got hung but didn't choke . . . Bob Dylan slung his rope. I sat down and listened quick . . . Gravy from that brain is thick." He concluded by calling out would-be detractors: "SHUT UP! . . . AND LET HIM SING!"[10] He and Dylan began writing each other; Cash's letters gush with enthusiasm, expressing how profoundly Dylan's songs have affected him. He opens a March 15 letter, which was mailed in an airsick bag, "I enjoyed your letter seven or eight times. I still feel that I need to read it at least 6 more times to level my own breezy brain to more of the levels of your multi-split-level genius." He says that June Carter listens to "Girl from the North Country" 83 times a day, and that Mother Maybelle is also a fan.[11]

Dylan made an equally strong and lasting impact on Allen Ginsberg, who, like Cash, was someone he admired and was eager to impress. Dylan and Ginsberg met in late 1963, after Ginsberg had been entranced by *Freewheelin'*. Ginsberg was also physically attracted to Dylan and feared after their first meeting that "I might become his slave or something, his mascot."[12] Like Cash, Ginsberg became a lifelong friend, and (again, like Cash) would later record with Dylan. (Ginsberg wrote to Dylan regularly as well up until his death in 1997.) These two admirers came from very different places in the American cultural cosmos; but the fact that both the radical beat poet and the country star saw Dylan as a kindred spirit and an inspirational figure attests to the broad, seismic shock of *Freewheelin'* and *The Times They Are A-Changin'*.

Amidst this growing fame and his ongoing relationship with Joan Baez, Dylan still hoped to hold on to Suze Rotolo, but, predictably, their relationship was unraveling. In her memoir Rotolo recalls vividly what it was like to be Dylan's girlfriend as he became an object of worship:

> Either people wanted to devour him or they offered themselves up for him to consume . . . Everyone craved his presence, his wisdom, his judgment. After *The Freewheelin' Bob Dylan* had been out awhile, at parties I noticed that people would approach him with reverence and tell him involved stories about their lives and then wait for him to speak.[13]

This adulation made Rotolo (and Dylan) deeply uncomfortable; ultimately she "couldn't handle being 'one step closer to God.'" Compounding this confusion was her knowledge of Dylan's unfaithfulness. She wrote in a journal at the time, "I believe in his genius, he is an extraordinary writer but I don't think of him as an honorable person."[14] They remained friends and possibly occasional lovers for another year or two, but by mid-1964 Suze had moved out of the West 4th Street apartment; after an intense argument that also involved Suze's sister Carla, who never trusted or got along with Bob, they ceased to be a couple.

Dylan played a half-dozen shows, mostly in New England, in April; returned briefly to California to perform at the Monterey Folk Festival in early May; and then, after visiting Eric Von Schmidt in Florida, flew to England for a short concert tour. He taped "With God on Our Side" for BBC television and played to a rapturous audience at the Royal Festival Hall in London, a set that included the first public performance of "Mr. Tambourine Man." At this point Dylan was still capable of being surprised by his own popularity, as he checked out the line of fans waiting to get in: "My God, I've never seen anything like it."[15] After the show Dylan tried to wait out the crowd, chatting and smoking pot with a small group of friends in his dressing room for a couple of hours, but even then, he was almost crushed as Maymudes led him through the throng of admirers.

"He was in a trance," Maymudes recalled, "and it was at that time that he first felt the true essence of the rock star; he knew from that moment forward that his life would never be the same."[16] Indeed Dylan could now enjoy the benefits of success and celebrity. He proceeded to Paris, where he had a brief affair with Nico, the model-actress who was about to embark on a singing career. Along with Maymudes, he traveled to Berlin, followed by Greece for a week's working vacation, writing most of his next album; then he returned to the States to record it.

That recording session has become the stuff of legend, thanks largely to Nat Hentoff's *New Yorker* profile, which focuses on Dylan at work in the studio. He recorded the album in one night, June 9, starting just after 7.00 p.m. and finishing up before 1.30 a.m. (in contrast to *Freewheelin'*, which took over a year). Producer Tom Wilson explained to Hentoff, "Usually, we're not in such a rush, but this record has to be ready for Columbia's fall sales convention," which sounds like Dylan is capitulating to his company, except that Wilson adds, "We think he's important enough to record whenever he wants to come into the studio."[17] Wilson hadn't seen or heard the songs Dylan was bringing in to record. The star showed up roughly on time, with a group of friends, out of whom Hentoff identified only Ramblin' Jack Elliott. More arrived during the session, and multiple bottles of Beaujolais were consumed.

Another Side of Bob Dylan, the result of this fast and loose approach, is often seen as a "transitional album," for obvious reasons: it's Dylan's last solo acoustic album (until the 1990s), yet many of the songs sound ready for full-band treatment. In fact, within a year three songs recorded that night would be top ten hits for other artists using rock arrangements: the Byrds' "Mr. Tambourine Man," Cher's "All I Really Want to Do," and the Turtles' "It Ain't Me Babe." Even the songs that weren't covered by others seem ready for a band: for instance with a different set of lyrics, "Motorpsycho Nitemare" is "Bob Dylan's 115th Dream," which got a full band arrangement on *Bringing It All Back Home*, and "I Don't Believe You (She Acts Like We Never Have Met)" would become a slow-burning rock song on Dylan's 1966 tour. More significantly, *Another Side* marks a very self-conscious transition away from "finger-pointin' songs," as this album mixes love songs, breakup songs, comic songs, and a new, visionary style that would solidify Dylan's reputation as a poet. As a result it's difficult to listen to this album without thinking about the masterpieces that came before and after it.

At the same time there is that spontaneous, ragged glory in *Another Side* that makes the album unique and suggests that the "transitional" tag is unfair. Paul Williams put it well: "The performances are sloppy, and uneven, and it seems reasonable to think the album could have been better if he'd taken more time with it. Except that that's like saying it'd be easier to fish if this boat were half-buried in sand in the desert, so it wouldn't roll around so much."[18] "All I Really Want to Do" presents the album's statement of purpose. It was recorded well into the session, and presumably well into the wine, but it's a perfect opening track, signaling with its off-the-cuff approach (yodels, impromptu laughter) as much as its lyrics that this "other side" of Dylan is going to insist that we not (always) take him so seriously.

As is often the case, the "you" of this song is both an individual, a would-be lover, to whom the song is directed, *and* the audience that expects so much from the singer, who asks, can't we just be friends? But through the negative statements that make up each verse Dylan also presents a way of being in the world that rejects the values he associates with the older generation's pursuit of the American Dream built on conquest, social climbing, discrimination, competition, and conformity. The song is a challenge to the ethos of the athletic field and the corporate ladder. There are, of course, many things I don't want to do to you, and they include dragging, draining, chaining, or bringing you down, locking you up, analyzing, categorizing, or advertising you. Saving what may be most important for last, you don't have to feel, see, or be like me. As Dylan steps away from songs drawn from headlines and specific "causes," he lays out a broad quasi-political agenda that hippies and individualists would embrace: tuning in and dropping out of a culture of capitalist competition and domination.

Even the slight, comic songs reiterate the challenge to "straight" conformist America. In "Motorpsycho Nitemare" the Dylan figure has to escape a farmer's daughter situation, so he baits the predictably conservative farmer by praising Fidel Castro; the farmer responds by throwing a *Reader's Digest*, the ultimate mainstream middlebrow publication of mid-century America, at his head. In "I Shall Be Free No. 10" Dylan fantasizes about growing his hair down to his feet and riding a horse onto a country club golf course.

"My Back Pages" rejects not just the expectations of the establishment but the pieties and self-righteousness of their opponents. According to Mike Marqusee, "no song on *Another Side* distressed Dylan's friends in the movement more than 'My Back Pages,' in which he transmutes the rude incoherence of his ECLC rant into the organized density of art."[19] Like "All I Really Want to Do," "My Back Pages" enumerates ways of thinking and being that the singer rejects, but in this case it's the mindset of intellectuals, leftist folk singers, and political activists. As he told the ECLC, they're old, and he is determined to be young. The song is life-affirming and refreshing, but it's understandable why many people heard it as a cop-out, or an invitation to believe in nothing. The new, younger man rejects the us-versus-them mentality; moreover he claims that by preaching—telling other folks what to do—he becomes the very authority figure he had rebelled against. But this new understanding is all negation; the chorus's disposition—just be young—could signal either a liberating embrace of empathy and instinct over abstract doctrines, or a kind of selfishness, a refusal to align oneself with collective action based on those abstractions.

The album closes with yet another great song of negation, a perfect bookend to "All I Really Want to Do." "It Ain't Me Babe" would quickly become one of Dylan's most covered songs—Johnny Cash and Joan Baez released versions of it before the end of 1964, and after the success of the Turtles' single, everyone from Nancy Sinatra to Flatt and Scruggs recorded it within a few years. On *Another Side* it's as if the singer is now ending the no-strings relationship he initiated with the first song because his friend/lover can't accept those terms. And of course, like the previous album's "Restless Farewell," "It Ain't Me Babe" is also a statement to fans: I'm not your leader, you can't depend on me. As the sing-along, no-no-no chorus makes clear, this is not a personal failing or character flaw but a sort of affirmative negation, a deliberate decision to be radically free.

However, on the album's most experimental song the concept of freedom is presented as an active, if ephemeral, force rather than negation or rejection. In "Chimes of Freedom" the singer is not alone; although there is one reference to "I" in the last verse, the song emphasizes the perception of a couple or, in my reading, a group. Unlike the other anthems on *Another Side*, "Chimes" presumes a collective identity; moreover its central image is one of hope for a more just world, a "freedom" associated with justice and inclusion. The chimes flash, toll, and strike for people who are hurting and people who are marginalized and oppressed—not exactly the *opposite* conception of freedom from that of "My Back Pages," but certainly one that the Old Left would find more reassuring.

The term *poetic* is so imprecise and loaded with value judgments that I hesitate to use it here, but more than any song Dylan had released since "Hard Rain," "Chimes of Freedom" plays with language, deploying vivid but surprising metaphors and images. The first line for instance refers to "midnight's *broken* toll," suggesting not just the suddenness of a loud bell "breaking" the silence but being broken down or defective. The central conceit of chimes flashing similarly attributes a visual quality to sound. It makes sense because the image is one of lightning *and* thunder. It is as if the sound is creating a visual effect, a sensation known as synesthesia. These visionary and sometimes frightening combinations continue throughout the song: walls tightening, rain dissolving, sky cracking. The synesthetic, symbolist language makes the hopeful refrain all the more compelling. Time stands still for the "spellbound" watchers until the storm passes, underscoring the way this song, like "Blowin' in the Wind" and "Hard Rain," transcends its immediate context, even as it was born in the aftermath of Kennedy's assassination (its reference to "soldiers whose strength is not to fight" seems like a direct reference to Martin Luther King and the Student Nonviolent Coordinating Committee).[20] The song's timeless message of hope was highlighted when Bruce Springsteen performed it during Amnesty International's Human Rights Now! Tour in 1988; the organization later made it the title song of a fundraising four-CD Dylan tribute collection in 2012.

At the June 9 session Dylan also tried two takes of "Mr. Tambourine Man," a song he had taped at Eric Von Schmidt's house and performed in London the previous month. Dylan later said he had worked on it in New Orleans during Mardi Gras and that additional inspiration came from a large Turkish tambourine owned by Bruce Langhorne, who later played guitar on the official recording of the song. Suze Rotolo claimed that Dylan wrote the song "about a lonely night Bob had spent wandering the streets after the two of us had quarreled." His friend Al Aronowitz was with Dylan the night of that quarrel, and Dylan typed out a draft of the lyrics in Aronowitz's apartment between midnight and dawn after raiding his fridge.[21] But the Mardi Gras influence still seems clear, as the singer wants to abandon all care and be swept up by music and revelry. Like "Lay Down Your Weary Tune" and "Chimes of Freedom," this song describes and invokes transcendence; it's about joining the parade and surrendering to a mystical experience that temporarily removes you from time.

In "Mr. Tambourine Man" it's not so much what he says as how he says it—the rhythm and alliteration of the lines, the image of dancing on a beach as the past (memory) and future (fate) are cast beneath the waves—and of course the melody, which is one of Dylan's strongest, and which would help make this another of his most popular and most frequently covered songs. But on June 9 it wasn't quite working, at least partly because of an ill-advised harmony vocal on the chorus by Jack Elliott (who didn't know the song and had no chance to rehearse). Dylan must have known he had written a masterpiece, but he decided to hold it over for his next album.

Another Side of Bob Dylan was released two months after it was recorded, with a sleek, modern cover design featuring a photograph (by Sandy Speiser) shot near Times Square but, unlike *Freewheelin'*, posed and pensive. Ironically the album that revolves around not taking oneself too seriously and being "younger than that now" features a more mature-looking singer/poet on the sleeve. And to underscore the "poet" part, once again the liner notes consist of free verse, titled "Some Other Kinds of Songs . . . Poems by Bob Dylan." The poems are untitled, mostly narrative, mostly in first-person, suggesting dreams. Their surreal rush of imagery was starting to make its way into Dylan's songwriting, and the refusal to be pinned down or even acknowledge meaning had become prominent, as it would in his mid-1960s songwriting:

> i know no answers an' no truth
> for absolutely no soul alive
> i will listen t'no one
> who tells me morals
> there are no morals
> an' i dream a lot

Despite the buzz surrounding Dylan, the album was a slower seller than its two predecessors, peaking at number 43 on the *Billboard* album chart, with no single to boost sales. (It performed better in the UK, where it reached number eight.) Between the recording session for *Another Side* and its release, Dylan returned to the Newport Folk

With Joan Baez on the cover of *Broadside*, September 1964.

Festival in July. There he met his admirer and pen pal Johnny Cash, who performed "Don't Think Twice, It's Alright" in his own set Friday night and then spent the rest of the evening recording songs with Dylan in Joan Baez's motel room.[22]

At Newport's "Topical Songs Workshop" the first afternoon Dylan played two not-very-topical new songs, "It Ain't Me Babe" and "Mr. Tambourine Man"; rather than play something from his own protest repertoire, he then covered Phil Ochs's anti-death-penalty song "Iron Lady." He joined Baez onstage that night for a duet on "It Ain't Me Babe" and returned for the final evening session to play four songs from *Another Side* before bringing up Baez for "With God on Our Side." Dylan was of course an even bigger star than he had been the previous year, and the audience flocked to him. Film from the festival shows him fully engaged with his new songs, singing "Chimes of Freedom" with power and conviction; at the end of his evening performance the crowd drowned out emcee Peter Yarrow's attempt to introduce the next performer until Dylan returned; beaming, he waved and told the audience that he loved them.[23]

But not everyone was pleased. Robert Shelton said that Dylan was so stoned that he was "out of control" and that Shelton and others thought at the time that it was a lackluster, sloppy performance. Predictably, some in the political folk establishment objected to the more personal and visionary songs that declared independence from causes and politics. In November Irwin Silber, one of the editors of *Sing Out!*, published an open letter to Dylan: while assuring him that the letter was written "out of love and deep concern," the concern was that Dylan was losing touch with his audience, which is to say, his old audience of traditional folk singers and enthusiasts:

> You seem to be in a different kind of bag now, Bob—and I'm worried about it. I saw at Newport how you had somehow lost contact with people. It seemed to me that some of the paraphernalia of fame were getting in your way. You travel with an entourage now—with good buddies who are going to laugh when you need laughing and drink wine with you and ensure your privacy—and never challenge you to face everyone else's reality again.[24]

The gap that Dylan's January letter to *Broadside* was meant to bridge had, for Silber at least, become a chasm.

It's easy to understand why Silber and others who had supported Dylan as he learned the ropes of the Greenwich Village-based folk scene would feel betrayed, especially by Dylan's increasing exclusivity and condescension. Van Ronk recalled that "a sort of hierarchy was established of knights of the round table, princes of the blood, all paying court to this emperor with the long, bushy hair. And because of who he was, that became a pretty nasty scene . . . He was always testing the loyalty of the people who were near him, and it could really get vicious at times." At one such session, after his former protégé dispensed career advice to him at the Kettle of Fish, Van Ronk, in his telling, walked out after asking, "Dylan, if you're so rich, how come you ain't smart?" Both men would remember each other fondly in their published memoirs, but they were never really close after that.[25]

When he wasn't holding court in the Village, Dylan retreated more frequently to Woodstock, NY, where Albert Grossman owned a large house. According to John Hammond, Jr., "Grossman began creating a mystique of exclusiveness. He secluded him away up in Woodstock and that changed Bob."[26]

It's fair to say that success had indeed changed Dylan, but, with a rapidly growing legion of fans, he had little reason to care what his

Dylan at the Café Espresso in Woodstock, NY, with friends including his future wife Sara Lownds (in striped shirt), John B. Sebastian (center), and Victor Maymudes (right), 1964. Photo by Douglas Gilbert.

brother folk singers or Irwin Silber thought about his career decisions. Months before "going electric," Dylan was already a rock star. And in August he would have his first encounter with the band that was redefining rock stardom. Beatlemania swept the USA with the group's first appearance on the Ed Sullivan Show in February; at one point in April the Beatles held all top five positions on the *Billboard* singles charts. Their first feature film, *A Hard Day's Night*, was released in July to critical acclaim and life-changing effect on young musicians everywhere. They would spend the second half of 1964 playing concerts around the world, with a North American tour in August and September. On August 28 and 29 the Fab Four played the Forest Hills Tennis Stadium in Queens, where Dylan had made a guest appearance at Joan Baez's concert earlier that month. They had discovered *The Freewheelin' Bob Dylan* in early 1964, and Dylan had become a Beatles fan during his cross-country road trip around the same time.

After the Beatles' concert on August 28 Dylan, Victor Maymudes, and journalist Al Aronowitz, who had arranged the meeting, were ushered into their suite at the Delmonico Hotel in Manhattan. Everyone present knew this was a big deal, so they were all trying to be cool. The Beatles had been avid consumers of amphetamines for as long as they'd been a group, but, surprisingly, they had little or no experience with marijuana. Dylan's posse brought along a sufficient quantity of weed, so the 1960s could now get started for real. Paul McCartney later recalled believing that he had discovered the meaning of life that night and made sure to write it down. The next morning he found a piece of paper on which he had scribbled, "There are seven levels."[27] Dylan himself passed out fairly early in the proceedings.[28] He and the Beatles would cross paths occasionally and influence each other deeply throughout the decade. The Beatles had revived and modernized the rock and roll music he fell in love with as a teenager, clearing the path for more adventurous young musicians just as Dylan was clearing it for songwriters. As is often noted, John Lennon's songwriting in particular became more introspective and lyrically sophisticated starting around this time. And George Harrison would become Dylan's close, lifelong friend and collaborator.

Dylan's concert schedule for the remainder of 1964 was far less grueling than the Beatles', but he spent the late fall touring the Northeast, Midwest, and California. On Halloween night he played New York's shiny new Philharmonic Hall at Lincoln Center, a concert that was recorded by Columbia and finally released in 2004 as volume VI of the Bootleg Series. Playing his first full concert in New York in over a year, Dylan was at his crowd-pleasing best, mixing older protest songs ("Who Killed Davey Moore?," "Lonesome Death of Hattie Carroll," "With God on Our Side"), political satires ("Talkin' John Birch," "Talkin' World War III Blues"), about half of *Another Side*, and a few mesmerizing songs that hadn't been released yet: "Mr. Tambourine Man," "Gates of Eden," and "It's Alright, Ma (I'm Only Bleeding)." Historian Sean Wilentz, who attended the concert at age thirteen, recalled of these new songs, "At the time, it just sounded like demanding poetry, at times epic narrative, proving once again that Bob Dylan was leading us into new places, the exact destination unknown but still deeply tempting."[29]

Dylan moved back and forth between these dense new songs and lighter material, interacting jovially with the audience throughout the evening. Joan Baez joined him for the last four songs of the second set. Their duet on "Mama, You Been on My Mind," an *Another Side* outtake, is charmingly loose, with a few miscues, and after well over a year of singing together, the blend of their mismatched voices had become more comfortable, or at least more familiar. At one point early in the evening, acknowledging the holiday, Dylan quipped that he had on his Bob Dylan mask and then added, "I'm masquerading." It was an offhand joke that now resonates with insight. The same man who was privately becoming more difficult to know or even to access was performing as the ingenious but warm and unpretentious Bob Dylan before an adoring audience. And even that public mask would soon be tossed off for another.

Dylan spent much of the next month playing colleges and large theaters in the Northeast and Midwest. A visit to Kenyon College was chronicled by future screenwriter Jay Cocks, who tagged along as Maymudes ("who looked like a hip version of Abraham Lincoln") and a student promoter ushered Dylan from airport to motel to concert hall and back, keeping the wine flowing and the fans at bay. Dylan was cooperative, even personable, with the young reporter who was not from a major publication and didn't feel the need to explain the Dylan phenomenon. In fact Dylan told Cocks that his friend Al Aronowitz had tried to write a profile of him for the *Saturday Evening Post* but that "he knew it would be cut to shit by the *Post* and he wouldn't get to say what he'd want to be sayin', only what they wanted." When Dylan tried to collaborate with Aronowitz on the article, the piece got "really weird, surrealistic, and the story never got written." Mentioning that he had visited the Actors Studio, home of the Method, he dismissed the idea of "tryin' too hard to be someone else. You can't learn to be someone else. It's just gotta be inside." Dylan falls back on the dichotomy between a singular, "real" inner self and various kinds of pretense—acting, showing off, conforming to social expectations.

He must have known better. The singer who joked about "masquerading" at the Halloween concert was already demonstrating how much more complex the process is: an artist or performer recasts what's "inside" him to create a virtual copy of an existing template (Guthrie) or an original combination of styles (Guthrie plus Ginsberg, with a little bit of Charlie Chaplin and an undying memory of Little Richard). To put it another way, he was still a bit "hung up" on the primacy of authenticity, even as he was playing with it as just another pose.

A week after the concert at Kenyon Dylan played Yale, and again, a student journalist interviewed him. But this time, perhaps because of the interviewer's approach, Dylan's mood was different—the headline read "I Don't Want to Know Anything." He's quoted early in the article saying, "It's all a joke . . . I'm not attached to anything. I can't even talk to you, because all our definitions of words are different."[30] At the end of 1964 Dylan was both the nihilistic enigma and the authentic, introspective bard who just happened to be a cultural phenomenon. The contradiction wouldn't be resolved anytime soon.

In August photographer Daniel Kramer had managed to get Albert Grossman on the phone and received permission to visit his house in Woodstock to spend an hour photographing Dylan. Kramer recalled the sign at the entrance to the property: "IF YOU HAVE NOT TELEPHONED, YOU ARE TRESPASSING." Dylan rode up on a motorcycle a few minutes later, greeted Kramer, and told him he could "do what [he] needed to do." According to Kramer, Dylan was cooperative but was not going to pose for a portrait or let the photographer control the session: "It was evident that he was a man who set his own marks and resisted being manipulated. He knew what he wanted to do and what he wanted to produce." The session extended well beyond an hour, and Kramer went on to photograph Dylan extensively over the next year, joining him at concerts and in the studio, most famously producing the photographs for his next two album covers.

While Kramer immediately perceived Dylan's insistence on control and self-determination, he also witnessed a kind of work ethic that he didn't expect from a "freewheelin'" writer and singer. He was struck by Dylan's "ability to make the best use of almost any time he could extract from his busy day. Often he would write in his small black notebook as he did for a while during the car trip to Philadelphia [for a concert] . . . He spent a great deal of time writing new material." Kramer saw Dylan's professionalism as his other defining trait, which he used to maintain a non-professional image: "Dylan's appearance, his casual dress, the pile of hair on his head, and the legend of the folksinger as a free spirit led me to believe that his life was similarly carefree. Observing the process of putting everything together . . . quickly taught me that my impression was wrong."[31]

Already the consummate American success story, Dylan was deeply driven and hard-working, as he had been from the time he arrived in New York four years earlier. At the same time Dylan had come both to embody and to express various kinds of freedom: freedom not to be the same person or say essentially the same things to every reporter for instance, but, more broadly, the freedom to change musical and personal style and the freedom from any kind of organization, movement, or cause. But he also represented the goals of a more idealistic freedom for marginalized groups of people. He had gone from *The Freewheelin' Bob Dylan*, which included the comic song "I Shall Be Free," to "Chimes of Freedom" and "I Shall Be Free No. 10." On *Another Side* he concludes the otherwise regrettable "Ballad in

Plain D," transparently about his breakup with Suze Rotolo, asking if even birds are free from the sky's chains. Throughout 1964 Dylan explored and struggled with the many valences of "free" and "freedom." He could continue this exploration; in fact it is the principle that would underwrite his entire career.

5
1965: Electricity

stay in line. stay in step. people
are afraid of someone who is not
in step with them.

So begins "Advice for Geraldine on Her Miscellaneous Birthday," the poem that Dylan published for the program of his Philharmonic Hall concert on Halloween night 1964. Shot full of absurdism and irony, "Advice" vents Dylan's frustrations with his audience's and the press's expectations; but at the same time it invites readers to share a series of jokes at the expense of the establishment. He encourages and enacts nonconformity by itemizing its perils, and near the end of the poem he warns, "do Not create anything, it will be/ misinterpreted. it will not change./ it will follow you the/ rest of your life."[1]

In January 1965 Dylan carried the ethos of "Advice for Geraldine" into Columbia's Studio A in the form of "Subterranean Homesick Blues," which would be the opening track on his next album. The song's lyrics combine description of what's happening on the street with survival advice—accordingly its working title was "Look Out Kid." The cadence, a rapid-fire delivery with heavy emphasis on the "one" of each four-beat measure, was not entirely new, a clear precedent being Chuck Berry's "Too Much Monkey Business." And yet it sounded totally fresh and somehow still does.

The lyrics mash up facetious advice with paranoia born of avoiding trouble with authorities, which involves speaking in code, especially about drugs—the "medicine" that Johnny's mixing up, the rumor of a bust in early May. It may be simplistic to compare "Subterranean Homesick Blues" to rap performances of later generations, but the similarity is there: the lyrics are declaimed rather than sung; it's built around a syncopated rhythm and insistent rhyme, and it's about life on the street. The delivery is as important as the words themselves, and Dylan's vocal is sneering and deadpan, hilarious and confrontational.

Dylan recorded a solo acoustic version of "Subterranean Homesick Blues" along with ten other new songs on January 13, 1965. Unlike most of the tracks he put down that day, this one really sounds like a demo. He doesn't quite have all the phrasing in place, and the acoustic setting doesn't do justice to the rap. But the next day Dylan and producer Tom Wilson brought in a band—Bobby Gregg on drums, Bill Lee (father of Spike) on bass, Bruce Langhorne and John Hammond, Jr. on guitar—to re-record half a dozen songs. With virtually no rehearsal, the band nailed "Subterranean Homesick Blues," which introduced the world to electric Dylan. (He had briefly "gone electric" in late 1962, recording "Mixed-Up Confusion" and "That's Alright, Mama" during the *Freewheelin'* sessions, but the failed single was a forgotten footnote by the time of *Bringing It All Back Home*'s release in March 1965.) Dylan had already departed from earnest "finger-pointin' songs" on *Another Side*, but the full-band arrangements of *Bringing It All Back Home* distanced him further from the folk scene he had conquered just a couple of years before.

The electric blues sound that defines *Bringing It All Back Home*'s side one had been developed by the Chicago bands backing Muddy Waters, Sonny Boy Williamson, Howlin' Wolf and others throughout the 1950s, providing much of the basis for early rock and roll. By January 1965 this hard-edged sound had found new commercial potential through white British bands who discovered and imitated the Chicago style. The Animals had hit number one in the USA and the UK with "House of the Rising Sun," a bluesy electric version of a traditional song—incidentally based on the acoustic arrangement Dylan had copied from Dave Van Ronk and recorded on his debut.

Another song from Dylan's first album, "Baby, Let Me Follow You Down," became the electric "Baby Let Me Take You Home," the Animals' other 1964 hit in the UK. The Rolling Stones had released their first two albums of blues and R&B covers in 1964, topping the British charts and making inroads in the USA as well. The Yardbirds' raucous *Five Live Yardbirds*, consisting almost entirely of Chicago blues standards and featuring Eric Clapton on lead guitar, had been released in December 1964. Young, white American blues aficionados were also discovering the sound, albeit with less commercial success. John Hammond, Jr. had recently recorded an album called *So Many Roads* with a blues band that included three recent departures from rockabilly singer Ronnie Hawkins's band—Levon Helm, Garth Hudson, and Robbie Robertson—joined by Charlie Musselwhite on harmonica and, on piano, Michael Bloomfield. Bloomfield, who would soon make a big impact on Dylan's sound, had a more prominent gig playing lead guitar for the Paul Butterfield Blues Band, a group that made their Chicago roots a calling card.

These bands—the raw, blues-based representatives of the "British Invasion" and their American counterparts—were at the cutting edge of popular music when Dylan recorded *Bringing It All Back Home* in January. And these musicians, along with the (more polished, less bluesy) Beatles, would become Dylan's new musical network: Bloomfield and other members of the Butterfield band would back him later that year at Newport, followed on tour by Helm, Hudson, Robertson, and their bandmates, then known as the Hawks. Dylan admired the Animals enough to consult them before releasing "Subterranean Homesick Blues" as a single.[2] As for the Stones, like any band that wanted to be taken seriously after 1965, they would follow Dylan in writing their own material—and it's particularly hard to imagine their breakthrough hit "(I Can't Get No) Satisfaction," recorded in May 1965, without "Subterranean Homesick Blues" showing the way.[3]

Among the other half-dozen electric tracks on *Bringing It All Back Home*, "Maggie's Farm," "Outlaw Blues," and "On the Road Again" stick closely to the urban blues sound and structure. These songs sound a lot like what the Stones and the Butterfield Blues Band were playing; the difference of course is the lyrics. "Outlaw Blues" is a comic riff on the language of the blues, with winking references to Sonny Boy Williamson's "Nine Below Zero" and Robert Johnson's "When You Got a Good Friend" as well as the opening line of the traditional song "I'm a Stranger Here." Similarly "On the Road Again" opens with a variation on the classic blues floater "I woke up this morning," but in Dylan's blues you wake up with frogs in your socks.

The lyrics to "On the Road Again" and "Maggie's Farm" are built around the singer's mistreatment while staying with a certain woman's relatives. Both complaint songs are played for absurdist, comic effect, but "Maggie's Farm" also denounces the mistreatment of powerless workers; Dylan's itinerant laborer emphasizes the sadism of his bosses, Maggie's brother and father, who humiliate "you" under the watchful eye of the National Guard. The slapstick humor of these scenarios recalls not only Guthrie's hobos but Charlie Chaplin's and Harold Lloyd's everyman characters, who endure unspeakable abuse at the hands of bullies and bosses but somehow manage to skate through unscathed. In both "On the Road Again" and "Maggie's Farm" the Dylan character is already gone. His humor targets the abuse of power while declaring freedom—the freedom to walk away, to be on the road again—as the core value.

Cartoonish misadventures also drive "Bob Dylan's 115th Dream," a six-and-a-half-minute epic that riffs primarily on the American discovery myth and Melville's *Moby-Dick*, with Captain A-rab (pronounced AY-rab, an echo of Ray Stevens's 1962 novelty hit "Ahab the Arab") at the helm of the *Mayflower*. It's one of Dylan's funniest songs, a series of unfortunate events shot full of wordplay, creative anachronism, and absurd humor. A kitchen explodes from boiling fat; a foot comes through a telephone line; a bowling ball knocks the sailor off his feet. Along the way Dylan mocks American mythology and pieties. Captain A-rab's first act upon landing in the New World is to try to buy it with beads. Later the singer is threatened with violence when he asks for help at a house decorated with the American flag. The song ends with the *Mayflower* in retreat, spying "three ships a sailing" toward the land they had just escaped. He extends a sardonic good luck wish to Columbus.

Dylan and producer Tom Wilson had worked quickly—to great effect—on *Another Side*, and they continued that approach on *Bringing It All Back Home*, knocking out the album's eleven tracks in three days. The band's nearly unhinged sound on "Bob Dylan's 115th Dream" and the other up-tempo blues rockers resulted from what would become a career-long strategy in the studio: Dylan didn't want to rehearse or do a lot of takes, and Wilson accommodated him by bringing in musicians who could intuit the songs' direction and feel. According to Bruce Langhorne, "There was a whole bunch of studio cats, and we were unrehearsed . . . No lead sheets. Everyone would just start playin'. I don't even remember Bob runnin' through the songs once. It was sort of telepathic—'Let's do a take.'"[4]

And yet Dylan was in control, determined to get the right sound while keeping it fresh. Daniel Kramer, who photographed the sessions, recalled that "between takes, Bob would work individually with musicians until he was satisfied with what was happening. He was patient with them and they were patient with him. His method of working, the certainty of what he wanted, kept things moving."[5] At a time when studio recording was all about perfection and precision Dylan and Wilson countered with an aesthetic of spontaneity. When the band missed their entrance on an early take of "115th Dream," singer and producer both cracked up. They later spliced the breakdown and laughter onto the master take, giving the track even more of an unpolished, "live in the studio" feel.

The other two full-band tracks are love songs but strikingly unconventional: both describe a kind of relationship, and a kind of lover, that had never existed in popular song before. The ironically titled "She Belongs to Me" sketches a woman who can't be possessed—a self-sufficient artist, a sorceress. Her powers include control over men, but Dylan defies the masculine songwriting tradition by not running from or putting down this powerful woman, much less warning other men not to fall under her spell. The song never condemns the artist/lover's narcissism; instead it offers a sincere recognition of this woman's supremacy, offering religious, patriotic tribute and musical gifts, better suited for her than for God and country.

The woman in "Love Minus Zero/No Limit" is even more enigmatic. Dylan had teasingly described his new songwriting as "mathematical" to interviewers, and the song's title (the slash separates the numerator from the denominator) is a formula for infinite love. Instead of a vivid description of his lover, the singer casts her mainly in terms of what she manages to avoid, such as sentimentality and materialism. Accordingly Dylan defies the clichés on which love songs are typically built, and as the song progresses the imagery seems to have less and less to do with "my love"—crumbling matchsticks, bankers' nieces, trembling bridges. But in a surprising turn for a song that has insistently broken from traditional imagery he evokes perhaps the most famous symbol in American poetry in the last line. Like Poe's raven she is both present and, symbolically, absent or lost; more "real" than the contrivances of other love poems but, in her own way, still an untouchable ideal.

Side two of *Bringing It All Back Home* is nearly all solo-acoustic, the exceptions being Bruce Langhorne's gentle electric guitar fills on "Mr. Tambourine Man" and Bill Lee's melodic bass accompaniment on "It's All Over Now, Baby Blue." But the decision to split the record into "hot" and "cool" sides was hardly an artistic compromise—the songs on side two make sense in the acoustic settings, and they continue the poetically charged trajectory of *Another Side*'s "Chimes of Freedom." Having rejected a solo take of "Mr. Tambourine Man" from *Another Side*, Dylan tried it with a full band but wisely abandoned the experiment; on the outtake released on the Bootleg Series, volume XII, he can be heard stopping mid-verse to complain "the drumming is driving me mad." Like "Blowin' in the Wind," "Mr. Tambourine Man" was well known to Dylan's audience by the time an official recording was released; and, like its predecessor, it would soon become a pop phenomenon, thanks to another landmark cover version.

But the change in Dylan's songwriting and public persona in the two years between those two hits is remarkable. According to one reviewer, "Dylan used to sound like a lung cancer victim singing Woody Guthrie. Now he sounds like a Rolling Stone singing Immanuel Kant."[6] In his history of the 1960s counterculture Peter Doggett observes, "In 1963, Dylan was popularly believed to be leading a nationwide crusade for justice and equality. In 1965, he was seen as a visionary whose songs carefully disguised the secret of life."[7] The visionary quality may have been evident in the abstractions of "Blowin' in the Wind" and the surreal imagery of "Hard Rain," but the four songs on side two of *Bringing It All Back Home* offer a stream of symbolism and logic-defying bits of narrative unprecedented in popular songwriting; as Doggett suggests, they practically demanded that listeners try to decode them in a quest for enlightenment.

Each verse of "Gates of Eden" presents a new scenario, leading up to the title's refrain. And each scenario is like a snippet of a dream or a vision inspired by marijuana or LSD. Taken individually the nine verses hint at profundity but escape any clear, convincing interpretation. Collectively they depict a world (ours) of confusion, pain, and unhappiness, contrasted with Eden, where there are no kings, no sins, no trials, but there are truths. While evoking a fundamental religious

With Allen Ginsberg and Sally Grossman, 1964. Photo by Douglas Gilbert.

concept, "Gates of Eden" is anything but moralistic or preachy. There may be a better world on the other side of those gates, but there's no instruction for attaining it or even a suggestion that it *can* be attained—the biblical Eden is a *lost* paradise, after all.

"It's Alright Ma (I'm Only Bleeding)" might be Dylan's version of Allen Ginsberg's "Howl," a condemnation of the social forces that punish free spirits and individual expression. Ironically referencing Elvis Presley's first single "That's Alright, Mama," the song lays out everything Dylan and his fans, or perhaps his followers, were rebelling against, mainly consumerism, conformity, and obedience. Here again Dylan is asserting the need to be free, in a non-conformist, self-actualizing Emersonian sense, as the essence of life itself.

Like Dylan's two previous albums *Bringing It All Back Home* ends with a song about ending something. It probably doesn't matter whether "It's All Over Now, Baby Blue" is addressed to some other real or imagined person or to Dylan himself: the song is about the difficult passage to a new life. It doesn't look back fondly on the old one or hopefully ahead to the new one—it just describes, in evocative, Freudian imagery, the disconcerting but inevitable need to start over. "It's All Over Now, Baby Blue" is a sequel to "The Times They Are A-Changin'," with the focus shifted from establishment figures to the young person who is beyond their command. Baby Blue's future is unwritten but in their own hands. And leaving is necessary, since the alternative is to work on Maggie's Farm.

By the time he recorded *Bringing It All Back Home* Dylan had grown even closer to his manager Albert Grossman, often staying with him or, in Grossman's absence, staying at his home in Woodstock, New York, a couple of hours north of the city, or at his Gramercy Park townhouse in Manhattan. Through Sally Buehler, who married Grossman in November 1964, Dylan got to know Sara Lownds, who worked as a secretary for Time-Life Films and did some modeling for magazines. Born Shirley Noznisky, she had changed her name to Sara at the insistence of her husband Hans Lownds, from whom she was now separated. David Hajdu describes her as "well-read, a good conversationalist and better listener, resourceful, a fast study, and good hearted." While she had a model's striking good looks, she was also a private person, not a scenester or even a big music fan; Hajdu also notes that when Sally Grossman asked her to watch Dylan on television, Sara thought she was talking about Bobby Darin.[8] By the end of 1964 Sara and Bob were falling in love. She moved into the Chelsea Hotel with her daughter Maria; Dylan was soon renting an apartment there too, complete with piano. When he wasn't traveling in late 1964 or 1965, this was Dylan's world: Woodstock, the Chelsea and nearby Gramercy Park, with occasional jaunts a few blocks south to the Village, where he would still hold court at the Kettle of Fish.

And yet when *Bringing It All Back Home* was released in March it was not Sara Lownds but Sally Grossman who appeared with Dylan on the cover. It's hard not to contrast Kramer's cover photograph to the *Freewheelin'* photograph with Suze Rotolo two years earlier. No longer dressed like a hobo in a too-thin jacket, out in public on a downtown street, sheepishly averting his eyes with his real girlfriend clinging to his arm; the new Dylan is inside a private, upscale living room (the Grossmans'), wearing a nice blazer, holding a Persian cat and looking up at the camera with a slightly annoyed expression, as if the photographer had interrupted whatever he was doing. Meanwhile his not-real girlfriend sits behind him on the divan wearing a fashionable red jumpsuit, her posture sexy and regal, holding a cigarette and casting a cool gaze towards us. Dylan has clearly traded one persona for another, the new one being far less inviting and more sophisticated. But there's also an ironic vibe to the image of Dylan "back home" in this domestic, bourgeois setting, complete with an ornate fireplace mantle and a very cute little cat. Dylan and Kramer arranged the shot carefully, experimenting with the placement of random objects on the mantle and the divan, so the cover image features, conspicuously, a fallout shelter sign, an issue of *Time* magazine (depicting Lyndon Johnson as Man of the Year) and a Hollywood gossip sheet (which Dylan is holding), along with record albums by Eric Von Schmidt, Lotte Lenya, Robert Johnson, the Impressions, Lord Buckley, and Bob Dylan (*Another Side*). Kramer used a double-exposure technique to create a blurred ring around the image of Bob and Sally; the photographer described it as "the visual effect of a spinning record," but it also suggests a keyhole in reverse, looking in rather than out.[9]

Along with the scattered records and magazines and the expression on Bob's and Sally's faces, it heightens a feeling of voyeurism, as if we've invaded Bob Dylan's privacy by buying his record.

For Dylan's fans, the very fact that there was a woman with him on his new album cover *and it was not Joan Baez* might have been the photograph's most striking feature. Ironically the cuff links Dylan is wearing on the cover were a gift from Baez (a detail she would later include in her song "Diamonds and Rust")—but by early 1965 their relationship as performers and as lovers was running on fumes. They played several shows together, mostly colleges, in February and March, Dylan still performing solo, but his heart was no longer in it. He would later complain that the audience she attracted was "morgue-y . . . It was like playing in a funeral parlor," he said, for "little flashlight people."[10]

Baez remained enamored of Dylan's songwriting—*Farewell, Angelina*, the album she released later that year, included four Dylan compositions, including the title song—but she did not like Dylan's new musical direction or his cynical posture. At one point, according to Baez, "I asked him what made us different, and he said it was simple, that I thought I could change things, and he knew that no one could."[11]

So it seems strange that Dylan invited Baez to join him on his tour of England that spring. Baez accepted, reasonably assuming she would be brought onstage to perform with Dylan. Dylan had no such intention, which made the invitation a little cruel. But relegating Baez to his entourage is in keeping with the bratty behavior reported by many acquaintances and captured in the documentary film devoted to the English tour, D. A. Pennebaker's *Dont Look Back*.[12] Dylan and Grossman allowed Pennebaker, a pioneer of *cinema verité*, to film onstage, backstage, at press conferences, in limos, and, perhaps most crucially, in his hotel suite. Although he never looks into or speaks to the camera, Dylan is always performing—for the film but also for whatever group of people surrounds him. Marianne Faithfull recalled the bizarre scene created by the film crew and the parade of young British pop stars who came to pay homage:

> We all sat on the floor of Bob's room talking and drinking and playing guitars while Bob pretended none of this was happening. He would walk in and out of the room, he would sit down and type, he would talk on the phone, he would even answer incredibly stupid questions, but only if he felt like pulling that particular thing into focus.[13]

Indeed, while Dylan never provides straight or predictable answers to baffled journalists, his attitude ranges from playful and amused to belligerent, depending apparently on his impression of the interviewer and his own fluctuating moods. And when Donovan, then a new sensation who modeled himself on Dylan, shows up and plays "To Sing for You," a sort of watered-down "All I Really Want To Do," an unimpressed Dylan answers with "It's All Over Now, Baby Blue," clearly demonstrating that he is not to be challenged as a songwriter.[14]

Baez disappears about a third of the way through *Dont Look Back*; she left the tour not long after writing to her sister Mimi:

> I can't stand to be around him. Everyone traveling with him is going mad—He walks around in new clothes with a cane—Has tantrums, orders fish, gets drunk, plays his record, phones up America, asks if his concert tonight is sold out—stops all three limousines every morning to buy all the newspapers that might have his name in them. He won't invite me to sing with him even when the kids yell out my name and send petitions to him to have me sing.[15]

Baez left London for Paris; she had her own shows to do, and both she and Dylan remained in Europe (separately) for a couple of weeks after Dylan's tour. But when she learned that Dylan was in a London hospital with a stomach ailment, she went to visit him. At his hospital room, she met Sara Lownds, whose existence she had been unaware of until then.[16]

Dylan's illness might have been brought on by the fact that he was substituting amphetamines and alcohol for food. He had gotten thinner, his face losing its slight pudginess, and his eyes, when not shielded by Ray-Bans, were sunken with sleeplessness. The drugs also help explain the erratic behavior Dylan displayed in Pennebaker's documentary. He seems unable to keep his leg still while listening to Donovan, and he becomes enraged when he learns that someone has thrown a glass out the window of his suite (admittedly, a serious offense). Late in the film his tirade directed at journalist Horace Freeland Judson from *Time* magazine is cruel without being clever or even coherent.[17]

It wasn't sustainable, but Dylan's rock-and-roll lifestyle was somehow fueling an amazing level of creativity and artistic growth. He was cranking out brilliant new lyrics. He was also eagerly embracing electric music and, along with it, a jaded hipster persona. The famous montage that Pennebaker filmed of Dylan flipping cue cards along with "Subterranean Homesick Blues"—arguably the first true music video—is a wonderful piece of postmodern art, a deconstruction of popular song performance. Like so much of what Dylan did in the mid-1960s, it proved so influential that it's hard to appreciate how original it actually was. Rather than lip-sync, Dylan stands with his mouth closed and a bored expression on his face, displaying cues that would normally be off-camera. And of course the cards sometimes playfully deviate from the lyrics (notably, "suck-cess" for "success"). Meanwhile Allen Ginsberg and Bob Neuwirth can be seen across the alley from Dylan, but they're ignoring him, engaged in their own conversation. At the song's end all three simply stroll off in different directions. When *Dont Look Back* was finally released in 1967, the cue card sequence was attached as a prologue.

Just a few weeks after *Bringing It All Back Home* hit the record stores, Columbia released the first single by a young Los Angeles band called the Byrds, an electric arrangement of "Mr. Tambourine Man" featuring one of the most memorable opening guitar riffs that ever flew across the airwaves. To make the song a radio-friendly two and a half minutes, Dylan's four double-length verses were reduced to one. Even more than Peter, Paul and Mary's "Blowin' in the Wind," the Byrds' "Mr. Tambourine Man" translated Dylan to a wider audience, topping both the British and American charts over the summer of 1965. Amidst the mid-1960s flood of Dylan covers the Byrds' stood out in terms of both quantity and quality. "Mr. Tambourine Man" was the title track and one of four Dylan songs on their debut; they would record another half dozen of his songs by the end of the decade.

With that first hit the Byrds popularized a sound that was immediately dubbed "folk rock," a marriage of two genres that had previously seemed irreconcilable. Although the term had begun to appear by late 1964, it became *the* sound of 1965.[18] The Beatles' albums *Help!* and *Rubber Soul*, both released that year, include a number of songs that fit the new genre ("I've Just Seen a Face," "I'm Looking Through You," and "If I Needed Someone," for instance). Simon and Garfunkel's "The Sound of Silence," originally released in an acoustic "folk" arrangement, became a number-one hit thanks to Tom Wilson, who stayed in the studio after a session with Dylan to record an electric backing track (to the duo's surprise and Simon's initial dismay). Barry McGuire would also top the singles chart in late 1965 with "Eve of Destruction," a protest song so overblown that it sounds like a parody of the genre, set to a standard folk-rock beat with brief, Dylanesque harmonica flourishes. The Turtles' and Cher's hit Dylan covers were also given folk-rock arrangements.

As a musical trend folk rock was somehow both short-lived and eternal. In the fast-moving music scene of the late 1960s it would quickly be supplanted by psychedelic rock and harder blues-based music, so that no significant band was embracing the folk-rock label two years after the Byrds ushered it in. At the same time the new sound—gentler, laid-back beats, a combination of acoustic and electric guitars, the latter more likely to "chime" than to snarl—became a permanent fixture of pop and rock music, as did lyrics that reflected new countercultural mores and social consciousness, with poetic intentions (or pretensions).

Of course Dylan rejected the label, as he would all labels—when asked in late 1965 if he planned to "stick to folk rock" he replied curtly, "I don't play folk rock."[19] And it's fair to say he really didn't: his electric bands were playing something much bluesier and grittier than the Byrds or Simon and Garfunkel. Even so, as the man most responsible for pushing folk in the direction of rock and popularizing the idea that writing one's own songs was a meaningful sign of authenticity, he was rightly seen as the figurehead of the new movement. Even before the release of *Bringing It All Back Home* a January 1965 headline in the British magazine *Melody Maker* summed it up: "Beatles Say—Dylan Shows the Way." The article featured admiring comments from John Lennon and George Harrison, who remarked, "I like his whole attitude . . . the way he dresses, the way he doesn't give a damn."[20]

Dylan returned to New York from the tumultuous tour of England in early June and spent two days in the studio with Tom Wilson and a band that included Bobby Gregg on drums, Joseph Macho, Jr. on bass, Paul Griffin on piano, and on guitar, the flamboyant Michael Bloomfield from the Paul Butterfield Blues Band. They worked on three songs for Dylan's next album, two of which were up-tempo electric blues: "Phantom Engineer," which would later be slowed down and retitled "It Takes a Lot to Laugh, It Takes a Train to Cry"; "Sitting on a Barbed Wire Fence," which was shelved until its release on the initial Bootleg Series installment; and a song that had emerged from what Dylan called "this long piece of vomit, about twenty pages long," set to waltz time, called "Like a Rolling Stone."[21]

For Dylan—and for popular music in general—"Like a Rolling Stone" was a milestone. When interviewer Martin Bronstein asked him (in February 1966) to name a song that was a "particular breakthrough," Dylan went so far as to say that he had "quit singing and playing" before he wrote "Like a Rolling Stone," and he was trying to focus on other kinds of writing. But then he realized "I had never written anything like that before, and it suddenly came to me that that was what I should do."[22]

Perhaps the closest thing Dylan had written previously was the last track of his last album, "It's All Over Now, Baby Blue." In fact "Like a Rolling Stone" follows Baby Blue, now identified as "Miss Lonely," into a new life without the comforts of home or any kind of safety net. The lyrics are undeniably cruel, taunting a formerly privileged young woman who has left home and is now living a hard life on the streets. And yet, even as Dylan himself would refer to "hatred" and "revenge" as the song's themes, he would add, "in the end, it wasn't hatred, it was telling someone something they didn't know, telling them they were lucky."[23]

And that is the miracle of "Like a Rolling Stone," that on paper it's a vicious rant, the "piece of vomit" Dylan called it, and yet, when sung, it's an anthem, in which "How does it feel" can just as easily be answered "It feels exhilarating" as "It feels like hell." It's what Bruce Springsteen, a decade later, would later call a "runaway American dream" and, a century earlier, what Huck Finn called lighting out for the territories: to have no direction home might signal alienation, but it's also the ultimate freedom. A rolling stone gathers no moss, has no attachments and nothing to slow it down, which is why Muddy Waters used the image to describe himself and why the Rolling Stones appropriated it.

It's not just the singing but the entire sound of the recording that creates the miracle of "Like a Rolling Stone." The Bootleg Series volume XII, traces the recording's development from the lilting, somewhat hesitant waltz Dylan originally imagined to the thick stew of guitar, organ, and Macho's melodic, climbing bass line following Bobby Gregg's steady, driving 4/4 beat, with off-the-beat tambourine accents. In his often-cited speech inducting Dylan into the Rock and Roll Hall of Fame, Springsteen recalled first hearing the song's opening "snare shot that sounded like somebody'd kicked open the door to your mind." That "shot" on the "four" echoes while Gregg taps the kick drum on the off-beat, just before the band kicks in on the "one," creating instant excitement. Both the verses and the pre-choruses feature enough space at the end for the band to churn, building tension as Dylan pauses to spit out the last word or phrase, barreling into the chorus. And then there's Al Kooper's slightly stoned Hammond organ part, which according to his own account was a kind of fluke: invited to the session as a guitarist, Kooper was intimidated by Michael Bloomfield's chops, but he was determined to be part of the recording. When Frank Owens was moved to piano, Kooper took Owens's position, uninvited, at the organ, successfully testing Tom Wilson's indulgence. Listening to the playback, Wilson wanted to bury Kooper in the mix, but Dylan liked the simple, slow-moving organ lines and insisted that they be pushed up.[24]

Columbia was reluctant to issue a single clocking in at six minutes, a length unheard of at the time. But the label's coordinator of new releases took an acetate of the recording to a popular Midtown discotheque, where "the effect was seismic"; the crowd demanded that the song be played again and again.[25] A couple of influential radio DJs in attendance called on Columbia to send them the record, so a single was hastily pressed with the song split into halves for each side, and by summer's end "Like a Rolling Stone," reissued with the complete track on the A-side and the nearly-as-long "Gates of Eden" on the B-side, was perched at number two on the *Billboard* singles chart, topped only by the Beatles' "Help." It was, by far, the greatest commercial success Dylan had achieved with one of his own recordings.

Less than a week after the official release of "Like a Rolling Stone" Dylan appeared for the third consecutive year at the Newport Folk Festival. The mythology surrounding his set on July 25 is dense, most of it reinforcing the image of Dylan committing a shocking but noble sacrilege by "going electric" before a sea of uncomprehending folkies who booed him off the stage. The reality was more complicated. While it's true that Dylan hadn't performed his new music live with a band, the half-electric *Bringing It All Back Home* had been out for four months, and the rocking "Like a Rolling Stone" was all over the airwaves, so it was clear that he was moving in that direction. Moreover the Newport Festival, while predominantly acoustic, had featured plugged-in blues performers in the past, and in 1965 Lightnin' Hopkins, the Chambers Brothers, and the Paul Butterfield Blues Band all appeared onstage with electric guitars. Nevertheless when Dylan took the stage with his Stratocaster, backed by Bloomfield, Sam Lay on drums, and Jerome Arnold on bass (all currently members of the Butterfield Band), along with Kooper on organ, it did seem like a betrayal to many—but certainly not all—in the audience.[26]

Dylan was unhappy that he was slated to perform early in the long evening program rather than as the night's closing act—which might have contributed to the edginess he brought to the stage.[27] He began a quick, jangly strum before shouting "let's go" as the band leapt into "Maggie's Farm," led by Bloomfield, who added searing fills at the end of each line of the song. The rest of the band chugged along, sometimes remembering the quick chord change at the end of each verse, sometimes not. Dylan delivered the lyrics forcefully, nearly shouting, in a duet with Bloomfield's blues licks. They hadn't worked up many songs, and Dylan's time slot didn't allow for a full set anyway, so after barreling through "Maggie's Farm," "Like a Rolling Stone," and "Phantom Engineer," he turned to the band and said, "Let's go, man, that's all," and they walked off.

Inevitably, the performance was met with a wide range of responses. There were about 17,000 people listening, and, as Elijah Wald points out, "What anyone experienced depended not only on what they thought about Dylan, folk music, rock 'n' roll, celebrity, selling out, tradition, or purity, but on where they happened to be sitting and who happened to be near them, and in the end the disputes and conflicting memories may count for more than the evidence preserved on tape and film."[28] Wald emphasizes that the sound was cleaner and more balanced farther from the stage, but fans up close were getting the direct, distorted blast of the amplifiers with indistinguishable vocals. The sound backstage and in the wings, where festival organizers and performers gathered, was probably even worse.[29] Poor sound quality, an under-rehearsed band, and, yes, philosophical objections to Dylan's new style all may have been responsible for the booing that mixed with the usual applause.

If some of the audience had been unhappy with the performance, more of them were unhappy with its abrupt conclusion. Murray Lerner's film footage, compiled on the DVD *The Other Side of the Mirror*, shows Peter Yarrow, who was serving as emcee, pleading alternately with the crowd (to accept Dylan's departure and let the show go on) and with Dylan (to return and placate the crowd). Dylan finally reappeared with a borrowed acoustic guitar to play a poignant "It's All Over Now, Baby Blue" and "Mr. Tambourine Man." The booing stopped.

"They were just like little babies," Dylan recalled several years after the fact. "They wanted to hear that, and that's all they wanted to hear. So I went out and sang it for them. At that time I just knew they were a bunch of fucks, and I just thought, 'Well, forget it!' if that's all they want you to do is sing 'em to sleep."[30]

Folk music fans tended to be politically liberal but musically conservative, valuing tradition and purity. Dylan was driving a chisel into the crack of that paradox, first by forsaking "finger-pointin' songs" and now by going electric. One of the left-wing traditionalists he offended at Newport was Pete Seeger, who had inspired and supported him during his Guthrie phase. Legend has Seeger threatening to cut the audio cables with an axe during Dylan's set; he later insisted his objection was strictly to the distorted sound blaring from the amps, which rendered Dylan's lyrics unintelligible.

Taking a broader view, Wald argues that Seeger and Dylan had come to represent conflicting values associated with the countercultural left: democracy and collective action for Seeger, radical individualism for Dylan. That conflict didn't matter much as long as Dylan was opposed to what the left-leaning folk community was opposed to—the military-industrial complex, consumerism, corporate narrow-mindedness, racism—but, as the incident at the Tom Paine Award dinner had shown, Dylan's independence was absolute, and he was just as determined not to be "owned" by the Emergency Civil Liberties Committee as by Columbia Records. Seeger's take, a couple of years after Newport, was that "the left tried to lionize him; he reacted violently against this, saying fuck you to them all."[31] That gesture of quasi-political defiance, Dylan's shift to rock music, was at the same time seen as a kind of sell-out, a capitulation to the more "commercial" rock and roll sound—and in fact it did gain him a wider audience. But for a certain cohort of fans and elder statesmen of folk music it was absolutely the "fuck you" Seeger perceived.

Then again, Dylan did come back out to play those two acoustic songs. With the valedictory "It's All Over Now, Baby Blue" as his song choice, he clearly wasn't apologizing for going electric, but he was at least signaling that he hadn't completely abandoned the solo acoustic format—in fact he had also performed an acoustic set at the Contemporary Songwriters Showcase the day before. He would reverse the order of this electric/acoustic split set when he went back on tour, in a move that epitomized his show-business savvy. The effect was not to ease the public into his new sound but to heighten the contrast between these two approaches. Fans could choose sides, or they could embrace both styles.

Four days after Newport Dylan returned to Columbia's Studio A in New York, and in one week he completed one of the greatest albums of all time, *Highway 61 Revisited.* Tom Wilson, who had produced Dylan's last four albums as well as the single "Like a Rolling Stone," was gone, probably at Dylan's behest, although Dylan later claimed that he couldn't remember the circumstances: "all I know is that I was out recording one day, and Tom had always been there—and I looked up one day and Bob was there."[32] "Bob" was Bob Johnston, a relatively inexperienced staff producer who was not inclined to tell Dylan what to do. His supportive, hands-off approach worked, and he remained Dylan's producer for the rest of the decade. Otherwise the band (with Harvey Brooks replacing Joe Macho on bass) picked up where they had left off in June, blending piano and organ with Dylan's and Bloomfield's guitars, leaning into basic blues chord progressions on five of the remaining eight tracks.

"Tombstone Blues" and "Highway 61 Revisited," slotted in as either side's second track, are both rollicking blues in which each verse presents a different bad-dream scenario. Mark Polizzotti aptly refers to the world of "Tombstone Blues" as "at once recognizable and wholly alien, an outsized American landscape made up not only of our daily reality, but also of our myths, dreams, cultural archetypes, and barely formed nightmares."[33] The description applies to both songs, which are inhabited by a cast of characters from the Bible, the underworld, folklore, and various musical and literary traditions, rendered with Dylanesque wordplay. They glide by as if on parade floats, delighting us even as they almost invariably represent vice and corruption. As is nearly always the case for Dylan, the wrong people are in power: in "Tombstone Blues" Jack the Ripper heads the Chamber of Commerce, the blowhard Commander in Chief (an oblique reference to President Lyndon Johnson) has made John the Baptist a torturer, the doctor's cold-hearted advice to the "hysterical bride," who apparently has just been raped, is "to not let the boys in." All is absurdity, cruelty, and corruption.

Highway 61, known as the Great River Road and the Blues Highway, represents America in the twentieth century much as the Mississippi River itself had in the nineteenth. And Dylan's vision of the highway that cuts through the middle of the country echoes the depiction of Mark Twain in *Huckleberry Finn* and Herman Melville in *The Confidence-Man*. Everyone on the road is shifty, morally compromised, looking out for number one, whether it's the biblical Abraham, who agrees to follow God's order strictly to save his own skin, or Mack the Finger and Louie the King, who are scheming to make a buck on a bunch of worthless merchandise, not coincidentally including shoestrings in the colors of the American flag. Adding to the song's absurdist, carnivalesque effect, Dylan substituted a police whistle where his harmonica fills would normally go.

The other tracks on *Highway 61 Revisited* might also be considered in pairs. "It Takes a Lot to Laugh, It Takes a Train to Cry" and "From a Buick 6" are the album's love songs. "It Takes a Lot to Laugh," a revision of Newport's "Phantom Engineer," is now a slow drag blues with a tack piano up front in the mix. In contrast to the overflowing imagery and verbal gymnastics of, say, "Tombstone Blues," this one is built on simple statements that sound almost like conventional lyrics borrowed from train songs. Pasted together, these lines form non-sequiturs (like the title), and yet each verse ends with an expression of devotion or lust. With its slinky, after-hours arrangement and the lyrics' pastiche of trains, landscapes, and longing, "It Takes a Lot to Laugh" deliberately rejects coherence.

"From a Buick 6" is a more straightforward blues collage, voiced by a man who spends a lot of time on the road and on the edge, a tribute to an equally mythical "junkyard angel" who knows what he needs and is bound to put a blanket on his bed.

"Queen Jane Approximately," which opens side two, could be a prequel to "Like a Rolling Stone." It's a come-on or offer of a different kind of life, made to a woman—in various stanzas a daughter, a mother, an actual queen—who seems to have everything but feels nothing. When you're tired of all the bullshit, come see me, he says. (Although Queen Jane hints at Queen Joan Baez, it's worth noting that Dylan had experimented with "Lord Jim" and "Queen Anne" in earlier drafts.)[34]

As Mark Polizzotti observes, Queen Jane is also the "counterpart" of a more infamous character interrogated at the end of side one, Mr Jones of "Ballad of a Thin Man". Here too it's tempting to identify a specific real-life inspiration, but Dylan's target is broader, and, unlike

Queen Jane, Mr Jones receives no sympathy or welcome from the singer. The pencil-packing Jones is presumably a journalist, someone like Horace Freeland Judson from *Dont Look Back*—representative of the mainstream media, failing to comprehend what's happening with Dylan and his generation of artists and musicians. And yet Mr Jones could be anyone from the square world, virtually anyone over thirty (to invoke the dividing line drawn by the Free Speech Movement). Like a character out of a John Cheever story, Mr Jones has all the credentials of an educated, sophisticated member of the managerial class, but now he is confronted with a world that rejects his conventional values. To him, it's part traveling circus and part nightmare, weird and more than a little threatening. The music is appropriately menacing but also a little campy, from the opening piano riff that sounds like it would accompany the villain walking into a saloon in a low-budget western to the organ swirling and punctuating beats to the descending chord progression of the verse. "Thin Man" is a tour de force, a summation of Dylan's disdain for people on the wrong side of the 1960s cultural divide.

On the album's last two songs it's the singer who confronts a world of alienation and confusion. "Just Like Tom Thumb's Blues" and "Desolation Row" are sober, downbeat echoes of "Tombstone Blues" and "Highway 61 Revisited," offering one bad encounter or bad dream after another, verse by verse. "Tom Thumb's Blues" begins in Juarez in the rain; whether all of its miseries and misadventures take place there, though, is anyone's guess. Saint Annie and Sweet Melinda could hustle you anywhere, and the same goes for the cops on Housing Project Hill and the blackmailing authorities.

The eleven-minute "Desolation Row" closes *Highway 61 Revisited*, the only song without a full band. Russ Savakus backs Dylan on acoustic bass, and in a stroke of genius or luck on Bob Johnston's part, Charlie McCoy accepted the invitation to provide acoustic guitar embellishments to Dylan's rhythmic strumming (he would play on Dylan's next four albums as well). On an album loaded with incongruous, unsettling images "Desolation Row" still stands out for its bleak depiction of a world gone wrong. Dylan opens the song with a dry, matter-of-fact reference to postcards of a hanging and a traveling circus. As many Dylanologists have noted, he was likely familiar with an infamous lynching, two decades before his birth in his hometown of Hibbing, of three Black men who were with the John Robinson Show Circus. As was often the case, the mob posed around the victims for photos, which were reproduced as postcards.[35]

Although Dylan professed to dislike T. S. Eliot—who is in fact mocked in this song, fighting with Ezra Pound while being laughed at by calypso singers—"Desolation Row" resembles Eliot's "The Waste Land" in its extensive use of historical, religious, and literary allusions and its depiction of a fallen, hopeless world. The refracted characters—an "easy" Cinderella, the Good Samaritan, Ophelia, Einstein disguised as Robin Hood, and many more—are out of place, diminished. State-sanctioned violence and petty cruelty are accompanied by cheap entertainment. Residents/inmates get used to it all, and nobody cares. Like the Waste Land and other dystopias, "Desolation Row" is an unreal city that feels uncomfortably familiar.

Highway 61 Revisited was released on August 30, less than a month after the last recording session. Like its predecessor, the album featured a cover photograph by Daniel Kramer, this time a close-up of Dylan wearing a Triumph motorcycle T-shirt under a stylish, patterned pink-and-blue overshirt, holding his Ray-Bans, looking out at us with an expression slightly more annoyed than the one he wore on the cover of *Bringing It All Back Home*. Behind him is Bob Neuwirth, visible only from waist down, holding one of Kramer's cameras. Dylan appears as Marianne Faithfull described him around this time: "nothing less than the hippest person on earth."[36] The album sold well, its number three position on *Billboard* the highest for Dylan up to that time, and it remained on the charts for most of the next year.

Two days before its release Dylan played his first concert since Newport, at the Forest Hills Tennis Stadium in Queens. Bloomfield was committed to the Butterfield Band, so Dylan recruited Robbie Robertson, a guitarist he had met through John Hammond, Jr. Robertson also had his own band, the Hawks, but he wanted the Dylan gig, so he asked Dylan to book the Hawks' drummer/singer Levon Helm as well. Along with Kooper on organ and Harvey Brooks on bass, this new group would back Dylan for the second half of the

Forest Hills concert. Before the show Dylan instructed Robertson and the other musicians, "Don't stop playing, no matter what."[37] They followed his orders, despite persistent booing and chants of "We want Dylan!" (that is, the "real" Dylan) between songs, some fans making it past barricades and onto the stage, knocking Al Kooper off his stool.[38] It was an extended version of the Newport set, only this time there was little doubt that the reason for the crowd's hostility was their disapproval of the electric band itself. Dylan took the same band to Los Angeles to play the Hollywood Bowl about a week later, expecting a more receptive audience. No such luck. Robertson recalled:

> After we played the first song, I looked out at the crowd and noticed something odd. People would look around and try to boo louder than one another, laughing and screaming with anger like this was a game or part of the show. Individually they didn't seem offended by the music; it was more of a mob mentality—"When Dylan goes electric, you boo." Jeering was just a thing to do.[39]

If confrontation had become part of the Dylan concert experience, it was also the trademark of his hit singles, as he followed up "Like a Rolling Stone" with "Positively 4th Street," a song recorded during the *Highway 61 Revisited* sessions but left off the album. Like the album closers "Restless Farewell," "It Ain't Me, Babe," and "It's All Over Now, Baby Blue," "Positively 4th Street" is a parting song, but it's much more bitter than its predecessors. The title suggests that the song is directed at someone from the old Greenwich Village scene (Gerde's Folk City and Dylan's apartment were on West 4th), but it could just as easily be *everyone* from the old folk community. There are no biblical or literary allusions here, no obscure references to mystery tramps or Napoleon in rags—just a straightforward telling-off of a fair-weather friend. Joni Mitchell later credited "Positively 4th Street" with her "revelation" that "you can write about anything in songs";[40] while it's less obviously groundbreaking than many songs Dylan had already written, there was still nothing else like it on the radio in 1965 in terms of lyrical content—not to mention there is no direct reference in the lyrics to the song's title, no chorus, no bridge, no refrain, not even consistent end rhyme. Musically, though, the song is catchy, driven by Al Kooper's descending organ motif and a laid-back "folk-rock" beat. It made the top ten in both the USA and UK.

A rolling stone gathers no moss. "Positively 4th Street" was in part a reflection of Dylan's attitude toward people who wanted to cling to him and bask in reflected glory. But it was also an attempt to free himself, yet again, from his recent past by pissing certain people off. Izzy Young, who had championed Dylan early in his career, later told biographer Anthony Scaduto that "at least five hundred people in a few months' time asked me if I was the one in the song." Young didn't necessarily think he was, but he expressed the anger many of Dylan's old companions must have felt: "he comes in and uses my resources and everyone else's resources in the Village . . . the bars and the clubs, and then he leaves. He gets bitter, he writes the bitter song. Dave Van Ronk never wrote something saying what a cocksucker Bob Dylan was. No one has ever said anything about Dylan. He's the one that's complaining. He's the one that left."[41]

Young's anger is understandable, but I would conjecture that Dylan's petulance was more strategic than personal. In order to continue to grow artistically he had to be free of the past and disconnected from whatever aid and comfort he could get from old friends like Van Ronk and Young. Maybe "writing that bitter song" wasn't really necessary, but it made his self-reinvention complete . . . and it's a great song.

6

1965–66: Acceleration

Following the pattern established by pop singers in the 1950s, when the LP record was a new format, rock stars in the mid-1960s cranked out new music at what seems now like a ridiculous pace. The Beatles delivered five albums—*A Hard Day's Night* through *Revolver*—in just over two years, July 1964 to August 1966. The Rolling Stones produced four—their rapid evolution from *Rolling Stones #2* through *Between the Buttons*—from January 1965 to January 1967. Dylan kept pace with four releases over nineteen months from *The Times They Are A-Changin'* in February 1964 through *Highway 61 Revisited* in August 1965 and a fifth, the double album *Blonde on Blonde*, coming in June of 1966.

While the Stones were just beginning to write their own songs and the Beatles were still mixing in covers in 1964 and '65, Dylan was writing all his own material throughout this period. My point though is not to compare Dylan's work ethic to his most prominent contemporaries' but to marvel at the expectations record companies and managers placed on all of them and at what they achieved when they were still in their early twenties. Like all pop stars, they juggled this prolific studio output with concert tours, interviews, and other personal appearances. The prevailing logic, accepted by the performers themselves, was that their time at the top of the pops was fleeting and that the public—especially younger record-buyers—would move on if a performer or group disappeared for even a few months.[1]

Working constantly, Dylan continued to stretch the limits of pop songwriting and produce albums with zero filler, in addition to stand-alone singles. In two sessions in the fall of 1965 he cut his next single, the rollicking "Can You Please Crawl Out Your Window?," along with "I Wanna Be Your Lover" and another song called "Freeze Out." He was backed by the Hawks, who also endured the often-hostile crowds at about two dozen concerts they played with Dylan over the last months of the year. "Window," a more light-hearted putdown song than "Positively 4th Street," bristled with energy but flopped as a single. "I Wanna Be Your Lover" (which riffed on "I Wanna Be Your Man," the Beatles song that had been a UK hit for the Stones) was shelved indefinitely, but "Freeze Out" would later be re-recorded and retitled "Visions of Johanna," a cornerstone of Dylan's next album.

Dylan's celebrity had continued to grow since Newport and *Highway 61 Revisited*, as he was now regarded as both a poet and a rock star. In September 1965 he appeared on the cover of *Esquire* magazine—specifically, the upper right quadrant of his face appeared as part of a composite image of "4 of the 28 Who Count Most with the College Rebels." Dylan was number one, his visage combined with those of Malcolm X, Fidel Castro, and the late John F. Kennedy. In December 1965 Ken Kesey (author of *One Flew Over the Cuckoo's Nest* and leader of the "Merry Pranksters"), Allen Ginsberg, and fellow poets Michael McClure and Gary Snyder attended Dylan's concert and after-party in San Francisco, along with Joan Baez and various prominent Hell's Angels. As if that VIP section weren't surreal enough, giant teddy bears appeared on the amps during the electric set, and someone from the crowd tossed a boot onstage, where it landed upright and remained.[2] While in San Francisco Dylan, with Robbie Robertson along for the ride, was feted and photographed with Ginsberg, McClure, and Snyder at Lawrence Ferlinghetti's City Lights bookstore.[3]

The same weekend Dylan held court at a press conference filmed for the public television station KQED, probably the most entertaining broadcast interview of his career. With friends and admirers—including Ginsberg—in attendance, a laconic but amiable Dylan answered, or played with, questions from students and professional journalists alike.

Do you think of yourself primarily as a singer or a poet?
Oh, I think of myself more as a song and dance man, y'know.

What poets do you dig?
Rimbaud, I guess; W. C. Fields; the family, you know, the trapeze family in the circus; Smokey Robinson; Allen Ginsberg; Charlie Rich—he's a good poet.

What do you think of people who analyze your songs?
I welcome them—with open arms.

What do you bother to write the poetry for if we all get different images? If we don't know what you're talking about.
Because I got nothing else to do, man.

If you were going to sell out to a commercial interest, which one would it be?
Ladies garments.[4]

Throughout the interview Dylan tended to play along with any questions from young people and any oddball questions but bristled at older, well-dressed attendees asking him to explain his own method or his popularity.

Around the same time he was interviewed for *Playboy* by Nat Hentoff, who had previously written a revealing but respectful *New Yorker* profile centered on the recording of *Another Side*. They colluded on an article that satirized the questions Dylan was tired of answering. Explaining his switch "from folk to folk rock" Dylan proclaimed, "Folk music is a bunch of fat people." He was probably only half-joking or exaggerating to say what he really meant:

> I have to think of all this as traditional music. Traditional music is based on hexagrams. It comes about from legends, Bibles, plagues, and it revolves around vegetables and death. There's nobody that's going to kill traditional music. All these songs

With Robbie Robertson, Michael McClure, and Allen Ginsberg outside City Lights Bookstore, San Francisco, December 5, 1965. Photo by Dale Smith.

> about roses growing out of people's brains and lovers who are really geese and swans that turn into angels.

The serious element in this hilarious response is that Dylan continued to be drawn to the mysteries and hard wisdom of traditional songs, which by this point had nothing to do with what people were calling "folk music." Asked again why he took up rock and roll, he told a shaggy dog story that begins, "Carelessness. I lost my one true love. I started drinking. I wind up in Phoenix. I get a job as a Chinaman . . ." and ends "The first guy that picked me up asked me if I wanted to be a star. What could I say?"

> *Playboy*: And that's how you became a rock-and-roll singer?
> Dylan: No, that's how I got tuberculosis.[5]

Meanwhile he and Sara Lownds had married on November 22 at a courthouse on Long Island. The ceremony and marriage itself remained a secret, if not particularly well kept. Less than a week afterward Dylan remarked to an interviewer with the *Chicago Daily News*, "Getting married, having a bunch of kids, I have no hopes for it. If it happens, it happens." He flatly denied the marriage—in front of Sara—when Jack Elliott tried to congratulate him in the Kettle of Fish around the same time.[6] From her previous marriage, Sara had custody of her daughter Maria, whom Bob would adopt, and in January she gave birth to Jesse, their first child. Whether it was to protect her and their children's privacy or to maintain Dylan's own sense—and image—of youthful freedom, Sara Dylan would not be part of Bob Dylan's public life until they were on the brink of divorce a decade later.

The new father and husband spent the first three months of 1966 recording *Blonde on Blonde* and playing numerous shows in the USA and Canada. By now Levon Helm had left the band, later explaining that he "began to think it was a ridiculous way to make a living: flying to concerts in Bob's thirteen-seat Lodestar, jumping in and out of limousines, and then getting booed."[7] For the winter shows he was replaced by the drummer who had replaced him in Ronnie Hawkins's band, Sandy Konikoff.

The remaining Hawks accompanied Dylan in Studio A for three *Blonde on Blonde* sessions in January, but things weren't quite coming together. January 21 yielded sixteen takes of "She's Your Lover Now," which Dylan ultimately rejected altogether.[8] The New York sessions' only keeper was the gorgeous rock ballad "One of Us Must Know (Sooner or Later)."

Then, at Bob Johnston's urging, Dylan moved the operation to Columbia's Nashville studios in mid-February, bringing only Robertson from the Hawks and inviting Al Kooper to play organ. The rest of the musicians were Nashville session pros: Charlie McCoy, Wayne Moss, Jerry Kennedy, Joe South and Henry Strzelecki on guitars and bass, Hargus "Pig" Robbins on piano, and Kenny Buttrey on drums. While the mythology surrounding Dylan's relocation presumes a clash of musical cultures, historian Sean Wilentz points out that the Nashville players were themselves in their mid-twenties and certainly would have known Dylan as a songwriter, at least; and

McCoy had played with Dylan the previous year, contributing the lead acoustic lines on "Desolation Row."[9]

As anyone who has heard *Blonde on Blonde* can attest, the Nashville crew were prepared to play anything Dylan threw at them. In a 1978 interview Dylan singled out *Blonde on Blonde* as the album that best captured "the sound I hear in my mind" when conceptualizing his songs. He famously referred to it as "that thin, that wild mercury sound. It's metallic and bright gold, with whatever that conjures up."[10] Although he added that this ideal sound was present in his two previous albums as well, the phrase "thin, wild mercury sound" has attached itself particularly to *Blonde on Blonde*.

Whatever the Nashville players might have thought of Dylan's new material or his style, what really surprised them was that they had been booked indefinitely—not, as usual, on a tight recording schedule—and that they would spend a lot of time getting paid to wait for Dylan to finish writing songs. On day two for instance they spent an entire evening and early morning in the studio playing ping-pong, waiting and dozing before Dylan arrived to cut the eleven-and-a-half-minute "Sad-Eyed Lady of the Lowlands" at 4.00 a.m.—and then nailed it almost immediately, finishing up at 5.30.[11] For other sessions Al Kooper would join Dylan in his hotel room to work out piano arrangements as he wrote the songs, which Kooper would teach to the musicians while Dylan finished writing, so they could hit the ground running when he showed up. The arrangements were informal, and the players didn't always know how many verses Dylan had up his sleeve.

Kenny Buttrey recalled being more amused than frustrated, explaining how, on the longer songs, the band would have to muster one sonic build-up, then another and another: "After about five, six minutes [of 'Sad-Eyed Lady of the Lowlands'] we start looking at the clock, everyone starts looking at each other, we'd built to the peak of our limit and, bang, [there] goes another harmonica solo . . . After about ten minutes of this thing we're cracking up at each other, at what we were doing. I mean, we peaked five minutes ago. Where do we go from here?"[12]

But perhaps the oddest moment occurred at the last session, when Dylan described the Salvation Army band sound he wanted on the song that would later be titled "Rainy Day Women #12 & 35." He briefly considered bringing in an actual Salvation Army band, but Buttrey thought they could do a better job themselves (suspecting that the genuine article might sound a little too polished).[13] A local trombonist arrived in the middle of the night (in coat and tie, according to Al Kooper), Charlie McCoy demonstrated his ability to play bass and trumpet simultaneously, Henry Strzelecki worked the organ pedals with his hands, Kooper grabbed a tambourine, and it seems possible that some substance or other was passed around to lighten the mood.[14]

The track is so familiar now that it's hard to appreciate how radical and unexpected it must have sounded as a Bob Dylan single and then as the album's opening track. This isn't folk *or* folk-rock but a wacky street-corner revival. Dylan chuckles as he declaims all of the things you'll get stoned for doing, and then lands the joke with the gleeful double-entendre at the end of each verse. As Andy Gill notes, Dylan's use of "stoned" marks the mid-1960s transition from the term meaning drunk (Ray Charles's "Let's Go Get Stoned," which refers explicitly to drinking, was a hit the same year) to meaning high on weed. There was no not-getting the joke, but the "persecuted" meaning of "stoned" gave the song a kind of alibi; it was not widely banned, and it peaked at number two on the *Billboard* charts.

Starting with that out-of-left-field track, the sound of *Blonde on Blonde* is more wide-ranging than Dylan's previous albums, yet it has a definite (thin, wild, mercury) sonic consistency. Urban blues, which had inspired much of *Bringing It All Back Home* and *Highway 61 Revisited*, is the template for about a third of the album, with musical and lyrical references to Lightnin' Hopkins (whose "Automobile Blues" hovers over "Leopard-Skin Pill-Box Hat") and Robert Johnson ("Come On in My Kitchen" echoes through "Pledging My Time"), among others. On the blues rave-ups, especially "Obviously 5 Believers," Robbie Robertson is the guiding force, playing sharp, stinging leads in dialogue with Dylan's harp and vocals. On other tracks there is a stronger folk-rock vibe—the soft, straight rhythms, blended acoustic and electric guitars and catchy hooks featured on "I Want You," "Just Like a Woman," and "4th Time Around" particularly.

The production bears little resemblance to the country music that was being made in Nashville in 1966—there's little echo, no backing vocals, no pedal steel, and only an occasional hint of a two-step beat, and few country records featured organ or a blaring harmonica. And yet the modern country music influence seeps in, through delicate electric guitar fills, Pig Robbins's gospel-tinged rolling grace notes on piano (especially on "Temporary Like Achilles"), and the musicians' abiding casual precision.

But the instrument that most clearly defines *Blonde on Blonde* is Dylan's voice, which is less caustic and much breathier than on his previous albums. Wilentz describes it as "by turns sibilant, sibylline, injured, cocky, sardonic and wry," to which I would just add that he always sounds a little bit stoned.

The album's themes are a significant shift from *Highway 61*'s interrogation of the pressures of conformity and the pervasiveness of corruption. For the most part *Blonde on Blonde* is about romantic relationships, revolving around the figure of a frustrated lover in an absurd universe—playful but disconcerting love songs. The unequivocal directness and repetition of the chorus of "I Want You" follow verses packed with surreal imagery: cracked bells and washed-out horns, a dancing child with his Chinese suit, etc. "Pledging My Time" references several blues "floaters"—phrases that show up with slight variations in numerous songs—but, as with earlier Dylan blues compositions, they get twisted into new shapes. The ardent pursuer in "Temporary Like Achilles" faces a series of obstacles, including multiple doors, a scorpion, and Achilles himself, as emblems of his would-be lover's hard-heartedness.

The whole point, throughout *Blonde on Blonde*, seems to be the avoidance of songwriter clichés or predictable word choice. If there's a downside to this approach it's that Dylan makes it hard to identify with the personae of songs like "Pledging My Time" or "Absolutely Sweet Marie." He's deliberately not writing "The Tracks of My Tears" or "Funny How Time Slips Away," beautiful, poignant songs that are more conventional and more emotionally direct but not as cool or clever.

Perhaps the best example is "4th Time Around," which features a gorgeous melody and arrangement but comes across as a kind of joke, a parody or answer song to the Beatles' "Norwegian Wood." Dylan had developed a friendly rivalry with John Lennon, whose songwriting began showing a strong Dylan influence around 1965 with songs like "You've Got to Hide Your Love Away" and "I'm a Loser." Picking up on the one-night stand narrative of "Norwegian Wood," Dylan imitated its matter-of-fact stream of small, random details, while deliberately allowing rhyme to govern the action. The acoustic, waltz-time arrangement was similar to the Beatles song as well, with intertwined acoustic guitar lines played by McCoy and Moss in place of the sitar. Years later George Harrison speculated that "Bob had listened to ["Norwegian Wood"] and wrote the same song again, calling it 'Fourth Time Around.' The title suggests that the same basic tune kept bouncing around over and over again."[15]

Other songs on the album though are more intimate and emotional, inspired to various degrees by Dylan's real-life relationships. "Just Like a Woman" may refer to Edie Sedgwick, a model and actress closely associated with Andy Warhol's "Factory"—Sedgwick and Dylan had met in December 1964 and become friends when Sedgwick lived at the Chelsea Hotel in late 1965. The fact that she was a fashion icon and wealthy socialite, a "youthquaker" according to *Vogue* magazine, resonates with the song's emphasis on vanity and selfishness. The reference to her fog, amphetamine, and pearls also conjures images of Sedgwick's drug use, which would lead to her tragic death in 1971.[16]

Of course, like any great song, "Just Like a Woman" transcends its immediate frame of reference; in this case its power lies as much in its melody and arrangement as in its lyrics. Dylan was just beginning to employ bridges (or "middle eights") in his songs—other examples on *Blonde on Blonde* include "I Want You," "Absolutely Sweet Marie," and "Most Likely You Go Your Way and I'll Go Mine"—embracing a convention associated more with pop music than folk. And the intensity of "Just Like a Woman" builds on that bridge, where the singer shifts from speaking (singing) *about* "baby" to speaking *to* her. He recalls her sheltering him when he was in need, but now he needs to get away. The musical shift and the band's vamping at the end of the bridge create a tension broken by the sound of the final verse, whose lyrics reflect resignation, imagining a future meeting when they avoid talking about the singer's embarrassing past self.

Over the years "Just Like a Woman" has been a flashpoint for the sexism of its chorus. The assumption that "taking" is a definitive womanly trait, along with the dismissive phrase "just like a woman," implying that they're all alike, is hard to defend. Even so, the contrast is not between women and men but between the things she does like a woman and her breaking, emotionally, like a little girl. In fact, the song hinges on that parallel between the singer and the girl/woman. Combined with his own "breaking" (in the bridge), that final line of the chorus connects the two of them and ultimately evokes sympathy for her.[17]

If Edie Sedgwick possibly inspired "Just Like a Woman," the leading candidate for the title role in "Visions of Johanna" would be Joan Baez, as suggested by the embedding of "Joan" in "Johanna" and the depiction of Johanna as an absent, Madonna-like figure, presumably a past lover, who haunts the singer. Whether Baez still had that kind of power over Dylan's imagination when he drafted the song in late 1965 is uncertain, but "Visions" certainly transcends its real or imagined backstory as well as the common songwriting trope of being with an available lover while dreaming distractedly of someone else.

"Visions" is one of Dylan's most compelling and most admired songs because, as Andy Gill explains, "it so perfectly sustains its position on the cusp of poetic semantics, forever teetering on the brink of lucidity, yet remaining impervious to strict decipherment."[18] Even my general description of the song's subject—the singer is with someone while dreaming of someone else—isn't quite right, and it ignores about two-thirds of the lyrics. Louise, the available, present woman, is "entwined" with a lover, but the lover might be a third person rather than the singer. And the song wanders through other scenarios: the ladies playing blind man's bluff in the empty lot, the "little boy lost" who "speaks of a farewell kiss" (from Johanna? Louise?), and an imaginary tour of an art museum, where we see the *Mona Lisa* (with the highway blues), jelly-faced sneezing women, and a mule wearing jewels and binoculars.[19]

What ties all these stanzas, all these real and imaginary women, together is the return to "visions of Johanna" at the end of each verse, the poet/artist's obsession. Gill sees the song as being about "the artist's search for transcendence, the constant attempt to locate inspiration outside of the physical world, in some more spiritual aesthetic realm." The artist may not succeed—probably won't—because he is living and working in an absurd, fallen world, waiting for Johanna. But he continues, says Gill, "whatever the cost and whatever the outcome," because these visions give their life purpose and meaning.[20]

In June 1966 *Glamour* published the lyrics to "Visions of Johanna," which seems incredibly strange, but it testifies to the esteem granted Dylan as a *writer* by the summer of 1966, not just by devotees and aging Beat poets but by the editors of a glossy fashion magazine. As Greil Marcus notes, "If you happened to have read 'We sit here stranded, though we're all doing our best to deny it' in *Glamour* in 1966, without having ever heard the line in a song, you could feel stranded in the white spaces between the words."[21] That feeling remains, even in a time when lyrics are much easier to access (in 1966 they weren't printed on a sleeve or insert to *Blonde on Blonde*, which was also the case with Dylan's previous albums). And part of the confusion stems from the fact that this search for transcendence is delivered in language that alternates between elevated and silly, at times almost comically straining for rhyme.

It still works, more or less, on the page, although even reading it silently we are reminded that this is a *song*, after all, a form in which heavy rhyme for instance is far more conventional and effective than in modern poetry. Moreover Dylan reminds us in the final lines that this is a musical performance, referring to skeleton keys played on harmonicas. Then comes the concluding harmonica solo itself. Punning on musical keys, "skeleton keys" played on harmonicas open every lock. Dylan had recorded a fiery, up-tempo version of "Visions" with the Hawks in November 1965. It absolutely grooves, but compared with the slower, supple arrangement that the Nashville cats lay down in the hours just before daybreak, the faster version sounds crazy, wonderfully perverse for being, in hindsight, so inappropriate for the song, and for Johanna.

Blonde on Blonde is virtually tied with the Mothers of Invention's *Freak Out!* (produced by Tom Wilson, interestingly enough) for the honor of being the first rock double album. The expanded format allowed Dylan to devote side four to a single epic song, "Sad-Eyed Lady of the Lowlands." In this case the song's inspiration is clearly Sara Dylan, whose previous surname, Lownds, is contained in "Lowlands." Other details in the song point toward Sara as well, but the clincher came a decade later when, in the song "Sara," Dylan stated outright that he wrote the song for her in the Chelsea Hotel. Although he seems to have written most of it not at the Chelsea but in Nashville's Studio A, it's a rare case of Dylan spelling out the source for a song. "This is indeed the music of marriage," writes Paul Williams; biographer Robert Shelton refers to it as "virtually a wedding song," and indeed it is a testament of devotion.[22]

That's not to say that "Sad-Eyed Lady" is straightforward, or that the subject is narrowly limited to Sara Dylan. The sad-eyed lady has a "mercury mouth" in the first line but a "cowboy mouth" later in the song; she has "sheets like metal" as well as a "sheet-metal memory of Cannery Row." Christopher Ricks and others have traced allusions and literary models for "Sad-Eyed Lady," but many lines remain inscrutable (which is just fine).[23] For instance the reference to dead angels hidden by "farmers and businessmen" could be a deeply personal reference to something in Sara's past, or it could be a deliberately obscure line with no foothold in Dylan's or Sara's experience, simply designed to further the mystery of the sad-eyed lady and to fill out a verse.

The soul-bearing drama of "Sad-Eyed Lady" is inseparable from the musical arrangement, with Buttrey tapping out 6/8 time on the high-hat, three indistinguishable acoustic guitars, bass, and piano creating a gentle wall of sound, above which float Kooper's organ motifs. The band creates a musical peak in each chorus, and then quiets again for the final refrain, caressing the singer's humble queries.

Blonde on Blonde completed a trilogy of mind-blowingly original and influential albums, and once again the sleeve design contributed to its effect. Jerry Schatzberg had replaced Daniel Kramer as Dylan's preferred photographer; Schatzberg's cover portrait, taken on a bitterly cold day on the western edge of Greenwich Village, is slightly out of focus, which is apparently what drew Dylan to this particular shot. The cover displays no text—to find the title you would have to read the narrow spine, which bisects the full, blurry image of a blank-staring Dylan when the gatefold cover is unfolded and turned the "wrong" way. The records emerge from Dylan's head.

The inner gatefold featured several black-and-white photographs of Dylan, all but one by Schatzberg, along with a picture of Schatzberg himself and a rather large shot of Italian actress Claudia Cardinale, chosen by Dylan because he had seen the photo in Schatzberg's studio and liked it. (Cardinale objected to the unauthorized use of her likeness, so it was removed from later pressings, along with another photograph of Dylan and an unidentified woman whose face is turned from the camera.)[24] The unconventional artwork, the double-album format and even the title were new and inscrutable.

Dylan had established a habit of assigning odd working titles to songs in the studio and then coming up with "real" titles when the albums were mixed. For *Blonde on Blonde* he continued a bit of schtick (begun on *Highway 61* with "Just Like Tom Thumb's Blues"

With Robbie Robertson at a press conference in Copenhagen, April 1966. Photo by Björn Larsson Ask.

and "Queen Jane Approximately") to attach seemingly random modifiers to song titles: "Absolutely Sweet Marie," "Temporary Like Achilles," "Obviously 5 Believers," and "Most Likely You'll Go Your Way and I'll Go Mine." But the album title was still more mysterious: a visual design reference or a personal one (who is the blonde? who is the other blonde?), "on" as in "referring to" or "on top of" or "set against"? Suze Rotolo had appeared in George Tabori's off-Broadway play *Brecht on Brecht* in 1963, so that title construction might have stuck with Dylan.[25] And, as many fans have noted, the title's initials spell "BoB."

Between and after the *Blonde on Blonde* sessions, Dylan continued playing half-acoustic, half-electric shows—nineteen North American dates throughout February and March—with the Hawks minus Levon, plus Sandy Konikoff. On April 9 the band played a one-off in Honolulu, now with Mickey Jones replacing Konikoff on drums; then they set out for a six-show tour of Australia, opening in Sydney on the 13th. Then there were another seventeen shows in Europe, wrapping up at the end of May. That European tour rivals the electric set at Newport as a symbol of Dylan's rebellious art and an object of fans' obsession. (In 2016 Sony Music released a 36-disc box set of all available recordings of Dylan's shows from 1966 to preserve its copyright protection, and it was met with rave reviews from fans even though the setlists are mostly the same from show to show.) Dylan would play a seven-song acoustic set consisting of three songs from *Bringing It All Back Home*, "Desolation Row" from *Highway 61 Revisited*, and three songs from the not-yet-released *Blonde on Blonde*. In other words it was very much "New Dylan" material, but acoustic. Then, after an intermission, he would reappear with the band—Robertson on guitar, Rick Danko on bass, Richard Manuel on piano, Hudson on organ, Jones on drums—and play the loudest, most aggressive music most of the audience had ever heard.

While that second set tended to get most of the attention, and still does, the acoustic set was magical. Despite having four solo acoustic albums to draw from, Dylan adapted "She Belongs to Me" from the *electric* side of *Bringing It All Back Home* for the acoustic opener, followed by the not-yet-released "4th Time Around" and "Visions of Johanna," which had also been recorded with a band for *Blonde on Blonde*. You can almost hear the audience's reverence and concentration as they take in this new material. Dylan sounds quite stoned, but as Paul Williams observes, that works to his advantage: "this is what his drugs (at who knows what price) have temporarily bought him: an unimaginable freedom from self-consciousness, a total willingness to share in his performance everything he's feeling and everything each song means to him, to give it all away without any conditions to anyone who happens to be listening."[26]

Mickey Jones recalled the excitement Dylan brought to the band for the electric set each night: "As soon as he strapped on that black Telecaster, he was ready to rock. He would jump around in the dressing room. He could not wait to get on that stage."[27] The second set's opener throughout the European tour was "Tell Me Momma," a new song that would never appear on a Dylan studio album and that he would never play live after this tour. An up-tempo blues in the spirit of "From a Buick 6" and "Obviously 5 Believers," "Tell Me Momma" features lyrics that come close to William Burroughs's cut-up technique, defying coherence and presaging some *Basement Tapes* songs. Not that anyone in the audience could make out these words. What mattered, on top of the ferocious energy of the band, was the way Dylan wailed the chorus: "TELL me momMAAAH . . . what is it . . . what's WRONG . . . with YOU . . . this . . . TIIIIIIIIIME!"

The next two songs on the standard setlist were more familiar—sort of. "It used to be like that, and now it goes like this" was how Dylan introduced *Another Side*'s jaunty "I Don't Believe You (She Acts Like We Never Have Met)," now slowed to a hard-rock stomp driven by Jones's powerful drumming. Knowing that a portion of the audience would be hostile to his new sound, Dylan did not try to appease them with familiar electric songs from his last two albums—no "Subterranean Homesick Blues," "Maggie's Farm," or "Tombstone Blues"; "Positively 4th Street" had been dropped before leaving the States. *Now* he was digging into his back catalog, reworking "Baby, Let Me Follow You Down" from his debut album and, later in the set, "One Too Many Mornings" from *The Times They Are A-Changin'*. Only three of the eight songs in the electric half had appeared on a record as full-band recordings: "Just Like Tom Thumb's Blues" and the set closers, the defiant "Ballad of a Thin Man" (with a more menacing sound than the studio version) and "Like a Rolling Stone."

While most European fans were excited by Dylan's embrace of rock music, the opposition was determined to be heard. Between songs audience members would slow-clap in unison, an established gesture of disapproval. Dylan deliberately took his time finding the right harmonica or tuning between songs, seeming to egg on the crowd. Although I would give anything to have been at one of these shows, I have to admit that it's easier to appreciate their gloriously raucous sound today, listening to professional recordings that allow us to hear every instrument and to make out Dylan's lyrics, which we already know anyway. In 1966 fans were listening to mostly unfamiliar songs or arrangements on overdriven speaker systems in halls that had never hosted rock music before. Again, many loved it, but a common theme emerges in the interviews C. P. Lee, who was there himself, conducted for his book *Like the Night*:

> "I couldn't believe it. It was so loud it physically hurt me."
>
> "It was loud."
>
> ". . . I felt like I was being forced back into my seat, you know? Like being in a jet when it takes off."
>
> "The level of sound was something that I'd never heard before, especially being so close up to it. I was just blasted out of my skin. It was physical rather than just listening to music. It took a long time before I could recognize what the tunes were."[28]

We should also remember that "hard rock," that thick, heavy, distorted, non-swinging sound that was redefining popular music, was in its infancy. The Kinks, the Who, and the Yardbirds were experimenting with guitar distortion in 1966, but Jimi Hendrix had not recorded an album yet, nor had the Doors or Cream. American garage bands like the 13th Floor Elevators and the Seeds were just getting started. The Stones had just released *Aftermath* and the Beatles were recording *Revolver*—breakthrough albums, to be sure, but more psychedelic

Mugging for the camera in Stockholm, April 1966. Photo by Björn Larsson Ask.

than hard rock. While fans, especially in England, accused Dylan of selling out or "going pop" by adding a band, that band was playing music that was heavy and abrasive, absolutely at the cutting edge. For that reason too—knowing in hindsight where the music went in the late 1960s—it's easier to appreciate what Dylan and crew were producing onstage in the spring of 1966.

One show where the tensions came to a head has, like Newport, become an infamous/celebrated moment in Dylan lore. The Manchester Free Trade Hall was especially unprepared for Dylan's show, surprised that afternoon (because no one had warned them) by the arrival of not only sound equipment but a film crew.[29] As usual, the acoustic set was well-received, but after the intermission there was much booing, slow-clapping, and anti-slow-clap shouting. At one point between songs Dylan, as he had done on previous nights, began mumbling nonsense into the microphone to get the audience to listen, and, when they became quiet enough, he concluded his gibberish by slurring the phrase "if only you wouldn't *clap* so hard." After a modest ripple of laughter from the audience he and the band lurched into "One Too Many Mornings." After that song and "Ballad of a Thin Man," in the relative quiet before the final number, an angry audience member by the name of Keith Butler shouted "Judas!"—a pointed accusation of selling out and, directed at a man who by then was known to be Jewish, a particularly insensitive one.[30]

As the band revved up "Like a Rolling Stone" Dylan snarled back with the title of an earlier song from the setlist—"I don't believe you"—and then punctuated it—"You're a liar!" Turning to the band, he instructed, "Play fucking loud!" Which they did, with Dylan practically screaming out the lines of his electric anthem. (For decades bootleg recordings of the Manchester show were mislabeled as the Royal Albert Hall concert; both recordings, along with all known recordings of the tour, have since been officially released.)[31]

The tour wrapped up with six more shows, shuttling between England, Scotland, and Paris before concluding in London. Although American audiences had famously booed the electric set as well, Dylan began to make his own kind of patriotic point regarding the European hostility toward his new sound. In Paris he used a giant American flag as a stage backdrop. At a press conference at Paris's George V hotel an interviewer suggested that his early albums were better than his current albums; Dylan asked if he was American, and when the interviewer replied that he was French Dylan responded, "That's probably why you think that."[32] At the tour's final show at the Royal Albert Hall he told the audience, "This is not English music you're listening to. You haven't really heard American music before."[33] While at that point Dylan might have been looking for any way to provoke his audiences, who certainly had heard American music before, he was also indirectly alluding to the British Invasion bands' mining American blues and R&B for a sound that was, at that moment, selling extremely well. It was also a kind of foreshadowing of Dylan's next chapter, in which his music would become even more deeply "American."

As on the 1965 English tour, D. A. Pennebaker followed Dylan around with a camera, this time not for his own film but for one that Dylan had agreed to edit and deliver to the ABC network for broadcast. Anyone who watches that film, titled *Eat the Document*, will understand why ABC rejected it: there was no way a mainstream American TV audience would accept a video collage with little discernible structure, even from someone as popular as Dylan. *Eat the Document* might be described as a shorter, less coherent *Dont Look Back*, shot in color. Footage of Dylan and the band onstage is interspersed with press conferences, street scenes (with and without Dylan), footage on trains and buses, footage *of* trains and buses, interviews with mostly disgruntled British concertgoers (including Keith Butler of "Judas" fame, who declares "He wants shooting—he's a traitor"), random close-ups of people on London streets, and many brief shots of the exterior of the Royal Albert Hall.[34]

The concert footage is riveting though, completely redeeming the otherwise directionless film. Among the notable offstage scenes are a slurry duet with Johnny Cash on "I Still Miss Someone" and a snippet of a long limo ride with Dylan and Lennon, both of them clearly under the influence of some combination of substances (in a much

On stage in Paris, May 1966.

later interview Lennon claimed that they were using heroin).[35] Sadly the two geniuses were too wasted to muster any witty banter. In the outtakes of the limo sequence Dylan spends much of the ride with his head in his hands and openly contemplates vomiting into the camera.

The footage from *Eat the Document* provides strong evidence, if any were needed, that Dylan was exhausted but propped up with a steady diet of drugs, especially amphetamines, which no doubt helped him bring almost unhinged energy to the stage each night. In his description of the extensive outtakes from the film Clinton Heylin notes how frequently Dylan says that he wants to go home, a refrain that adds poignancy to the pro-American provocations toward the tour's end. (Heylin also mentions Dylan, on camera, slagging T. S. Eliot, who renounced his American citizenship in the 1920s, as well as the celebrated British writer Robert Graves.)[36] He looks completely drained and strung out.

Despite his apparent homesickness and recent animosity toward the Old World, Dylan spent a couple more days in England, hanging out mainly with the Beatles, before returning to New York. Once back home he kept a low profile throughout June and July, staying mostly at his new house in Woodstock, dubbed Hi Lo Ha, with Sara and Jesse, now six months old. He was supposed to be editing his tour film for ABC—predictably it never saw commercial release. His other project was to review the galleys of a book he had written and which the publisher Macmillan was ready to release.

The book, *Tarantula*, was every bit as nonlinear as *Eat the Document*; biographer Howard Sounes rightly describes it as "a hundred and thirty-seven pages of liner notes for a Dylan album that did not exist," referring to the experimental poetry and prose Dylan had included on the back covers of four of his previous albums. The chapters combine prose and verse, but it's all stream-of-consciousness, fractured narratives and Dadaist wordplay. Dylan ends each piece with a verse letter signed by someone who seems to have stepped out of "Highway 61 Revisited": Homer the Slut, Popeye Squirm, Hector Schmector, Zeke the Cork. Occasionally he echoes his own songs, as in the titles "Ballad in Plain Be Flat," "Sacred Cracked Voice & the Jingle Jangle Morning," and "Subterranean Homesick Blues &

the Blond Waltz"—and in one particularly intriguing selection called "The Vandals Took the Handles (An Opera)" he inserts his own epitaph:

here lies bob dylan
murdered
from behind
by trembling flesh
who after being refused by Lazarus,
jumped on him
for solitude
. . .
God rest his soul
& his rudeness

Tarantula was, in part, another instance of Dylan's ongoing dialogue with John Lennon, who by this point had published two well-received books of literary nonsense, *In His Own Write* and *A Spaniard in the Works*. It was also an attempt to cash in on Dylan's sudden fame and widespread acclaim as a "poet." Although he would later suggest that Grossman arranged the book contract without his consent, for Dylan *Tarantula* was a means of capturing the overflow of his torrential creativity. He was writing constantly in the mid-1960s, as many friends and associates attest, and not all of that writing was channeled into his songs, or could be.

Paul Williams, one of the most perceptive commentators on Dylan's work, contrasts the success of Dylan's songwriting, and even his liner notes, with the "failure" of *Tarantula*, while recognizing that "in this same period Dylan was using not-unrelated techniques to produce masterpieces like 'Desolation Row' and 'Gates of Eden.'" For Williams it's a lack of sincerity that dooms *Tarantula*, despite its relentless cleverness: "*Tarantula* is show-off stuff, and it is very interesting to discover that Dylan, for all his genius with language, is not impressive when he's just showing off."[37]

Dylan asked for a couple of weeks to make last-minute changes to the galley proofs, but he seems to have had second thoughts about

At Kronborg Castle, Denmark, the setting of *Hamlet*, May 1966.
Photo by Björn Larsson Ask.

allowing the book to be published at all. Perhaps it already didn't seem like *him* anymore. He was similarly frustrated with the editing of *Eat the Document*. Meanwhile he had only a few weeks before going back on the road; Grossman had booked more than sixty concerts for late summer and fall, including a mid-August performance at Shea Stadium in New York.[38]

But the tour would be cancelled, and the publication of *Tarantula* would be postponed indefinitely. On July 29 Dylan crashed his Triumph motorcycle on the way from Grossman's house to his own home in Woodstock. Accounts vary as to what happened and how serious Dylan's injuries were, and he and Grossman revealed almost nothing at the time.

Dylan told Robert Shelton, long after the fact, "It happened one morning after I'd been up for three days. I hit an oil slick."[39] He told the playwright Sam Shepard, about twenty years after the accident, "I can't even remember how it happened. I was blinded by the sun for a second . . . and I kind of panicked or something, I stomped down on the brake and the rear wheel locked up on me and I went flyin'."

Sara Dylan was following Bob in a car, presumably because they were originally taking the bike to a mechanic for repairs. She (or someone else) either took him to a hospital, as Dylan told Shepard, or directly to his doctor Ed Thaler's house in Middletown, New York, over an hour away. Howard Sounes, who interviewed Sally Grossman and Ed Thaler, concludes that Dylan was not seriously hurt and was not hospitalized. But he did spend several weeks at the Thalers' house before returning to Woodstock, and he was seen wearing a neck brace when he re-emerged.[40]

At the time of the accident, with little real information in the press, fans feared Dylan's life was in danger. In hindsight some have speculated that the accident was nothing more than an excuse for Dylan to escape and perhaps to detox. It seems most likely that while his injuries were not life-threatening, they were serious enough to justify a long recovery and the cancellation of tour dates. (Reportedly Grossman's response to the news was, "How could he do this to me?"[41]) During his recovery at Dr Thaler's and back home in Woodstock Dylan also realized he now had an opportunity to rethink his priorities and the direction of his career. In *Chronicles* he acknowledged as much: "I had been in a motorcycle accident and I'd been hurt, but I recovered. Truth was that I wanted to get out of the rat race."[42]

7
1967–68: Withdrawal

Dylan's disappearance coincided with the advent of a true rock music culture, chronicled and to some extent created by a wave of serious writing about the music. In early 1966 Paul Williams started the mimeographed magazine *Crawdaddy!*—named for the London club that launched the Rolling Stones' career—boasting a circulation of 20,000 by the end of 1967.[1] Jann Wenner established *Rolling Stone* in the fall of that year, the magazine's name simultaneously invoking the band, the Muddy Waters song that inspired them, and of course Dylan's breakthrough hit. *Rolling Stone*, which exhibited a near-obsession with Dylan, would see six-figure circulation by the end of the decade. Barry Kramer's *Creem*, which provided an early platform for Lester Bangs, Dave Marsh and other passionate, new-journalism-inspired music writers, would follow in 1969. Meanwhile established publications like the *Village Voice* and *Melody Maker* were devoting regular space to thoughtful rock criticism, and even major daily newspapers were no longer treating the music as a lightweight teenage fad.[2]

Although hard rock and psychedelia are often referred to as the "soundtrack" of the 1960s, they were much more than background music. Power chords from solid-body electric guitars, blaring through six-foot-tall Marshall stacks; sharp, hypnotic riffs on electric pianos or Hammond organs; thunderous drums borrowing licks from the most aggressive post-bop jazz—the new sounds symbolized countercultural identity as immediately as tie-dyed tunics or men's shoulder-length hair, but they cut deeper into the baby-boomer consciousness.

Musicians, particularly songwriters, were thought-leaders: not only Dylan and the Beatles but Paul Simon, the Byrds, Buffalo Springfield, Donovan, and others could be quoted reverently and discussed at length in college dorms across America. A few years earlier Dylan had proclaimed to the older generation that their sons and daughters were beyond their command. If that hadn't quite been true in 1964 it certainly was in 1967, the year of Human Be-ins and the "Summer of Love"; race riots and anti-war protests; the Monterey Pop Festival; *Hair*; *The Graduate*; *Bonnie and Clyde*; debut albums by the Doors, the Grateful Dead, and the Jimi Hendrix Experience. And of course *Sgt. Pepper*.

But Dylan, who was widely seen as the oracle of the counterculture, was nowhere to be found, at least not in the flesh. He did not perform live or release any new music from mid-1966 to the very last week of 1967. He spent most of his time with his family at Hi Lo Ha, his house on the outskirts of Woodstock. The singer Maria Muldaur, a Woodstock neighbor, recalled the relaxed atmosphere: "They had a nanny, like a domestic helper, but everything was very casual. When we had dinner I noticed that the plates didn't match. Everything was not real hippyish, but it was casual and not all put-together."[3] At some point Allen Ginsberg delivered a supply of books, and Dylan got a visit from his parents, who noticed a large Bible prominently placed in his study.[4] According to Happy Traum, a musician who knew Dylan from his Greenwich Village days and was now a Woodstock neighbor, "I never met such a dedicated family man . . . Dylan shut out the world of show business and all the Manhattan craziness and turned into such an ordinary guy that he was actually a little boring to be around."[5]

Dylan would have agreed. In *Chronicles* he explains, "Outside of my family, nothing held any real interest for me and I was seeing everything through different glasses. Even the horrifying news items of the day, the gunning down of the Kennedys, King, Malcolm X . . . I didn't see them as leaders being shot down, but rather as fathers whose families had been left wounded." As for the counterculture, "I had very little in common with and knew even less about a generation that I was supposed to be the voice of."[6]

While Albert Grossman no doubt mourned the lost revenue from Dylan's cancelled tour dates and other projects, he must have also seen the silver lining of his client's new reclusiveness: his absence and the mystery surrounding it only added to the mystique. When Dylan granted Michael Iachetta an interview for the *Daily News* in May (nine months after the accident) the resulting article was focused more on the difficulty of getting to Dylan than on any revelations *from* Dylan, who did at least offer this account of his activities:

> What I've been doin' mostly is seein' only a few close friends, readin' little 'bout the outside world, porin' over books by people you never heard of, thinkin' about where I'm goin', and why am I runnin', and am I mixed up too much, and what am I knowin', and what am I givin', and what am I takin'. And mainly what I've been doin' is workin' on gettin' better and makin' better music, which is what my life is all about.

In Iachetta's rendering 1967 Dylan sounds a lot like 1963 Dylan, down to the stream of gerunds with dropped Gs. Dylan promised that he was focused on his music but insisted that his songs were "not goin' to get written down until some things are evened up," probably a reference to his record company, which was trying to re-sign him, and his manager, with whom he was becoming disenchanted.[7]

Meanwhile that record company and manager made sure to keep Dylan in the public consciousness throughout 1967. Columbia not only reissued all of Dylan's previous albums but released a new compilation, *Bob Dylan's Greatest Hits*, in March. The ten tracks were logical choices, singles that charted for Dylan or for other artists, and yet the haphazard sequencing and "greatest hits" approach didn't serve the prototypical "album artist" very well. There was clearly a strong market for the album, though: it peaked at number ten on the *Billboard* charts (number six in the UK) and eventually sold over 5 million copies in the USA alone.

The artwork aided the collection's popularity: the front cover photograph by Rowland Scherman caught Dylan in profile, playing

Poster for *Dont Look Back*, 1967.

harmonica, a dark silhouette defined by stage lighting that creates an aureole around the head of famously bushy hair. Dylan's untamed hair was also the focal point of a large poster inserted in the record sleeve. Now a pop art classic, Milton Glaser's design presents Dylan's profile in solid black with a stylized, multicoloured swirl of hair clearly symbolizing the songwriter's wild creativity, the psychedelic freedom of hair and mind. But that was Dylan as the 1967 counterculture wanted to see him—by the time of *Greatest Hits*' release in March, he looked more like a small-town preacher or gentleman farmer, with close-cropped hair and a thin beard.

In May *Dont Look Back*, D. A. Pennebaker's *cinema verité* treatment of the 1965 tour of England, was released in theaters, giving fans another fascinating encounter with a Dylan who no longer existed. The same might be said of Daniel Kramer's wonderful book of black-and-white photographs, first published in April 1967. Already these images of Dylan from 1964 to 1965—onstage, backstage, in the studio, on the street, in his apartment—were like the contents of a time capsule. Dylan's image and influence were everywhere in the spring of 1967, but Dylan himself was out of the public eye.

Meanwhile Dylan's contract with Columbia was about to expire, and Grossman was negotiating with MGM records. But Columbia's new president, Clive Davis, recognized the importance of holding on to Dylan and ultimately re-signed him for another five years, increasing his royalty rate from 4 to 10 percent.[8]

Dylan might have seemed like a risky investment, given the accident and his retreat from the spotlight. But in relative seclusion Dylan had the most productive year of his career, composing around 75 new songs and recording over a hundred tracks that would seemingly have their influence multiplied by remaining officially unreleased. And he would conclude the year by quickly writing and recording another (officially released) masterpiece.

In February Rick Danko and Richard Manuel, veterans of Dylan's tumultuous 1965–6 tours, came to Woodstock, ostensibly to perform with Tiny Tim in an experimental film called *You Are What You Eat*. Grossman and Dylan still had Danko, Manuel, Garth Hudson, and Robbie Robertson on retainer, so they suggested that the band (not yet the Band) move to the Catskills so they could work with Dylan on whatever new material he came up with; they would also participate in filming additional scenes for Dylan's own ill-fated experimental film, the coincidentally titled *Eat the Document*.

That spring Danko, Manuel, and Hudson rented a pink split-level house on a large tract of land near Woodstock, in West Saugerties, while Robertson and his girlfriend rented their own place nearby. They began getting together with Dylan every afternoon, running through an unpredictable array of old folk and pop tunes, spontaneously generated nonsense songs, and, eventually, new, completed Dylan songs. Their assignment was to record demos of those new songs so that Grossman could offer them to other performers. But their process took on a life of its own, as over the next eight months the five musicians, joined toward the end by drummer Levon Helm, created a new sound and a collection of recordings that came to be known as the Basement Tapes.

The early sessions took place at Dylan's house, in a den called the Red Room (even though the previously red walls had been painted over). Most of the songs they recorded there were oldies, gospel, and blues; others consisted of improvised lyrics over standard chord progressions. After a month or two, they moved the operation to the Danko-Manuel-Hudson house, nicknamed Big Pink. Most days Dylan would show up around noon, make a pot of strong coffee, and lead the sessions in the basement-level garage. According to Hudson, they would run through "seven, eight, ten, sometimes fifteen songs a day," recording somewhat sporadically but mainly trying to preserve the better stuff, typically at the session's end.[9]

Dylan would reflect on the Big Pink sessions in a later interview: "You know . . . that's really the way to do a recording—in a peaceful, relaxed setting—in somebody's basement. With the windows open . . . and a dog lying on the floor."[10] According to Robertson, an area rug was the only effort they made to dampen the acoustics. The group would sit in a circle to record: "No monitors, no nothing, except if you played too loud you couldn't hear the vocal and that meant you were playing too loud."[11]

Posterity owes a special debt to Garth Hudson for serving as the recording engineer as well as the organist for these summer-long sessions. He had good equipment but nothing like a modern recording studio to work with, and he seems to have done all the work himself. According to Danko, "Garth ran the tape recorder and we had a little mixing board with four or five inputs going into the 2-track machine."[12] With musicians and mics close together and no partitions, sounds bled together—or perhaps "blended" is a better word, because no one ever hears these recordings and wishes they were cleaner. The sound is warm and direct; as music journalist and critic Greil Marcus describes it, "a sound that makes you feel you're in the room, that places the room around you as you listen."[13]

Marcus doesn't stay in the room though: in his 1997 book *Invisible Republic*, republished years later as *The Old, Weird America*, he describes—or, you might say, creates—"the World of Bob Dylan's Basement Tapes" (the book's subtitle). For Marcus the Basement Tapes conjure a mythical lost landscape of Harry Smith's *Anthology of American Folk Music* (described in Chapter Two), an "old, weird America" that is decidedly anti-modern, with a penchant for murder-ballad violence, illusion, and shaggy dog stories. Departing from conventional music criticism, he extrapolates from Smith's *Anthology* and the Big Pink basement a pair of similar (but not identical) neighboring towns, Smithville and Kill Devil Hills. This out-of-time, carnivalesque small-town America is evoked as much by the recordings' sound and attitude as by their often-bizarre lyrics. Since his book's publication, Marcus's mythology has influenced how reader-listeners respond to the Basement Tapes. Dylan himself acknowledges the book in *Chronicles*, and Todd Haynes's film *I'm Not There* places one of its six Dylan avatars in a setting clearly borrowed from *The Old, Weird America*.

Although the musicians switch up instruments, it's usually Dylan on lead vocals and acoustic guitar backed by Robertson on electric, Danko on bass, Manuel on piano, and Hudson on organ. "We didn't try to overplay anything," said Richard Manuel. As part of that ethos, there are few instrumental solos. Most of the 138 tracks made commercially available in 2014 as volume XI of the Bootleg Series are drummerless, but Manuel played drums as needed until Levon Helm rejoined the band toward the end of the sessions in early fall. The sonic glue that holds the sound together—and to a great extent provides its mysterious, timeless feel—is Hudson's Lowrey organ, which swirls around the other instruments while thickening the soup. His style suggests church music—classical and gospel—more than 1960s soul or rock, furthering the sense that this isn't like any other music anyone was making at the time.

"Dylan was rediscovering the joys of music—old songs, improvised songs, crafted songs: they all provided him with evident satisfaction and pleasure as he performed them," writes Paul Williams. "Dylan and the Band could move from a boisterous sea chantey to an Elvis Presley pop ballad without missing a beat or shifting realities. You are what you feel like singing and playing, and you can sing and play anything you like."[14]

Especially in the early weeks of recording, Dylan and company goofed around a lot—a doo-wop parody called "I'm Your Teenage Prayer," the wonderfully conceived but undeveloped "See You Later Allen Ginsberg," a couple of John Lee Hooker covers in which Dylan imitates Hooker, a wacky arrangement of that nineteenth-century classic "They Gotta Quit Kickin' My Dog Around." The humor is thoroughly good-natured, in contrast to the edgier satire of "Highway 61 Revisited" or "Leopard-Skin Pill-Box Hat," and the silliness spills into several of the songs that would be offered up as demos. For instance the rollicking "Odds and Ends" sounds like the result of someone challenging Dylan on the spot to write a song about spilled orange juice. "Open the Door, Homer" borrows its chorus from a comic vaudeville tune called "Open the Door, Richard" (recorded by several Black artists, notably Count Basie and Louis Jordan in the late 1940s), while the verses offer unrelated bits of nonsensical pseudo-wisdom. Absurd non-sequiturs are the building blocks of many Basement Tape songs, such as "Yea! Heavy and a Bottle of Bread" and "Lo and Behold!"

"Clothes Line Saga" parodies Bobbie Gentry's "Ode to Billie Joe," which saturated the airwaves that summer. The family members in Gentry's "Ode" reveal their lack of compassion for the suicidal Billie Joe through mundane remarks at the dinner table; Dylan pushes that device to absurd lengths, with an insipid conversation about the vice president going mad and the wet clothes drying on the line.

While "Clothes Line Saga" is clearly a spoof, it's often not easy to sort the basement songs into comic and serious stacks. And especially when it comes to Dylan, one listener's charming nonsense song is another's key to enlightenment. Indeed Dylan's songs were still open to a range of interpretations, but they were truly *open* in a way they hadn't been before—they were spacious and abstract; the lyrical voice was calmer and, goofy songs notwithstanding, more mature. The structure and arrangement of "Nothing Was Delivered" comes out of the 1950s doo-wop and R&B that the band had been fooling around with, but the lyrics are a confrontation that seems beyond the realm of teenage romance. Instead it sounds as if the listener is a small-time crook on the wrong end of a mob interrogation, or an Old Testament prophet getting cursed by a king—or perhaps it's an argument between old and young generations about false promises.

"Tears of Rage," which, when re-recorded with Manuel on lead vocals, would be the opening track on the Band's first album, is clearly a generational confrontation—or, more specifically, a lament voiced by the parents of a daughter who has taken on the life of Miss Lonely in "Like a Rolling Stone," or the young woman in the Beatles' "She's Leaving Home" (released early that summer). At the same time, with the opening reference to carrying "you" on Independence Day, the song has often been heard as a parable of despair over a nation that has lost its way. Prophecies and confrontations turn apocalyptic in "This Wheel's on Fire," with its recurring image borrowed from a vision of God's judgment in the book of Daniel, and "Crash on the Levee," warning of a devastating flood.

If Dylan was thinking in terms of biblical punishment, he was also thinking about redemption, although (again) it's sometimes hard to tell how seriously to take him. The lyrics of "Sign on the Cross" read like the kind of song he would write a little over a decade later, during his gospel phase, but he delivers it almost like another parody. The performance walks a thin line between genuine religious searching and a lampoon of popular religion, but a spoken-word passage in which Dylan imitates a TV preacher tips the scale toward the ironic.[15]

"Quinn the Eskimo (The Mighty Quinn)" offers another kind of salvation, something like the promises of a carnival barker, but the parallel with evangelical pitchmen is clear enough. The prevailing theory that the chorus and title refer to actor Anthony Quinn as Inuk the Eskimo in the 1960 film *The Savage Innocents* only reinforces the parodic effect: people need something to believe in, like a Mexican-American movie actor playing an Eskimo.[16] Dylan would later say of the song, "I don't know what it was all about. I guess it was some kind of nursery rhyme."[17]

Faith in personal redemption is not ironized, although it is also not explicitly religious, in "I Shall Be Released," perhaps the most enduring of the Basement Tapes songs. The title echoes Dylan's earlier comic talking blues "I Shall Be Free" and "I Shall Be Free No. 10," but this time he's serious. The scenario—a prisoner confidently anticipating release—might sound like an outtake from *The Times They Are A-Changin'*, evoking the literal and metaphorical concerns of the Civil Rights Movement. But that's not exactly what this is. "I Shall Be Released" isn't about freedom-as-justice; it's about the condition of imprisonment and the longing for redemption. As with his early anthems, the images are concrete but highly evocative and open to interpretation.

Significantly there's no reference to a crime or to the speaker's guilt or innocence. He remembers the face of "every man who put me here," which could be judge and jury, or it could be every man he's ever met, all of them contributing in some small way to putting him where he is now. But he doesn't say that they've wronged him or that he's going to get even, only that he remembers them. In the third and final verse a man next to him cries out that he was framed, but the singer offers no comment on the matter. Everybody's been framed, but that's not the point; imprisonment is an existential condition.

His light shines from west to east rather than east to west. Why? Andrew McCarron emphasizes the religious associations of the "light," titling his study of Dylan's transformations *Light Come Shining*. For McCarron the light "moves in reverse" because it represents a spiritual upheaval, a total change in perspective: "When the release comes, it will be like nothing the poet/singer has experienced up to that point."[18] For Mike Marqusee, finding his "light" in the west "reinforces the sense that here, as elsewhere in the Basement Tapes, the yearning for freedom is also a yearning for oblivion, for death, for immersion in the setting sun."[19] Rebirth or death—the release may be either or both.

Possibly the most mysterious song in this mysterious trove is "I'm Not There," which was largely unknown until Todd Haynes used it for the title of his 2007 Dylan-inspired film. At a little over five minutes, it's one of the longest of the Basement Tapes tracks, and yet it might have been even longer than what we have, as the recording starts in progress. Dylan's already in the middle of a word, it's not even clear that this is the first verse, and the lyrics seem far from finished. He fills out lines with filler words or just syllables, slurring his way through what he hasn't worked out. But the performance is devastating, Dylan's delivery understated yet weighted with pain and resignation, while Danko, Manuel, and Hudson slowly build the musical intensity around him. As Greil Marcus observes, "Words are floated together in a dyslexia that is music itself—a dyslexia that seems meant to prove the claims of music over words, to see just how little words can do." The power of the refrain, "I'm not there, I'm gone," is enhanced by the fact that we can't quite make sense of the words that lead up to it. About all we know is that he has abandoned a woman he adores and he's not going back—and that's all we need to know. Meanwhile Dylan's simple device of singing alternate verses an octave apart creates uncanny emotional force.

The sessions at the Red Room, the Big Pink basement, and, for a brief period in early fall, a different house Danko and Helm rented allowed Dylan to reset his musical gears, relax, and get back to doing what he loved. In August Hudson compiled ten of the best new songs onto a single tape and sent it to Albert Grossman's office so that it could be distributed to selected musicians and managers; sometime before October he had supplemented that batch with another five tracks, one of which ("Get Your Rocks Off") was lost in transmission. That widely circulated tape (or, in some cases, acetate record) consisted of fourteen songs: "Million Dollar Bash," "Yea! Heavy and a Bottle of Bread," "Please, Mrs. Henry," "Crash on the Levee," "Lo and Behold!," "Tiny Montgomery," "This Wheel's on Fire," "You Ain't Goin' Nowhere," "I Shall Be Released," "Too Much of Nothing," "Tears of Rage," "Quinn the Eskimo," "Open the Door, Homer," and "Nothing Was Delivered."

The first result was a flurry of new Dylan songs performed by other artists. Peter, Paul and Mary released "Too Much of Nothing" as a single in November; Manfred Mann's ebullient version of "The Mighty Quinn" was a big hit in early 1968, followed by Julie Driscoll with Brian Auger and the Trinity's cover of "This Wheel's on Fire." The Byrds, revamped under the influence of Gram Parsons, would release a countrified "You Ain't Goin' Nowhere" as a single in April and include that song and "Nothing Was Delivered" on their landmark *Sweetheart of the Rodeo* album in the summer of 1968. Joan Baez would include three basement songs on her 1968 all-Dylan album whose title, *Any Day Now*, nodded to "I Shall Be Released." Dozens more interpretations of Basement Tapes songs followed, including within just a few years Flatt and Scruggs, Lulu, the Four Tops, Fairport Convention, Julie London, and the Hollies.[20]

A delayed but more significant result was the birth of the rock bootleg album. In mid-1969 two guys who worked for a Los Angeles record distributor pressed a couple thousand double albums of Dylan material that they called *Great White Wonder*. They included ten songs from the "Minnesota Hotel Tape" recorded at Bonnie Beecher's apartment in 1961, a smattering of early studio outtakes, and seven Basement Tapes tracks. *Great White Wonder* did great business, almost entirely because of the Basement Tapes material, and other bootleggers soon got in on the act, making the rest of the fourteen tracks from Hudson's compilation available to fans who knew where to look. As Clinton Heylin explains in his history of the bootleg industry, the practice of trading and selling tapes of live performances had existed in classical and jazz circles prior to 1969, but it was the Basement Tapes that provided the impetus for the rock bootleg, which would become a significant underground economy and a source of fascination, sometimes obsession, for fans.[21]

Even before the tapes began circulating through independent record stores they had attained legendary status, with *Rolling*

Stone reporting on "The Missing Bob Dylan Album" in June 1968 and calling for an official release. Jann Wenner, who wrote the article, dubbed the recordings "Dylan's Basement Tape." Paul Williams recalled that "In 1967–68, simply having heard this tape conferred status on a person."[22] After the release of *Great White Wonder* that status required ownership of the LP version.

The West Saugerties sessions also had the lasting effect of transforming the Hawks into the Band. Helm returned when Grossman landed them a recording contract with Capitol; he played on only a handful of songs with Dylan, but he loved Woodstock and fell right into the groove the rest of the band had established over the summer. While the former Hawks had deepened Dylan's (already considerable) appreciation for rhythm and blues, Dylan had exposed them to a lot of country music, which would become an important ingredient in the Band's sound. Robertson recalled, "Up to that point The Hawks were so anti-country music. All of a sudden I looked at old-timey music like the Carter Family differently. Before that we would have been, 'That's like hillbilly shit.' Now we weren't looking at it like that anymore . . . I think Bob had a terrific influence on us having the ability to combine The Impressions and the Stanley Brothers into the same flavor."[23]

"The boys had also discovered how to write songs," recalled Helm, crediting Dylan's influence. Robertson concurs: "I remember the barriers coming down . . . It was no longer two verses, bridge, verse and out. All of a sudden it was like, 'Hey, if you want you can write eight verses.'"[24] The Band continued to rehearse and record at the Danko–Helm house in the fall of 1967 and then took their new songs and basement sound to a professional recording studio in New York in early 1968 to record the classic *Music from Big Pink*. Although not recorded in the basement, the album is a natural extension of the sound "the boys" had developed over the summer. It opens with "Tears of Rage" and ends with "This Wheel's on Fire" and "I Shall Be Released."

In *Chronicles* Dylan recalls being appalled when Robertson, riding with him in a car in Woodstock, had asked,

"Where do you think you're gonna take it?"
I said, "Take what?"
"You know, the whole music scene." The whole music scene![25]

Without intending or even wanting to, Dylan—along with Robertson, Hudson, Danko, and Manuel—was in fact taking the scene in a new direction: roots-oriented music that was distinctly *not* "folk rock." The casual, lo-fi aesthetic, the blending of folk and popular styles, including some that predate rock and roll, would be absorbed by the Flying Burrito Brothers, the Grateful Dead, Little Feat, and others; it would run through much of what was called country-rock in the seventies and later alt-country and Americana. Meanwhile the stripped-down approach to recording—everyone in a circle, no overdubs—was famously picked up by the Beatles for the *Get Back/Let It Be* sessions.[26] It might be giving Dylan and the Band too much credit to trace every "live in the studio" recording back to Big Pink, but they did popularize the concept of trading studio craft for intimacy and spontaneity in recording.

Incredibly Columbia Records left on the table (or in the pockets of bootleggers) money that could have been made from an official release—until 1975 when the *Basement Tapes* double album was planned following Dylan and the Band's reunion and tour. Dylan had little involvement in that project, leaving it mostly to Robertson, who, with the help of sound engineers, remastered the tapes, greatly reducing the separation in Hudson's two-track recordings to produce a compressed, nearly mono sound; the Band added a few overdubs to "fix" some rough spots as well. Eight of the 24 tracks on the double album were by the Band without Dylan—some songs recorded during the *Music from Big Pink* sessions, others made from scratch in 1975. The resulting album sold well and earned rave reviews, although, as Sid Griffin notes, critics at the time did not mention (or didn't notice) the extent to which the tapes had been "cleaned up" and re-recorded.[27] While it might not be the "raw" artifact that record-buyers thought they were getting, the 1975 *Basement Tapes* still ranks with Dylan's and the Band's best work. Fortunately, with the 2014 release of the six-CD *Basement Tapes Complete*, fans have access not only to the untampered-with recordings but to dozens of great and/or interesting covers and Dylan originals.

On October 3, 1967, Woody Guthrie died in a psychiatric hospital in Queens. He had been Dylan's greatest musical influence, providing a model for songwriting that was simultaneously personal and political, as well as a singing style that defied popular standards with a stunning, plain-spoken directness. In his own songs Dylan had moved away from Guthrie's vision of collective action for social justice, and he had discontinued his visits to Guthrie once he became famous. Yet Guthrie's death undoubtedly moved him, coming at a time when Dylan was living in relative sobriety and quiet reflection. He called Harold Leventhal, Guthrie's manager (and an old friend of Dylan's who had produced the 1963 Town Hall concert), encouraging him to organize a benefit concert and volunteering to participate.

Two weeks later Dylan was back in the studio, returning to Nashville with producer Bob Johnston. While still on good terms with the Band, he had decided to record an album of all new songs and to lay down the basic tracks with two of the studio pros who had generated the "thin, wild mercury sound" of *Blonde on Blonde*: drummer Kenny Buttrey and bassist Charlie McCoy. But this album would sound nothing like its predecessor, nor would it sound like the Basement Tapes. *John Wesley Harding* is spare and stark, just bass, drums, and Dylan on acoustic guitar or piano, his harmonica piercing the gentle soundscape as the only solo instrument.

A few years later Dylan told biographer Anthony Scaduto, "I would have liked a good sound, more musical, more steel guitar, more piano, more music . . . I didn't sit down and plan that sound."[28] In fact he brought the Nashville tracks back to Woodstock expecting Robertson and Hudson to add some overdubs and flesh things out. Robertson recalled telling Dylan, "I wouldn't know what to add to these songs." He went on: "They sounded complete to me in their bold, minimalist way. Bob shrugged, as if to say, '*Maybe you're right*.'"[29]

Uncharacteristically Dylan wrote the lyrics and then attached melodies, most of which are borrowed or inspired by folk songs and hymns. None of the songs have choruses, and only one has a bridge. The last two ("Down Along the Cove" and "I'll Be Your Baby Tonight," the one with the bridge) are love songs; Pete Drake's steel guitar, added for just these two, gives them a distinctly country feel. The other ten songs are parables, stories of outlaws, saints, and prophets, set in dreams, the biblical past, or the Old West.

In a perceptive early review the *Village Voice*'s Richard Goldstein wrote that the album "not only eludes, but dares interpretation. It sits like a heavy lead safe guarding its precious innards with bolts of cryptic cool. Reach for the handle and it seems to hiss from within itself: 'I am inscrutable.' Give the lock an undaunted shove, and it taunts, 'I may be empty after all.'"[30] Goldstein makes it clear that he does not find *John Wesley Harding* to be empty, and most listeners over the years would agree. But he captures the way Dylan's use of archetypal figures, biblical or otherwise antiquated language, cryptic conversations, and unresolved conflicts seem to insist that we perform some kind of exegesis—but frustrates us if we try to turn the songs into allegories.

For example in "As I Went Out One Morning," the singer meets a fair damsel; although she offers to "secretly accept" him he resists temptation, suspecting that she is dangerous. That seems simple enough, but the meaning is complicated by the fact that the woman is in chains. How do we square that fact with the singer's belief that she means to harm him? Is it the chains that make him think she's dangerous? There's no other clue, so what else could it be? Does the danger lie in getting too involved with a damsel in distress? Another complicating factor—in this seemingly simple, three-verse story-song—is Tom Paine, who is introduced in the first lines. In fact the opening lines rhyme "Paine's" with "chains." Many commentators see "Tom Paine" as an intentional reference to the Tom Paine Award that Dylan received from the Emergency Civil Liberties Committee back in 1963, when he drunkenly insulted and then shocked the organization by suggesting his own affinity with Lee Harvey Oswald. But it could just be Tom Paine, revolutionary pamphleteer and radical proponent of individual freedom.

In any case Paine calls off the girl, and the song ends with him apologizing for her. But all she's done is try (very politely) to seduce the singer. So . . . if Tom Paine represents the *abstract* ideal of fighting for freedom, then the damsel in chains, for whom he feels he must apologize, could represent *real* situations in which a man such as the singer, who may be Bob Dylan, might get seduced—join the struggle! Remove my chains! She suggests they fly south, possibly further referencing the Civil Rights Movement. That interpretation —getting "seduced" by the movement is the temptation-to-be-resisted—sort of works, especially in light of Dylan's distancing himself from protest. But even as I work through what I just wrote it feels overwrought: that message sounds more like the Dylan of 1964 than 1967. And of course the "I" isn't necessarily Dylan at all. It's possible that he just liked the way "Paine's" and "chains" rhymed and improvised from there.

Other songs on *John Wesley Harding* are even more enigmatic. "I Dreamed I Saw St. Augustine" evokes the union organizing song "Joe Hill" ("I dreamed I saw Joe Hill last night/ Alive as you and me"). But unlike Joe Hill the historical Augustine was not a martyr; the fourth-century convert to Christianity became a respected theologian, known for his *Confessions* and philosophical treatises on a variety of subjects. In Dylan's rendering he carries a blanket and a golden coat; he has little to say before he is put to death. In the third and final verse the singer dreams that he was among those responsible for Augustine's supposed martyrdom and then concludes by bowing his head and crying. Some dreams defy interpretation.

The trajectory of "The Wicked Messenger" is a bit clearer, and it carries the most Christian message of any song on the album. In the Book of Proverbs (13:17) "A wicked messenger falleth into mischief, but a faithful ambassador is health." Dylan's messenger is a flatterer and someone whose mind presumably makes simple things complicated. Moreover this wicked messenger comes from Eli, who in the Book of Samuel is punished for caring more about his own sons than God's commandments. The setting may be the Old Testament, but the wicked messenger seemingly experiences a revelation associated with the New Testament. After he is stricken with burning feet, unable to continue in his role as messenger, he experiences conversion as he is told "If ye cannot bring good news, then don't bring any." The song is still ambiguous—not all "good news" is the Good News of Christian salvation—but clearly the messenger, like a character in a Flannery O'Connor story, has been radically changed, his blinders removed, his heart opened.

"The Ballad of Frankie Lee and Judas Priest" is another quasi-Christian parable, complete with a concluding moral and an admonishment, neither of which is really supported by the story the song tells. As if to emphasize this avoidance of clarity, Dylan introduces a neighbor-boy character to deliver a single, cryptic line near the end of the song: "nothing is revealed."

Nothing is revealed either in the album's most famous and most intriguing song. The first two verses of "All Along the Watchtower" consist of dialogue between the Joker and the Thief. The Joker's opening lines, longing for escape amidst the confusion, resonated with the chaotic and frightening environment of late-1960s America: the escalation of U.S. involvement in the Vietnam War, the 1968 assassinations of Martin Luther King and Bobby Kennedy, riots in major cities following King's shooting, the protests and violent response at the Democratic National Convention that summer. Not that Dylan mentions any of those current events. All we know is that this Joker is desperate, but the Thief is resigned: they have an errand, some work to do, and time is running out. The third verse pans back to the watchtower, where in the last lines we see the two riders in the distance, presumably the two we've been listening to.[31] We don't know where the watchtower is or when any of this is taking place, but the coming of the Joker and Thief is linked with ill omens; they are not bringing good news. We can speculate as to what the wildcat, the howling wind, and other details mean, but what matters is the atmosphere of foreboding Dylan creates with these obscure but suggestive images. The times they are a-changin', and not for the better.

"All Along the Watchtower" became one of Dylan's best-known songs, thanks largely to Jimi Hendrix's brilliant version, a hit single in the USA and Britain the following year. Dylan has performed "Watchtower" well over 2,000 times, more than any other song in his catalogue—almost always with an arrangement borrowed from Hendrix.

John Wesley Harding sold well, reaching number two on the U.S. album charts and number one in the UK, with no singles, no tour, and relatively little publicity. Especially with Dylan's mystique more powerful than ever (almost no one outside the Woodstock area had seen him for the past eighteen months), the sleeve design fascinated fans. Dylan posed for the cover photograph in Woodstock with two members of the Bengali Bauls, a group of Indian musicians Grossman had invited to the States, and a local carpenter named Charlie Joy. Dylan wears what looks like the same coat he wore on the cover of *Blonde on Blonde*, his hands jammed into the pockets, giving the camera a toothy grin (as opposed to the blank stares of his last few albums). Like the music, the cover of *John Wesley Harding* could not be less psychedelic: a slightly overexposed black-and-white photograph on a grey background, and nothing but text on the back. And yet fans insisted there must be something groovy hidden in the cover photograph—hold it upside down and you might make out the faces of the Beatles in the bark of the tree behind Dylan. Or perhaps there was a hidden message in the title, which was also the album's first track. While Dylan fabricated a noble character for the real-life outlaw John Wesley Hardin and added a "g" to his last name, did he deliberately choose a name whose initials suggest the tetragrammaton —JHWH—the Hebrew theonym for God?

Mocking just that kind of search for something hidden in his work (while also providing more grist for interpretation), Dylan's liner notes, the last he would write for 26 years, tell the story of three kings who believe the key to Dylan's new album is neither faith nor froth but . . . Frank. They visit Frank and ask him to "open [the new record] up for us." When he asks how far they would like to go, they tell him, "Not too far but just far enough so's we can say that we've been there." Frank obligingly performs a series of random gestures, finally punching his fist through a plate glass window. The kings are not only satisfied but delighted; moreover "the first one's nose had been mysteriously fixed, the second one's arm had healed, and the third one was rich."

On January 20, 1968, three weeks after the release of *John Wesley Harding*, Dylan performed onstage for the first time in a year and a half with the Band (temporarily calling themselves the Crackers) at the Woody Guthrie tribute organized by Harold Leventhal, with proceeds going to the Committee to Combat Huntington's Disease. Levon Helm remembers that "the crowd gasped when we all walked onstage. Bob's hair was cut short and combed, and we were all dressed in grey western-cut suits and cowboy boots. This time there wasn't any booing." They had worked up basement-style arrangements of "I Ain't Got No Home," "Dear Mrs. Roosevelt," and "The Grand Coulee Dam," Dylan's impassioned vocals paying tribute to his hero without imitating him, instead "spitting out Guthrie's 16-syllable lines as if they were watermelon seeds," as Paul Williams put it.[32] They delivered their set for both the afternoon and evening programs, at the latter of which, according to Helm, they "brought down the house." Afterward Dylan chatted comfortably with old friends at a party in Central Park West.[33] Dylan was "back," but he was much more subdued, and he wasn't interested in touring or in rushing out another record.

He continued to live a quiet life in Woodstock, reading, visiting with friends, and spending time with Sara and their growing family—Maria was seven, Jesse two, and Anna one year old when Samuel Dylan was born in July 1968. Dylan's friend, the journalist Al Aronowitz, recalled, "During this period, Bob and Sara grew to be one of the tightest twosomes I've ever known . . . Bob acted like a romantic cornball when he was with her."[34]

He also took up painting, receiving guidance from his neighbor Bruce Dorfman, who taught at the Art Students League of New York. Dylan's first major work, a colorful, primitive-style depiction of musicians and an elephant, became the cover of the Band's *Music from Big Pink*, released in July.

His amazing productivity as a songwriter in 1967 had run its course though, either by choice or lack of inspiration. Throughout 1968 he wrote almost nothing and, with the exception of the Guthrie tribute in January, did not perform in public or record in a studio.

He did agree to a couple of interviews after the release of *John Wesley Harding*. Surprisingly he spoke with Hubert Saal, *Newsweek*'s music critic, despite his anger over that magazine's 1963 article exposing his conventional middle-class upbringing. He confirmed, "I won't be giving any concerts for a while . . . I went around the world a couple of times. But I didn't have anything else to do then." And he confessed to being an undisciplined songwriter, but added, "I've always tried to get simple. I haven't always succeeded. But here [on *John Wesley Harding*] I took more care in the writing."[35]

That summer he gave an interview to his old friends John Cohen and Happy Traum for *Sing Out!* magazine, even contributing artwork for the cover when the interview was published in October. Here Dylan is polite, even friendly, but for most of the interview he reveals little if anything. Frequently he seems to be putting Cohen on—at one point he tells him he is not especially interested in recording his own songs:

> I was going to do a whole album of other people's songs, but I couldn't find enough . . . I shy away from those songs which repeat phrases, bars and verses, bridges . . . so right there it leaves out about nine-tenths of all the contemporary material being written, and the folk songs are just about the only ones that don't . . . I don't know, maybe then too I'm just too lazy to look hard enough.[36]

In other words it was only because he wanted to record songs without choruses, bridges, and refrains that he was forced to write his own material for *John Wesley Harding*. The interview gets testy near the end, when Traum presses Dylan on the lack of social and political engagement of his recent work, suggesting that artists have an obligation to speak out against the Vietnam War. Dylan replies, "I know some very good artists who are for the war," and after a bit more banter, "Anyway, how do you know I'm not, as you say, for the war?"[37]

Dylan's concerns in 1968 were understandably closer to home. In June his father died at the age of 56. Despite their distant relationship "we had more in common now [just before Abram's death] than ever," he would later write. "I, too, was a father three times over—there was a lot that I wanted to share, to tell him."[38] Dylan flew to Minnesota for the funeral, bringing his mother back to Woodstock, where she began spending more time with Bob and his family. Bob and Sara gave their son Samuel the middle name Abram.

Dylan had also wanted to rename Dwarf Music, his music publishing company, to celebrate Samuel's birth, but he learned that because Albert Grossman owned half the business he could not make that change on his own.[39] He had already been chafing under Grossman's management—the song "Dear Landlord" on *John Wesley Harding* is often heard as an expression of his discontent—and by mid-1968 he and Grossman rarely spoke to each other, despite being neighbors. But the discovery that Grossman owned half of Dylan's publishing (something Dylan should have known already) was the breaking point, the start of a years-long effort to divorce himself legally from the businessman who "drink[s] my wine." The aggressive, competitive Grossman had been the ideal manager for a young performer who was ready to conquer the world—by taking care of Dylan's business, he had allowed Dylan the artistic freedom and control he needed. But now that Dylan was taking stock, thinking about his family, and not obsessively creating new "product," he wanted control over the Bob Dylan business as well.

8

1969–71: Reinvention

Throughout his career Bob Dylan jotted down ideas in cheap, spiral-bound notebooks, as well as the backs of envelopes, hotel stationery, and almost any other stray pieces of paper that were at hand. One notebook entry, from around 1968, reads,

I been movin' too much
So I don't wanna be
Moved for awhile
I beg you please
To just
Let me be
I'll do anything you say
That will make you happy . . .
The times have changed

On another page in the same notebook, he writes,

Everybody asks you,
"Where have you been?"
Everyone will ask, "Why? and, "when
Are you going back again?"[1]

These forthright but banal lyrics never made it into a completed song, but they seem to reflect Dylan's state of mind, not wanting to move too often or too far from his home in Woodstock. Although the "you" that he's begging to "To just let me be" is probably the public and the press, the "you" he'll do anything for is more likely his wife. Meanwhile "The times have changed" in a general sense—the social and political upheaval forecast in Dylan's 1964 song had certainly occurred—but he had changed too into a mellow family man, a country squire in his late twenties.

The second excerpt reflects Dylan's awareness that his fans were asking when he's going (or coming) back, while Columbia Records—with whom he had recently signed on for another five years—was eagerly awaiting a follow-up to *John Wesley Harding*. But unfortunately the creative juice that had produced that album and the summer of 1967's Basement Tapes had all but dried up.

"One day I was half-stepping," Dylan told an interviewer a decade later, "and the lights went out. And since that point, I more or less had amnesia . . . It took me a long time to get to do consciously what I used to be able to do unconsciously."[2] He may have written only two songs over the course of 1968, but both were very good: the mournful "I Threw It All Away" and a song he later said he wrote for Barbra Streisand, "Lay Lady Lay."[3]

Another song he had tinkered with was a collaboration with his friend George Harrison. Harrison, who had loved *Music from Big Pink*, visited the Band and Dylan in Woodstock in November 1968; near the end of the sojourn the Dylans hosted a Thanksgiving gathering. They must have played some Basement Tapes for George, who sent a letter soon afterward to "Tiny Montgomery," playfully addressing Dylan as the title character of a Basement Tapes song. The note includes a chord progression for the song they were working on, "I'd Have You Anytime,"[4] which would eventually open Harrison's epic triple album *All Things Must Pass*. But Harrison found Dylan surprisingly subdued during the visit, recalling later that he was "very quiet, and he didn't have much confidence—that's the feeling I got with him in Woodstock. He hardly said a word for a couple of days."[5]

On February 13 Dylan returned to Nashville to start recording his next album, with just four completed songs. He wrote and recorded another five songs over the next few days; then he was joined by Johnny Cash in the studio on the 17th and 18th. He and Cash, who had maintained their friendship and mutual admiration throughout the decade, might have had an album-length collaboration in mind—they ran through over twenty songs, from "Mountain Dew" to "Just a Closer Walk with Thee" to "I Walk the Line." But historic as the session was, the results are mostly awkward and uninspired. As Colin Escott puts it (in the Bootleg Series volume XV liner notes), "If the Everly Brothers were consummate duettists, creating subtle overtones between their two voices, Cash and Dylan were two guys singing together."[6]

The sessions did yield what became the opening track of Dylan's next album, a duet version of "Girl from the North Country." A few others had potential—most notably a mash-up of "Don't Think Twice, It's Alright" with Cash's 1964 rewrite of that same song, "Understand Your Man"; and "Big River," which Dylan had recorded at Big Pink with the Band a year and a half earlier—but no one seems to have been in charge of the session, and neither singer had the patience to keep working on the more promising ideas.

Fittingly the new album was called *Nashville Skyline*, as it embraced the style of music the city was known for. Dylan and Bob Johnston brought back the rhythm section of Kenny Buttrey and Charlie McCoy, along with Pete Drake, who had played pedal steel on the last two tracks of *John Wesley Harding*. They added Bob Wilson on piano, along with Norman Blake and future star Charlie Daniels on guitar to create a fuller, modern country sound. Dylan was deeply rooted in country music, devoted particularly to Jimmie Rodgers and Hank Williams, but *Nashville Skyline* wasn't exactly the high lonesome, old-school country or honky-tonk he had absorbed as a teenager listening to the radio. It was not quite countrypolitan, the polished style associated with 1960s Billy Sherrill productions, either—but it was smooth and generally upbeat thematically and musically. He even adopted a new voice for the occasion—a clear, mellow croon that he had kept in his back pocket since his days singing in Minneapolis coffeehouses.

There was an equally radical shift in Dylan's songwriting. Having gone from streams of satirical and surreal imagery on his classic electric albums to spare, quasi-biblical parables on *John Wesley Harding*,

Dylan was now delivering straightforward love songs. "I Threw It All Away" might be the first Dylan song to express unequivocal regret over losing a lover. "Tonight I'll Be Staying Here with You" could have been written thirty or forty years earlier, if the promise of casual sex weren't quite so obvious. "Lay Lady Lay" would certainly have had a hard time getting past censors even a decade earlier, but its unabashed carnality was right in step with the times—it became Dylan's fourth top ten hit in the USA, his sixth in the UK. (Dylan admitted that he had objected to releasing it as a single, but Columbia's president, Clive Davis, had insisted: "He thought it was a hit single, and he was right."[7])

Dylan would later claim to have "put an end to" Tin Pan Alley, the symbol of standard pop songwriting, but on *Nashville Skyline* he worked strictly within its conventions. For the first time in his recording career he was delivering songs that could have been written by someone other than Bob Dylan; he came up with a few gems but also some of the most vapid lyrics of his career.[8] On "Peggy Day" and "Country Pie" he flaunts his embrace of simple pleasures and simpler turns of phrase, spending the night with Peggy Day and, in another verse, spending the day with Peggy Night. Dylan told Hubert Saal of *Newsweek*,

> These are more the type of songs that I always felt like writing. The songs reflect more of the inner me than the songs of the past. They're more to my base than, say, "John Wesley Harding." There I felt everyone expected me to be a poet so that's what I tried to be. But the smallest line in this new album means more to me than some of the songs on any of the previous albums I've made.[9]

He may have actually felt that way at that moment, but Dylan had made similar claims—they expect me to write one way, but I'm moved to write this other way—throughout his career.

Needless to say, many fans were disappointed. Ed Ochs wrote in *Billboard*, "Dylan, the satisfied man, speaks in clichés and blushes as if every day were Valentine's day . . . So goodbye, Bob Dylan, I'm glad you're happy though you meant more to me when you were . . .

confused like everybody else."[10] Yet many critics loved it, and the album sold well, hitting number two in the USA and number one in the UK. Nat Hentoff, who had interviewed Dylan for the *New Yorker* and *Playboy* earlier in the decade, sent him a congratulatory note: "Dear Bob: I just wanted to tell you that *Nashville Skyline* is just plain pleasure and I wanted to thank you for it." Broadway producer Stuart Ostrow inquired with Columbia Records about doing a "musical theatre piece" based on the album. George Harrison's review came on a card from England: "Dear Bobbie, Thanks for Nashville Skyline, it is beautiful."[11]

Even if the songs are evidence of a creative drought, *Nashville Skyline* works as a lightweight, *fun* album. You can listen to "Nashville Skyline Rag" and gripe about it being filler—an instrumental, by-the-numbers bluegrass jam—or you can relax and enjoy the session players' musicianship. You can scratch your head over Dylan's use of pie fillings as lyrical filler in "Country Pie," or you can just sing along, loving that country pie.

Dylan would later tell Tony Glover that, in a reversal of his process for *John Wesley Harding*, this time he wrote the tunes first. He suggested thinking of the words *as* music: "If you were to isolate the words for a minute, and just think of the sound of the voice, the sound of the music and the vocal—suppose you couldn't understand English at all and you just heard the sound of it—the sound of it would be pretty much what the words are. You know, a lot of dreamy kind of stuff, nice, pleasant, soothing type of music, I'd imagine."[12]

In an odd way, Dylan's embrace of mainstream country music mirrored his embrace of electric rock music four years earlier, in that he was allying himself not just with a sound or genre but a culture that was alien to many of his fans. Country music aligned with conservative values, especially support for the war but also traditional gender roles and hair styles, antipathy toward Civil Rights protests, and disapproval of illicit drug use. Later that year Merle Haggard's "Okie from Muskogee" would epitomize this cultural divide as it became a rallying cry for the conservative "silent majority" (although, ironically, the song originated as a joke among Haggard's pot-smoking band members).

Yet Dylan wasn't the only "rock-oriented" performer reaching across that divide. A year earlier the long-haired International Submarine Band, led by Gram Parsons, had released *Safe at Home*, an album combining songs by Haggard and Johnny Cash with Parsons's honky-tonk originals. Soon afterward Parsons joined forces with the Byrds, moving them into country territory with *Sweetheart of the Rodeo*, an album that opened and closed with Basement Tapes songs bathed in Lloyd Green's gorgeous pedal steel playing. The year 1968 also saw the release of Townes Van Zandt's first album; his songs and arrangements leaned to the "western" side of country and western, but they also reflected the poetic singer-songwriter ethos that Dylan had pioneered.

Meanwhile country music was incorporating rhythms and musical textures from folk-rock—you can hear it in 1969 releases by Bobbie Gentry, Waylon Jennings, Glen Campbell, and others. Musically there was increasing crossover between country and rock, but culturally the barriers remained high. Columbia Records managed to get the Byrds a spot on the Grand Ole Opry in 1968, but, as Lloyd Green recalled, when the audience "saw this young group of hippie-looking guys and with longer hair than what they were used to, they literally booed. Welcome to Nashville."[13] And now Dylan, the musical figurehead of the counterculture (much to his chagrin), was not only dabbling with steel guitar and songs about heartbreak—he was calling attention to it all with the album title, the back-cover photograph of Nashville, and a front-cover photograph that exudes the warm, down-home affect of the music, Dylan hoisting a Gibson hummingbird guitar with one hand and tipping his broad-brimmed hat to us with the other.

And, of course, Johnny Cash at the height of his popularity was not only singing with Dylan on the first track but contributing a poetic tribute to him on the back cover, extolling his friend's Whitmanesque individualism:

There are those
Who are beings complete unto themselves
Whole, undaunted,—a source
As leaves of grass, as stars

As mountains, alike, alike, alike,
Yet unalike . . .

Herein is a hell of a poet.
And lots of other things
And lots of other things.

Nashville Skyline was released on April 9, 1969. Dylan returned to Nashville two weeks later to record a new song, "Living the Blues," and several covers; then on May 1 he taped an appearance at the Ryman Auditorium for the first episode of *The Johnny Cash Show*, which aired in June. Cash used the show to break down some of those musical-cultural barriers—the first broadcast featured not only Dylan but Joni Mitchell and Cajun fiddler Doug Kershaw; that first summer alone saw appearances by Melanie, the Staple Singers, Linda Ronstadt, the Monkees, and Creedence Clearwater Revival. Kenny Buttrey, who played at the taping, said of Dylan, "I've never seen anybody that scared."[14] Indeed Dylan, who hadn't performed on television since *The Steve Allen Show* in 1964 (and had only performed before an audience once since 1966) appears nervous as he sings "I Threw It All Away," looking away from the camera at all times—but his "new" voice is clear and strong, as it is when he is joined by Cash for "Girl from the North Country."

Back in Woodstock Dylan was becoming increasingly uncomfortable with aggressive fans and pilgrims—not just gawking and following him around town but trespassing and even breaking into his house, apparently thinking he'd be cool with it. The family moved to a more secluded house on the other side of town in late spring, and Dylan bought as much of the surrounding property as he could. They spent a portion of that summer on Fire Island, NY, where Dylan frequently jammed with the eclectic composer and multi-instrumentalist David Amram; Paul Simon visited as well, as did Bob's mother.[15] In August Dylan went back to Hibbing for—incredible as this may seem—his ten-year high school reunion. Sara came along and even got to meet Dylan's old girlfriend Echo Helstrom.[16]

As if Woodstock were not already attracting enough unwelcome hippies, the summer of 1969 was destined to be forever linked with the town's name. Organizers of the Woodstock Music and Art Fair originally planned to hold the event in or very near the town, which already had countercultural cachet through association with Dylan and the Band, in addition to its history as an artist colony. But locals wisely blocked the proposed festival, so it was eventually moved to a farm in Bethel, NY, about 40 miles (64 km) away. That was still close enough to increase the magnetic power of Woodstock (the town) and certainly close enough to generate hype over the possibility of an appearance by Dylan. Not only was the festival virtually in his backyard but several performers strongly connected to Dylan—notably Joan Baez and the Band—were scheduled to perform. He was having none of it.

Meanwhile brothers Ron and Ray Foulk were organizing a similar festival on the Isle of Wight, to be held two weeks after Woodstock, and they made an attractive pitch to Dylan: $50,000 plus expenses and a relaxing family vacation at a sixteenth-century country house

Talking with reporters and fans, Isle of Wight, August 1969.

in the land of Tennyson. As part of the deal Dylan agreed not to play any other summer festivals, i.e. Woodstock, a "concession" he must have been happy to make.[17] Although the Dylans had originally planned to bring the kids with them, crossing the Atlantic on the *Queen Elizabeth II*, a temporary health issue with their son Jesse delayed the trip, and Bob and Sara flew to London a week and a half later, several days before the concert on August 31. Staying at historic Forelands Farm, he rehearsed with the Band and hosted three-fourths of the Beatles (John, George, and Ringo) and their wives. At one point Dylan and Lennon faced off against Harrison and Starr in doubles tennis; according to Al Aronowitz, who had accompanied Dylan as road manager, they were not very good at it (but what a scene!).[18]

As he had been with *The Johnny Cash Show* taping, Dylan was nervous about the Isle of Wight gig. And especially considering all the changes in his music before and after the motorcycle accident, his audience did not know what to expect—but rumors circulated, amplified by the press, raising expectations of a marathon set with guest appearances by various Beatles and Stones.[19] On the night of Dylan's appearance the tension and expectations were heightened by delays, which, according to Aronowitz, made Dylan anxious and belligerent.[20] Yet when he took the stage around midnight he settled right in with the Band (who had played their own set just before his), told the crowd it was "great to be here, it really is," and delivered a solid seventeen-song performance. If not quite career-spanning, the setlist went back as far as 1964's *Another Side* ("It Ain't Me Babe" and "To Ramona," both solo acoustic) and featured hits such as "Mr. Tambourine Man," "Like a Rolling Stone," and "Rainy Day Women #12 & 35." He didn't try to replicate the *Nashville Skyline* sound with the Band, but he did weave in and out of his country croon throughout the performance, and he included the recently released "I Threw It All Away" and "Lay Lady Lay." The performance lacked the intensity and menace of the 1966 tour, but it was pleasantly loose, even slightly ragged, and pretty close to the sound Dylan and the Band created on the Basement Tapes—which were represented in the setlist by "Quinn the Eskimo" (already familiar thanks to Manfred Mann) and "Minstrel Boy."

The crowd seemed appreciative, but many, including the Foulk brothers, were disappointed that Dylan didn't play longer or jam onstage with rock luminaries. The following day London papers reported fans setting fires at the concert site and threatening to riot because Dylan had played only about an hour.[21]

Not long after his return to the USA the Dylans bought a townhouse on MacDougal Street in Greenwich Village. Given his recent quest for privacy and frustration at being pursued even in semi-secluded Woodstock, the move to Manhattan seems counterintuitive, especially with another child, Jakob, due in December.

"Looking back," Dylan would recall later, "it really was a stupid thing to do."[22] It might have made sense at the time though, considering that New York City has often allowed celebrities a strange kind of freedom. Like other world cultural capitals, it's so big and there are so many famous people that it provides a kind of invisible shield, as if there's a code among other residents to give the notable residents some space.

Except that not everyone follows the code. A fan by the name of A. J. Weberman proclaimed himself the world's leading Dylanologist (coining and simultaneously tarnishing the label) and began stalking Dylan, rummaging through his garbage, phoning him, recording the conversations, and writing about his "discoveries" in a paper called the *East Village Other*. Weberman was obsessed, writing painfully intricate and idiosyncratic analyses of Dylan's lyrics, but he was also hostile, believing that Dylan had completely sold out by turning his back on protest and the needs of his fans. On Dylan's birthday in 1971 he would lead a small mob that he called the "Dylan Liberation Front" to their anti-hero's house to present a cake with hypodermic needles for candles—part of Weberman's theory was that Dylan was a heroin addict. Fortunately the Dylans were out of the country, on a visit to Israel, but on several other occasions Dylan engaged directly with Weberman, finally confronting and pummeling him on the street.[23]

That incident came later though; in 1969 Dylan knew Weberman only as an eccentric interpreter of his lyrics. When Jann Wenner asked about him Dylan replied, "Is this the guy who tears up all my songs?

On stage at the Isle of Wight Festival with Rick Danko and Robbie Robertson, August 1969.

Well, he oughta take a rest. He's way off." That interview for *Rolling Stone*, published in November, was the most extensive Dylan had given since his exchange with Cohen and Traum for *Sing Out!* the previous year. In this one too Dylan is alternately candid and evasive, keeping his interviewer off balance, often with what seems like mock chumminess. And he's as funny as he had been in his better-natured press conferences circa 1965.

At one point Wenner remarks on the "awkwardness of this interview," and Dylan replies, "Well, I don't find anything awkward about it. I think it's going real great." Asked why he called his album *John Wesley Harding* he says, "I called it that, Jann, 'cause I had the song 'John Wesley Harding,' which started out to be a long ballad . . . But in the middle of the second verse, I got tired." Wenner asks what other album titles he considered, so Dylan pivots, revealing (speciously) that the original title for *Nashville Skyline* was *John Wesley Harding,*

Volume II, and a little later he riffs on other possible album titles: "Certainly couldn't call the album *Lay, Lady, Lay*. I wouldn't have wanted to call it that, although that name was brought up. It didn't get my vote, but it was brought up. *Peggy Day—Lay, Peggy Day*, that was brought up. A lot of things were brought up. *Tonight I'll Be Staying Here with Peggy Day*. That's another one." And so on.

Wenner asked, "Have you ever thought of doing an album . . . a very arranged, very orchestrated album, you know with chicks and . . . ?" Dylan's cryptic reply was, "Gee, I've thought of it . . . I think about it once in a while. Yeah." Did Wenner realize how prescient that question was? Dylan's next album would have the kind of old-fashioned sound he alludes to, with occasional orchestration, lots of overdubs, and women as backing vocalists ("chicks"). Dylan had already recorded several tracks in Nashville that would find their way to that album, *Self Portrait*, but he opted to resume recording in New York in March 1970 rather than return to Nashville.

Self Portrait remains the oddest album of Dylan's career. It was not particularly divisive in 1970 though, because fans and critics were united in disliking it. I have yet to find later commentary on *Self Portrait* that doesn't cite the first line of Greil Marcus's review for *Rolling Stone*: "What is this shit?," which both was and wasn't a rhetorical question—Marcus's review is pretty negative, but he does proceed to contemplate the 24-song double album track by track, trying to figure out what this shit actually is. In the middle of this exploration he observes,

> *Self Portrait* most closely resembles the Dylan album that preceded it: *Great White Wonder*. The album is a two-record set masterfully assembled from an odd collection of mostly indifferent recordings made over the course of the last year, complete with alternate takes, chopped endings, loose beginnings, side comments, and all sorts of mistakes . . . A bit from Nashville, a taste of the Isle of Wight since you missed it, some sessions from New York that mostly don't make it, but dig, it's Dylan . . .

Marcus also saw the project as "a curious move toward self-effacement: Dylan removing himself from a position from which he is asked to exercise power."[24] Dylan would later concur with both claims: "A lot of worse stuff was appearing on bootleg records," so he made "so to speak, my own bootleg record."[25] He would also later claim that it was an attempt to get rid of his fans, who were bothering him just as much on MacDougal Street as they had in Woodstock: "I said, 'Well, fuck it. I wish these people would just *forget* about me. I wanna do something they *can't* possibly like, they *can't* relate to.'"[26]

These are both intriguing ideas—that *Self Portrait* is Dylan's own Dylan bootleg and that it was a deliberate effort to alienate fans. He could have produced a "bootleg" that fans would have loved—for instance an official *Great White Wonder*, although Columbia probably wouldn't have gone along with it. *Self Portrait* does work kind of like a bootleg, especially with the inclusion of four songs recorded at the Isle of Wight concert sprinkled in among studio tracks, a heavy dose of covers, two instrumentals, an opening track sung entirely by "chick" singers, plus two "Little Sadie"s and two "Alberta"s. The lack of continuity seems intentional.

But what's very un-bootleg about *Self Portrait* is the high degree of studio polish, which was also the feature most likely to make fans run away. For the most part the studio sweetening took place in Nashville, without Dylan's participation: the feathery backing vocals and "polite" countrypolitan or light-rock rhythm arrangements on "I Forgot More Than You'll Ever Know," "Take Me As I Am," "Take a Message to Mary," and others, and the orchestrations on "Belle Isle" and "Wigwam." Finally there's not only the preponderance of covers but the odd choice of covers, which included "Blue Moon" (a standard that had been cut by everyone from Ella Fitzgerald to Elvis); Gordon Lightfoot's "Early Morning Rain," which had recently been a country hit for George Hamilton IV; and Simon and Garfunkel's "The Boxer," on which two Dylan vocals are clumsily double-tracked. Fans who, two years earlier, had pondered, "What do the Joker and the Thief represent?" now pondered, "What *is* this shit?"

And yet the album has aged extremely well, a testament to the importance of social and historical context in shaping how we hear music. While there were Dylan fans (and new converts) who easily warmed up to the country sound of *Nashville Skyline*, the quirkiness and the corniness of *Self Portrait* were a bridge too far in 1970. Young people defined themselves through the music they loved and against the music they hated, which included anything their parents were listening to. Marcus imagines a teenage Dylan fan getting *Self Portrait* as a birthday gift from his parents: "He considers giving it back for Father's Day."[27] While young (and old) people still build musical preferences into their identities, the lines are more permeable now, especially between generations—witness for instance the number of fans under thirty at Dylan shows in the 2020s.

Mocked and despised by young people, easy listening music was a cultural force in 1970, for instance as the preferred musical setting for great country players like Floyd Cramer and Chet Atkins. Today most of us only hear Andy Williams or the Ray Conniff Singers during the holidays, but Williams had his own network television show and sold millions of albums in the late 1960s. *The Lawrence Welk Show* was not yet in syndication—it was a network (ABC) program consistently among the top thirty shows in the Nielsen Ratings. "Elevator music" was seemingly everywhere, with its inobtrusive percussion, soft choral singing, and tame orchestrations. *Self Portrait* isn't Muzak, but the schmaltzy arrangements, especially of well-known pop hits, sounded heretical coming from someone like Dylan. That shock has worn off as the "easy listening" of the late 1960s and early '70s has all but disappeared, having been replaced in elevators and grocery stores by nostalgic classic rock and pop programming.

Moreover, in the wake of *Highway 61 Revisited*, albums had come to be seen as musically and thematically unified statements by important artists—think *Sgt. Pepper* or *Tommy* or *John Wesley Harding*. And what statement was *Self Portrait* making? Conceptually it might have been that Dylan's musical "self" was, after all, a composite of Tin Pan Alley pop, folk, blues, country, and a surprising array of other people's music. Or the concept might have been, "Fuck it. I wish these people would just forget about me." But it was hard to hear this album, track by track (all 24 of them), as unified. *Self Portrait* seemed trivial, an over-produced bunch of covers and second-rate live recordings.

But it's easier over half a century later not to worry about what the album says about Dylan's state of mind, the future of popular music, or really anything else. Its eclecticism and don't-give-a-damn vibe seem pretty compelling in fact. If, like me, you were baffled at first by the Clash's *Sandinista!* (three records, styles ranging from Motown to swing to dub and reggae, lots of what seemed like filler) but then started to think, "this just might be the coolest thing the band ever did," you can appreciate how, over time, *Self Portrait* starts to make sense. And it doesn't hurt that some of the tracks have been nicely recontextualized themselves; for instance "Wigwam" was used to great effect in Wes Anderson's *The Royal Tenenbaums*, and a cover of "All The Tired Horses" by Lisa O'Neill was featured at the end of the last episode of the series *Peaky Blinders*.

Volume x of the Bootleg Series, *Another Self Portrait* (2013), also enhances one's appreciation of the original album, even as it encourages listeners to imagine a better version of it—perhaps with more traditional songs like "Pretty Saro," "Spanish Is the Loving Tongue," and "This Evening So Soon," as well as the half-dozen or so tracks that are presented without overdubs. Hearing more of what Dylan was up to in early 1970 draws this listener at least back to the original album. Maybe, like *Sandinista!*, it should have been a triple. If nothing else *Another Self Portrait* reflects the way most of us consume music in the twenty-first century—the sequencing doesn't matter, and we're more likely to cherry-pick songs to listen to anyway. It's another way in which the original *Self Portrait* works better in the streaming/playlist era, when an album's sonic and thematic unity is not such an important measuring stick for quality.

The fluidity of *Self Portrait* is even clearer in light of the fact that a month before its release Dylan was already back in the studio—Columbia's Studio B in New York—recording more covers as well as lackluster versions of his own famous tunes. At the afternoon session on May 1 Dylan, Al Kooper (piano), Ron Cornelius (guitar), Charlie Daniels (bass), and Alvin Rogers (drums) were joined by none other than George Harrison for part of the session. Unfortunately on the recordings released by Sony Music (in 2021) you can hardly tell Harrison is there. That evening, with Russ Kunkel replacing Rogers on drums (and Harrison departed), Dylan began laying down tracks for his next album. The first week of June, just as *Self Portrait* was about to hit the shelves, he returned with the same group and continued playing a mix of covers and new originals, which was presumably the plan for the *Self Portrait* follow-up. But, possibly because of the hostile reception to *Self Portrait*, he ultimately opted for an all-originals set, calling the album *New Morning*. Following the radical *Self Portrait*, *New Morning* is one of Dylan's safest albums, but it came at a time when he might have needed to play it safe.

Dylan had virtually invented the "singer-songwriter," which was rapidly becoming not just a self-evident descriptive term but a distinct musical genre. Carole King's breakthrough album *Tapestry* would be released in early 1971 (and spend fifteen weeks at the top of the *Billboard* album chart), but her solo debut *Writer* was already out in mid-1970, as King transformed herself from a Brill Building songwriter into a performer of her own songs. Joni Mitchell, who had built a reputation as a songwriter with "Both Sides Now" and "The Circle Game," released her own breakthrough, *Ladies of the Canyon*, in April 1970, around the same time *Sweet Baby James* made James Taylor a star with the hits "Fire and Rain" and "Country Road." And of course Leonard Cohen, whose poetic lyrics were often praised alongside Dylan's, had already released two albums that made him a critics' favorite. The genre was defined not just by the fact of writing one's own songs but by the prevalence of introspection and at least occasional reference to the singer's personal life, as well as a poetic sensibility that ventured beyond uncomplicated love-and-breakup songs. The musical backing was what would come to be called light rock, a mix of acoustic and electric instruments, drums optional, with arrangements that foregrounded vocals rather than guitar or keyboard solos. Dylan had written all the songs on *Nashville Skyline*, but those weren't exactly "singer-songwriter" songs. With *New Morning* though, he got more personal.

The most overt example is the last song he wrote and recorded for the album, "Day of the Locusts." In June, not long after laying down most of the tracks for *New Morning*, he had driven to Princeton University to accept an honorary degree at the school's commencement. His traveling companions were Sara Dylan and David Crosby, with whom he smoked "some killer weed."[28] The honorary doctorate attested to Dylan's stature among academics, especially literature professors who were eager to cross the generational divide by devoting class time to Dylan's lyrics. But academia's love was not requited—in his 1966 *Playboy* interview with Hentoff for instance he had quipped, "Colleges are like old-age homes; except for the fact that more people die in colleges than in old-age homes, there's really no difference."[29]

Suspicious though he was, Dylan donned an academic robe and sat onstage among other honorees, including Coretta Scott King and the political writer Walter Lippmann. Princeton's president read a citation: "Although he is now approaching the perilous age of 30, his music remains the authentic expression of the disturbed and concerned conscience of young America."[30] Dylan's reaction, as he recalls in *Chronicles*, was predictable and priceless: "Oh Sweet Jesus! It was like a jolt. I shuddered and trembled but remained expressionless. The disturbed conscience of Young America! There it was again. I couldn't believe it!"[31]

Dylan's song commemorating the experience echoes Nathanael West's novel *The Day of the Locust*, whose title evokes the biblical plague to suggest a violent comeuppance for a decadent society. The locusts that were "singing for me" during the ceremony in Dylan's song might represent the plague he wishes upon his Ivy League captors; at the very least they are singing a "sweet melody" that takes him away from the discomfort and anxiety he feels. The song ends with Dylan's escape, reminiscent of songs such as "Maggie's Farm" and "On the Road Again." The difference from those earlier songs is that this "I" is less a character created by Dylan and more the "real" Bob Dylan who had just driven away with a diploma he hadn't even asked for.

Other songs, despite being less clearly autobiographical, come across as genuine personal reflections. "Went to See the Gypsy" is often presumed to be about Elvis Presley, but other than the fact that the Gypsy "did it in Las Vegas" there's nothing in the song to support that inference (and, for what it's worth, Dylan saw but never met Presley). But the dreamlike scenario does present the singer as someone who needs help and the Gypsy as someone, a traveler and possibly a performer, who can provide it. After his first fruitless meeting with the Gypsy, a dancing girl advises him to try again. His hope rises—he sees lights in the distance, hears music—but when he goes back to the Gypsy's hotel room he finds an open door and an empty room. No dancing girl, no Gypsy. Whether this is a dream or a memory or a little of both, the song set in a Minnesota town, about seeking guidance only to end up back on your own, seems deeply personal, coming from someone who had been struggling at his craft for the past couple of years.

The singer of "Sign on the Window" similarly finds himself alone and confused—the opening verse poignantly conveys the feeling of self-absorbed loneliness after someone has left you. While other *New Morning* songs ended in the Black Hills of Dakota or a little Minnesota town, "Sign on the Window" ends with a fantasy of family life in Utah, with a wife he hasn't met yet and kids that will "call me 'Pa.'" The song seems to confirm faith in the domestic life Dylan himself had embraced since the motorcycle accident three years earlier. But the singer of "Sign on the Window" sounds uncertain, as if trying to convince himself that it's the life he wants.

That spring Dylan had met with the poet Archibald MacLeish, then in his late seventies, who wanted him to contribute songs to a play he was writing. (The connection probably stemmed from the earlier inquiry from Stuart Ostrow about developing a musical from *Nashville Skyline*, since Ostrow was now producing MacLeish's play.) Dylan would later make their meetings the centerpiece of the *New Morning* section of *Chronicles*, expressing the awe that he felt in being summoned by the great poet but also the futility of the experiment. This invitation was another indication of Dylan's stature as a writer, but MacLeish understandably seemed to have fixed his attention on the mid-1960s Dylan of "It's Alright, Ma" and "Desolation Row." MacLeish's play, *Scratch*, concerned the nature of evil, so while it might have jibed with 1965 Dylan it was thematically darker than 1970 Dylan.

"The play itself was conveying some devastating truth," wrote Dylan, "but I was going to stay far away from that. Truth was the last thing on my mind, and even if there was such a thing, I didn't want it in my house."[32] Even so Dylan offered MacLeish three songs—"New Morning," "Time Passes Slowly," and "Father of Night." They were apparently far from what the older poet was looking for: the first two are full of love and hope, and the last is a prayer to a supreme deity. All three songs found a place on Dylan's album, one serving as the title track and "Father of Night" as a closing statement.

Those songs and others balance out the despondency of "Sign on the Window" and "Went to See the Gypsy." "The Man in Me" and "If Not for You" are both lyrically and musically uplifting, perhaps not coincidentally the two most recognizable songs on the album. The former was resurrected in 1998 as the opening theme for *The Big Lebowski*, a film whose details are cherished by its fans in a way that resembles the avidity of Dylanologists. (With that in mind, I must note that on another *New Morning* track, "Winterlude," Dylan refers to himself as "Dude.") Pre-*Lebowski*, "The Man in Me" seemed like the most disposable of Dylan songs, as lightweight as anything on *Nashville Skyline*; post-*Lebowski*, it has become one of Dylan's most often-heard recordings (through TV shows, movies, and ads); it was one of the six songs featured in the original permanent exhibit at the Bob Dylan Center in Tulsa. "If Not for You," a sweet, straightforward love song, didn't have to wait as long to become part of the soundtrack of our lives. Not long after *New Morning*, George Harrison included it on the bestselling *All Things Must Pass*, and the following year it became the first hit single for Olivia Newton-John.

Critics and fans were relieved, even elated, by *New Morning*, which was released in October, just four months after *Self Portrait*. Although the album had a few quirks—including two spoken-word tracks, one of them ("If Dogs Run Free") accompanied by Maeretha Stewart's scat singing in a jazzy beat-poetry setting—it was still a collection of new, non-country Dylan songs, some of which were catchy and some of which seemed to reveal his actual state of mind. At the very least he wasn't selling out or sabotaging his own career this time.

Writing in *Rolling Stone*, the respected critic Ralph Gleason declared, "We've got Bob Dylan back again . . . This is a hopeful album, and, my God, we need it." Ed Ochs, who had disparaged

Nashville Skyline, wrote in *Billboard*, "Dylan is dancing, singing to the sun, and you can really love him."[33] That kind of praise seems a bit excessive (and possessive) today, but it's also easy to understand the enthusiasm. Not only were there some good, hopeful songs on *New Morning* but it *sounded* great and very much of its moment, Dylan switching between guitar and piano, backed by highly capable players who could have almost passed for the Band. This was not the Old Dylan, but it was a New Dylan that old fans could live with.

Having released three studio albums in a year and a half (similar to his mid-1960s pace) Dylan was, in some sense, "back," but he would resist the temptation to tour for several more years, even as he continued to show up occasionally as a performer. He appeared in a 1970 television documentary focused on bluegrass banjo master Earl Scruggs, who had recently parted ways with his longtime partner, guitarist Lester Flatt. (One of Flatt and Scruggs's last albums had featured four Dylan songs; Flatt reportedly did not like this new direction Scruggs was pursuing, courting younger listeners.) In the opening scene Dylan sings "East Virginia Blues" and plays guitar in a quartet with Scruggs and his sons Gary and Randy.

Living in Greenwich Village may not have been ideal, but at least Dylan could easily make the rounds of clubs and larger music venues—old haunts like the Gaslight, where he saw his former henchman Bobby Neuwirth perform; but also the Bitter End, where he checked out Jackson Browne around the time of his first album's release; and the Fillmore East, where he caught, on various occasions, Eric Clapton (with Delaney and Bonnie), Elton John, and Frank Zappa.[34]

Dylan was now a published author as well—*Tarantula* had its official publication, finally, in November 1970. Partly because it had already circulated on the black market for over four years, the book created little stir. Reviews tended to be harsh, but they fueled discussion about Dylan's stature as a literary figure. Music critic Robert Christgau, writing in the *New York Times*, argued that Dylan was after all a performer. Citing the simpler, more condensed lyrics of Dylan's recent albums, he concluded, "More and more, Dylan asserts the value of the popular and sensual over the verbal. This book will find its way into A. J. Weberman's concordance and doubtless become a cult item, but it is a throwback. Buy his records."[35]

For those who wanted to buy his records there wouldn't be a true follow-up to *New Morning* for a few years, but there would be some new recordings in 1971. In March Dylan had Leon Russell assemble a band for a few days' work at the recently opened Blue Rock Studio in Manhattan. With Russell on piano, Jesse Ed Davis on guitar, Carl Radle on bass, and Jim Keltner on drums, Dylan recorded "Watching the River Flow," "When I Paint My Masterpiece," and a handful of covers. The hard-driving, bluesy "Watching the River Flow," which Dylan wrote in the studio, would be released as a single in June but would not quite crack the Top Forty. As Clinton Heylin notes, "Watching" reflects Dylan's lingering writer's block, or at least his awareness that he was no longer able to write the kinds of songs he had written before the motorcycle accident four years earlier.[36] Like John Lennon's "Watching the Wheels" almost a decade later, Dylan's song is about taking an extended break, though he seems less content with it than Lennon later would. Within a single verse he sounds both frustrated by his situation and resigned to it. The "when" of "When I Paint My Masterpiece" also emphasizes the distance between an unproductive present moment and a wished-for period of creativity. And yet the creativity is already evident. The imagery—of European travel, but mainly Rome—is audacious and playful: dating Botticelli's niece, dodging lions in the Colosseum, chasing wild geese on a hilltop.

Both songs would be included on his second greatest-hits collection, released in November 1971. Columbia wanted to repeat the success of the first *Greatest Hits* and get another Dylan album on store shelves while he was watching the river flow; Dylan agreed but insisted on selecting the tracks and making it a double album. To that end he enlisted Happy Traum to join him in September to record new versions of a few Basement Tapes songs that had been popularized by other artists. While it's hard to understand why he and Columbia boss Clive Davis didn't just release the Basement Tapes versions of these songs—"I Shall Be Released," "You Ain't Goin' Nowhere," and "Down in the Flood (Crash on the Levee)"—the new duet versions were welcome additions to the canon, uncluttered, unplugged, and sung with conviction. Dylan added another unreleased recording to the collection: "Tomorrow Is a Long Time," from his 1963 Town Hall concert. That lovely early song had already been covered by about a dozen artists, notably Elvis Presley in 1966 and Rod Stewart on *Every Picture Tells a Story*, an album that spent four weeks atop the *Billboard* album charts the month before *Greatest Hits Volume II* appeared.

There was no poster this time, but *Volume II* gave fans an album-side's worth of material that had not been released on a previous LP. The other "hits" were well chosen and well sequenced; they included omissions from the first collection such as "Hard Rain" and "Don't Think Twice, It's Alright" alongside the more recent "Lay Lady Lay" and "If Not for You."

Between the completion and the release of *Greatest Hits Volume II* Dylan recorded the single "George Jackson," arguably his first "finger-pointin' song" since *The Times They Are A-Changin'*. While serving time for his role in a gas station robbery, Jackson was radicalized by the racism and violence of the prison system. In early 1970 he and two other inmates were charged with murdering a guard, possibly in retaliation for an earlier killing of three Black inmates during a racially charged fight. While awaiting trial in San Quentin, Jackson led a violent escape attempt, during which he was shot and killed. He had published a book, *Soledad Brother*, about his prison experience and was aligned with the Black Panthers and Angela Davis, so his case received a good deal of media attention.

While Dylan had no direct connection to Jackson, his earlier music had reflected and inspired the revolutionary ethos of the Panthers. Huey P. Newton, the group's founder, had contacted Dylan a year earlier, expressing his appreciation—"I always tell people that we never would have gotten out the first issue of our paper, if it hadn't been for you, especially 'Ballad of a Thin Man'"[37]—and inquiring about the possibility of a benefit concert for the legal defense fund. The concert never occurred, but Dylan held on to the letter (now in the Bob Dylan Archive); despite shunning politics and activism he clearly remained attuned to systemic racial injustice and sympathetic to the Movement.

Performing at the Concert for Bangladesh with Ringo Starr, George Harrison, and (partly visible) Leon Russell.

"George Jackson" is written in the topical song tradition, Dylan siding unequivocally with Jackson and in the final verse describing the world as a prison yard where if you're not a prisoner you're a guard. It's as effective as some of his early protest songs, but, this being 1971, the subject and the circumstances had changed. Unlike Hattie Carroll (or Emmett Till or Medgar Evers), Jackson, while clearly a victim of a racist justice system, was not only an activist but a revolutionary who advocated and perpetrated violence. That may or may not be the reason, but despite scratching the *Billboard* Top Forty and despite its being a return to the protest mode for which Dylan was celebrated, "George Jackson" all but vanished from the Dylan canon not long after its release. He never performed it live and never included it on an album, although both the acoustic version and the band version (which served as the B-side) finally reappeared in 2013 on the *Side Tracks* compilation.

If "George Jackson" revealed a Dylan willing to re-engage with the fight for racial justice, his participation in George Harrison's hastily assembled Concert for Bangladesh on August 1, 1971 showed him coming off the bench for a philanthropic cause. Harrison and Ravi Shankar organized the event, an afternoon and evening show at Madison Square Garden, to raise awareness and funds for refugees displaced by the Bangladesh War of Independence. Dylan was nervous once again, to the point where even on the day of the show Harrison wasn't sure he would participate (and had been careful not to announce that he would perform). Accompanied by Harrison on electric guitar, Leon Russell on bass, and Ringo on tambourine, Dylan delivered a five-song set of old favorites for a rapturous audience: "Hard Rain," "Blowin' in the Wind," "It Takes a Lot to Laugh, It Takes a Train to Cry," "Love Minus Zero/No Limit," and "Just Like a Woman." (For the evening set he subbed "Mr. Tambourine Man" for "Love Minus Zero.") Dylan was in good voice, essentially the voice of 1964–5, with Harrison supplying unobtrusive licks between vocal lines—not exactly a challenging set, but a comforting one for both performer and audience.

On a more musically raucous occasion in late October and early November, Allen Ginsberg recruited Dylan—along with David Amram (French horn, recorder) and Happy Traum (banjo)—to be part of a makeshift band backing him on semi-improvised songs, both in a professional recording studio and on a New York public television broadcast. A few songs from a mid-November session with Dylan among the strummers would eventually be released on Ginsberg's *First Blues* album, on which the poet has an all-star band jamming behind him as he sings about flying to Puerto Rico on the "Vomit Express" and giving head to a newspaper boy. Ginsberg was thrilled to have Dylan's participation in his own singer-songwriter venture, and Dylan was apparently happy to ride along and encourage his old friend and champion. As Sean Wilentz observes, "Ginsberg would, for the rest of his life, see Dylan's work . . . as aligned with his own practice of vocalizing poetry, in a vernacular, idiomatic, self-expressive form."[38]

Dylan's final performance of 1971 actually rang in 1972, onstage with the Band, whose New Year's Eve show culminated a four-night stand at New York's Academy of Music. By this point the Band had released four studio albums; they were a fixture in the rock firmament and arguably at their peak as a live act. The New Year's Eve show was recorded for the album *Rock of Ages*, but that album would not include the four-song encore with Dylan, which became available only with the CD release of the full concert in 2013. In contrast with the Bangladesh concert, which was anchored by Dylan's acoustic guitar, this full-Band electric mini-set melded the 1966 tour with the Basement Tapes, with a bit more intensity (encore! New Year!) than the 1968 Guthrie tribute. Dylan half shouts his way through "Down in the Flood," "When I Paint My Masterpiece," and a song, he announces, they haven't played in six years (it was actually two and a half), a blistering "Like a Rolling Stone."

At the beginning of a new year Dylan, at age thirty, was entering what then seemed like middle age, even a little beyond middle age for a rock star. But with a still-adoring audience growing up along with him he remained the most respected figure in rock music, and he could electrify a crowd at Madison Square Garden or the Academy of Music. Paradoxically, despite releasing three albums in very different styles over the past three years, plus another *Greatest Hits* collection, he seemed to be in a holding pattern. He could still sell millions of albums and potentially concert tickets, but he was no longer at or even very close to the cutting edge, and he never really would be again.

9

1972–74: Resurgence

In the early weeks of 1972 Don McLean's "American Pie" topped the *Billboard* charts for four weeks and reached number two in the UK. McLean's allegory for the decline of rock and roll amidst the turbulence of the 1960s featured Bob Dylan as "the Jester" who stole the thorny crown from "the King," replacing Elvis as the center of the popular music universe. Later, as "the players tried for a forward pass," attempting to advance rock music, the Jester is "on the sidelines in a cast," a reference to Dylan's recovery from the motorcycle accident.

In the six years since the accident Dylan had been fairly productive, releasing four studio albums, a couple of singles, and a few new tracks for his second greatest-hits package, but in the public imagination he remained where McLean left him: sidelined. His creative output had decelerated considerably; he had made a few live appearances but was no longer touring; he was still revered, but he was no longer writing breathtakingly original songs.

Another hit song from 1972, Rick Nelson's "Garden Party," is a kind of anti-"American Pie." Nelson's title refers to an oldies concert at Madison Square Garden at which he performed. He was trying to move past his 1950s teen idol image with a country-rock sound and shoulder-length hair, but the audience, for whom the music died with Buddy Holly in 1959, did not approve. Nelson concludes that if he's only there to evoke memories, he'd rather drive a truck.

"Garden Party" challenges the nostalgia that underwrote McLean's hit. But like "American Pie," Nelson's song references Bob Dylan, with a "Mr. Hughes" wearing Dylan's disguise. "Howard

Hughes" was a traveling alias for George Harrison, and Nelson, Dylan, and Harrison were all friends, so Nelson seems to be gently teasing Harrison (who at the time may have been planning an album of Dylan covers) about being a little too enamored of his friend. If so, Harrison could have said the same about Nelson. Describing his own performance in "Garden Party," Nelson alludes to his 1961 hit "Hello Mary Lou": "She belongs to me." That line has two meanings: Mary Lou belongs to Nelson, and Dylan's "She Belongs to Me" had been Nelson's last Top Forty hit. Nelson had also recorded covers of "I Shall Be Released," "If You Gotta Go, Go Now," and "Love Minus Zero/No Limit." And it was clear from his new song that he had been inspired by Dylan's example, willing to be booed for following his own muse.

While neither "American Pie" nor "Garden Party" is primarily about Dylan, these references say something about Dylan's place in the popular imagination at that moment: an inspiration and a guide but also a performer who was still on the sidelines. As one indication of Dylan's low profile, Clinton Heylin's day-by-day Dylan chronicle, *A Life in Stolen Moments*, includes just four pages on 1972, in contrast with for instance 24 pages for 1965.[1]

Dylan still owned a home in Woodstock, as well as a house in the Hamptons, a ranch in Arizona, and the townhouse in Greenwich Village.[2] Occasionally he would show up at a concert in or around New York. In October he joined Doug Sahm, formerly of the Sir Douglas Quintet, in a Manhattan studio to play various instruments and provide backing vocals on the delightful *Doug Sahm and Band*—Dylan's song "Wallflower" got its first release on the album, whose cover features a cartoon illustration of the musicians, with Dylan in a wide-brimmed cowboy hat, smiling and cradling a Telecaster. Otherwise his presence on the album is subdued, in keeping with a period when he was biding his time and avoiding the spotlight.

Around the same time screenwriter Rudy Wurlitzer and Kris Kristofferson coaxed Dylan into writing music for, and then acting in, Sam Peckinpah's film *Pat Garrett and Billy the Kid*. Dylan loved Peckinpah's *Ride the High Country* and *The Wild Bunch*, and he had always been drawn to outlaw lore, from Jesse James to John Wesley Hardin(g) to Pretty Boy Floyd.[3] Coincidentally Kristofferson had worked as a janitor and gofer at Columbia's Nashville studios when Dylan recorded there—he held the bongos and cowbell in place for Kenny Buttrey on "Lay Lady Lay"—but in the early 1970s he had suddenly become famous as a country singer-songwriter, and he was now making the leap to film acting in the role of Billy. Peckinpah had no idea what a coup it was to have Dylan involved, but when Wurlitzer brought him to the set in Durango, Mexico, to play a few songs the director was floored. According to James Coburn, who played Pat Garrett, "There was just the two of them in there . . . And Bobby played three or four tunes. And Sam came out with his handkerchief in his eye: 'Goddamn kid! Who the hell is he? Who is that kid? Sign him up!'"[4]

That kid Dylan provided instrumental music for the film, aided by old associates Bruce Langhorne and Roger McGuinn, as well as Booker T. Jones, bassist Terry Paul, and drummer Jim Keltner. He also sang two songs—"Billy," which alludes to the film's plot while romanticizing the outlaw hero, and the somber "Knockin' on Heaven's Door," which plays as Slim Pickens's character, Sheriff Colin Baker, dies after a gunfight.

Jerry Fielding, the film-scoring pro who had been hired to work on the film, was not impressed. "Everybody loved it," he said of "Heaven's Door." "I thought it was shit. That was the end of me."[5] It may be Dylan's simplest song, lyrically and structurally, but the arrangement—Keltner's steady beat like a horse's walking gait; the blending of acoustic guitar strumming and Carl Fortina's harmonium; the soft, melancholy chorus of background singers; and Dylan's own understated vocal, heavy on the echo—gives it an uncanny power. And generations of listeners have found the conceit of a tough old man knockin' on heaven's door as poignant as an answer that's "blowin' in the wind."

Dylan was given the role of the appropriately named "Alias"—when asked "Alias what?" he replies, Brando-like, "Alias anything you please." A printer's apprentice who joins up with Billy, Alias has few lines, but in one memorable scene set in a general store Pat Garrett orders him to recite the labels of jars of food (spoiler: there are a lot of beans) while Garrett interrogates and then kills another member of

Billy's gang. Dylan recalled that "there wasn't any dimension to [Alias] and I was very uncomfortable in this non-role." But appearing alongside the charismatic Kristofferson as Billy and Coburn as the overbearing Garrett, Dylan's/Alias's discomfort is actually quite charming.

Life in Durango during filming was not charming. The weather was bad, a case of the flu went around, there were frequent delays, and there was little for the cast and crew, nearly all male, to do but drink.[6] Peckinpah himself drank heavily and was a demanding, erratic taskmaster. "There I was trapped deep in the heart of Mexico with some madman, ordering people around like a little king," Dylan recalled—but he also praised the director (in the same interview) as "a wonderful guy . . . an outlaw. A real hombre. Somebody from the old school."[7]

Dylan's mixed feelings about Peckinpah were probably compounded by his attempt to temporarily relocate the family to Durango during filming, an arrangement that understandably did not appeal to his wife: "She'd say to me, 'What the hell are we doing here?' It was not an easy question to answer."[8] Meanwhile Dylan witnessed the conflicts between Peckinpah and MGM, which resulted in a hastily edited theatrical version that was a commercial and critical flop. The lesson, for Dylan, was not to let producers or executives make artistic decisions: "Sam himself didn't have final control and that was the problem . . . Someone other than Sam had taken a knife to some valuable scenes."[9]

The filming stretched from late November into February, the Dylans' only break being a brief January trip to visit George and Pattie Harrison in England. Upon leaving Mexico Dylan recorded most of the soundtrack, including "Knockin' on Heaven's Door," in Los Angeles in February. At the same session Dylan recorded a spontaneous song—actually just a repeated chorus that began "Rock me Mama like a wagon wheel . . ." He never went back to it, but about 25 years later a teenager named Ketch Secor heard it on a bootleg recording and added verses; eventually his band Old Crow Medicine Show recorded it, with Dylan credited as co-writer, and it went on to become an inescapable bar-band request, the "Free Bird" of the twenty-first century.

After recording *Pat Garrett and Billy the Kid*, Bob and Sara decided to stay in California, renting a house in Malibu and then buying property near Zuma Beach. Working with architect David Tobin, they began constructing an elaborate, sprawling mansion whose most prominent design feature was a gigantic onion dome.[10]

In May a photograph of Dylan on the set of *Pat Garrett and Billy the Kid* appeared on the back cover of *Writings and Drawings*, essentially his collected lyrics and liner notes, with Dylan's own illustrations that tended to be comically literal references to song and album titles. (For *Bringing It All Back Home* Dylan drew a man struggling to carry an impossibly large pile of indistinct objects, plus a bicycle, with a small house in the distance.) To have (nearly) all of Dylan's lyrics in a single book was a big deal. He had never included them on his album sleeves or as inserts; the practice had been unheard of prior to *Sgt. Pepper*, mainly because sheet music was big business and printing lyrics on inner sleeves was seen as giving away something publishers wanted to sell. By 1973 the industry had changed along with the singer-songwriter movement, providing lyrics for albums by Simon and Garfunkel, Leonard Cohen, James Taylor, Carole King, Joni Mitchell, and others, but Dylan would continue to hold out until, oddly enough, the live album *At Budokan* in 1978.

The publication of a handsome collection of lyrics seemed like a statement, a claim to higher literary merit, so it revived the question of Dylan's status as a poet. Reviewing the book for the *New York Times* Albert Goldman acknowledged that the lyrics were meant to be performed rather than read before commenting at length on how flat they fall on the printed page: "They sputter and stutter with the clumsiness and monotony of bad beat poetry, phony folksongs, home-made surrealism and sentimental, side-of-the-mouth valentine verse."[11] Clive James in *The Guardian* was gentler but made essentially the same argument: "It's only by keeping the sound of the song in one's head that one can refrain from blaming the lyric for formal lapses which are in fact part of its fluent strength: the real formal lapses aren't in the fake-naïve syntax, which is nearly always eminently singable, but in the aberrant diction and slap-dash construction."[12] Both Goldman and James point to "Blowin' in the

Wind" as an example of a lyric that appears trite on the page—and maybe they have a point. And yet both critics carefully make the distinction between song lyrics and poetry but then proceed to critique Dylan's song lyrics *as poetry*. Perhaps by issuing his "writings" as a handsome hardback book with a distinguished publishing house (Knopf) Dylan left himself open to this kind of criticism. At the same time he sold a lot of books, and he did the book his own way, right down to the drawings.

Dylan had relocated to Malibu at a time when Los Angeles was arguably supplanting New York as the nation's cultural capital—a shift chronicled by Ronald Brownstein in *Rock Me on the Water: 1974, The Year Los Angeles Transformed Movies, Music, Television, and Politics*. The opening scene of Brownstein's book is a party for David Geffen, attended by (among others) Warren Beatty, Jack Nicholson, Ringo Starr, Harry Nilsson, Bianca Jagger, and promoter Bill Graham; it also featured an impromptu performance by Bob Dylan and the Band, along with Cher, who was dating Geffen at the time. The previous year Geffen had strategically befriended Robbie Robertson and through him Dylan.[13]

Following Robertson's and Dylan's leads the other members of the Band moved from Woodstock to Los Angeles in 1973, adding to a list of transplanted musicians that also included Joni Mitchell, Linda Ronstadt, Jackson Browne, and the Eagles.[14] All four of those acts recorded for Geffen's Asylum label, which had become synonymous with the Southern California musical zeitgeist. When Neil Young inaugurated the Roxy, a new Sunset Strip theater co-owned by Geffen, Dylan attended with Geffen and Robertson.

With the possible exception of the Rolling Stones (who had already partnered with Geffen's mentor Ahmet Ertegun at Atlantic Records), there was no greater trophy artist than Bob Dylan for someone out to conquer the music industry, and Dylan happened to be near the end of a contract with Columbia. He agreed to record an album with the Band for Asylum and—the big news—tour with them, producing an additional live album from the tour. Geffen and Bill Graham would join forces to promote what became known, unimaginatively, as Tour '74.

The reuniting of Dylan and the Band was mutually beneficial. The Band was still very popular, but they were in a creative slump, fueled by substance abuse and infighting. Their late 1973 album *Moondog Matinee* was a half-hearted covers collection, and their previous studio album, 1971's *Cahoots*, had been met with lukewarm reviews. According to Levon Helm, Dylan "knew that The Band was not in great shape, and he wanted to help us out of the sense of goodness he felt for us. Bob could've had his pick, but he chose us out of loyalty."[15] It's true that Dylan could have had his pick, but there was no band he felt as comfortable with—it was after all the Band with whom he had confronted the world with hard rock, then developed new songs and a new sound at Big Pink, and returned to the stage for the Woody Guthrie tribute and Isle of Wight performance.

Along with the success of "Knockin' on Heaven's Door," which was a Top Twenty hit in the USA and UK that fall, the reunion with the Band and return to touring signaled a comeback. Dylan was still in a bit of a songwriting drought, but he came up with enough new material for an album whose working title, *Ceremonies of the Horseman*, alluded to a song from his creative peak, "Love Minus Zero/No Limit." Dylan recalled writing "about twelve or fifteen songs in about three days," and the album was recorded in about a week.[16]

No producer is listed on the album sleeve, but Rob Fraboni, credited as engineer, oversaw the sessions, negotiating with Dylan and Robertson on the major decisions. That informal arrangement reflects the recording process itself, Dylan's preferred method of working quickly with little preparation and few overdubs—inspired, fresh playing taking precedence over technical precision.

"We'd run through 'em once, and then Bob wanted to cut," said Helm. And that worked just fine—the album, which Dylan retitled *Planet Waves*, has the Band's trademark warm but hard-edged sound, a rock album that proudly lets its roots (country, blues, swing, gospel) show through. Garth Hudson's accordion on the opener, "On a Night Like This," defines the song more than Dylan's lyrics. In his draft of the liner notes, Dylan wrote of the song, "This brings back the old polka days for me. Beer halls & pin balls. Land of 1000 lakes. Of fat gals dancing with smeared lips doing the hula & the dirty can-can . . ."[17]

"Going, Going, Gone" is about reaching a point of no return, perhaps reflecting Dylan's state of mind as he prepared to go back on tour. Robbie Robertson tests the limits of the whammy bar and the end of each verse, a sonic refrain that lets you know the singer really is gone. *Planet Waves* may be the only album in Dylan's catalog on which he seems to be *in* a band—the singer, the songwriter, the leader, but still one of the band rather than a solo artist with a backing band. That's partly because the Band is a confident, assertive unit, not a bunch of hired studio musicians, and because Dylan had established such a strong rapport with them. But it's also because the lyrics don't demand our attention—it's even more true than on *New Morning* that these are (mostly) songs plenty of other people could have written.

But of course other people *didn't* write them, and in some cases the songs resonate more with listeners simply because the words come from Dylan. The album's most personal-sounding songs are the diametrically opposed "Dirge" and "Wedding Song," the only songs recorded without the Band. The "Dirge" is for a love that's died—the singer hates himself for the "weakness" of having loved whoever he's singing to. He seems to be trying to convince himself that he's moved on. There is little in the song to suggest that the "love" was romantic though—as with "Like a Rolling Stone" and "Positively 4th Street," "Dirge" vents its anger at an unspecified target, possibly a former friend or an amalgam of people who attract him but hold him back.[18] "Wedding Song," which closes the album, is an expression of gratitude and devotion clearly written for Sara—a sweet gesture, but rather mechanical in its execution.

The album's most enduring song manages to be both personal and universal. Dylan wrote "Forever Young" for his children, in the form of a blessing. As such it's conventional enough, but the overarching sentiment—stay young in spirit—jibes with the outlook Dylan had professed throughout his early career, most memorably in "The Times They Are A-Changin'" and "My Back Pages" but also in interviews and the infamous Emergency Civil Liberties Committee speech. The wish that you stay forever young is appropriately dedicated to children, but it struck a chord with Dylan's generation, who were having kids of their own and confronting the pressures of adulthood in their late twenties and early thirties. Like other great songwriters of the period—Paul Simon, Jackson Browne, Joni Mitchell—Dylan was reflecting on that transition: how do you hold on to the sense of freedom and possibility when your life becomes increasingly part of a network of responsibilities? "Forever Young" doesn't really delve into that question, but the song is a wish for some kind of answer.

Tellingly Dylan almost left "Forever Young" off the album because of an offhand remark—suggesting that he must be getting old—made by a visitor to the studio. A friend of Dylan's boyhood pal Louie Kemp asked Bob, "Are you getting mushy in your old age?"[19] Dylan didn't want to hear that, but luckily Rob Fraboni persuaded him to keep the song. There still remained the question of which "Forever Young" to use. With several takes to choose from, very different feels and tempos, they settled on the idea of closing side one with the now-familiar slow, solemn version, and opening side two with a shorter, up-tempo arrangement, making the song a kind of hinge to the album. (A third distinct version, a solo demo, provides a touching final track of the 1985 *Biograph* box set.) Although it was not released as a single "Forever Young" joined the list of Dylan anthems, included on every subsequent "best of" collection and in hundreds of his concert setlists.

With Dylan now recording for Asylum, Columbia released what has come to be known as the "revenge album," a collection of covers left over from the *Self Portrait* and *New Morning* sessions. As if to call him out, his old record company titled the album simply *Dylan*. Although there might not be much difference conceptually between Dylan performing, say, "Big Yellow Taxi" (which is on *Dylan*) as opposed to "The Boxer" or "Early Morning Rain" (which are on *Self Portrait*), the cover versions on *Dylan* seem charmless and dull compared to those on the earlier album. Besides, the context is different: this time it's not Dylan deliberately pushing boundaries (or his audience's buttons) but his former record company making a quick buck with recordings he did not want released. While not quite unlistenable, *Dylan* is correctly deemed by most fans the worst official LP in his catalogue. Despite terrible reviews, it achieved gold record status and cracked the top twenty on *Billboard*'s album charts—it was, after all, *Dylan*.

Dylan and the Band spent the last weeks of the year rehearsing for Tour '74, which kicked off in Chicago on January 3. Geffen and Bill Graham set up a mail-in (pay-in-advance) lottery system for tickets, which generated hype, allowing them to boast that 5 million people were vying for 650,000 seats. Dylan was on the cover of not only *Rolling Stone* (for the sixth time) but *Newsweek* (with a banner reading "Dylan's Back!"). The excitement was genuine, since Dylan hadn't toured since 1966 and was reunited with one of the best rock groups on the planet.

Over six weeks they played forty concerts in 21 cities (sometimes performing an afternoon and evening show), hitting every region of the country. There were celebrity sightings, especially in New York (John and Yoko, Miles Davis) and Los Angeles (Warren Beatty, Jack Nicholson, Ringo). In Atlanta Jimmy Carter invited Dylan and the Band to the Governor's Mansion, where Carter quoted Dylan's lyrics from memory and Dylan, in a private conversation, asked Carter what his Christian faith meant to him.[20] (Levon Helm recalled fondly that Rosalynn Carter made them breakfast and that Bob "enjoyed a good southern breakfast with the Carters as much as any of us."[21])

The shows were generous, consistently over two hours, opening with Dylan fronting the Band on half a dozen songs; a similar-length set from just the Band; then another, brief Dylan/Band set followed by several songs performed by Dylan solo and about four more songs from the Band before Dylan rejoined them for the finale. Dylan's song selection was career-spanning and crowd-pleasing. "Most Likely You'll Go Your Way and I'll Go Mine" established itself as the opener about a week into the tour and for a while closed the set as well, an old-fashioned bookend reprise. "Lay Lady Lay," "Rainy Day Women #12 & 35," "It Ain't Me, Babe," "Ballad of a Thin Man," "All Along the Watchtower," "Knockin' on Heaven's Door," "The Times They Are A-Changin'," "Don't Think Twice, It's Alright," "Highway 61 Revisited," and "Like a Rolling Stone" were regularly featured, with a full-band "Blowin' in the Wind" as an encore. Meanwhile *Planet Waves* shot up the charts, reaching number one in the USA just as the tour wrapped up in mid-February, but most shows featured only two or three songs from the album, "Forever Young" being the mainstay.

On stage at Boston Garden with the Band, January 1974. Photo by Peter Simon.

With the exception of Dylan's five-song solo set it was a full-on rock show, with mostly new arrangements of songs that were already considered classics. The approach wasn't as heavy or as caustic as the 1966 shows (which had Mickey Jones pummeling the drum kit), but this was still an aggressive sound that could fill large arenas, with Dylan semi-shouting most of the lyrics. In the midst of the Watergate scandal (Nixon would resign that August) the line from "It's Alright, Ma" about the president having to stand naked always got a surge of applause, as it has ever since. And audience members began a practice that soon became standard at big rock concerts, holding up matches and cigarette lighters like candles when the houselights went down.

While Dylan and the Band were playing much like they had when they were booed in 1966, this time they were received with worshipful applause. There was no "shock of the new" in the music or sense of betrayal—after all in 1974 the Band's style represented mainstream rock, and Dylan hadn't made a solo acoustic album in ten years. There was no sense of confrontation, but neither was there a feeling of risk or intimacy at these arena shows.

Daniel Mark Epstein, who saw the tour at Madison Square Garden, later wrote in his Dylan biography, "[T]he show was fascinating—full of rage, terror, and ironic humor—but it was pitiless, lacking the pathos everyone knew was in the blood of the songs themselves." Paul Williams, also recognizing the almost manic energy of the performance, described Dylan's vocal delivery on "Most Likely You Go Your Way" as fulfilling the "non-relationship" of the song's title, "as if to say, 'I want to make it clear that you [audience] and I really have no connection with each other, and as long as we remember this we can have a good time here tonight.'"[22]

The audience, the performers, and the rituals of concertgoing and touring had changed. Journalist Lucian Truscott IV reported that fans "lit up $40-an-ounce grass, snorted $75-a-gram coke, flashed gold rings and fancy platform boots, wore prefaded jeans and enough Indian jewelry to have bought Wounded Knee . . . and shelled out upwards of $100 to scalpers [face value was typically $8.50–$9.50] for tickets."[23]

For their part Dylan and the Band saw a big payday, and, Helm recalls, "We lived and travelled like six kings amid the excesses of all that mid-seventies rock and roll money: the fastest jet, the longest limos, the biggest suites, tons of white powder." But he also remembered the exhaustion that came with it: "The amount of energy that playing for those big audiences required was incredible. I know I felt wrung out like a sponge."[24] Dylan did not recall Tour '74 fondly: "I wasn't comfortable and I wasn't happy," he said. He later reflected, "I think I was just playing a role on that tour . . . I was playing Bob Dylan and The Band was playing The Band. It was all kind of mindless. The people that came out to see us came mostly to see what they missed the first time around . . . We were cleaning up but it was an emotionless trip."[25]

Something else bothered Dylan about Tour '74: "I wasn't really in control of the situation," he recalled about two years later. "Nobody was in control. We were just shuffled around from airport to limo to hotel lobby to hockey rinks. I felt like Willis Reed [the great New York Knicks center]. And in order for me to do whatever it is that I do, I have to have control and I didn't have too much control on that specific tour."[26] He had been there before, under Grossman's management prior to the motorcycle accident, and more recently he had seen Peckinpah lose control over his own film. Dylan was returning more fully to a business where many people would try to manipulate him, limiting his artistic and contractual freedom. He was determined to regain that freedom, in the form of legal control.

He performed at the birthday party for Geffen a week after the tour ended in February, but the album-to-album contract with Asylum didn't last. *Before the Flood*, the double live album commemorating the tour, would be released on Geffen's label in June, but in August Dylan re-signed with Columbia. In addition to a better royalty he gained control of the master tapes of his previous albums.[27]

The tour was a turning point in other respects. Dylan would never again stay off the road for as long (almost eight years) as he had before Tour '74. His marriage might have been under stress before, but for the most part he had been a family man during the non-touring years; that would now change as well. And whether the tour or something else was responsible, he would enter a new, highly creative phase in the mid-seventies.

That spring, while his mansion was being built in Malibu, Dylan returned to New York and for several weeks focused his attention on painting. His interest in visual art had grown over the years. After making the cover art for the Band's first album in 1968 he had created his own covers for *Self Portrait* and *Planet Waves*, and he had also added drawings (mocked by some reviewers) to his collection of lyrics. Friends had told him about a painter, teacher, and philosopher named Norman Raeben, who happened to be the son of Sholom Aleichem, the Yiddish writer whose stories provided the basis for *Fiddler on the Roof*. Raeben conducted small classes daily in a studio on the eleventh floor of Carnegie Hall, lecturing and berating students as they stood at their easels. He apparently didn't recognize Dylan when he showed up one day and certainly didn't treat him differently than the other aspiring artists ("rich old ladies from Florida—standing next to an off-duty policeman, standing next to a bus driver, a lawyer. Just all kinds," according to Dylan.)[28]

Dylan did not suddenly start painting masterpieces, but he credited Raeben with changing his artistic vision and even how he thought about himself. He told a reporter a few years later, "I had met magicians, but this guy is more powerful than any magician I've ever met. He looked into you and told you what you were. And he didn't play games about it . . . After that I wrote *Blood on the Tracks*."[29] He told another interviewer that Raeben "put my mind and my hand and my eye together in a way that allowed me to do consciously what I unconsciously felt."[30]

Raeben's teaching would have a profound effect on Dylan's songwriting, but it also contributed to his emotional estrangement from Sara Dylan, as he acknowledged: "I went home after [Raeben's classes] and my wife never did understand me ever since that day. That's when our marriage started breaking up."[31] Dylan had a secret affair with one of the other students in Raeben's class, and a more open one with Ellen Bernstein, who worked in A&R (artists and repertoire) for Columbia Records.[32] Bernstein was single and, at 24, nine years Dylan's junior. Throughout the summer they spent weekends at Dylan's farm in Minnesota, near his brother David Zimmerman's house. "He had a painting studio out in the field, and the house was far from fancy, out in the middle of nowhere," Bernstein told biographer Clinton Heylin. "He was very relaxed, and that's where and when he was writing *Blood on the Tracks*."

Dylan's songwriting "amnesia" had suddenly ended. Over the course of the summer he wrote more than enough songs for an album—many of them lyrically complex and long, with seven or more verses. He worked hard on them, playing them for Bernstein, revising and recopying them. His small, spiral-bound notebooks from that year have become holy relics, housed in the Morgan Library in New York and the Bob Dylan Archive in Tulsa. The red notebook owned by the Morgan contains fair copies of most of the songs that made it onto *Blood on the Tracks*, including three versions of "Idiot Wind" and several others that he didn't record (including notably "Church Bell Blues" and "Don't Want No Married Woman").[33]

Dylan was excited enough about his new songs to play them for musician friends on several occasions. Crosby, Stills and Nash, bluegrass guitarist Peter Rowan, bassist Tim Drummond and guitarist Michael Bloomfield were among those who got a preview. Dylan had been blown away by Bloomfield's blues chops when they played together at Newport and on *Highway 61 Revisited*, and he may have been auditioning him to play on the new record. But according to Bloomfield Dylan made it impossible:

> He took out his guitar, he tuned to open D tuning and he started playing the songs nonstop! . . . [H]e was selling the whole thing and I was saying, "No man, don't sing the whole thing, just sing one chorus and if it's not gonna change let me write it down so I can play with you." And he didn't. He just kept on playing[;] he just did one after another and I got lost; they all began to sound the same to me, they were all in the same key, they were all long, I don't know, it was one of the strangest experiences of my life. And it really hurt me.[34]

The songs Dylan wouldn't let Bloomfield play were chronicles of love that didn't last. Discussing *Blood on the Tracks* in a radio interview with Mary Travers a few months after its release he said, "A lot of people tell me they enjoy that album. It's hard for me to relate to that—people enjoying that kind of pain, you know?"[35] At other times Dylan bristled at the suggestion that the songs on *Blood on the Tracks* were autobiographical, even claiming in *Chronicles* that they were based on Chekhov stories (which is probably not true, but it kind of works). It's probably best not to obsess over the autobiographical correspondences of the songs—I take the Chekhov dodge as a reminder that the songs are ultimately works of fiction—but it's fair to say that these tracks reflect the "kind of pain" that Dylan experienced and caused in his relationships.

Having workshopped the songs through the late summer, on September 16 Dylan returned to the studio where he had made his first six albums—Columbia's Studio A, now under new ownership and renamed A&R Studios. Over three days he recorded and re-recorded twelve new songs, experimenting with the musical settings—first solo acoustic, then a full band (Deliverance, named for the film that had made a star of their leader, multi-instrumentalist Eric Weissberg)—and then settling in with just bassist Tony Brown and

Dylan on acoustic guitar and harmonica.[36] As he had done with past studio bands (and more recently with Michael Bloomfield), Dylan gave little to no guidance before recording.

Keyboard player Tom McFaul remembered, "There was virtually no rehearsal. Dylan would play part of a song, then he'd say, 'It's got a bridge, like any other bridge, you'll get it'; then we would record."[37] They got multiple good takes of four songs, but "Meet Me in the Morning" would be the only Deliverance track to make the final cut. Dylan found the sound he wanted with just Brown on bass and occasionally McFaul on keyboards. Working with engineer Phil Ramone he selected takes of ten songs (eliminating "Call Letter Blues" and "Up to Me"). Except for the hard-edged blues "Meet Me in the Morning," the arrangements were spare and quiet—some organ on a couple of tracks, a little steel guitar on "You're a Big Girl Now," but otherwise either solo ("Lily, Rosemary and the Jack of Hearts") or just Dylan and Brown.

The album had been recorded and mastered quickly, but Columbia's pressing plants were backed up, and the release date was pushed to the new year. For better or worse that gave Dylan time to reconsider the arrangements: "I hadn't listened to it for a couple of months . . . The record still hadn't come out, and I put it on. I thought the songs could have sounded different, better, so I went in and rerecorded them."[38] Once again Dylan was asserting creative control.

The slightly longer version of the story is that in December, when he visited his farm in Minnesota for the holidays, Dylan played an acetate of the album for his brother David, who produced and recorded music for TV and radio. David told him that the sound wasn't exactly radio-friendly. Taking his brother's advice Dylan allowed him to recruit some of Minneapolis's top studio players for two days of sessions, during which they re-recorded five of the songs: "Idiot Wind," "You're a Big Girl Now," "Tangled Up in Blue," "Lily, Rosemary and the Jack of Hearts," and "If You See Her, Say Hello." All five of these Minneapolis remakes replaced the more austere versions Dylan had recorded with Tony Brown and Tom McFaul. The Minneapolis band handled their assignment well—the album did become more radio-friendly, and it's hard to imagine a world where their version of "Tangled Up in Blue" doesn't exist. On the other hand many insiders and fans who heard the album as originally planned (it was of course widely bootlegged before the New York sessions were officially released in 2018) were baffled by Dylan's decision, mainly because his vocal performance on the original sessions was so raw and expressive. Joni Mitchell's later assessment, for instance, was that "He took the vulnerability out of [*Blood on the Tracks*], and in the process he took the depth out."[39]

That seems like an overstatement: the *Blood on the Tracks* that has sold over 2 million copies and continues to make every greatest-albums-of-all-time list is undeniably a masterpiece. And yet, when you listen to the New York versions of the re-recorded songs—"Idiot Wind," "You're a Big Girl Now," and "If You See Her, Say Hello" especially—you realize it would have been even better if Columbia had gotten the album pressed before the end of 1974.

Whether inspired by his marital crisis, competition from Mitchell and other confessional singer-songwriters, or the conceptual breakthrough he experienced with Norman Raeben, Dylan's new songs were unlike anything he had written before. One of his best and most beloved songs, "Tangled Up in Blue," most clearly demonstrates the impact of Raeben's teaching.

"I guess I was trying to make it like a painting where you can see the different parts but then you also see the whole of it," Dylan later explained. The version that Dylan recorded in New York began in third person and shifted to first person, whereas the Minneapolis version is all "I," but both versions are actually a series of disconnected vignettes in which "I," "he," and "she" may or may not be the same person from one verse to the next. Specific places are mentioned—in one verse the great north woods, New Orleans, and Delacroix; in another Montague Street—but specific times are not. One stanza features a "topless place" with a spotlight, suggesting the recent past, but two stanzas later a reference to slave-dealing denotes a more historically distant setting. And yet the man and woman involved in each encounter somehow seem to be the same man and woman, suggesting that all of these stories of chance meetings, ill-fated romances, hookups, and break-ups are essentially the same story. (The fluidity of the situations described in "Tangled" is multiplied by the fluidity of the lyrics themselves. Not only did Dylan make changes between New York and Minneapolis in 1974; he has continued rewriting the song ever since, most dramatically on his 1984 tour.)

Like a classic Frank Sinatra concept album—*In the Wee Small Hours*, *Only the Lonely*, *No One Cares*—*Blood on the Tracks* dwells on lost love. "Simple Twist of Fate" (another song whose lyrics Dylan has repeatedly revised) describes either a one-night stand or a breakup, but the refrain suggests regret that "fate" prevented a more lasting relationship. As in some versions of "Tangled Up in Blue," here the third-person perspective switches to first-person, suggesting that the "he" we've been observing has really been "I" all along. The song was at least partly inspired by memories of Suze Rotolo—the parenthetical title in the red notebook was "4th Street Affair," and on one occasion (in 1981) Dylan referred to "Suze" while performing the song.[40] But really we learn nothing about the woman in the song, which is focused from the beginning on the man's feeling of emptiness and abandonment.

Other songs add variations on the theme of lost love. "You're Gonna Make Me Lonesome When You Go," inspired by Ellen Bernstein, comes close to being an upbeat breakup song—upbeat possibly because it was Dylan who actually controlled the terms of that relationship.[41] In fact the song is closer to a traditional love song, a celebration of an affair, than a lamentation over its end. The refrain simply provides perspective—this fulfilling relationship isn't going to last. "If You See Her, Say Hello" is an updated "Girl from the North Country" and perhaps the most beautiful and heartbreaking song on the album, partly because it's one of the most melodic but also because the singer's regret is so direct and genuine. Unlike those two songs, "You're a Big Girl Now" wallows in heartache, one minute desperately pleading for another chance, the next minute pointing an accusing finger at the unfaithful lover.

The singer has only fondness and gratitude for the woman who provides "Shelter from the Storm," but here too the relationship was impermanent, and the song is partly a reflection on what went wrong. It's a seemingly ancient story: the song's title is taken from a prophecy in the Book of Isaiah, the shelter being a pavilion on Mount Zion for the survivors of Israel. As in "Tangled Up in Blue," it may be that the

"I" and "she" are not confined to a single place and time—the first words of the song in fact refer to another lifetime. In two separate stanzas the singer is either Christ or a Christ-like figure, with a crown of thorns and soldiers gambling for his clothes. In whatever guise he takes the singer is persecuted, living in times of "toil and blood." It's in this fallen world, during perhaps multiple lives of trouble and persecution, that he needs the emotional shelter she provides. But he's on his own again at the end of the song, wishing he could go back in time "to when God and her were born."

"Lily, Rosemary and the Jack of Hearts" is a cinematic story song, set in a Wild West town with a hanging judge, a cabaret, bank robbers, card games, and, improbably, a diamond mine. The Jack of Hearts, whose name ends every verse, is the essential character—both Lily and Rosemary love him and hate "Big Jim," the man who controls them both. The Jack of Hearts is a lover but also a thief, the leader of the gang who break into the bank's safe. The song is a frolic, but in keeping with the album's theme of love's hazards it ends with Big Jim dead, Rosemary about to be hanged for his murder, and Lily still thinking about the Jack of Hearts, the object of desire, who is paradoxically "the only person on the scene missing."

But the album's most searing track, also presumed to be the most confessional, is "Idiot Wind," its title borrowed from Norman Raeben's stream of verbal abuse.[42] No song changed as much in Minneapolis as this one. Dylan revised about half the verses, but what really transformed the song was the full-band arrangement and a vocal delivery that went from being primarily pensive and somber to being, above all, angry. "Idiot Wind" begins as a story-song, perhaps an outlaw ballad, but it soon becomes a one-sided account of a failed relationship, directed at the former partner. Like a Symbolist poet Dylan braids together decontextualized images that convey personal anger, confusion, and pain. On the Minneapolis version he says that he's sorry that he'll never really know her pain, and yet it's on the New York version that he actually *sounds* sorrowful, even though he doesn't say it. In either version "Idiot Wind" is the emotional core of the album, the song that tracks closest to Dylan's comment about people "enjoying that kind of pain."

Columbia released *Blood on the Tracks* on January 17, 1975. The front cover featured a heavily manipulated photograph of Dylan taken about a year earlier, during the tour with the Band. The drab colors and pointillist effect of the image heighten the sense that Dylan, wearing dark glasses and showing no expression, is once again inscrutable—no more smiling country singer doffing his hat. The back cover went through three iterations, due partly to the fact that Pete Hamill, who wrote the liner notes, quoted lines from the test pressing of "If You See Her, Say Hello" that Dylan changed in Minneapolis.

Hamill's essay, which won a Grammy, is an encomium to Dylan that situates him as a survivor of Vietnam War-era America and a visionary poet: "To enter [his] envisioned world is like plunging deep into a mountain pool, where the rocks are clear and smooth at the bottom." A display ad that Columbia ran in *Rolling Stone* played up Dylan's legend while establishing *Blood on the Tracks* as the ultimate confessional singer-songwriter album:

> Now, suddenly, here's this startlingly *exposed* figure standing in the sunlight. Could this be "the real Bob Dylan"? We still can't know.
>
> But we do know there's something profoundly different about this album.
>
> We don't know what change has come about in Dylan's life. Maybe he doesn't. In any case, he isn't saying.
>
> But there's evidence. And you can judge for yourself.[43]

There *was* something profoundly different about the album, as evidenced by glowing reviews and strong sales—it was Dylan's second consecutive number-one studio LP in the USA. With the last line of "Up to Me," another outstanding song that was originally slated to close *Blood on the Tracks*, Dylan sings that no one else could have played his tune: "you know it was up to me." And in fact he was once again writing and playing songs that no one else could create.

10

1975–78: Revelation

The marital discord that lay beneath *Blood on the Tracks* would continue for two more years after the album's release, fueled by Dylan's serial infidelity. As he matter-of-factly explained to an interviewer in 1978, "[Y]ou meet a lot of people that are attracted to you, and also you become attracted to quite a few people, and you can't really be sure many times whether that's true or not, so you just have to let the situation run its course."[1] Before divorcing in 1977 the couple went through periodic reconciliations. They were still building a family mansion (the design kept changing) at Point Dume in Malibu, and they appeared in public together occasionally, for instance in March 1975 when Dylan performed at a benefit for SNACK (Students Need Athletic and Cultural Kicks) in San Francisco and at Paul McCartney's launch for the album *Venus and Mars* on the *Queen Mary* in Long Beach. In May Dylan spent about two weeks in the South of France with David Oppenheim, whose artwork was featured on the back cover of *Blood on the Tracks*.[2] Dylan called Sara every day, but according to Oppenheim, "We lived an adventurous life. No complications. We screwed women, we drank, we ate . . ."[3]

Dylan spent most of the summer of 1975 back in New York, carousing with old friends and making new ones. His base of operations was the Bitter End nightclub, which had recently re-opened as the Other End. When Patti Smith played there in late June Dylan showed up and chatted awkwardly with her, beginning what would become a lifelong friendship. Smith, like Dylan about a dozen years earlier, was now an underground sensation in New York, about to break out nationally; she would record her debut album, *Horses*, later that summer. Dylan also sat in with Ramblin' Jack Elliott at the Other End and then tried out a little new material, notably the ominous breakup song "Abandoned Love."

On another night, driving through the East Village, he spotted a young woman with long black hair carrying a violin. He pulled over and asked her if she could play it. The violinist, Scarlet Rivera, came along to Dylan's loft and played with him for about an hour, at which point he asked if she would like to go hear a friend of his. "We jumped back in his car, went a few minutes away to the club The Bottom Line," Rivera recalled. "His friend that was playing was Muddy Waters. I was expecting to watch the whole show from the bar. He went up and did one song with Muddy. At the end of that song, he went to the microphone and said, 'Now I want to bring up my violinist.'"[4] Rivera passed this very public audition, and her violin would become the distinctive new voice on Dylan's next album.

Dylan's old running partner Bob Neuwirth played a series of shows at the Other End that July, often with Dylan in attendance, sometimes onstage. Other musicians made their way to the club to play with Neuwirth, who was unofficially assembling a band for a tour he and Dylan were planning. David Mansfield, a multi-instrumentalist who was just nineteen at the time, was among the musicians who were being auditioned and recruited; he reported that "most of the people who'd played with Bobby [Neuwirth] ended up playing with Bob Dylan. The stage at The Bitter End was so crowded you could barely find a place to stand."[5]

Meanwhile Dylan had struck up a friendship with Jacques Levy, whose claims to fame at that point were co-writing a few songs that appeared on the Byrds' 1970 album *Untitled* and directing the risqué off-Broadway revue *Oh! Calcutta!* One evening Levy ran into Dylan on his way to the Other End and joined him for a drink; before the night was over they were collaborating. Unlike many songwriting teams Dylan and Levy literally wrote together, each contributing lines to the songs and bouncing ideas off each other. Eventually Levy would type them up and Dylan would revise. To escape the distractions of the city they retreated for part of the summer to Dylan's house in the

Hamptons, where, according to Levy, they completed about fourteen songs together.[6]

Columbia released *The Basement Tapes* that June, giving Dylan his second critical and commercial triumph within six months. Dylan seemed to take little interest in the preparation or release of the eight-year-old *Tapes*, but he was soon ready to record the songs he and Levy had just written. The first, unsuccessful attempt came on July 14 with members of singer-guitarist Dave Mason's band. Then two weeks later Dylan and his new producer, Don DeVito, invited somewhere between fifteen and twenty musicians to the studio, all at once, including no fewer than five guitarists (one of whom was Eric Clapton). Predictably the studio was too crowded and the proceedings too unfocused to accomplish anything, and after two unproductive sessions Dylan had only one take ("Romance in Durango") that would make it onto the album.

He asked bass player Rob Stoner, "What would you do if this was your session?" Stoner recalls telling him, "I would send everybody home. Come back fresh tomorrow night with a much smaller group." Dylan took Stoner's advice: the group for the July 30 session consisted of Stoner, drummer Howie Wyeth, Rivera, singer Emmylou Harris, and, on percussion, Sheena Seidenberg. No electric guitar—the only solo instruments would be violin and harmonica. The smaller band clicked, and they recorded the rest of the album (plus several good takes of songs that wouldn't make the cut) over the next two nights.

True to form, Dylan provided little preparation or guidance for the band. "There were times when I didn't even know I was supposed to come in and had to jump fast," recalled Harris. Wyeth, who got the last-minute call on Stoner's recommendation, was at a particular disadvantage. He told biographer Clinton Heylin,

> [Dylan] wouldn't even tell us the names of the tunes . . . the first song we started to do—I had just barely met him—I think they were recording it, we played the song and we sort of fumbled the ending . . . He said, "Okay, we're gonna do that again." And I said, "Bob, are we gonna end this or is it gonna be a fade?" And he went into such a lengthy explanation, he went on and

> on, that everybody got so confused, it ended up we didn't even do the song [again]. He said, "Let's not even do it." And Stoner said, "Don't ask him anything. Just play."[7]

But once again Dylan's method—prioritizing spontaneity by deliberately not preparing the other musicians—paid off. You can hear just a trace of uncertainty and a little extra room in the groove, but it provides the tension that gives the band its unique sound. Stoner and Wyeth were very much in sync; the space created by the absence of electric guitars brought Stoner's melodic bass lines to the forefront, and Wyeth did not shy away from adding aggressive fills between vocal lines, especially leading into choruses. Sheena Seidenberg's percussion and Rivera's violin provide a lot of what's often referred to as the band's "Gypsy" sound. And the contrast between Dylan's voice, which often strains against the melody, and Harris's clear, effortlessly perfect pitch, like a second violin, adds to the exotic feel of the album, which would be called *Desire*.

Levy later identified storytelling as the strength he brought to the songwriting partnership, and to a great extent *Desire* is an album of story-songs. The most significant of the Dylan-Levy narratives at the time was "Hurricane," which Dylan was inspired to write after reading Rubin "Hurricane" Carter's book, *The Sixteenth Round*. Carter, a professional middleweight boxer, and his friend John Artis had been convicted for a triple murder in Paterson, New Jersey, in 1966. After key witnesses recanted their testimony against Carter and Artis in 1974, freelance writer Richard Solomon and advertising executive George Lois (who coincidentally had designed the 1965 *Esquire* cover combining the faces of Dylan, Malcom X, Castro, and JFK) founded a committee to campaign for Carter's retrial, sending copies of *The Sixteenth Round* to influential people—like Dylan. Thus the case was becoming a cause célèbre in the summer of 1975, and Jacques Levy was already well aware of Carter when Dylan told him he wanted to write a song about the case.

Dylan recorded versions of "Hurricane" on three successive nights in late July, but Columbia's lawyers were worried about being sued over the lyrics—most conspicuously the song's original version had witnesses Alfred Bello and Arthur Dexter Bradley robbing the *bodies* of the murder victims, when in fact they had only confessed to robbing the cash register in the bar.[8] (Other inaccuracies such as inflating Carter's standing as the top contender for the middleweight title were legally less problematic.) The rewritten version that was released as a single and included on *Desire* was recorded in an all-night session on October 24, almost three months after the rest of the album, with Wyeth, Stoner, Seidenberg, and singer-actress Ronee Blakley (replacing Harris on vocals).

"Hurricane" lays out Carter's defense forcefully: he and Artis, both Black, were convicted by an all-white jury, largely on the basis of questionable testimony from three witnesses, also white, who did not see the shooting itself. No forensic evidence tied Carter and Artis to the murder. The song opens like a script with stage directions, appropriate to Levy's background in theater. In his summation Dylan indicts the racist justice system itself for the framing of Carter. Dylan was committed to Carter's cause, meeting with him, keeping in touch, and getting the "Hurricane" single out within weeks of its recording, well ahead of the album.

Desire's other true-crime story-song, "Joey," whitewashes the career of the mobster Joe Gallo, who had been shot to death in a Little Italy restaurant a few years earlier. The sensational nature of Gallo's slaying, along with heightened interest in the Mafia following the first two *Godfather* films, surrounded Dylan and Levy's depiction of Joey as a noble, compassionate warrior. Dylan said he got the idea for the song when he and Levy had dinner with the actor Jerry Orbach and his wife Marta, who regaled them with stories about Gallo—they had been friends and had gone to the Copacabana with him just hours before he was killed.[9] While rehabilitating Gallo's reputation was not as righteous a cause as crusading for Carter's release, Dylan saw the eleven-minute "Joey" as a continuation of a folk tradition celebrating outlaws, one that he had engaged in repeatedly throughout his career.[10]

"Romance in Durango" pays homage to Marty Robbins's classic "El Paso," a song Dylan would later discuss lovingly in his 2022 book *The Philosophy of Modern Song*. "Durango" is pure South-of-the-Border romance, from the cinematic opening image of "Hot chili peppers in the blistering sun" to the singer's inevitable, tragic death at the song's conclusion. "Durango" segues musically into another story-song set in an exotic (and purely fictional) location, "Black Diamond Bay." In this postmodern anti-narrative, characters interact randomly but without clear motivation or logic—then a volcano erupts, burying them all. If there's a point to all this it's made in the final verse, in which the singer, watching "old Cronkite" on television, sees a news item about the island's destruction and shrugs it off as a distant tragedy in a place he was never going to visit anyway. The randomness and dark humor of the story are heightened by this reminder of the way tragedy is mediatized, becoming just another story on TV.

The exoticism of the lyrics blends with the "Gypsy" sound throughout the album, as on "One More Cup of Coffee (Valley Below)," in which the singer woos the daughter of a powerful man described as an "outlaw," "wanderer," and protective king. (Dylan said the song was inspired by a Gypsy festival he attended in southern France on his 34th birthday, earlier that year.[11]) "Mozambique," an old-fashioned postcard song in the tradition of "Moonlight in Vermont" and "Old Cape Cod," was actually written about Marseille, where Dylan had spent time with David Oppenheim earlier in the year. The name Mozambique had the right rhythm and rhyming potential, but the Southeast African country was not exactly a tourist destination in 1975, as it was just ending a decade-long war of independence and would continue to experience violent unrest for years. Whether this irony was intended is unclear.

But the most captivating story-song on the album is "Isis," the first set of lyrics Dylan and Levy co-wrote. The narrator shifts back and forth between an account of his marriage and an expedition he undertakes with a mysterious stranger. The story has biographical overtones—the lure of a fortune to be made on the road set against the desire to return to his "mystical" wife—but the song's appeal lies in its playfulness, the clipped cinematic dialogue and odd turns of phrase. Naming the title character after an Egyptian goddess sets off allegorical alarm bells, especially since the expedition turns out to be an attempt to grave-rob a pyramid (embedded in ice!). But the moment of that revelation is also the point where you know this is really just a good, cartoonish yarn—Levy later called it a "cowboy story."[12] The singer returns to Isis empty-handed but apparently able to take up where they left off.

Desire closes with another love song: "Sara," Dylan's intensely personal tribute to his wife. The song is beautiful, full of specific memories (like writing "Sad-Eyed Lady of the Lowlands" at the Chelsea Hotel) and pledges of devotion. At the same time the singer doesn't acknowledge his own infidelity as the main cause of the rupture he's trying to mend. As Sean Wilentz points out, "Even as he rhapsodized about Sara's charms, wisdom, and devotion, Dylan seemed self-absorbed and all too willing to place responsibility on her for the marriage's souring . . . 'Whatever made you want to change your mind?' Dylan sang, as if he didn't know."[13]

Sara Dylan might have judged her husband's sincerity for herself, as she attended the recording session. Jacques Levy said, "It was extraordinary. You could have heard a pin drop."[14] Another witness, Larry Sloman, added that "People eyed Sara for a reaction but she seemed impassive. And then Dylan came into the control room and a friend of Sheena's broke the spell, asking him the name of the song. 'Sara,' Dylan shot back, annoyed, 'Part One.'"[15]

Desire would wait until January for release, but in the meantime Dylan and Neuwirth were cooking up a tour that would contrast dramatically with the previous one. They hoped to dispense with the hype of the big rock show, instead conceptualizing an old-fashioned "revue" with multiple performers who would just show up in your town, rent a hall, hand out some advertising flyers, and play. The atmosphere would be loose and unpredictable, with guest artists joining the band from time to time. Dylan would obviously be the big draw, but Neuwirth would do a set of his own, as would a few other invitees, including Roger McGuinn, Ramblin' Jack Elliott, and—billed second only to Dylan—Joan Baez.

Although her career had been eclipsed by Dylan's in the mid-1960s, Baez had re-emerged in the early 1970s, having scored a hit single in late 1971 with her version of the Band's "The Night They Drove Old Dixie Down." In April 1975 she released the album

Diamonds & Rust, which included a soft-rock cover of "Simple Twist of Fate," complete with a verse mimicking its author's voice, and the hit title track, a fond musical memoir of her relationship with Dylan. Their reunion was big news, the resulting hype to some extent foiling the tour's "let's just show up and play" ethos.

Dylan never acknowledged (and it may not have been the case) that his Rolling Thunder Revue borrowed its name from the U.S. aerial bombardment campaign over Vietnam (1965–8), known as Operation Rolling Thunder. The fact that the Revue's house band adopted the moniker Guam, which was the site of an important U.S. Air Force base, seems like a hint, but it's worth noting that throughout 1975 Guam was home to a processing center for more than 100,000 Vietnamese refugees—so if the band name was anything more than a joke it might have been a symbolically humanitarian counterbalance to "Rolling Thunder."

Guam was anchored by the core group of Stoner, who served as de facto musical director, Wyeth, and Rivera, but there would be no shortage of guitarists: Neuwirth and Dylan were joined by Steven Soles, T-Bone Burnett, and Mick Ronson, whose previous gig was with David Bowie's Spiders from Mars. Wunderkind David Mansfield played steel guitar, dobro, and mandolin, and Luther Rix added his own rolling thunder with congas and other percussion.

Dylan rehearsed with the band at SIR studios in New York in late October, preparing to open the tour, symbolically enough, in historic Plymouth, Massachusetts, on October 30. A week before that first show they gathered at Gerde's Folk City in the Village for owner Mike Porco's birthday party. The long night was a reunion of old folk luminaries—Dave Van Ronk, Eric Anderson, Phil Ochs, David Blue, and of course Ramblin' Jack—and a scene for rising stars such as Tom Waits, Patti Smith (who was invited to join the Revue but later dropped), and Bette Midler, who had recently recorded "Buckets of Rain" as a boozy duet with Dylan for her next album. The birthday party/jam session lasted all night, a rowdy, unofficial start to a different kind of tour.

Over five and a half weeks the Rolling Thunder Revue hit 23 cities, all in New England with the exception of a few dates in

On stage at Harvard Square Theatre with the Rolling Thunder Revue, November 1975. Photo by Peter Simon.

Canada and a few in western New York. The informal traveling-band concept held up in spirit, but the tour did include some large venues, and the entourage included a film crew Dylan brought along to work on an experimental side project. About seventy musicians, crew, and family traveled mainly by bus: a customized Greyhound, playfully named "Phydeaux," for the musicians, a less glamorous Delmonico bus, nicknamed "Ghetteaux," for everyone else—except for Dylan, who traveled with his family and dog in a Monaco Executive camper known as the "Green Machine." (He also brought along a red Cadillac.)[16] There was plenty of sex and drugs (cocaine especially) to go along with the rock and roll, but there was also family—Baez's son, Sara and Bob's kids for part of the itinerary, and, toward the end, Dylan's mom.

Dylan brought in his boyhood friend Louie Kemp as tour manager; Jacques Levy was the stage director; Allen Ginsberg and Peter Orlovsky were originally slated as performers but became baggage handlers (why not?); and Larry "Ratso" Sloman, covering the tour for *Rolling Stone*, became its chronicler . . . and a kind of mascot. As Sloman describes it he was treated as a nuisance at first, especially by Kemp, and was frequently denied access to the musicians, but by sheer persistence he won Dylan's trust, which allowed him to interview everyone on the tour and produce the detailed and entertaining book *On the Road with Bob Dylan*.

The Revue's theatrical touches included a stage curtain that looked like it had been borrowed from a nineteenth-century county fair or traveling circus. Dylan's stage apparel always included a vest and a wide-brimmed hat with an arrangement of flowers fixed to the hatband and often included white face paint. (The face paint was explained variously as a nod to commedia dell'arte or to Jean-Louis Barrault's mime character in the film *Les Enfants du Paradis*, or, somewhat implausibly, a way to make his facial expressions more visible to fans in the cheap seats.[17]) Rivera painted gothic designs on her face as well; Baez occasionally dressed as Dylan, and at other times danced like a 1960s go-go girl while McGuinn played "Eight Miles High." T-Bone Burnett wore aviator goggles onstage and would lasso McGuinn at the conclusion of the song "Chestnut Mare."[18]

But mostly there was the theatricality that comes with any good rock show: musicians—Dylan especially—reacting to each other, playing to the audience, mugging, posturing, and just generating energy. Dylan seems to have taken seriously the great pre-tour advice Patti Smith had given him: "Use your fists."[19]

When the curtain lifted Guam would open the show with a set that featured various vocalists, including Blakley, who had recently released a new album and was winning rave reviews for her role in Robert Altman's film *Nashville*. Neuwirth, who emceed this part of the show, would take center stage for a few numbers, including "Mercedes Benz," the song he wrote with Janis Joplin. Ramblin' Jack would join the group to sing a few, and then Dylan would appear, unannounced, and launch into "When I Paint My Masterpiece" with Neuwirth sharing vocals. Dylan's set featured torrid arrangements of mid-1960s classics—typically "It Ain't Me, Babe," "Hattie Carroll," and either "Hard Rain" or "It Takes a Lot to Laugh"—and conclude with the not-yet-released "Romance in Durango" and "Isis."

The curtain would fall for a fifteen-minute break and then rise, dramatically, only after Dylan and Baez could be heard singing "Blowin' in the Wind" together. After a five-song duo set ending with "I Shall Be Released" Baez would perform her own mix of traditional and contemporary songs, including "Diamonds & Rust" and closing with "The Night They Drove Old Dixie Down," joined by McGuinn, who would then do his own short set. Dylan would return for a couple of solo numbers and a few songs with the core *Desire* band before being joined by full Guam for a finale of "Just Like a Woman," "Knockin' on Heaven's Door," and "This Land Is Your Land."[20] It was a good, long evening, four hours at least, with occasional special guests added to the line-up. Those guests included Ronnie Hawkins, Gordon Lightfoot, and for the last eight stops of the tour Joni Mitchell, who, not coincidentally, was working on songs for an album, *Hejira*, largely about life on the road.

The freshness and energy of the music comes through clearly in audio recordings of the tour, both the two-disc Bootleg Series volume v and the fourteen-disc box set released in 2019. As great as the chemistry between Dylan and the Band was, he sounds more comfortable here than on *Before the Flood*. He still enjoys belting out certain lines, especially on "When I Paint My Masterpiece" and "Isis," but he *sings* more than he shouts. The textures and rhythms are different—where the Band had two keyboardists, the more nimble Guam has steel guitar, violin, and congas. "It Ain't Me, Babe" had been converted to a rock arrangement on the previous tour, but now it featured a buoyant, country-inflected gallop. And then there's "Isis," its piano-based studio arrangement replaced by multiple guitars swirling and churning, Rivera's violin screaming above the maelstrom and in the breaks between verses, which Dylan delivers with increasing intensity as the story progresses.

Dylan had cameras rolling for these performances, some of which would be included in the film *Renaldo and Clara*. Like *Eat the Document* this new work-in-progress would combine concert footage with scenes shot at various locations during the tour. But this time most of those scenes were staged, directed (more or less) by Dylan but largely improvised. On Patti Smith's recommendation Dylan enlisted Sam Shepard to join the tour as a screenwriter, but as *Renaldo and Clara* had no script Shepard had little to do. (Dylan ultimately credited himself as the writer as well as director.) Inspired by auteurs such as François Truffaut and Luis Buñuel, Dylan clearly took his film seriously at times, but it was a self-indulgent exercise or, in Baez's view, a "monumentally silly project."

She recalled, "Bob would stand in back of the camera and chuckle to himself and get everyone to run around and act out his mind movies. The filming happened in gleeful little happenings, enacting whatever dream Dylan had had in the night."[21] And that's pretty much how *Renaldo and Clara* comes across: riveting concert excerpts interspersed with random documentary footage, tour members improvising mostly love scenes and quarrels, and David Blue playing pinball while telling stories about Dylan.

Surprisingly the usually private Sara Dylan plays a significant role—multiple roles in fact. She and Baez, along with the poet Anne Waldman, play prostitutes in one sequence of scenes; in another sequence Baez plays the "Woman in White" and Sara, wearing a brown wig and make-up that evoke Sophia Loren, plays Clara. Dylan, supposedly in the role of Renaldo, is torn between these two lovers. In the film's most infamous scene Baez as the Woman in White enters Renaldo and Clara's apartment; over the course of this encounter the Woman in White watches while Renaldo and Clara kiss and fondle each other on a bed, and then the two women temporarily team up to confront the unfaithful Renaldo before the Woman in White finally leaves. In the film's next-most-infamous scene Dylan and Baez, not clearly "in character," meet in a bar and discuss their past, as Baez's "Diamonds & Rust" plays in the background. "What do you think it would have been like if we'd gotten married?" she asks. "I dunno. I haven't changed that much," Dylan replies.

As compelling as these scenes are for fans, most of the dialogue is pointless and repetitive, and the non-linear collage of fiction, non-fiction, and concert performance is a challenge to sit through (especially since it's available only as a bootleg with grainy video and muffled sound). Unable to persuade a studio to distribute the film, Dylan released it independently in early 1978—to hostile reviews. He tried editing it down to a more manageable two hours ("just took it and . . . hacked it up," he said), but *Renaldo and Clara* never found a wide audience.[22]

Some of *Renaldo and Clara*'s highlights though were restored and repurposed for Martin Scorsese's 2019 film *Rolling Thunder Revue: A Bob Dylan Story*. With Dylan's cooperation Scorsese spliced together some of the best footage shot for Dylan's film with fresh interviews and a few fake storylines, the most amusing of which has a teenage Sharon Stone meeting Dylan in 1975 and joining the entourage. *Renaldo and Clara* is never mentioned; instead a fictional director, the pompous and bitter Stefan Van Dorp (played by Martin Von Haselberg), is credited with filming the tour. While Scorsese's mockumentary is in no way a remake of *Renaldo and Clara*, it does suggest what the earlier film could have been: genuinely funny and playful in its blurring of reality and fiction—and thoroughly entertaining.

Both films foreground Dylan's efforts on behalf of Rubin Carter, which included a concert at the women's correctional facility where Carter was temporarily housed and a benefit at Madison Square Garden, the December 8 tour finale known as "Night of the

Hurricane." Ken Regan's widely circulated photograph shows Dylan, dressed for the stage, separated from a smiling Carter by a pull-down security gate—symbolizing his imprisonment although at the minimum-security prison Carter was not actually confined to a cell (much less a 10-foot (3 m) cell, as the song claims).[23] While Dylan had famously turned away from organized protest a decade earlier, it's worth noting that he had occasionally re-engaged with humanitarian campaigns, going back to his participation in the Concert for Bangladesh and his advocacy for George Jackson, and more recently (in May 1974) by joining Phil Ochs and others at a benefit for political prisoners and other victims of Augusto Pinochet's reign of terror in Chile.

But he took a much more active role in the campaign to free Carter, already with the "Hurricane" single and now as the organizer behind a fund- and consciousness-raising event. In addition to the usual Rolling Thunder Revue line-up the Night of the Hurricane featured appearances by Coretta Scott King and Muhammad Ali (who gave a rambling speech and stumped for political candidates who had nothing to do with Carter's case). Roberta Flack and Ritchie Havens were added as musical guests, and Robbie Robertson showed up to jam on "It Takes a Lot to Laugh, It Takes a Train to Cry." Baez not only masqueraded as Dylan but at another point ran onstage in a blonde wig and shorts, pretending to be an overzealous groupie. True to her activist principles she also made a plea for putting an end to prisons.[24] Rumors circulated through the crowd that the Governor of New Jersey was about to grant Carter clemency, and Carter himself was on the phone with Dylan during the intermission conveying the same message.[25] But it wasn't true: Carter and Artis were granted a retrial in 1976 but were again found guilty. Artis was paroled in 1981, but Carter would not be freed until 1985, when a U.S. District Court set aside the convictions, citing the racism that underlay the previous trials.

About a week after the Night of the Hurricane the Rolling Thunder Revue crashed Norman Mailer's Christmas party. As Lucian Truscott tells the story, he (Truscott) secured an invitation for his friend Bob Neuwirth, who then asked to bring Dylan (*of course* you bring Dylan!), who then showed up with a Winnebago full of musicians. They made their way to Mailer's apartment, where Dylan hobnobbed with the New York literati—Joseph Heller, Mario Puzo, Susan Sontag, Lillian Hellman, and E. L. Doctorow were among Mailer's guests. According to Truscott, the band got a bit antsy, but Dylan was in his element: "I remember standing for about an hour around 3 a.m. listening to Dylan and Mailer heatedly discuss one of the lesser-known campaigns in World War II . . . As we got back on the tour bus at about 5 a.m., Mailer was standing at the door holding a bottle of bourbon, imploring us to stay." Instead they retreated to the Other End, woke up the owner and had breakfast.[26]

Desire was finally released the first week of 1976 to strong reviews, and it became Dylan's third album in three years to hit number one on the U.S. chart. Days after its release he hosted Night of the Hurricane II in Houston, with the added star power of Ringo, Stephen Stills, Dr. John, and a full set by Stevie Wonder.

After a few months' respite Dylan and Guam regrouped for rehearsals in April and began a southern U.S. tour in Lakeland, Florida, on April 18. The line-up had changed slightly: Ronee Blakley returned to her acting career, with singer-songwriter Donna Weiss taking her spot. Jack Elliott recalled asking if he could come along again, but Dylan was evasive: "He said, 'I don't know what the plan is. I heard that Joan Baez is going to be there. And Kinky Friedman . . .' He was letting me know that I wasn't going to be on the tour."[27] Even with the Revue's chummy, everyone-gets-a-turn-at-the-mic vibe, Dylan was the boss, and the boss isn't always your friend. Blakley, who *was* chummy with Dylan, told Howard Sounes that she once gushed to lead guitarist Mick Ronson, "Isn't Bob wonderful?" to which Ronson replied, "I don't know. He's never spoken to me."[28]

The consensus among the musicians who played both legs of the Rolling Thunder Revue is that the 1976 version was significantly less fun. No more face paint and improvised movie scenes and just a generally darker mood. In an effort to maintain the regional, road-trip feel of the first tour, the '76 Revue moved slowly across the Deep South and Southwest, hitting eight cities in Florida, seven in Texas—it seems crazy that this legendary tour never played the Mid-Atlantic, the Midwest, or the West Coast. The excitement that met the tour in medium-sized New England cities did not carry over to the South, and it didn't help that they played so many shows in the same region, often scheduling afternoon and evening performances. In fact several concerts were cancelled because of poor ticket sales.[29] Dylan had changed the setlist significantly, leaning into the lost-love songs from *Blood on the Tracks* and playing only two or three from *Desire*, even though the new album (unreleased during the first leg) was enormously popular. Even "Hurricane" disappeared from the set after the second Night of the Hurricane. And the closer was no longer Guthrie's "The Land Is Your Land" but instead a less idealistic folk standard, Paul Clayton's "Gotta Travel On." This oblique tribute to Clayton, Dylan's friend and admirer who had taken his own life in 1967, may have been spurred by a more recent tragedy: Phil Ochs, another friend and admirer who had hoped to be part of the Rolling Thunder Revue, hanged himself in April, not long before the beginning of the tour's second leg.

While the music on the 1975 tour was hardly mellow, it became harder-edged in the South in 1976. "It's got its own vibe," Rob Stoner recalled. "Much more of a punk-rock vibe than the '75 stuff. It just evolved that way. It definitely wasn't just a repeat . . . it was more rocking."[30] Although the 1975 shows are now accessible thanks to official archival releases and the Scorsese documentary, it was a pair of concerts from the end of the 1976 tour that provided the tapes for Dylan's second live album, *Hard Rain*. Dylan had contracted with NBC to deliver a concert special for prime-time broadcast; he rejected the first attempt, made with network oversight while the band rehearsed in Florida, so he had to finance the filming of a later concert himself.

Arrangements were made to film an outdoor performance in late May at Colorado State University's football stadium, but the weather did not cooperate. Stoner remembered it as a "terrible weekend," with Dylan in a bad mood and everyone drinking heavily: "We were supposed to do the gig two or three consecutive days—each time the 'rain date' was supposed to be the next day—but it was pouring for days and days. Meanwhile it's costing Bob a lot of bread. Everybody's holed up in this little hotel up in the mountains in the middle of nowhere, with nothing to do but get drunk."[31]

The rain continued, and the band went on with the show, giving an impassioned, gleefully angry performance. As Stoner recalled, "Everybody's soaked, the canopy's leaking, the musicians are getting shocks from the water on the stage . . . It was awful. So everybody is playing and singing for their lives, and that is the spirit that you hear."[32] On the NBC broadcast, as on much of the tour, Dylan wears a Middle Eastern head scarf in place of the hat-with-flowers; other band members adopt variations on the leader's headgear (Baez wears a red turban). The TV program actually begins with the encore, the appropriately chosen "Hard Rain" (which oddly is not included on the album—sort of a ghost title track). The last song before the credits roll is a searing version of "Idiot Wind," with Dylan's nearly manic delivery of the lost-love diatribe, filled, as David Mansfield said, "with such black energy and venom."[33]

Even at a time when late-night music showcases such as *The Midnight Special* (on NBC) and *In Concert* (on ABC) were popular with younger audiences, airing an hour-long prime-time rock show—with no emcee or interviews or surprise guests or backstage tomfoolery—was newsworthy and risky. *Hard Rain* landed Dylan on the cover of *TV Guide*, but the show itself got a lukewarm reception. The album, whose release coincided with the TV special, didn't fare much better with critics, but it contains some ferocious performances, and it documents the "punk" energy of Rolling Thunder II well. Dylan and producer Don DeVito mixed in a few songs from a previous concert and did not include any of the three acoustic duets with Baez from the broadcast. But they wisely included high-octane versions of songs that were not part of the previous year's tour. A rewritten "Lay Lady Lay" was less seductive than insistent. Three of the four songs on side two of *Hard Rain* are lost-love tales from *Blood on the Tracks*, and the fourth, "I Threw It All Away," fits the same pattern, the wistful country croon of the original replaced by a desperate howl on the refrain. The regret of "I Threw It All Away" leads into the accusations and anger of the final track, "Idiot Wind."

Of course it wasn't just bad weather (hard rain, idiot wind) that drove the performance, and the "black energy" wasn't confined to the Colorado State concert. While 1976 was not quite 1966 Dylan was once again at a creative and popular peak that coincided with self-indulgent and sometimes cruel behavior. Sara Dylan dropped in on the tour occasionally—significantly she was there for the filming of *Hard Rain*—but didn't travel with Bob. She knew that he was cheating on her and with more than one partner: on-and-off relationships with Ellen Bernstein, the actress Sally Kirkland, and others. After the tour the Dylans tried to live together at the Point Dume mansion, but, according to Sara, Bob became "continually quarrelsome" and even abusive. When she filed for divorce the following spring she asserted that he had struck her on one occasion. "I was in such fear of him," she said, "that I locked doors to protect myself from his violent outbursts and temper tantrums."[34]

In late 1976 Dylan turned his focus to editing some eighty hours of film down to the four-hour *Renaldo and Clara*. His collaborator was Howard Alk, who had previously worked on *Dont Look Back* and *Eat the Document* and had shot and edited *Hard Rain*. They continued assembling the film throughout much of 1977, arranging scenes with an obscure symbolic structure in mind.

Dylan's one remaining live performance in 1976 would be part of a much more celebrated rock music film. For the Band's "Last Waltz," their star-studded Thanksgiving Day farewell extravaganza at San Francisco's Winterland Ballroom, Robbie Robertson had teamed up with director Martin Scorsese. Warner Brothers agreed to finance Scorsese's film on the condition that Dylan would appear. Dylan agreed to the concert but wouldn't commit to being part of the film because he and Alk knew that *The Last Waltz* would be released around the same time as *Renaldo and Clara*. According to Levon Helm, the filmmakers "went ahead and told Warners that Bob was in on the whole deal." But about fifteen minutes before taking the stage Dylan made his position clear: he did not want to be filmed.

"Scorsese went nuts," recalled Helm. "Without Bob there would be no movie."[35] In the nick of time Bill Graham, who was producing the concert, convinced Dylan to allow filming for two of the five songs he was scheduled to perform, "Forever Young" and the grand finale, "I Shall Be Released." With Louie Kemp monitoring the film crew, cameras were turned away from the stage for "Baby, Let Me Follow You Down," "Hazel," and "I Don't Believe You," but then Dylan threw one last curve. After "Forever Young" he spontaneously led the band into a reprise of "Baby, Let Me Follow You Down," forcing Scorsese to risk losing "I Shall Be Released" (with all the stars back onstage) if he kept filming. Over Kemp's objections Graham and Scorsese kept the cameras rolling, and all three songs made it into *The Last Waltz*.[36] Dylan's performance was the climax of the evening—he and the Band clearly still had a unique chemistry, and their brief set at the end of the film provides a bookend to the onstage footage from *Eat the Document* a decade earlier.

The Dylans' divorce proceeded quickly, but the custody battle was a preoccupation for much of 1977, reaching its nadir when Sara attempted to forcibly remove her children from school, at one point chasing them down the hallway and allegedly striking a teacher.[37] Dylan meanwhile became involved with Faridi McFree, the kids' art-therapy teacher who had been hired by Sara. In a kind of repeat of the summer of 1974 with Ellen Bernstein, Dylan, his children, and McFree vacationed at his Minnesota farm, where he worked on new songs and tried them out on his new love interest. This was not a good look for a man trying to win custody of his children, and in fact Sara did prevail in court.

In September Dylan began leasing a rehearsal space in Santa Monica, naming it Rundown Studios. The Rundown would become his base of operations for the next several years, but his immediate concern was to put together a new band for a world tour. His new manager, Jerry Weintraub, arranged for a series of dates in Japan, where Dylan had never played, as the start of a tour that would occupy him for most of 1978. Weintraub, who would eventually become a major film and television producer, had previously managed tours for Elvis Presley, Frank Sinatra, and most recently Neil Diamond.

Presley's death that August had hit Dylan hard. "He didn't speak for a couple of days," McFree recalled. "He was really grieving."[38] It might have been the new manager's suggestion or memories of latter-day Elvis or Neil Diamond's flashy stage show that inspired Dylan to front a large band very unlike the loose, medicine-show, no-such-thing-as-too-many-guitars outfit from Rolling Thunder. Instead the band that Dylan would take to Japan in February would be rock-based but much more mainstream, with arrangements that David Mansfield, who played in both groups, would describe as "more straightforward and straightlaced than anything we'd done" on the previous tour. Along with Mansfield and guitarist Steven Soles, the rhythm section of Stoner and Wyeth returned for rehearsals, but Wyeth bowed out of the tour because of Japan's stringent drug policy. Stoner once again served as musical director, rehearsing the band-in-progress before Dylan's arrival.

After numerous musicians, especially back-up singers and drummers, had auditioned at the Rundown, Dylan had a new band for Japan and beyond: Stoner, Mansfield and Soles, flashy lead guitarist Billy Cross, keyboard player Alan Pasqua, drummer Ian Wallace, reed player Steve Douglas, percussionist Bobbye Hall, and on vocals Helena Springs, Jo Ann Harris, and Debi Dye Gibson. The shows were lucrative enough that when the Japanese promoter sent Dylan a list of songs he should play, Dylan complied, a rare relinquishing of artistic control.

Another contractual provision was that Dylan would record the concerts at Nippon Budokan Hall in Tokyo for an album. Originally released exclusively in Japan in August 1978, *Bob Dylan at Budokan* presents Dylan in a musical setting unlike anything he had tried before. Mansfield's description of the music as "straightlaced" suggests correctly that it sounded tame, designed to appeal to a more musically conservative audience, which of course old Dylan-heads found disturbing. Western audiences would experience the new approach in person between June and December and on vinyl when Columbia gave *Bob Dylan at Budokan* worldwide release in April 1979.

Indeed there was nothing gritty in these new arrangements, which tend to be bouncy, at times cloying and at other times bombastic. The backing singers have great voices, but they're generally confined to unimaginative oohs and aahs. Similarly Steve Douglas is a virtuoso reed player, but having him deliver fills on the flute makes songs like

"Love Minus Zero" and "All Along the Watchtower" sound like what's now called yacht rock. "Don't Think Twice, It's Alright" becomes a light reggae confection, and the haunting acoustic guitar lick that runs through "It's Alright Ma" becomes a heavy riff delivered by the full band between each verse. For the most part it's all very slick and a little busy; Dylan sounds engaged, at times eager to please, but rarely passionate. The pleasure of *Budokan* comes from the sheer audacity of the arrangements, which radically recontextualize some Dylan classics, something he would do repeatedly in live performances for the rest of his career. Ultimately it's kind of a fun album, and Dylan seems to enjoy messing with his own sacred texts. But the fun is never very intimate, and *Budokan* remains a hard set to warm up to.

After eleven shows in Japan and twelve in Australia Dylan and the band took a working break from the road to record his next album, *Street-Legal*. He would make it without his right-hand man Stoner—the bass player who had been the onstage intermediary between Dylan and his bands on both Rolling Thunder tours had had enough. There might have been personal conflicts involved, but the fact that Stoner had already teamed up with rockabilly revivalist Robert Gordon, whose group also included Wyeth and the legendary guitarist Link Wray, suggests that he wanted to follow a more raw, rootsy musical direction than the one Dylan had chosen.[39] The new bass player, who would also join the tour, was Jerry Scheff, who significantly had played with Elvis throughout the 1970s. Meanwhile Carolyn Dennis replaced Debi Dye Gibson in the trio of background vocalists.

Critics and fans have been divided on *Street-Legal* since its release. In *Rolling Stone* Greil Marcus gave the album a scalding assessment, more negative than his famous "What is this shit?" review of *Self Portrait* eight years before. Marcus argued that Dylan's singing was no longer natural—"emotion has been replaced by mannerism, subtlety by a straining to be heard"—and that the lyrics, seemingly rich and complex like those of his classic period, were actually meaningless.[40] Michael Gray conversely has hailed the album's "astonishing complexity and confidence, delivered in one of Dylan's most authoritative voices."[41] Comparing it to *Blonde on Blonde* Gray describes *Street-Legal*'s language as "packed tight with characters, incident, biblical allusion, surreal flights of fantasy and a restless emotional thrust."[42]

It's not hard to fall somewhere in between these opinions: I don't find Dylan's singing as emotionally flat as Marcus did, but I agree that the lyrics, especially on the most ambitious (wordy) songs, don't really add up no matter how many times you listen to and read them. I'm thinking particularly of "Changing of the Guards," "No Time to Think," and "Where Are You Tonight? (Journey through Dark Heat)," all of which feature apocalyptic imagery depicting a world of misery and injustice that may or may not allow love to endure. But the scenarios they describe, the stories they hint at, even the chains of imagery they contain are fragmented beyond comprehension; we're left grasping at straws. Then again coherence isn't everything—"Changing of the Guards" is still irresistible, thanks to its propulsive sound, the backing vocals echoing the first lines of the verses, and the poetically bleak situations that parade by. And "Where Are You Tonight?" (a sly allusion to "Absolutely Sweet Marie") succeeds on its own terms as a song about desperately searching for someone to love in a world gone wrong—and here the band digs a deep, soulful groove, kicked off by Bobbye Hall's congas and sustained by Alan Pasqua's Hammond organ.

In "Señor (Tales of Yankee Power)" the singer is either a prisoner or an escapee in transit, a victim of Yankee power who doesn't know what the future holds for him. The song's bridges heighten the drama as he remembers the moment of separation from his lover and his own capture and perhaps torture; the story ends with his desperate plea for help in an escape. Sean Egan observes that "the outward-looking nature of *Desire* departed along with Jacques Levy, and when Dylan turned his view back onto himself he saw a wasteland."[43]

Indeed that wasteland theme pervades this uneven album, filtering into the tracks that may or may not qualify as love songs. The title of "True Love Tends to Forget" sums up that song's sentiment—if we love each other there's a lot that we're going to have to overlook or ignore. There's nothing particularly attractive (or distinctive) about the insistent lovers or the situations depicted in "Baby Stop Crying," "Is Your Love in Vain," and "We Better Talk This Over," all of which are pretty forgettable songs. Musically the album's best moment is "New Pony," Dylan's rewrite of "Pony Blues" by Son House.[44] The song is full of sexual innuendo and menace, amplified by the band's dirty blues playing, which would not be out of place on an early-seventies Stones album. Raising it to another level, the backing vocal trio answers each line with the eternal question, "How much longer?"

One common complaint about *Street-Legal* was that the sound was awful—not the band itself but the recording and mixing. Under pressure to complete the album and get back on the road, Dylan decided to record at Rundown, which was not a proper recording studio, using mobile equipment. His impatience with acoustic dividers, headphones, and other modern contrivances didn't help, and the resulting mix "sounded like it had been recorded under wet cardboard," as Howard Sounes described it. A remaster in 1999 helped the album's overall reputation, but the muddy mix probably influenced a lot of the initial negative reactions.

The band reconvened for a weeklong residency at Los Angeles's Universal Amphitheatre and then began the tour's European leg on June 15, the day *Street-Legal* was released. After a month in Europe they took another two-month break and then resumed the tour for 65 dates over three months throughout North America. The 25–30-song setlist evolved and varied slightly, but Dylan continued to devote much of the show to his greatest hits, augmented by a few selections from *Street-Legal*, an R&B cover (usually either Tampa Red's "She's Love Crazy" or Muddy Waters's "I'm Ready"), and a terrific new original blues, "Am I Your Stepchild?" (later memorably recorded by both Solomon Burke and Jerry Lee Lewis).

Dylan was still fairly reclusive, but he seemed more comfortable hanging out with band members on this tour. He even did some between-song patter onstage, introducing "Tangled Up in Blue" as a song "I wrote three years ago about three people in love with each other all at the same time" and leading into "Maggie's Farm" by referencing the infamous Newport 1965 performance—"I got kicked out of town . . . Smoke was flying everywhere." He also indulged in a little Vegas nightclub schtick, introducing the backing vocalists as his ex-girlfriend, current girlfriend, and fiancée.[45] (That was sometimes more than a joke.)

Dylan also made himself much more available to interviewers before and during the 1978 tour—not just agreeing to talk but answering a wide range of questions candidly and at length. He discussed why musicians like to smoke pot, coined the phrase "thin, wild mercury sound," criticized the film *Dont Look Back*, explicated *Renaldo and Clara*, explained his pre-*Blood on the Tracks* breakthrough with Norman Raeben, and acknowledged his failure as a husband. Responding to criticism that he was doing "Las Vegas showroom music," he told Pete Oppel of the *Dallas Morning News*, "Well, maybe it is. But you know who plays Vegas? B. B. King. Merle Haggard plays Vegas. Willie Nelson plays Las Vegas. You play where there's a crowd of people."[46] Asked by Australian journalist Craig McGregor if he really liked being on the road, he replied, "It's not that I like it or dislike it; it's what I'm destined to do. Muddy Waters is still doing it, and he's sixty-five. In the States there's a lotta old guys that are doing it, and I kinda feel that when I'm that old, as long as

Performing with the "Budokan" band at Carolina Coliseum, Columbia, SC, 1978.

I can do it I guess I will do it, because it's all I did ever do, or want to do."[47]

He also discussed religion with various interviewers. In March a question from Ron Rosenbaum for a *Playboy* article prompted a series of questions from Dylan: "What would Christ be in this day and age if he came back? What would he be? . . . He would have to be a leader, I suppose."[48] When McGregor asked if he's getting into religion, Dylan explained that he didn't actually have much religious background, Jewish or otherwise. "No, no dedicated religion, I have not gotten into that. No dogma. I don't usually do that, I usually play my guitar."[49] He would continue to play his guitar, of course, but his feelings about religion—and dogma—would change dramatically before the end of the tour.

11

1978–84: Conversion

By the end of 1978 the punk explosion had changed the rock music landscape, even though (in the USA at least) bands such as the Sex Pistols, the Ramones, and the Clash barely dented the album charts and were non-existent on commercial radio. As had been the case with Dylan in the early and mid-1960s, the new groups defined themselves against the mainstream, which was part of their appeal. The broader aesthetic that punk spearheaded—essentially DIY, with energy and simplicity taking precedence over musical virtuosity and complexity—was becoming more widely accepted. That aesthetic was soon rebranded as New Wave, an umbrella term covering everything from the funky, cacophonous onslaught of Ian Dury and the Blockheads to the cool, almost robotic sound of the Cars. But at that moment, if not for much longer, punk and New Wave presented a challenge to what most people thought of as rock music and particularly to the generation of musicians who were now pushing forty. If you were Elton John or the Who you could still sell millions of records and play to arenas full of fans, but, to borrow a key word from the Clash's slogan, you might no longer *matter*—at least not to critics and trendsetters.[1]

And Dylan was certainly part of rock's old guard. Throughout the 1970s he was invoked by music marketing campaigns for a series of singer-songwriters vying to be the "New Dylan"—a phrase used so often that it became a kind of joke by the end of the decade. But one particular "New Dylan" seemed to occupy the space previously held by the old Dylan. Following a protracted battle over his management in 1978 Bruce Springsteen followed up the simultaneous *Time*-and-*Newsweek*-cover success of 1975's *Born to Run* with the stunning *Darkness on the Edge of Town* and a tour that featured three-to-four-hour sweat-drenched sets.

Dylan and Springsteen had crossed paths occasionally—they met backstage at a New Haven Rolling Thunder Revue show—and they had a few conspicuous things in common. Springsteen had been signed to Columbia by John Hammond, the same executive who had signed Dylan. They shared an association with another rock and roll poet, the female "New Dylan" Patti Smith—who had her first and only big hit with "Because the Night," co-written with Springsteen. And while the E Street Band didn't sound like any of the groups Dylan had assembled for albums or tours, both bandleaders combined ambitious, literate songwriting with straightforward guitar-based rock. Most significantly, Springsteen in 1978 had achieved the kind of adulation as both a writer and performer that Dylan had known in his electric prime. He wasn't the bestselling artist in the world, but at that moment it was clear that in terms of originality and impact no one could touch him, just as it had been for Dylan in the mid-1960s.

While Springsteen was leaving crowds breathless and awestruck, what Dylan was offering audiences in 1978 was pretty close to a nostalgia show. His most recent studio album had been a critical flop with disappointing sales; *Renaldo and Clara* had been a daring artistic move, but it was even more resoundingly panned than *Street-Legal*, and few people even saw it. In his book subtitled "The Transformations of Bob Dylan" Andrew McCarron likens Dylan's situation at the end of 1978 to where he had been just before the motorcycle crash, "more than crestfallen and uninspired . . . chronically exhausted and physically ill, as he had been twelve years earlier."[2]

McCarron also sees what happened next as a repetition of the transformation "script" established with the earlier motorcycle accident and recovery. This time the transformation was symbolized by a silver cross that a fan tossed onto the stage in San Diego on November 17, 1978. Dylan would tell an interviewer (two years later) that he hadn't been in such bad shape at the end of the tour—"I was doing fine . . . relatively content"—but onstage a year after the fact he told a story of "feeling sick" the night he picked up the cross and feeling even worse the following night in Arizona: "I was used to all kinds of things, and I said, 'I need something tonight that I never really had before.' And I looked in my pocket and I had this cross that someone threw up on stage . . . And I put that cross on."[3]

The silver cross story suggests a sudden conversion, but Dylan's embrace of Christianity took some time and effort, aided by his circle of band members and acquaintances. Mary Alice Artes, Dylan's girlfriend at the time (credited as "Queen Bee" on the *Street-Legal* inner sleeve), is probably the one who introduced him to the Vineyard Fellowship, an evangelical Christian group based in Los Angeles. But David Mansfield and Steven Soles, Rolling Thunder Revue veterans who played on the 1978 tour, were also affiliated with the Vineyard, as was T-Bone Burnett. Dylan spent the early months of 1979 in the Vineyard Fellowship's Bible study class, three and a half hours a day, four days a week. As Paul Williams notes, it was a time commitment similar to what he had done with the art teacher Norman Raeben and in another group setting where he was essentially a novice.

"I had always read the Bible," he said, "but I had only looked at it as literature. I was never really instructed in it in a way that was meaningful for me."[4] Heavily influenced by the work of Hal Lindsey, author of the bestseller *The Late Great Planet Earth*, the Vineyard Fellowship emphasized a literal reading of the Book of Revelation; the apocalypse that was close at hand would be signaled by violent global conflict. Rebirth through Christ and preparation for his Second Coming were the central tenets, and while faith as opposed to works was the key to salvation, immoral behavior was evidence of Satan's presence and influence—on an individual or society as a whole.

Dylan's spiritual rebirth ignited a creative streak that produced over the course of the year enough songs for his next two albums and then some. At first he was hesitant to record and release these new songs himself and planned to have them recorded by Carolyn Dennis, another girlfriend who had sung back-up on the 1978 tour and was herself born again. But as he demoed the songs he became more comfortable with the idea of making his own gospel album. Teaming up with Jerry Wexler, the legendary producer who had overseen classic 1950s and '60s recordings by Ray Charles, Aretha Franklin, and countless other soul and R&B performers, Dylan made *Slow Train Coming* over the first two weeks of May at Muscle Shoals Sound Studio in northern Alabama.

He and Wexler recruited Mark Knopfler, who had just risen to fame with Dire Straits, to play guitar, along with Straits' drummer Pick Withers. (When Wexler suggested Knopfler, Dylan alluded to the similarity in their vocals: "Yeah, he does me better than anybody.")[5] Tim Drummond, a studio pro and veteran of Neil Young's Stray Gators, was enlisted as bass player, along with Jim Keltner on drums. Barry Beckett, a founding member of the famed Muscle Shoals Rhythm Section, played keyboards and, being intimately familiar with the studio, co-produced with Wexler. Helena Springs and Carolyn Dennis returned as backing vocalists, along with Regina (Havis) McCrary; the Muscle Shoals Horn Section punched up about half the tracks.

Gospel, R&B, and rock have been intertwined musically and culturally since the 1940s. Sister Rosetta Tharpe's arrangements and electric guitar sound like early rock and roll; Ray Charles could change the words to a gospel tune like "It Must Be Jesus" and deliver "I Got a Woman." Little Richard, Sam Cooke, Elvis Presley, Aretha Franklin, and Al Green crisscrossed the boundaries between gospel and secular music. Obviously gospel permeates the predominately Black genre that became known as soul music in the 1960s; a little less obviously, with blues as a common denominator, gospel's presence can be felt throughout predominantly white rock music of the late 1960s and early '70s—the Band, Clapton's post-Cream projects, Joe Cocker's Mad Dogs & Englishmen, the Allman Brothers, etc. So musically there was no reason listeners should have been unprepared for the bluesy gospel music that Dylan, Wexler, and the band were putting down in Muscle Shoals. Beckett, Drummond, and Keltner carve out deep grooves, and Knopfler's blues licks cut and jab through the air above them. Springs, Dennis, and McCrary, clearly at home in this musical style, provide a mostly smooth, polished foil to Dylan's grittier, half-spoken vocals. And unlike *Street-Legal* the recording quality and the mix are clean and clear—perhaps too much so for some tastes, but I think perfectly suited to the music, especially in doing justice to the outstanding rhythm section.

But of course it wasn't the music that would prove divisive. As a puzzled Mark Knopfler reported to his manager with comic understatement, "All these songs are about God."[6] More specifically they were about the importance of believing in the resurrection and second coming of Jesus Christ and the choice that all people must make to save themselves from eternal damnation. The metaphors and images are simple and biblical: light versus darkness ("Precious Angel"), sleep versus awakening ("When You Gonna Wake Up"), a thief in the night representing the sudden, disruptive return of Christ ("When He Returns"). The songs disparage earthly attainments as substitutes for salvation ("Gotta Serve Somebody," "Slow Train," "Gonna Change My Way of Thinking"). And they often set the Christian singer against the world of nonbelievers (most persistently in "I Believe in You").

There's no use searching for "the old Dylan" in these songs—in fact the whole point here is that he is not who he was, that he is wiping the slate clean to write only about what really matters—but there are certainly some lyrics capable of engaging and moving the unconverted. In the otherwise deadly serious "Gotta Serve Somebody" Dylan indulges in some schtick courtesy of comedian Bill Saluga, also known as Raymond J. Johnson, Jr., whose routine (widely circulated via Miller Lite TV ads) consisted of listing all the names you could call him by, ending with "But you doesn't have to call me Johnson." You may call Dylan Bobby, Zimmy, RJ, or Ray, but you're still gonna have to serve somebody. There are also many moments of great power in the album's straightforward expressions of devotion, especially as delivered through Dylan's aching, sincere vocal.

It's easier to admire and even love these songs almost half a century after they were released, knowing that Dylan would not spend the rest of his life repeating their message. At the time, though, it seemed to many listeners that he was not really embracing something new and meaningful but instead denouncing the aesthetic and philosophical ideals he had previously represented. Specifically Dylan had often espoused radical freedom and individualism, a rejection of authority and received wisdom. His promise, most explicit in "All I Really Want to Do" but implicit throughout his 1960s canon, was "I will not tell you what to believe or what to think." Now he was doing just that, embracing a belief system that epitomized submission to authority and acceptance of received wisdom. The resistance from his old fans had less to do with the basic tenets of Christianity (plenty of rock musicians were Christian) than with his evangelism and the cultural position of the evangelical Christianity he had embraced. The modern evangelical movement was conservative on a range of social and political issues—birth control and premarital sex, women's rights, gay rights, drug use, the death penalty, pacifism, environmentalism, and so on. However one might define the "counterculture," the conservative Christian church was a big part of what it countered. And on *Slow Train Coming* Dylan wasn't just celebrating his own awakening; he was laying down God's law that condemned those who did not heed the call.

The implicit bigotry of this view becomes explicit on "Slow Train," lamenting the newfound global power of anti-American "sheiks" from oil-producing Arab states. Not surprisingly reviews of the album, which was released in mid-August, were mixed. On one side Jann Wenner, *Rolling Stone*'s editor, wrote a review praising Dylan's newfound commitment, asserting that "the more I hear the new album . . . the more I feel that it's one of the finest records Dylan has ever made. In time, it is possible that it might even be considered his greatest."[7] Writing in *New West* Greil Marcus took the opposing view: "it's an initially commanding but ultimately slick piece of music," and when it comes to the message, "What we're faced with here is really very ugly."[8]

The divided response to *Slow Train Coming* continued when Dylan began performing his new songs live. On October 20 he debuted "Gotta Serve Somebody," "I Believe in You," and "When You Gonna Wake Up" on national television, NBC's *Saturday Night Live* (*SNL*). For *SNL* and the tour he was about to launch, he retained the mighty Keltner–Drummond rhythm section and added Fred Tackett of Little Feat on guitar (Knopfler having returned to Dire Straits); another Muscle Shoals legend, Spooner Oldham, along with Terry Young on keyboards; and the choir of Helena Springs, Regina McCrary, and Mona Lisa Young. On *SNL* Dylan looks a bit ill at ease, as one might expect considering he was performing religious songs for a hip late-night sketch comedy show, introduced by Eric Idle of the heretical Monty Python (*Life of Brian* was in theaters)—but the band and singers carry the performance, and Dylan delivers his new songs convincingly, especially "I Believe in You." Then it was back to Los Angeles for a week of rehearsals before opening the tour with a two-week residency at the Warfield Theatre in San Francisco.

At the Warfield, a historic 2,200-seat theater, Dylan worked out the kinks in his new set while, night by night, the audience reaction evolved. One constant, not only at the Warfield but over the next seven months of shows, was that Dylan would perform only his new, religious songs. At first it must have seemed like 1966 all over again. Jim Keltner told interviewer Ray Padgett,

> I'll never forget this one guy with a red bandana around his head [who] would stand up and say "Fuck you, Dylan! Rock and roll!" Then right next to him . . . was a guy sitting with a little sports coat on. He had his wife or his girlfriend and a little baby. He stood up after the "Rock and roll!" guy stood up and said, "We love you, Bob! We love your music!"[9]

Press reviews were similarly divided. The *San Francisco Chronicle*, calling it an evening of "religious studies, not rock and roll," complained that "Dylan has written some of the most banal, uninspired and inventionless songs of his career." But a journalist from the *San Jose Mercury News* was grateful that he was no longer performing as "some pained imitation of Neil Diamond" but rather was "singing from a hurt in the heart, from somewhere deep inside himself." The same writer noted that there were "loud boos" and numerous walk-outs.[10] But apparently word got around that while Dylan was absolutely not going to play any of his old songs, the performance was incredible. "After the first three nights," recalled Spooner Oldham, "all the rebels didn't come back or [they] accepted it. It calmed down and everybody seemed to enjoy it more."[11]

Over the next few weeks, Dylan and the band played small theaters in Santa Monica, Tempe, San Diego, Albuquerque, and Tucson.

Then after a month off for the holidays they resumed the tour in January, going from Seattle to Charleston, West Virginia, another nineteen dates in eight states. He would take another hiatus to record the new songs he'd been performing—the *Saved* album—then return for a month of concerts in the Northeastern USA and Canada. The official Bootleg Series box *Trouble No More* offers eight CDs' worth of testimony to the soulfulness and passion of those performances. Except for a slightly shifting cast of backing vocalists—at one point in 1980 their number was up to five—the band stayed intact through July 1981 and continued to burn through potent new songs like "Saved" and "Solid Rock," while simmering on the slow, heavy blues of "Cover Down, Pray Through" and the more meditative "What Can I Do For You?" and "Pressing On."

What we don't hear on the *Trouble No More* CDs are Dylan's infamous between-song "raps" or mini-sermons. At times he interpreted contemporary global politics in terms of the second coming, predicting an imminent war of Armageddon ("Russia is gonna come down and attack the Middle East. It says this in the Bible".[12]) At other times he disparaged detractors in the audience or previous audiences. At a Hartford, Connecticut, concert in May 1980 he fell into a rant about San Francisco being a gay mecca: "Anyway, it's a place for homosexuals. I mean, they have homosexual politics. It's a political party. I don't mean it's going on in somebody's closet. I mean it's political. You know I'm talking about? . . . I guess the iniquity's not yet full. And I don't wanna be around when it is!"[13] While gay-bashing was not a regular feature of his shows, these remarks demonstrate how narrow-minded and conservative Dylan's worldview had become during the hardcore "gospel" period.

When the band returned to Muscle Shoals in February to record *Saved* they had been playing the album's songs live for a few months—an unusual circumstance for Dylan, who nearly always recorded with little rehearsal, forcing spontaneity by throwing musicians into the deep end. *Saved* seems to justify Dylan's usual method, because the studio versions of these songs pale in comparison to the live versions that preceded them. The album was recorded at the same studio by the same producers who did *Slow Train Coming*, but, as Keltner put it, the music itself "didn't want to be anything like *Slow Train Coming.* It wanted to have a big, open, live, exciting sound to match the praise [in] the songs. And it didn't happen. It didn't come across [on] tape."[14] Some of the power comes through on "Saved," "Solid Rock," "Pressing On," and "Are You Ready," the album's more energetic, harder-edged songs, but Keltner is certainly right that they all sound better live.

For record buyers it didn't help that unlike its predecessor *Saved* lacked the element of surprise—having processed one Christian Dylan album, old fans were not especially intrigued by another one. And the cover art—looking like something out of a Christian comic book, the Lord's hand emanating light and reaching downward, pointer finger extended to touch one of the cluster of upstretched human hands—made it clear even before you split the cellophane that Dylan hadn't budged doctrinally. (The album was later reissued with a less garish cover, a manipulated photograph of Dylan performing onstage, taken from the original inner sleeve.)

On February 27, Dylan picked up his first Grammy award: Best Male Rock Vocal Performance for "Gotta Serve Somebody." The fact that this was his first (and even then in a narrowly defined genre category) is evidence of how out of touch the Grammys were in the 1960s and to a lesser extent the 1970s. Perhaps more significant than the award was the performance Dylan gave at the ceremony. Introduced to a standing ovation he led the band, decked out in tuxedos and black evening gowns, through a pulsating version of the Grammy-winning hit.

From *Saturday Night Live* the previous October through May of 1980 Dylan played more than seventy shows without doing a single pre-*Slow Train* song. Over the summer of 1980, though, he returned to writing songs without overt born-again messages, while continuing to compose Christian songs as well. In September he began rehearsing the band again at Rundown Studios, putting them through their paces on new material as well as some of his older songs and a range of covers that recalls *Self Portrait*—including the Temptations' "I Wish It Would Rain," Dave Mason's "We Just Disagree," the Little Willie John–Peggy Lee standard "Fever," and even the recent breakout hit from *The Muppet Movie*, "Rainbow Connection."

In the meantime he had found a new love interest in Clydie King, a renowned singer who had replaced Carolyn Dennis on *Saved* and the spring tour. (When King died in 2019 Dylan paid tribute to her as "my ultimate singing partner . . . No one ever came close."[15]) This wasn't the end of Dylan's "Gospel phase"—he would continue to perform his religious songs when he resumed touring in the fall and would never refer to it as a closed chapter in his life. But now the Christian songs would be part of, rather than the entirety of, his concerts, which he would approach with less missionary zeal.

In November 1980, after almost six months off the road, Dylan returned to San Francisco's Warfield Theatre, where he had started his Christian campaign a year earlier, for another two-week run. On the first night he opened with "Gotta Serve Somebody" and "I Believe in You," just as he had done a year earlier. But now the third song was "Like a Rolling Stone." Christian songs still outnumbered secular songs, but before the evening was over the crowd also heard "Girl from the North Country," "Just Like a Woman," "Señor (Tales of Yankee Power)," a lovely duet with Clydie King on Dion's 1968 hit "Abraham, Martin and John," a new love song called "Let's Keep It Between Us," and, closing the show, "Blowin' in the Wind." Gradually more old Dylan songs and covers made their way into the set, shifting the balance by the end of this second Warfield residency. He told an interviewer that fall that he had decided his old songs "weren't anti-God at all. I wasn't sure about that for a while."[16] Moreover close listeners like Paul Williams noticed "ambivalence" in the performance of the gospel songs, as if Dylan didn't want to give up on them but "hasn't found a way to reinvent them, to make them part of what he feels as a performer right now."[17]

Meanwhile Dylan had been filling up spiral notebooks and hotel stationery with new lyrics and eventually fully developed songs. "Every Grain of Sand," the most powerful of these new compositions, would anchor his next album. In structure and in its visionary, abstract imagery "Every Grain" recalls "Chimes of Freedom"; the insistence on the spiritual unity of all creation also evokes Dylan's early secular hymn "Lay Down Your Weary Tune," while gesturing to William Blake's poem "Auguries of Innocence," which begins,

To see a World in a Grain of Sand
And a Heaven in a Wild Flower
Hold Infinity in the palm of your hand
And Eternity in an hour . . .[18]

The song describes the singer's struggle with temptation, loneliness, and despair; the metaphors for these feelings are commonplace, but they're woven together effectively. Each refrain returns to the consolation that comes with recognizing a vast, ultimately coherent design governing the universe. It's a theistic message but not a specifically Christian one; "Every Grain of Sand" sounds more Unitarian than Pentecostal or Baptist. It has been one of his most enduring songs, frequently covered, and resurrected as the show closer throughout the *Rough and Rowdy Ways* tour from 2021 to 2024.

Another song Dylan worked on in the studio and played live several times that fall, "The Groom's Still Waiting at the Altar," features a chorus that vaguely hints at a second coming. The bridegroom in the chorus could be Christ but doesn't have to be—there isn't much in the verses to reinforce a Christian interpretation. Instead there's a

With Tim Drummond on stage in Paris, June 1981.

loosely structured, dark monologue describing a personal breakdown, violent political upheaval, and an ill-fated relationship with a woman named Claudette. Dylan had drawn heavily on blues structures for his gospel songs, but the sound of "Groom" is harder-edged, classic urban blues, harkening back to his early electric period.

Other new songs were unequivocally secular. "Let's Keep It Between Us" is a soulful blues that, as its title suggests, warns against the dangers of allowing a romance to "go public." If Dylan were writing about his own life in that moment, the recipient of this message would be Clydie King, but he had no shortage of recent and long-past romances that had been kept out of the public eye. Whatever relationship he might have had in mind, the song reveals little about it—the lyrics are really about the prying eyes and meddlers that surround them.

Another great new song, "Caribbean Wind," Dylan played live only once—at the Warfield on November 12, responding to a request from the music journalist Paul Williams. Dylan had told Williams privately that he was proud of this new song and shared the lyrics with him, but a few years later (in the liner notes to *Biograph*) he remarked, "That one I couldn't quite grasp what it was about after I finished it . . . I think there's four different sets of lyrics to this, maybe I got it right, I don't know. I had to leave it."[19] There are in fact many variations in the lyrics (live, studio, published), but suffice it to say that "Caribbean Wind" presents another story of a past encounter with a woman whose memory haunts the singer. As with certain *Blood on the Tracks* songs the lyrics dwell on disjointed fragments rather than forming a seamless, coherent narrative; as Williams argues, the song's success "depends not on the conveying of information but on the conveying of a *feeling*; what it's like to be inside this moment."[20] Intriguingly this moment would seem to be happening in a tropical film noir, perhaps *Key Largo* or *To Have and Have Not*. And like most of Dylan's songs from this period it sounded much better live than in the studio.

After a brief tour following the second Warfield residency Dylan took another extended break before returning to the studio in the spring of 1981. He had gotten used to recording informally at

Rundown since making *Street-Legal* there, but he also tried out other Los Angeles studios with new producers. At one point he brought in Jimmy Iovine, the future mogul who had worked with Springsteen and recently produced breakthrough albums for Patti Smith (*Easter*) and Tom Petty (*Damn the Torpedoes*), but the collaboration didn't work, mainly because Dylan wanted the musicians playing together in the same room. He tried the legendary Robert "Bumps" Blackwell, who had co-written and produced early hits for Dylan's teenage idol Little Richard. Their session did produce his next album's title track, "Shot of Love," but that was all that made the cut.

The remainder of the album would be recorded at Clover Studios in Hollywood with Chuck Plotkin more or less at the helm, aided by recording engineer Toby Scott and Dylan's recording assistant Arthur Rosato. Plotkin and Scott had recently mixed Springsteen's *The River*, which recommended them as a team that could get a "live" sound in a modern studio. But they were unprepared for Dylan's headstrong opposition to separating musicians and overdubbing, in addition to his refusal to wear headphones.

Scott recalled, "if Bob had a guitar in his hands, at any instant he [might] start playing, the band would join in and he'd get to a microphone—maybe—and start singing the song . . . On one song Chuck ran from the control room and picked up the vocal mike, stand and all, and followed Bob around the studio pointing the mike at Bob's mouth."[21]

The difficulties didn't end there. According to Scott, Dylan essentially refused to let him and Plotkin mix the tapes (that is, to blend and balance the multiple tracks that make up each recording), so that the album as issued was a rough or "monitor" mix.[22] As a result *Shot of Love* sounds "live" but also thin and a bit shrill.

And when collectors—and eventually everyone else, thanks to the official Bootleg Series—heard the songs that had been left off the album, *Shot of Love* became known for the great album it *could have been*, making the album it *was* even more of a disappointment. In addition to "Let's Keep It Between Us," "The Groom's Still Waiting at the Altar," and "Caribbean Wind," Dylan abandoned a wonderful rave-up called "Price of Love" and the haunting "Angelina," yet another fascinating ill-fated love story set against images of revolution and apocalypse. (Maybe he just had too many revolution-apocalypse-romance songs and decided to leave them all off?) Angelina is a sinister angel, a goddess who must be resisted at the peril of one's soul. As with other songs from late 1980 and early '81, this one takes place in a world of deception, where good and evil are hard to tell apart, evoking biblical and pseudo-biblical imagery to create an atmosphere of mystery and dread. But Dylan was no longer deploying that imagery to tell his listeners what to think or what to do.

Recorded with his touring band, *Shot of Love* begins and ends well—with the infectious, rousing title track and the beautiful "Every Grain of Sand." But most of the songs Dylan ultimately included were lyrically one-dimensional and musically run-of-the-mill. Powered by Keltner, Drummond, and Tackett, the band is tight enough to breathe life into songs like "Trouble" and "Dead Man, Dead Man" (one of only two songs, the other being "Property of Jesus," that presents an unequivocal born-again Christian message). Other tracks never seem to get off the ground. Ronnie Wood, Ringo, and Donald "Duck" Dunn (bass player for Booker T and the MGs) made guest appearances on "Heart of Mine," but you wouldn't really know it if they weren't listed on the album's credits.

Shot of Love improved significantly when "Groom's Still Waiting" was added in later pressings as well as CD and cassette releases—the song had gotten unexpected FM radio play as the B-side of the single "Heart of Mine." Still this potentially great album, which also had the attraction of being Dylan's transition away from hard-core sermonizing, is frustratingly mediocre. It raised the possibility, previously suggested by *Budokan* and the 1978 tour, that Dylan might finally be a regular, mainstream singer-songwriter. In his review Lester Bangs wrote, "If you suspend all expectations in any direction, and maybe if you even forget who made it, you can probably just throw *Shot of Love* on and enjoy a nice, bluesy, decidedly minor LP by a medium-level folk-rocker."[23] This was not a recommendation.

Shot of Love was released in August 1981, between the European and North American legs of a tour that continued to combine secular Dylan classics with his recent gospel songs. (Another regular feature of the European shows was a Dylan–King duet on the Jerome Kern–Otto Harbach standard "Let's Begin.") The fact that Dylan had embraced his pre-Christian catalogue was no secret, but it didn't create tremendous excitement or demand for tickets—in fact the very last scheduled tour date, in Tallahassee, was cancelled because of poor sales.[24] Dylan had been rejuvenated by his new calling when this series of tours began in fall 1979; by the end of 1981, while he was presumably still Christian, his career was more or less back where it had been before he picked up that silver cross.

Just after the new year Howard Alk, Dylan's longtime friend and filmmaking collaborator, died of a drug overdose. Dylan may have felt haunted as well by the tragic deaths of heroes and friends, which by now included the suicides of Paul Clayton and Phil Ochs, the drug-related death of Elvis Presley, and the assassination of John Lennon. He told Arthur Rosato, his longtime assistant, that he had decided to stay off the road until 1984. "He was upset," Rosato recalled, "and he talked a bit. He wanted to know if I was going to be okay . . . But he shut down the studio then and there."[25]

Dylan spent the next year out of the spotlight. He took several trips to the Caribbean, where he vacationed in Anguilla and sailed on a 68-foot (21 m) luxury schooner called the *Water Pearl*, which he co-owned with its builder, Chris Bowman.[26] He spent part of the summer, as he often did, in Minnesota with his children and occasionally showed up at concerts (Big Joe Turner, Squeeze, Stray Cats), sometimes joined by his son Jesse.[27] Meanwhile the Point Dume house in Malibu, which he retained in the divorce, had become his home base. In June he made a surprise appearance at the Peace Sunday anti-nuclear concert held at the Rose Bowl in nearby Pasadena, singing with Joan Baez and performing an unlikely cover of Jimmy Buffett's "A Pirate Looks at Forty" (he had recently turned 41 himself). All the while he was writing—filling notebooks with ideas and preliminary lyrics, as he had done for years.

In early 1983 Dylan was ready to record again. He sounded out a few famous musicians (reportedly Frank Zappa, David Bowie, and Elvis Costello) as potential producers, finally settling on Mark Knopfler—the logic being that a fellow performer would be more reliable than someone who mainly inhabited the studio. Knopfler was eager to work with Dylan again and agreed to devote a month's break from touring with Dire Straits to the project. He brought in Straits' keyboard player Alan Clark, while Dylan, fresh from the Caribbean, recruited the legendary Jamaican rhythm section of Sly Dunbar (drums) and Robbie Shakespeare (bass)—and, perhaps to challenge or push Knopfler, added former Rolling Stones lead guitarist Mick Taylor to the band. The combination of Sly and Robbie's pulsating drum-and-bass and the sleek, fluid modern rock of Dire Straits would give this album-only band a unique, enchanting sound.

Dylan's working title was *Surviving in a Ruthless World*, but by the time of its release it had become *Infidels*. Both titles make sense in reference to the songs' content, which is thematically bleaker than any Dylan album since *Highway 61 Revisited*. We live in a ruthless world inhabited by infidels—not in a narrow doctrinal sense but as a description of the modern human condition of faithlessness and the moral corruption that comes with it.

The opening track, "Jokerman," is one of Dylan's most compelling songs, one that he revised heavily in the weeks leading up to the recorded version—the numerous extant drafts (housed at the Bob Dylan Archive) are a testament to Dylan the obsessive craftsman. The title character, possibly a fleshed-out version of the Joker from "All Along the Watchtower," is described in contradictory terms: angelic and demonic, playful and nefarious, divine and degraded. The ruthless world he inhabits and for which he is a kind of emblem or figurehead is the world of Desolation Row, almost two decades later. Jokerman survives by being ruthless himself. He is beautiful, with features worthy of a Michelangelo sculpture, and he is a snake, shedding his skin when necessary. In my reading Jokerman is "man" (the gender-specific term seems appropriate to the song's outlook), gifted to the point of being in some ways superhuman but also inherently corrupt and confused, a true infidel.

Similarly "License to Kill" presents "man" fulfilling a self-destructive fate, a modern tragic hero. He is a victim of his own hubris and self-worship. The voice of warning—literally the chorus, as in a

Greek tragedy—is a woman, who repeatedly asks if anyone will take away "man's" license to kill.

Dylan, never known to embrace modern views of women, again posits a corrupt world of men threatening the innocence of a woman in "Sweetheart Like You." The refrain is a variation on the proverbial "What's a nice girl like you doing in a place like this?"—but this "place" seems to be not just a dingy nightclub but the material world itself. Unfortunately for the "sweetheart", the singer who is seducing her may be a representative character of that dangerous world. After kissing her he asks how much abuse she will be able to take. And at the song's chilling close the "permanent bliss" that he seems to be offering is one step down. I don't think she should trust this guy.

Apocalyptic imagery runs through *Infidels*, but the song that comes closest to the eschatology of Dylan's Vineyard Fellowship years is "Man of Peace." Like Jokerman, the Satan who comes as a man of peace is shape-shifting and beguiling—the Führer or a priest, who knows?—but he is also an entertainer who knows all the love songs. There's a lot of conventional wisdom here—Satan is a master of disguise, the road to perdition is paved with good intentions, peace-in-our-time might lead to greater future suffering. The song ends with a promise of apocalypse in the penultimate verse and salvation in the last verse, but even then a seemingly hopeful image of a blue-eyed boy finding Christ is undercut by the final refrain: Satan appearing as a man of peace.

"I and I," a song possibly even more opaque and fascinating than "Jokerman," epitomizes the album's somber outlook. Terry Gans reports that a pair of Bequian crew members on the *Water Pearl* used the phrase "I and I" prolifically; Dylan may also have been thinking of Rimbaud's famous anti-grammatical expression, "Je est une autre" (I is someone else)—in *Chronicles* he says that "bells went off" when he first read that sentence.[28] It is hard not to imagine Dylan as the double "I." The song plays out like a mid-century Existentialist novel, the narrator having slept with an unnamed stranger and now going out for a contemplative walk. While the sun should be rising higher as he walks, by noon the road is only getting darker. In another apocalyptic overture he muses that the world could end tonight; meanwhile the woman in his bed is probably still asleep. This time there's no suggestion of a

Christian second coming, just a meaningless end to everything. "I is someone else" because of a division in the self—public/private, active/contemplative, the mind (one "I") contemplating itself (the other). The two can never be completely reconciled. Like the "strange woman" in my bed I am a stranger to myself. In the poignant last line—appropriate for a song structured as an aimless walk—he complains that he makes shoes for everyone else but still goes barefoot. His fate is to live without the services he provides—whether those services include escape, insight, or something else.

Infidels was rounded out with a closing love song that reflects the album's cosmic despair—"Don't Fall Apart on Me Tonight"—and a pair of topical blues-rockers. "Union Sundown" protests the march of globalization in jingoistic, buy-American terms, but its lament of organized labor's decline also decried President Ronald Reagan's union-busting and promotion of free-market capitalism. Through thinly veiled allegory and sarcasm "Neighborhood Bully" offers a full-throated defense of Israel in the wake of the invasion of Lebanon in June 1982. Although the song's thrust is more political than religious, it added to speculation that Dylan was revisiting Judaism as he seemingly backed away from evangelical Christianity. In September 1983, between the album's completion and its release, he visited Israel on the occasion of his son Jesse's bar mitzvah and was photographed at the Western Wall. For *Infidels*' inner sleeve he included another photograph of himself on the Mount of Olives, with Jerusalem in the background. Significantly the photograph was taken by Sara Dylan, who had joined him on the trip, reconciled if not reunited.

With Knopfler as co-producer and state-of-the-art equipment at New York's Power Station, Dylan temporarily reversed his position against modern studio techniques, employing isolated instrument tracks, overdubs, even digital recording. In fact when Knopfler left New York to resume touring with Dire Straits the first week of May, Dylan spent two more months messing around with the mixes.[29] The album's sound is clear and punchy (very "digital"), with the drums, particularly the snare, pushed way up in the mix—something that became a fetish of 1980s production style but even so is unusually pronounced on *Infidels*.

After Knopfler's departure Dylan also reconsidered which songs to include on the album. In addition to the songs described above, another album's worth of new, original songs had been recorded during the April sessions. Even more than *Shot of Love*, *Infidels* left a trail of ghost albums that critics and fans have assembled on websites, fanzines, and homemade CDs. Among the unjustly excluded tracks are "Someone's Got a Hold of My Heart" (which reappeared as "Tight Connection to My Heart" on Dylan's next studio album) and the beautiful "Lord Protect My Child," which recasts the hopeful blessing of "Forever Young" as a prayer that reminds us (yet again) of the degenerate state of the world. But the two no-doubters, both of which Dylan inexplicably dropped, are "Foot of Pride" and "Blind Willie McTell."

In his comprehensive book on the making of *Infidels* Terry Gans describes how diligently Dylan worked on "Foot of Pride," going through sixteen written drafts and 47 takes of this six-verse song.[30] It's basically a rap performed over a blues progression, a return to *Highway 61*-era panoramas with multiple characters inhabiting a modern wasteland: the published lyrics start with an unnamed dead man and then proceed to another man named James, a businessman who goes by Red, Miss Delilah (a "philistine"), and assorted baby killers and hypocrites ("beautiful people"), before returning to the first dead man. As Gans observes, "an almost hazy evil pervades each of these verses."[31] There's no story, just one intriguing portrait of corruption and pride after another, consistent with the preoccupations of *Infidels*. The version released on the first installment of the Bootleg Series would have been one of the best tracks on the album, and the version released on *Springtime in New York* (Bootleg Series volume XVI) is even better, with a more elastic rhythm and more venomous vocal delivery from Dylan.

And then there's "Blind Willie McTell," which, since its official release on the premiere Bootleg Series, has become one of Dylan's most admired songs. For comparison consider Robert Hayden's poem "Homage to the Empress of the Blues" (1962), which alternates stanzas sketching out the pain of unfaithful lovers and a cold winter in a dilapidated house with stanzas describing the resplendent Bessie

Smith onstage: "She came out on stage in ostrich feathers, beaded satin,/ and shone that smile on us and sang."[32] At the risk of flattening the poem, the logic is that Smith sang the blues boldly, in extravagant costumes, to simultaneously express and offer relief from the hardships that her audience endured. Dylan does something similar to Hayden in "Blind Willie McTell," a song that pays homage to another great blues singer.

Best known for "Statesboro Blues," McTell recorded sporadically from the 1920s to the 1950s; although he was never as famous or as flamboyant as Bessie Smith, he made a good living as a performer, dressed well, and (like Smith) did not pander to white audiences' stereotypes of Black-blues-singer authenticity.[33] Dylan mentions McTell only in the refrain, but the repetition—no one can sing the blues like him—says it all. The rest of the lyrics commemorate suffering and despair, with particular reference to "the ghosts of slavery's ships" as well as modern African American life.[34] If no one can sing the blues like McTell it's not the subject-matter of his songs so much as his voice—which is clear and bright, "more obviously eloquent of poise than suffering," as Michael Gray puts it. It's that voice that conveys to Dylan, and to other white listeners, some understanding of African American history.

The melody of "Blind Willie McTell" echoes "St. James Infirmary," a classic blues that shares a lineage with "The Dyin' Crapshooter's Blues," recorded by Blind Willie McTell in 1940 and 1949. Both songs contemplate death and both end with the singer giving instructions for his own elaborate funeral. Dylan makes this connection explicit in the last verse, where the singer gazes out from the St. James Hotel. Like "St. James Infirmary" and "Homage to the Empress of the Blues," "Blind Willie McTell" attempts to convey, without explaining, what the blues mean, what the blues are for. Acknowledging the essentially African American experience of the blues, he offers a broad explanation of the suffering that fuels Blind Willie McTell's music.

According to sound engineer Neil Dorfsman, "Everyone was in shock when he dropped it."[35] Dylan would later claim that he left "Blind Willie McTell" off the album because "It was never developed fully, I never got around to completing it." Perhaps there was more he wanted to do with it, but it's hard to imagine this heartbreaking, powerful song, or the performance that was eventually released in 1991, as anything but complete—as Gray describes it, a "visionary requiem for America's past and everybody's future."[36]

In the two years since Dylan had released *Shot of Love*, MTV had rapidly changed the way rock music was promoted and was reshaping how it was performed and consumed. With the "Subterranean Homesick Blues" cue-card sequence Dylan had made one of the most influential music videos almost two decades earlier; now he would star in a much more conventional clip for "Sweetheart Like You," *Infidels'* first single. The filming took place long after the album had been recorded, so with the exception of bass player Robbie Shakespeare, musicians in the video are mimicking parts played by others on the record. Notably Clydie King, who does not even sing on "Sweetheart," appears as the organist. In a stage-set nightclub the band plays while an older woman, a "sweetheart" who sweeps up after the show, pauses to listen.

The following March MTV debuted the more ambitious video for "Jokerman," conceived by Dylan's old friends Larry "Ratso" Sloman and George Lois. Dylan carelessly lip-synchs most of the choruses, looking airbrushed and clean-shaven, wearing a stylish cream-colored jacket over a white T-shirt. But for most of the video song lyrics are superimposed on dozens of famous paintings, sculptures, and photographs, including images of Dylan through the years, along with Hitler and Ronald Reagan.[37] While many of the visual images are literal representations of specific lyrics, the cumulative effect is to illuminate the song's range of meanings.

Infidels was cheered by critics and fans—*Rolling Stone* gave it four-and-a-half stars with reviewer Christopher Connelly declaring it Dylan's best since *Blood on the Tracks*—and it sold better than *Saved* or *Shot of Love*. Somewhat like the reception of *New Morning*, there was a collective sigh of relief at the return of the Dylan "we" know. So it was a good time for him to do something a little perverse. On March 22, 1984 Dylan appeared on *Late Night with David Letterman*, which, along with MTV, was a defining phenomenon of early 1980s television. He brought in a backing band of young musicians he had been jamming with in Malibu for months—drummer Charlie Quintana and bassist Tony Marsico of the unsigned punk band the Plugz and like-minded guitarist JJ Holiday. Dylan did not rehearse the band specifically for the show or tell them ahead of time which songs they would play.

"I figured we'd play at least one from *Infidels*," recalled Marsico, "but when we were walking out onstage, he just said, 'Sonny Boy in E.' It was like, oh shit, here we go."[38]

"Sonny Boy in E" meant "Don't Start Me to Talkin'" by Sonny Boy Williamson, which they *had* played before at least. It was a raw, high-energy performance, as close to punk as Dylan would ever come, played with a trio of musicians half his age. When he did play songs from *Infidels* they were equally edgy—awesome renditions of "License to Kill" and "Jokerman" that bear little sonic resemblance to what's on the album. Near the end of "Jokerman" Dylan put down his guitar and picked up a harmonica in the wrong key; the band continued to bash out another wordless verse while Dylan searched for the right harp. The mishap somehow only enhanced the performance, after which Letterman jokingly asked if they could play the show every Thursday. (There's a Mailgram from him in the Bob Dylan Archive that reads, "Dear Bob, It's Thursday. Why aren't you here? Best Wishes, David Letterman."[39]) For the time being at least, Dylan was back.

12

1984–92: Restoration

On January 28, 1985, Bob Dylan joined a choir of musical luminaries—Michael Jackson, Stevie Wonder, Lionel Richie, Bruce Springsteen, Cyndi Lauper, Diana Ross, Ray Charles, Dionne Warwick, Harry Belafonte, Tina Turner, Paul Simon, Billy Joel, and many others—to record "We Are the World." USA for Africa's response to the British Band Aid's "Do They Know It's Christmas?" would play constantly on radio and MTV that spring and summer, topping the charts and raising millions for famine relief. The cause was worthy, even if the song itself was predictably smug and saccharine.

The recording session was like a high school prom for pop stars; no one—other than Prince—was too cool to show up. In the "making-of" documentary we see a profoundly uncomfortable Dylan surrounded by more eager participants, and when it's his turn to sing his solo line he needs a little help. Only after some coaching and a good-natured Dylan impersonation from Stevie Wonder does he manage to deliver his line about saving our own lives, after which it's all smiles and hugs, a star hobnobbing with other stars.[1]

Six months later Dylan performed at the conclusion of the fourteen-hour Live Aid concert at Philadelphia's JFK Stadium. As the "voice of a generation" and the songwriter who made social consciousness part of the pop music vocabulary, he was the obvious choice to cap off the event, even more so because he could play an acoustic set in front of a curtain while the all-star choir set up for a "We Are the World" finale. While Dylan himself probably wasn't concerned about what this performance meant for his career, it's worth noting that Live Aid was broadcast to almost 2 billion viewers worldwide, and, revered as he was, Dylan had not held a central place in pop culture since his mid-seventies comeback. He hadn't had a top-ten hit since "Lay Lady Lay" in 1969.

Originally Dylan was scheduled to perform "Blowin' in the Wind" with Peter, Paul and Mary, but after rehearsing with them he nixed the idea (leaving Peter, Paul and Mary off the program altogether), instead bringing out Keith Richards and Ron Wood—three amigos, three acoustic guitars.[2] The performance did not go well. They were all fairly wasted by the time they hit the stage, Dylan looking particularly spent and sweating profusely. The stage monitors were behind the curtain, so the trio were probably unable to hear themselves; the frantic herding of singers for the finale provided additional distractions. They played three songs, the inevitable "Blowin' in the Wind" preceded by two others from Dylan's "protest" phase—"The Ballad of Hollis Brown" and "When the Ship Comes In," which were appropriate to the occasion but probably unknown to 99 percent of the audience.

As the ballad of a desperately impoverished farmer, "Hollis Brown" also set Dylan up to make a pitch for diverting "some of the money . . . one or two million, maybe" to pay the mortgages of struggling U.S. farms. Live Aid organizer Bob Geldof was incensed: Dylan's remark undermined the promise that funds raised by the concert would go directly to African famine relief, while implicitly equating economic hardship in a wealthy nation with mass starvation in Ethiopia.[3]

Infidels had raised the hopes of his followers, but for the most part Dylan's 1980s were epitomized by his Live Aid appearance. He was an icon of the music industry but also a dissipated ghost from a generation of artists who had made their statements and were now just going through the motions—or so it seemed at the time. It would be a hard rut to escape. In *Chronicles* he assesses his mid-1980s career: "I was what they called over the hill. If I wasn't careful I could end up ranting and raving in shouting matches with the wall. The mirror had swung around and I could see the future—an old actor fumbling in garbage cans outside the theater of past triumphs."[4]

But he wasn't about to just quit. To support *Infidels* Dylan had gone back on the road in the summer of 1984 after a long hiatus, playing 27 stadium shows across Europe. Accentuating the "Woodstock Generation" vibe, promoter Bill Graham paired him with Santana for the tour, adding Joan Baez and Van Morrison for a few appearances as well. Dylan's latest band had a classic British rock sound built around former Stone Mick Taylor on guitar, Small Faces/Faces veteran Ian McLagen on keyboards, and Colin Allen, who had played with John Mayall's Bluesbreakers and Donovan, on drums, the token American being Gregg Sutton on bass. This was the most straight-ahead rock band Dylan had toured with since the Band in 1974, and their Stones/Faces swagger was particularly effective on blues-based classics like "Highway 61 Revisited," "It Takes a Lot to Laugh," and "Tombstone Blues." The setlist spanned Dylan's career but was weighted heavily toward old favorites, with only one or two songs from the trio of gospel albums and usually three from *Infidels*. A completely rewritten "Tangled Up in Blue," performed solo, was a highlight, along with a partially rewritten "Simple Twist of Fate" played with the full band.

Overall these were impressive shows delivered to large, enthusiastic crowds. At Wembley Stadium in London Dylan was joined onstage by Morrison, Eric Clapton, and Chrissie Hynde; at the final show in the grounds of Slane Castle in Ireland he sang "Blowin' in the Wind" with Bono, who had recently recorded *The Unforgettable Fire* there with U2. The tour is represented somewhat meekly by the official *Real Live* album, released in November 1984—ten songs from a setlist that was over twice as long, and not necessarily the best performances.

But *Real Live* served the purpose of maintaining Dylan's Columbia contract, which required an album per year. In interviews throughout the mid-1980s he would complain about studio recording—it had never been his favorite part of the job, but making records now seemed particularly painful. He still didn't like the artificiality that studio technology imposed on performance, but he was also struggling to generate worthy material to record. Although masterpieces like "Blind Willie McTell" and "Foot of Pride" remained unreleased, for his 1985 album *Empire Burlesque* he would recycle two other songs from the *Infidels* sessions, "Clean Cut Kid" and "Someone's

With Mick Taylor and Carlos Santana, 1984. Photo by Heinrich Klaffs.

Got a Hold of My Heart," the latter substantially rewritten as "Tight Connection to My Heart (Has Anybody Seen My Love)."

"Tight Connection," the lead track and unsuccessful single from *Empire Burlesque*, is intriguing but not quite coherent lyrically, partly because Dylan cut and pasted several lines from old Bogart movies and an episode of *Star Trek*.[5] It has a nice, soulful feel, though, and the vocals by Carolyn Dennis, Queen Esther Marrow, and Peggi Blu—it isn't fair to call them "background" vocals—are strong enough to overcome the song's shortcomings. That's true of *Empire Burlesque* as a whole: the songs are elevated whenever the trio of Dennis, Marrow, and Blu show up, and even more when vocalist Madelyn Quebec is featured ("Trust Yourself," "When the Night Comes Falling from the Sky," "I'll Remember You").

This being 1985 MTV videos were required, and the one made for "Tight Connection" comes across as an unintentional parody of the genre, which is to say, it's stagey and playful, it flaunts its large budget (shot in Japan with multiple sets and locations; Dylan wears at least six different outfits), it features several randomly placed beautiful women, it's directed by an accomplished filmmaker (Paul Schrader), and it makes no sense. The song's odd reference to a powder-blue wig becomes a visual motif, a clue to some non-existent mystery. Dylan can be seen on the streets of Tokyo, in an upscale hotel, at some sort of clothing warehouse; at various times he is engaged in earnest conversation with elegant women, interrogated and imprisoned by Japanese police, playing guitar in a lounge where another woman is singing "Tight Connection," miming the last chorus with karaoke singers, etc. It's fun to watch even now, but it's hard to imagine that any of this was Dylan's idea.

He had fought for artistic freedom and self-determination throughout his career, but now he seemed to be ceding control. It's not as if any one individual, a manager for instance, was telling him what to do—since Grossman's departure Dylan was supported by a number of loyal advisors for various parts of his business, a list that in the 1970s and '80s included Naomi Saltzman, Jerry Weintraub, Elliott Roberts, Gary Shafner, Jeff Rosen, and Debbie Gold. Instead he seems to have believed that in order to stay relevant he had to play along with new music-industry expectations, including stylish music videos and modern-sounding tracks.

Even more than *Infidels*, *Empire Burlesque* is mired in mid-1980s sound effects—drum machines and other amped-up percussion, synthesizers assuming the role of strings and horns, lots of echo, and an overall bright, busy sound. Musicians including Ron Wood, Al Kooper, Jim Keltner, and Sly and Robbie come and go, as the album was recorded piecemeal in Los Angeles and New York, with lots of overdubs. No producer is named on the album's sleeve or label, but Dylan hired Arthur Baker, best known at the time for dance remixes of pop hits, to oversee the mixing. He told Baker that he wanted "to make a record like Prince or Madonna."[6]

The Bootleg Series volume XVI: *Springtime in New York* offers stripped-down presentations of some of the stronger songs, including "Tight Connection" and "When the Night Comes Falling from the Sky," which was a staple of Dylan's setlists for the next couple of years. That song succeeds despite rather than because of the lyrics, which are a mash-up of abstractions, clichés, and mixed metaphors—rescued by the refrain, the repetition of the ominous title phrase.[7] "Seeing the Real You at Last" is a direct, in-your-face breakup song (which, like "Tight Connection," splices in old movie dialogue)[8]—and here too the lean, harder-rocking take included on *Springtime in New York* is a welcome alternative to what appears on the album. But regardless of the arrangements, writer's block is evident throughout *Empire Burlesque*'s mostly workmanlike songs. Even the feisty "Clean Cut Kid," which finds Dylan in familiar thematic territory—the violence of consumerism and conformity—comes across as an overwrought sermon.

But as if to set the rest of the album in relief Dylan concludes it with a solo acoustic performance, a meditation on beauty and artistic vision called "Dark Eyes." Each verse contrasts the workings of the material world with the non-temporal world of creativity, symbolized by the dark eyes. Ironically it was Arthur Baker's suggestion to include an acoustic song. According to Baker, "I was brought in to sort of 'modernize' Bob's sound. But I was still a fan and, as a fan, personally, I would have liked to strip the damn record down—but that wasn't what I was hired to do. Anyway, when I mentioned an acoustic song, and the very next day he came in with 'Dark Eyes,' I thought it was a song he already had . . . I think he only did two takes. It's one of his best songs of the 1980s."[9]

Released in June, a month before Live Aid, *Empire Burlesque* was greeted with mixed reviews and modest sales, which had become something of a pattern for Dylan albums since the mid-seventies. But a far more successful and influential collection was being prepared for Christmastime release: *Biograph*, a five-record box set spanning two decades. Curated by Jeff Rosen, who managed (and still manages) Dylan's publishing, *Biograph* offered new Dylan fans an introduction that included the big hits but was not restricted to his most famous songs. The tracks were sequenced neither chronologically nor thematically, yet each album side had its own logic and flow. It included eighteen previously unreleased recordings—including three live performances from 1966 and studio outtakes dating from 1962 ("Baby, I'm in the Mood for You") to 1981 ("Caribbean Wind")—justifying the purchase even for those of us who had all the albums. Not least, the lavishly illustrated booklet and sleeve notes were built from an extensive, often revelatory interview by Cameron Crowe.

Pop music had seen big multi-record sets before (mostly live albums) but *Biograph* was something new. Not coincidentally it came along just as compact discs were starting to claim significant market share, and it was available in that format as well as vinyl and cassette. Within a few years the major-artist career-spanning CD box set became a record-store fixture, an attractive way to repackage old recordings, mixing big hits with rare and previously unreleased tracks. For Dylan specifically *Biograph* also tested the market for the much more ambitious Bootleg Series that Rosen would launch on Dylan's behalf in the early 1990s.

In the months between the releases of *Empire Burlesque* and *Biograph*, Dylan's awkward suggestion that Live Aid proceeds be diverted to American farmers inspired Willie Nelson, Neil Young, and John Mellencamp to put together their own all-star concert event in Champaign, Illinois. Dylan could hardly turn down the invitation to appear at Farm Aid, where he would deliver a much stronger performance than he had in Philadelphia. He might have gained some perspective, or at least cleared his head, in the interim, having visited Russia to perform a few songs at a poetry festival in Moscow (other guests included James Ragan, Robert Bly, and Seamus Heaney). In *Chronicles* he would recall being allowed to ride Tolstoy's bicycle when he visited the author's estate.

At the suggestion of Debbie Gold, a tour manager who began working with Dylan around 1981, he teamed up with Tom Petty and the Heartbreakers for his Farm Aid set. "We rehearsed about a week, playing maybe a million different songs," he told an interviewer. "That was one of the best times I ever had. We were blazing."[10] Indeed Petty and the Heartbreakers were a great match for Dylan—a little younger and scrappier than the Mick Taylor–Ian McLagen band, a little older and more polished than the Plugz. Moreover the "big jangle" of Petty's Rickenbacker guitar recalled Roger McGuinn and the Byrds with an overlay of garage rock. Dylan was a few months away from touring, but their six-song set at Farm Aid convinced everyone involved that they should keep it going.

The "True Confessions" tour with Dylan and Petty began in February 1986 with a month of shows in New Zealand and Australia, followed by a week in Japan. After a break they would play arenas and stadia throughout North America over the summer. Petty's records were outselling Dylan's, but he was appropriately deferential onstage, playing mini-sets of his own songs and strumming along behind Dylan for the bulk of the show. They were joined by the "Queens of Rhythm," a quartet of singers that included Madelyn Quebec, Queen Esther Marrow, Carolyn Dennis, and Louise Bethune.[11]

"They were fabulous," recalls Stan Lynch, drummer for the Heartbreakers. "They also played rhythm, tambourine, and shakers. They were bringing the church to that shit." Lynch also believes Dylan raised the Heartbreakers' game: "We were all very reverent. I saw it immediately in the other guys, too. It was like, 'Oh, shit, we're in the presence of somebody who can really do this!' We thought we were seasoned vets, and we realized, 'This had been pre-cooked way before us. He's been good a long, long, long time.'"[12]

With Tom Petty and the Heartbreakers and the Queens of Rhythm, 1987.
Photo by John Atashian.

A one-hour, ten-song concert video from the Australian tour, first aired on HBO as *Hard to Handle*, offers some evidence of the band's fire: "In the Garden" (a holdover from the gospel period), "Just Like a Woman," "When the Night Comes Falling from the Sky," and "Knockin' on Heaven's Door" are particularly inspired. Unfortunately though, Dylan rushes carelessly through his solo performances of "It's Alright, Ma" and "Girl from the North Country." Dylan and the Heartbreakers never made a studio album together, but while in Australia they did record the title theme for the Paul Michael Glaser-directed *Band of the Hand*—both the single and the film disappeared quickly.

As with the 1984 European trek the "True Confessions" tour was a crowd-pleaser: a rock band with a big sound, playing a mix of recent songs and Dylan classics to huge audiences. Dylan might have been wondering if he could just keep touring and let the songwriting and recording slide. He had told Kurt Loder in 1984, "I'm just thankful I can play on stage and people will come and see me. Because I couldn't make it otherwise, I mean if I went out to play and nobody showed up, that would be the end of me. I wouldn't be making records, I'll tell you that. I only make records because people see me live."[13] And if anyone thought he had anything left to prove as a songwriter they need only delve into *Biograph*. But a record contract and a longstanding work ethic that revolved around writing kept him plugging away, trying to cobble together songs from random ideas and overheard phrases that filled spiral notebooks and scraps of paper.

Dylan seems to have become more unhappy and emotionally detached in the late 1980s. His former manager Albert Grossman died of a heart attack in January 1986. Dylan and Grossman hadn't been close for many years and were in litigation at the time of Grossman's death (Dylan would finally settle with Sally Grossman two years later to gain full control of his publishing).[14] And yet he and Grossman had once been a world-conquering team, and the passing of this one-time father figure held symbolic weight. He lost yet another friend, Richard Manuel, to suicide early that year, following many years of substance abuse and addiction.

Dylan meanwhile embraced the rock-and-roll lifestyle with perhaps more abandon than at any time since the mid-1960s, with alcohol and cocaine taking a heavier toll on a man now in his mid-forties. Lovers came and went, with numerous concurrent relationships. His long affair with Clydie King ended sometime in 1984.[15] Then in January 1986 he became a father again when Carolyn Dennis, who had sung with him on albums and tours dating back to *Street-Legal*, gave birth to a daughter, Desirée. Dylan and Dennis married on June 4 of that year but kept it secret (the marriage was later discovered by biographer Howard Sounes as he was researching his 2001 biography). He bought Dennis a house in suburban Los Angeles, where he also spent some time, but he continued to see other women, especially while on tour. He had another long-term relationship in the late 1980s with record executive Carole Childs. Britta Lee Shain, in an account of her own brief affair with Dylan in 1987, frequently mentions Childs as the acknowledged girlfriend but was unaware at the time that he was also married to Dennis. Shain's memoir is among other things a study in celebrity from the perspective of a hanger-on: Dylan effortlessly manipulates her and other members of his entourage and always gets what he wants.

At the same time other associates acknowledged the strain that comes with celebrity and adoration. David Was, who worked with Dylan a few years later, remembered, "There were times when he looked absolutely beleaguered, doing this stuff. It occurred to me that it was a continuous burden having to be 'Bob Dylan' after all these years."[16] He took to wearing a hoodie and ballcap and sometimes went off by himself incognito. He also rehired his old henchman Victor Maymudes to serve as chauffeur-gofer-bodyguard.

After the tour with Petty Dylan took another turn at film acting, with a role he was well prepared for—a burned-out rock star—in Richard Marquand's *Hearts of Fire*. Marquand was coming off major box office successes with *Return of the Jedi* and *Jagged Edge*, but nothing could save *Hearts of Fire* from critical and commercial failure. Dylan's character, Billy Parker, tries to guide the career of a promising young singer, Molly McGuire (played by Fiona Flanagan), but finds his mentorship—and Molly's affection—usurped by an arrogant, young New Romantic-style pop star (Rupert Everett). The wooden dialogue and slow, predictable storyline ensured the film's

Filming *Hearts of Fire* in Toronto, 1986.

early disappearance from theaters upon its release in late 1987. Dylan sleepwalks his way through it all, but at least he gets onstage a few times, his best moment being a barroom performance of John Hiatt's "The Usual." And in one uncanny bit of dialogue Billy Parker tells his protégée, "I guess I've always known I was never one of them rock and roll singers that was gonna win any Nobel Prize. Is that what you call it, Nobel Prize?"

Perhaps the best thing to come out of *Hearts of Fire* was a BBC documentary, *Getting to Dylan*, centered on Dylan's participation in the film. Director Christopher Sykes manages to interview a reluctant Dylan in his trailer while Dylan—either to put himself at ease or to psych out Sykes—sketches his interviewer's portrait (and it's a nice sketch). When pressed on the nature of his fame Dylan asserts that among all the famous people he knows "nobody seems to think it's what they really went after." As an example he says that if he looks into the window of a pub he can see people being "real" or natural, but he knows that if he walks in everyone's behavior will change immediately. Throughout the interview Dylan is in control but on edge, less hostile than in *Dont Look Back* but still defiant. He says he doesn't perform out of some need to be loved; rather "I do it because I *can* do it and because I think I'm good at it." And he insists that in a world where everyone wants to control you "I'm nobody's puppet, nobody pulls my strings," a claim that sounded somewhat hollow at this point in his career.

Dylan went back on the road with Petty and the Heartbreakers again in 1987—the "Temples in Flames" tour—just after a brief summertime run (six dates, all stadiums) with the Grateful Dead. The Dead appreciated Dylan's music and wanted to revisit some deep cuts from his catalogue, but Dylan didn't make it easy. He was unprepared or unsteady when the tour began, and he and the band butted heads over song selection. "It [was] as if we had never practiced," guitarist Bob Weir recalled. Dylan's setlist, he said, "didn't have much to do with what we had rehearsed."[17] *Dylan & the Dead*, the official live album released a year and a half later, attests to the band's struggle to make the collaboration work, as Dylan delivers some of the most uninspired vocals of his career.

When he wasn't on tour or on a movie set Dylan spent his time at his sprawling Malibu home, as well as the Minnesota farm and the Caribbean. In March of 1987 he sang to Elizabeth Taylor at her 55th birthday party and performed a beautiful solo rendition of a relatively obscure George Gershwin song, "Soon," at a Gershwin Gala at the Brooklyn Academy of Music. He seems to have been sort of floating along, but he still had albums to deliver to Columbia, so he rehearsed and recorded with various combinations of musicians and then cobbled together his next two records.

Released in August 1986, *Knocked Out Loaded* was a hodgepodge of an album that re-used some instrumental tracks from the *Empire Burlesque* sessions with new vocals and overdubs. The album's title, which comes from the blues classic "Junco Partner," suggests something sweatier and more daring than the finished product. At one point Dylan contemplated going all-covers—and in fact the album opens with a spirited version of Junior Parker's boogie blues "You Wanna Ramble" followed by Kris Kristofferson's "They Killed Him," an awkward spin-off of "Abraham, Martin and John" with Gandhi and Jesus Christ replacing the Kennedys. But the album's centerpiece is the eleven-minute "Brownsville Girl," which Dylan co-wrote with playwright and former Rolling Thunder chronicler Sam Shepard. A revision of an *Empire Burlesque* outtake called "New Danville Girl," "Brownsville Girl" opens with a dim memory of a Gregory Peck western, in which a dying gunfighter insists that his killer be allowed to go free, so he can know how it feels to face death every moment. That sentiment and the motif of a movie-as-dream, half-remembered, infuse the rest of the song, as he flashes back to his time with the Brownsville Girl. The singer also returns three more times to Gregory Peck, gradually blending his own memories with the movie's plot and dialogue. By far the most successful song on the album, it harkens back to the fractured, ill-fated love stories of *Blood on the Tracks*.

The remaining five tracks on *Knocked Out Loaded* are among the least interesting Dylan has ever released. They include two more collaborations (one song written with Petty, another with pop songwriter Carole Bayer Sager), a calypso version of the gospel standard "Precious Memories," and a pair of disposable, noisy rockers, "Driftin' Too Far from Shore" and "Maybe Someday." As with *Empire Burlesque*, no one is credited as producer, and again the sound is busy and bombastic. The Queens of Rhythm do their best, but aside from "You Wanna Ramble" and "Brownsville Girl" they don't get much to work with.

Almost two years later, when Dylan released *Down in the Groove*, not much had changed. There are more covers—six, if you count the traditional "Shenandoah"—and nothing that equals "Brownsville Girl." Moreover there's nothing to suggest that Dylan went into the studio with any kind of plan or even cared much about the results, which are spliced together from multiple sessions with over two dozen musicians and singers contributing. That said, *Down in the Groove* does have its pleasures, although they may differ from listener to listener. For me the opening cover of Wilbert Harrison's soulful "Let's Stick Together" is a nice surprise, as is the closing "Rank Strangers to Me," a country standard popularized by the Stanley Brothers. Still experimenting with songwriting collaboration, Dylan co-wrote two songs with Grateful Dead lyricist Robert Hunter, the regrettable "Ugliest Girl in the World" and the charming "Silvio," which also features Jerry Garcia and Bob Weir on backing vocals—Dylan sings about finding out what dead men know with the Dead along for the ride.

Dylan was never less independent in his career than he was in the years following *Infidels*. Writing with Hunter, Shepard, Petty, and Bayer Sager, touring with the Heartbreakers and the Dead—this was a period of collaboration for Dylan, and while some of the collaborations worked, his partners tended to cover for him, not to move him forward musically.

Probably the most enduring collaboration was also the most serendipitous. Dylan's old friend George Harrison had been kicking around the idea of an occasional supergroup with Jeff Lynne, and the opportunity presented itself in April 1988 when Harrison's record company asked him to come up with an original B-side for his next single. Harrison and Lynne were in Los Angeles at the time, and they managed to wrangle mutual friends Roy Orbison and Tom Petty to convene at Dylan's Point Dume home studio. The five of them wrote and recorded "Handle with Care" on the spot with Harrison taking the lead, and the Traveling Wilburys—as in, Wilbury it (we'll bury it) in the mix—were born. Warner Brothers, Harrison's label, saw that they had something too good and too marketable to "bury" as a B-side, and the quintet enjoyed the experience enough to expand the concept into an album.

The process was quick and easy, the songs lightweight and catchy. Further signaling that they weren't taking themselves too seriously, each member of the group adopted a Wilbury "family" moniker—Dylan got to be Lucky Wilbury (he can't help it if he's Lucky)—and they added drummer Jim Keltner in the role of cousin Buster Sidebury.[18] Dylan was the lead writer and singer on "Dirty World," "Congratulations," and "Tweeter and the Monkey Man," a playful story-song with multiple Springsteen references. *Traveling Wilburys Volume 1* sold far better than any 1980s Dylan album, and it hinted at more vitality and certainly more wit than his recent studio work.

Around the same time Dylan came to realize that something had to change. In *Chronicles* (and before that in interviews) he recalled a night onstage in Locarno, Switzerland, while touring with the Heartbreakers in October 1987, when he felt momentarily empty, unable to sing—and then suddenly felt reborn as a performer. "It's almost like I heard it as a voice," he said in a *Newsweek* interview. "It wasn't even like me thinking it. I'm determined to stand, whether God will deliver me or not . . . After that is when I sort of knew. I've got to go out and play these songs. That's what I must do."[19] He decided to start touring with a new, smaller band of his own, without the Queens of Rhythm, playing more modest venues and (re)building a fan base. He even imagined playing the same towns three consecutive years to build word-of-mouth and "form the nucleus of my future audience."[20]

While he didn't strictly follow that three-year plan, starting in 1988 Dylan *would* play about a hundred shows a year, mostly smaller venues, typically on the road six months at a time. His new approach would come to be known as the Never-Ending Tour, the term coined during a 1989 interview with *Q* magazine, though never embraced by Dylan himself.[21]

The first band he assembled consisted of guitarist G. E. Smith and drummer Chris Parker from the *Saturday Night Live* house band

(Dylan's promoters left Saturday nights open so that Smith and Parker could keep the *SNL* gig), along with bassist Kenny Aaronson—no keyboard, just the basic, stripped-down rock line-up. As usual, rehearsals were more like jam sessions, and the prime qualification for the job of Dylan sideman was the ability to follow his lead without instruction or advance notice. Setlists and arrangements changed frequently.

"He was standing directly in front of me," remembered Parker, "and I would watch his body language most of all. That was the only clue."[22] The versatile G. E. Smith was the ideal Dylan guitarist, with natural, dynamic stage presence and an encyclopedic knowledge of Dylan's catalogue as well as the range of folk, blues, and pop songs the boss might spontaneously decide to cover. At the first show of the tour in June Dylan opened with "Subterranean Homesick Blues," a song he had *never* played live before. On another, legendary night at Toad's Place in New Haven he played fifty (different) songs over four sets, mixing in surprise covers such as "Help Me Make It Through the Night," Joe South's "Walk a Mile in My Shoes," and Springsteen's "Dancing in the Dark."

Whatever visitation Dylan received in Switzerland, whatever switch had flipped, it also led him to try a new approach when it was time to record his 1989 album *Oh Mercy*. On Bono's recommendation he enlisted the help of Daniel Lanois, who (with Brian Eno) had produced U2's groundbreaking 1980s albums *The Unforgettable Fire* and *The Joshua Tree*. Lanois was in New Orleans recording the Neville Brothers' *Yellow Moon* when he first met with Dylan, and Dylan got to hear Lanois's treatment, with Aaron Neville's vocals, of "Hollis Brown" and "With God on Our Side." He was impressed: Lanois "seemed like the kind of cat who, when he works on something, he did it like the fate of the world hinged on its outcome."[23]

Dylan's prior experience working with strong-willed producers was mixed at best, and he and Lanois clashed frequently. And yet recording in an old New Orleans mansion with mobile equipment, only at night (Dylan's preference), they broke free from the harsh, sterile sonics of Dylan's recent albums. Lanois coaxed Dylan to deliver his best songs and vocal performances in years, and he surrounded them with a thick, swampy sound provided by a core group of New Orleans-based musicians, which included Willie Green on drums, Tony Hall on bass, Mason Ruffner on guitar, and Malcolm Burn on keyboards. "Everything in New Orleans is a good idea," Dylan writes in *Chronicles*, which might have been the guiding principle of *Oh Mercy*.[24]

The songs on *Oh Mercy* seem to be drawn from the same well as those on *Slow Train Coming* but with more subtle Christian messaging. The vocabulary and the song structures are simple, with vocals that are often more spoken than sung—but they never feel trite, lyrically or musically. "Where Teardrops Fall," for instance, sounds like a throwback to 1950s pop-R&B, but as Andrew McCarron argues, the seemingly straightforward love song also alludes to the Gospels and the letters of Paul. The place where teardrops fall may be Golgotha, the site of Jesus's crucifixion.[25] He still seems to have the end of days fixed in his vision, but the mood is gentler and more somber than on the evangelical albums or even *Infidels*. "Ring Them Bells" is a commemorative hymn that reminds us the end is near. The "Man in the Long Black Coat" who leads a woman away is a sinister figure—Death personified, if literary tradition has anything to say about it—but he is not out of place in the landscape Dylan evokes throughout the song, with trees bent over by hurricanes and smoke on the water. And there seems to be no redemption or repair for all the broken things in "Everything Is Broken," even though the swamp-rock arrangement makes you want to twist the night away and break a few more things. Other songs—"Most of the Time," What Was It You Wanted," "What Good Am I?," the outtake "Dignity"—are wistful, at times bitter, reflections on broken relationships and the meaning of it all.

Much like *Infidels* six years earlier, *Oh Mercy* was seen as a comeback. In the *New York Times* Stephen Holden paired it with Tracy Chapman's second album, *Crossroads*, citing Chapman as the most promising of the latest "New Dylans." But he concludes that "The halting, introspective voice [of *Oh Mercy*] heralds the appearance of another 'New Dylan,' one who is a bit more mature and careful than any we've met before." *Rolling Stone*'s Anthony DeCurtis reviewed it alongside the Stones' *Steel Wheels* album, calling both efforts "challenging and satisfying."[26] The *Village Voice* critics ranked it the fifteenth best album of 1989.

Dylan's next album, 1990's *Under the Red Sky*, didn't exactly sustain the "halting, introspective" mood of *Oh Mercy*. The first track, "Wiggle Wiggle," comes with dance-party instructions. The album was dedicated to Dylan's then-four-year-old daughter Desirée Gabrielle ("Gabby Goo-Goo"), which might explain the nursery-rhyme and once-upon-a-time motifs that run through almost all the songs, but especially "Under the Red Sky," "10,000 Men," "2 × 2," "Handy Dandy," and "Cat's in the Well." And yet like William Blake's *Songs of Innocence and Experience*, the songs on *Under the Red Sky* combine children's poem structures with a world-weary, jaded perspective on life and love. Not coincidentally Carolyn Dennis, increasingly estranged from the peripatetic Dylan, filed for divorce between the recording and release of the album.

In "Unbelievable" Dylan sings a once-upon-a-time story of a man with no eyes and a bleeding heart. Other songs feature sardonic, self-referential humor; in "T.V. Talkin' Song," a modern-day Woody Guthrie character listens to a speaker in Hyde Park rant against the dangers of television, prompting a riot. A film crew shows up, so at the end of the song he gets to watch the anti-TV riot on TV. But as with the Wilburys, with whom Dylan would record a follow-up just after *Red Sky*, the prevailing mood is light, not pushing the songs or the simple rock-and-roll arrangements too hard. The choice of producers Don and David Was, who had recently hit the top ten with "Walk the Dinosaur," underscored the more playful agenda. Numerous guest stars—George Harrison, Slash, Stevie Ray and Jimmie Vaughan, Elton John, David Crosby—stopped by to contribute parts, most of which are buried in the mix. Instead of really featuring the guest musicians, the album maintains a consistent, mostly rocking sound, anchored by Kenny Aronoff on drums and a tag team of Don Was and Randy Jackson on bass. Although it was less inspired than *Oh Mercy*, *Under the Red Sky* has considerably more character than most of Dylan's 1980s albums, and it deserved a better reception than it received from record buyers and all but a few critics.

Amidst recording and more extensive touring, Dylan made a number of other significant appearances as the 1980s turned to the 1990s. He was inducted into the Rock and Roll Hall of Fame in

1988, with a presentation speech by Bruce Springsteen: "Bob freed your mind the way Elvis freed your body. He showed us that just because the music was innately physical did not mean that it was anti-intellectual."[27] Dylan gave a brief acceptance speech, acknowledging his debt to Little Richard (who was there), and later led a stage full of rock stars through "Like a Rolling Stone." He taped another notable performance, a three-song set backing up his old Woodstock neighbor Van Morrison for Morrison's 1991 TV documentary *One Irish Rover*, on the Hill of the Muses in Athens.

In February 1990 he joined the Byrds onstage for "Mr. Tambourine Man" at a televised memorial concert for Roy Orbison, his fellow Wilbury who had died a little over a year earlier. He mumbled and wheezed his way through "Like a Rolling Stone," backed by an all-star band, on David Letterman's tenth anniversary show in 1992. Honoring his Jewish heritage, he appeared on three Chabad "To Life" telethons—he sent a tape in 1986 and performed in the studio in 1989 and 1991. In one of the in-studio performances he plays flute, recorder, and harmonica in a trio with the actor Harry Dean Stanton and singer Peter Himmelman (also the husband of Dylan's adopted daughter Maria), closing a three-song, all-Hebrew set with a rousing "Hava Nagila." In the second, he noodles on electric guitar, staring at his hands, while Kinky Friedman sings "Sold American."

Not many people saw the Chabad telethons, but millions watched an equally strange Dylan performance at the 1991 Grammys, where he received a Lifetime Achievement Award. Standing alongside Jack Nicholson, who presented the award, Dylan seemed unable to keep still, fidgeting and shifting his weight from side to side, and upon taking the plaque he at first turned away from the microphone as if looking for the exit. Then he gave a brief speech, recalling memorable words from "my daddy . . . a very simple man." Except that Dylan couldn't seem to recall those words, and after an awkward silence he broke the tension with expert comic delivery: "He said so many things, you know."

When the laughter died down he continued: "He did say, 'You know it's possible to become so defiled in this world that your own mother and father will abandon you, and if that happens, God will always believe in your own ability to mend your own ways.'" End of speech. His father's wisdom, it turned out, was identical to a nineteenth-century commentary on the book of Psalms (27:10) by Rabbi Shimshon Rafael Hirsch.[28] Did Dylan intend it as a reminder to everyone present that redemption was possible? Was he commenting on his own defilement, his own feeling of isolation and abjection? Or did the Hirsch quote just pop into his head at a moment when he had no idea what to say?

In his earlier appearance on that same Grammy telecast Dylan led his touring band through "Masters of War," a song choice clearly aimed at Operation Desert Storm, the USA's recent bombing campaign against Iraq. They blazed through an aggressive electric version of the 1963 protest song, but Dylan's delivery of the lyrics was atonal and indecipherable. Depending on your point of view it either undermined the song's message (by making it incomprehensible) or added another layer of protest to the protest. Only fans who had attended Dylan's recent shows knew that the performance was in fact par for the course.

Such was the state of Dylan's career as he entered his fifties: hit-or-miss albums, erratic appearances, and repeated acknowledgments of what he had already accomplished. If the Grammy appearance left a lot of the audience scratching their heads, the release of the Bootleg Series, volumes I–III, the following month served as a reminder of Dylan's genius. Unlike *Biograph* (released six years earlier), the first Bootleg Series box contained nothing that had already been officially released: 58 tracks, including radically different takes of classics and dozens of songs that only true bootleg collectors had previously owned. For the casual fan it was a revelation that Dylan had so much material as good or better than what had appeared on official albums—and few would have guessed that these first three volumes only scratched the surface. Like *Biograph*, the Bootleg Series inspired similar collections from other major artists, the six-disc *Beatles Anthology* in 1995 and Springsteen's four-disc *Tracks* in 1998 being the most worthy successors. But Dylan, or his team of curators led by Jeff Rosen, outdid them all: as of this writing the Bootleg Series is up to eighteen volumes, all of them multi-disc collections and all in some way revelatory.[29]

Around the same time this first collection of new-old songs hit the shelves Dylan gave a unique interview to *Song Talk*, the journal of the National Academy of Songwriters—unique because Paul Zollo, the interviewer, focused strictly on writing, and Dylan seemed completely on board. At one point he jokingly contrasted songwriters with poets, reinforcing while gently mocking the distinction: "Poets don't drive cars . . . Poets don't go to the supermarket. Poets don't empty the garbage . . . Poets don't even speak on the telephone. Poets don't even talk to anybody." At another he sounds like he's through with songwriting: "if nobody wrote any more songs from this day on, the world ain't gonna suffer for it. Nobody cares. There's enough songs for people to listen to, if they want to listen to songs." And yet at the interview's conclusion he takes pride in what he's been able to accomplish: "There's just something about my lyrics that just have a gallantry to them. And that might be all they have going for them. *[Laughs]* However, it's no small thing."[30]

It was a new but appropriate way of describing Dylan's songwriting: *gallant*, as in courageous, unyielding, steeped in traditional (songwriting) values. Unfortunately he was not producing many gallant new songs in the early 1990s, but he did have tradition on his mind. In the summer of 1992 he recorded another batch of covers—folk, blues, gospel, R&B—at Acme Studios in Chicago with multi-instrumentalist David Bromberg (who had played on *Self Portrait* and *New Morning* over two decades before) and Bromberg's band. But instead of mixing and releasing an album from those sessions Dylan returned to his home studio in Malibu to record a similar slate of songs with just an acoustic guitar, which he would release later that year as *Good As I Been to You*. On one level this was an easy way to fulfill a recording contract during a songwriting drought. And yet this album and its successor, 1993's *World Gone Wrong*, are much more than that. The symmetry with that first session for Columbia thirty years earlier—just a guy singing folk, blues, and gospel with an acoustic guitar—was clear enough, even though *Good As I Been to You* sounded completely different. The rasp in Dylan's voice was no affectation now, the eager energy of 1961 replaced by a mature intimacy with songs such as "Sittin' on Top of the World" and "You're Gonna

Quit Me." Dylan's guitar playing was more supple and nuanced as well. On these albums he planted the flag that he would fly for the rest of his career: perhaps he was still the rebel who killed Tin Pan Alley and revolutionized modern songwriting, but he was also the living, breathing, singing encyclopedia of American musical traditions, from nineteenth-century parlor songs such as "Hard Times Come Again No More" to pop standards like "Tomorrow Night" to murder ballads such as "Delia."

His delightful liner notes to *World Gone Wrong*—the first he had written since *Planet Waves*—reiterated his affection for the songs. About the Mississippi Sheiks, his source for "Blood in My Eyes" and "World Gone Wrong," he writes, "rebellion against routine seems to be their strong theme. all their songs are raw to the bone & are faultlessly made for these modern times (the New Dark Ages) nothing effete about the Mississippi Sheiks." While Dylan wasn't writing any songs that he was eager to record, these albums repositioned him as the keeper of the flame; it was clear, after a decade of erratic performances onstage and in the studio, that he was still devoted to his craft.

In October, between the two acoustic albums' releases, Dylan was celebrated yet again, this time with a gala concert at Madison Square Garden marking thirty years as a recording artist. Along with the Lifetime Achievement Grammy and the Bootleg Series box, the anniversary concert suggested a career coming to a close. Dylan worried that it would be "like goin' to my own funeral," but if that was the case, it was at least a money-making funeral—sponsored by Columbia Records, with a double CD and VHS to commemorate the event. The line-up for "Bobfest," as Neil Young called it, included Stevie Wonder, Eric Clapton, the Band (minus the estranged Robbie Robertson and the late Richard Manuel), Tom Petty and the Heartbreakers, Tracy Chapman, Willie Nelson, Johnny Cash, Roger McGuinn, Richie Havens, the O'Jays, Chrissie Hynde, and George Harrison; the house band fused Booker T and the MGs with all-star sidemen Jim Keltner and G. E. Smith, who had left the Never-Ending Tour but served as the evening's musical director.

The early part of the show was marred by the audience's hostility toward Sinéad O'Connor, who had recently torn up a picture of Pope

Dylan being awarded Commandeur des Arts et des Lettres by Jack Lang, French Minister for Arts, Paris, January 1990.

John Paul II on *SNL*; after silently absorbing the crowd's boos she substituted an *a cappella* recitation of Bob Marley's "War" (the song she had performed on *SNL*) for Dylan's "I Believe in You" (which she had rehearsed for the concert). O'Connor's protest might have reminded a few audience members of the honoree's more defiant early career, but that was not the intended mood for the evening. The celebration resumed, and a couple of hours later the man himself performed solo ("Song to Woody," "It's Alright, Ma," "Girl from the North Country") and with the assembled guests ("My Back Pages," "Knockin' on Heaven's Door"). He seems *almost* happy to be there and gives an engaging performance, even bowing to the audience before leaving the stage.

The after-party was held, appropriately, at Tommy Makem's Irish Pavilion on 57th Street. Singing and playing with the Clancy Brothers,

Makem had inspired Dylan during the folk revival, and they were on the bill that night at Madison Square Garden. Once again surrounded by folk stalwarts and rock stars, Dylan repaired to Makem's to continue the celebration until the break of dawn.[31]

13
1993–2006: Renewal

In the aftermath of the thirtieth anniversary concert, the Lifetime Achievement Grammy, and the release of the retrospective Bootleg Series box set, fans could be forgiven for thinking that Dylan had retired, at least as a songwriter. His 1992 and 1993 albums had contained no original songs, and his 1995 album would be another live set, comprised mostly of greatest hits. Dylan himself later recalled, "I really thought I was through making records. I didn't want to make any more."[1] There was little doubt that he would continue to tour, even without new material to promote—he consistently said that performing live was his priority. He told the *New York Times* in 1997 that touring was "as natural to me as breathing. I do it because I'm driven to do it, and I either hate it or love it. I'm mortified to be on the stage, but then again, it's the only place where I'm happy. It's the only place you can be who you want to be."[2] Setlists changed frequently, and band members changed occasionally, but through it all Dylan continued to average over a hundred shows a year.

One particular live performance venue, MTV's *Unplugged* series, had become a cultural phenomenon in the early 1990s, not just with viewers but with CD buyers. Among Dylan's contemporaries the greatest beneficiary of the format was Eric Clapton, whose 1992 *Unplugged* reinterpreted "Layla" as back-porch blues, sold 26 million copies, and made him a Grammy magnet. Dylan was interested in the unplugged concept—after all he had created a cultural earthquake by *plugging in* three decades earlier—but, true to form, he wanted to do it his own way, ideally without MTV branding. In November 1993 he booked the Supper Club in Manhattan's Theater District to perform four short (ten-song) sets over two dates, with two hundred tickets for each show distributed for free to fans who lined up at Tower Records. Playing acoustic instruments, Dylan and his band—John Jackson on guitar, Bucky Baxter on pedal steel and slide guitar, Tony Garnier on bass, Winston Watson on drums—were in top form, delivering new, unpredictable setlists to awestruck crowds and getting it all on film. Again, true to form, Dylan decided not to release it, and the Supper Club shows became yet another prized bootleg.

Exactly one year later Dylan came to terms with MTV and taped a set for *Unplugged* with the same band, supplemented by Brendan O'Brien on organ and guitar. Here Dylan seems to embrace the nostalgia, even wearing a polka-dot shirt and Ray-Bans reminiscent of his mid-1960s electric heyday. The MTV set makes more concessions than the Supper Club shows to casual fans—"All Along the Watchtower," "The Times They Are A-Changin'," "Rainy Day Women #12 & 35," "Knockin' on Heaven's Door," and "Like a Rolling Stone" are all included. But so is "John Brown," an early anti-war song from Dylan's catalogue that had not yet appeared on an official release, and a beautiful version of "Dignity," an outtake from the *Oh Mercy* sessions that he had recently released on *Greatest Hits, Volume III*. And while his eyes are hidden behind the shades, he seems very present, certainly not phoning in the performance. The Supper Club shows may have been more adventurous and compelling, but *Unplugged* (both the 1995 CD and the DVD released in 2004) represents mid-1990s Dylan well.

In the year between the Supper Club and MTV *Unplugged*, Dylan's shows were mostly electric, with embedded solo acoustic mini-sets and a final acoustic encore. One notable exception was his appearance in May 1994 at the Great Music Experience, a three-night festival at the Tōdai-ji temple in Nara, Japan. Sponsored in part by UNESCO, the event brought together Japanese and Western musicians from across the musical spectrum—other North American artists included Joni Mitchell, Ry Cooder, and Jon Bon Jovi. Dylan sang "Hard Rain," "I Shall Be Released," and "Ring Them Bells" backed (to beautiful effect) by the Tokyo New Philharmonic Orchestra. That August he appeared at another three-day festival that could hardly have been more different, the 25th anniversary Woodstock 1994. Given Dylan's conspicuous absence from the first one in 1969, there was considerable hype surrounding his performance. Adding to the pressure was that despite the inclusion of a handful of Woodstock-generation artists, most of the line-up and nearly all the audience were of the mosh-pit generation. The situation made him uncomfortable enough that he stalled for about half an hour on his tour bus, but when he emerged, the young crowd proved to be appreciative, even reverent, down to the final acoustic encore of "It Ain't Me, Babe."[3]

Notable appearances the following year included a performance at the opening of the Rock and Roll Hall of Fame Museum and at Frank Sinatra's eightieth birthday celebration, where he sang "Restless Farewell" at Old Blue Eyes' request. Despite spending so much time on the road, Dylan seems to have settled into a less reckless lifestyle; according to Victor Maymudes, he even quit drinking in 1994.[4] With the help of managers Jeff Rosen and Jeff Kramer he also made some shrewd business decisions, such as switching his licensing from ASCAP (American Society of Composers, Authors, and Publishers) to SESAC (Society of European Stage Authors and Composers) for a $2-million advance.[5] Early licensing ventures included a Bank of Montreal television ad featuring "The Times They Are A-Changin'" and a CD-ROM game, *Highway 61 Interactive*. He was also buying more real estate—according to biographer Howard Sounes, a total of about seventeen properties by the late 1990s.[6] Maymudes worked as Dylan's real estate scout after being relieved of his road-manager duties in 1995 following a statutory rape charge (which was dropped). But even their revised professional relationship ended badly after Dylan abruptly fired Maymudes's daughter for mismanaging a coffee shop he owned in Santa Monica.[7]

As I write this in the 2020s so many rock musicians who became famous in the 1960s and '70s press on through *their* seventies and eighties that it seems perfectly normal. But no one knew that was going to happen in the 1990s—the prevailing attitude toward the Stones, Clapton, Dylan, and others was already "Can you believe they're *still* at it?" Fans joked that the Stones' Steel Wheels tour in 1989–90 should be called "Steel Wheelchairs" even though Bill

Wyman was the only band member older than fifty.[8] In 1990 the average age of the Traveling Wilburys was 45 when, in the song "Wilbury Twist," they conjured up a self-effacing dance craze whose instructions included falling on your ass and putting your teeth in a glass. No one would have guessed that when Dylan celebrated thirty years as a recording artist he wasn't even halfway through his career.

Instead, what most people thought when they heard his 1997 release, *Time Out of Mind*, was that he must have had one more great album in him, and this was it. As with *Blood on the Tracks* and *Infidels* Dylan wrote most of *Time Out of Mind* at his Minnesota farm, during the winter of 1995–6. The following summer he went back to Daniel Lanois, who had produced *Oh Mercy* seven years before, with his new set of lyrics. He also gave Lanois a list of blues and early rock and roll records to use as reference points. Lanois understood that it wasn't just a musical style but a recording style Dylan was after, the style of 1950s studios that weren't set up for loud blues and rockabilly bands—a little too much echo, a bit of distortion, not much separation between instruments. Lanois was thrilled. He remembers thinking, "This could be the greatest record ever. Bob was at a lyrical peak, and as for myself, I saw the potential for a new level of sonics on the horizon. I became obsessed with the idea of making a heartfelt, dangerous, and monumental record."[9] Dylan and Lanois would tussle over creative decisions (as they had done on *Oh Mercy*), but they succeeded in making, if not the greatest record ever, something that was indeed heartfelt, dangerous and monumental.

They started recording in Oxnard, California, at Lanois's Teatro studio with a small group consisting of Dylan, Lanois, bassist Tony Garnier, and Tony Mangurian on drums. But then in January Dylan insisted on a change and moved the operation across the continent to Criteria Studios in Miami. The number of musicians multiplied—usually not a good development on a Dylan album, but in this case it worked. Jazz drummer Brian Blade played alongside the quintessential rock drummer Jim Keltner. Other key musicians included Augie Meyers, whose Vox organ defined the sound of the Sir Douglas Quintet; blues guitarist Duke Robillard; slide guitar player Cindy Cashdollar; Bucky Baxter from Dylan's touring band on pedal steel;

and Jim Dickinson, a founder of Criteria's house backing band, the Dixie Flyers (and a renowned producer himself) on electric piano and pump organ. Working in various combinations, they created a thick, spooky sound that evoked the fifty-year-old records Dylan had recommended to Lanois but without falling into any imitative "retro" trap. Lanois ran Dylan's mic through a small, old-fashioned guitar amplifier, deliberately overdriving the vocals.[10]

When *Time Out of Mind* begins it sounds as if the "record" button had been pressed a little late, or maybe a little early—a bass and organ are in the middle of a gentle chord progression, and then we hear a rhythm tapped out and then quickly picked up by the organ, at first a kind of reggae inflection but soon more suggestive of a ticking clock. That chilling opening moment of "Love Sick" sets the album's mood, as Dylan sings about walking through dead streets, tired and wired, driven by a ghostly energy. The landscape, the weather—which will be referenced in almost every song—is a projection of the singer's frame of mind. He's sick of love, he wishes he'd never met her, but in the song's last lines, he confesses, his voice almost breaking, that he'd do anything to be back with her.

Time Out of Mind is one of the bluesiest albums of Dylan's career, with "Dirt Road Blues," "Million Miles," "'Til I Fell in Love with You," "Can't Wait," and "Highlands" all built on standard blues forms. Accordingly the songs offer hard life-lessons, and they tend to focus on personal experience. That's not to say that they're autobiographical, just that there is an "I" in every song telling about his own experience and outlook. The songs are very much about how it *feels* (to borrow from a memorable song's chorus)—to be lovesick, to get old, to lose faith in humanity . . . These personal feelings are, if not universal, widely shared across time. The album's title, referring to a distant, imprecisely located past, is suggestive. Even with scattered references to a few specific cities, to Neil Young and novelist Erica Jong, these songs are hard to place—they could be happening anywhere, at any time. "These songs, I felt, were more all-encompassing," Dylan told Jon Pareles. "They were . . . filled with the dread realities of life."[11]

"Cold Irons Bound" follows the tradition of "I Shall Be Released" and "Señor (Tales of Yankee Power)" as a prisoner song, although the refrain is about the only clue to the singer's immediate situation. Perhaps the cold irons are metaphorical—it hardly matters, as the singer recalls betrayals and disappointments that put him where he is. But unlike "I Shall Be Released," "Cold Irons Bound" offers no hope for redemption. Everything is in its place, and his place is in cold irons.

Two tracks offer some respite from the mood of exhaustion and fatalism. "Make You Feel My Love" is a sweet love song with somewhat clumsy lyrics that has become one of Dylan's most frequently covered compositions. Billy Joel released his version (on *Greatest Hits, Volume III*) a month before *Time Out of Mind* appeared; then in 1998 Garth Brooks covered it for the soundtrack to the film *Hope Floats*. But it was Adele's 2008 version, which inspired *X Factor* contestants and millions of karaoke singers, that turned "Make You Feel My Love" into a standard. And then there's the album's closer, the seventeen-minute, twenty-verse "Highlands," which riffs on Robert Burns ("My Heart's in the Highlands"), wanders into a slow-moving encounter with a waitress in a Boston restaurant, and then ends this bluesy album on a note of renewal and possibility.

In May 1997, between the recording and the release of *Time Out of Mind*, Dylan was hospitalized with pericarditis, or swelling of the tissue surrounding the heart, caused by a fungal infection known as histoplasmosis. His condition was painful and potentially fatal, causing much concern for his family, friends, and of course millions of fans. "I really thought I'd be seeing Elvis soon," he quipped.[12] Dylan saved many of the cards and faxes he received during his hospital stay, including one from Frank Sinatra that reads, "Dear Bob, Give 'em hell in there . . . We're betting on you."[13] It was a good bet: Dylan fully recovered over the summer and was back on the road the first week in August, playing 56 shows before the end of the year. When *Time Out of Mind* appeared at the end of September, listeners (even those who knew the album had been completed before his illness) inevitably heard it as Dylan's meditation on his own mortality, especially with songs like "Tryin' to Get to Heaven" and "Not Dark Yet." Dylan clarified a few years later: "Well, it *doesn't* deal with my mortality. It maybe just deals with mortality in general. It's the one thing we all have in common, isn't it?"[14]

Time Out of Mind signaled Dylan's most significant comeback since Tour '74 and *Blood on the Tracks*. He hadn't released an album of new, original songs in seven years, and, good as *Oh Mercy* was, he had really been in a slump for seven years before that one, dating back to *Infidels*. Moreover *Time Out of Mind* made a big impact beyond the Dylan faithful, even before Adele recorded "Make You Feel My Love." It went platinum in the U.S., gold in the UK, and it garnered three Grammys, including Album of the Year. Adding to the hype was the sudden, overwhelming success of Dylan's son Jakob with his band the Wallflowers, whose album *Bringing Down the Horse* sold 4 million copies and yielded four hit singles—the biggest of which, "One Headlight," also won a pair of Grammys that year.

Dylan's performance of "Love Sick" at the Grammy ceremony made the news not because of anything Dylan did but because one of the young people hired to silently groove behind the band unexpectedly took off his shirt, revealing the words "Soy Bomb" scrawled on his chest, and proceeded to dance spasmodically alongside Dylan until he was escorted off the stage. "I had a few simple objectives," the Soy Bomber said years later. "To dismantle capitalism, to replace 4/4 with 11/4 as the dominant time signature (my dance was in 11/4), to abolish song verses in favor of a chorus-only reality, and to defame the soy industry to pave the path for oats."[15] The performance was summed up nicely by, of all people, Raquel Welch, who wrote a congratulatory note to her friend Bob: "Hey, you looked really spiffy in your suit and were super cool when that weenie, 'Mr. Soy,' appeared out of nowhere! . . . God, what a hoot! You didn't even flinch!!"[16]

Indeed not. Dylan was more unflappable than ever in his new role as Elderly Badass. He had spent most of the 1980s and early 1990s trying to look like a rock star, a muscular, vaguely Springsteenish presentation that involved leather vests and earrings. Toward the turn of the century, though, he adopted a look that critic Ann Powers aptly describes as "borrowed from a Western movie: wide-brimmed hats, three-quarter frock coats, and satin scarves or turquoise-studded bolo ties, his face adorned with a pencil-thin mustache. The mod Dylan was now presenting himself as an American version of timeless—eternally wandering at the nation's old New Frontier."[17] He wore a Stetson hat when he performed "Knockin' on Heaven's Door" in September 1997 at the World Eucharistic Conference in Bologna, Italy, which led to a brief conversation with Pope John Paul II. He showed up in a conventional tuxedo when he received the Kennedy Center Honor a few months later (alongside Charlton Heston and Lauren Bacall), but he must have been gratified to hear Gregory Peck present him as "something of a Civil War type, a kind of nineteenth-century troubadour and maverick American spirit." Citing "Brownsville Girl" and its reference to Peck's role in *The Gunfighter*, Peck affirmed that "Bob Dylan's never been about to get out of town before the shooting starts."

It would be four years between the release of *Time Out of Mind* and Dylan's next album—which would have been a lengthy "disappearance" a couple of decades earlier but by the late 1990s was not an usually long gap for a major artist. And Dylan had hardly disappeared. In 1998 he toured Europe, Australasia, and North America (twice), and played several dates in South America with the Rolling Stones. For the second North American leg he was joined by Van Morrison and Joni Mitchell (on her first tour since 1983). Despite the success of *Time Out of Mind*, Dylan generally included only one or two of his new songs in a classics-heavy set.

He spent even more of the following year on the road, highlighted by a series of shows with Paul Simon over the summer. The two superstars had never been close personally. Simon, whose style was so different from Dylan's, clearly did not like being compared to him, as he was throughout his career; he had even parodied Dylan with "A Simple Desultory Philippic" on 1966's *Parsley, Sage, Rosemary and Thyme*. But they respected each other, and they made for a compelling double-bill, alternating opener/closer roles and singing a couple of their signature tunes together, Dylan nailing (more or less) the harmony on "The Sound of Silence." (A 2010 handwritten note from Simon in the Bob Dylan Archive indicates that they were attempting to co-write a song at that time, but the collaboration seems to have been abandoned.[18])

Dylan also kept the momentum going with a song he recorded in mid-1999 for the film *Wonder Boys*, starring Michael Douglas as a cynical, middle-aged writer who can't finish his anticipated second novel. Dylan's new song, "Things Have Changed," worked well for the film, and it also epitomized his own not-entirely-new but updated image as a dyed-in-the-wool rebel with nothing to prove and no one to answer to. The song got a good bit of airplay while climbing *Billboard*'s "Adult Alternative" chart, and its clever music video spliced Dylan into scenes from the film. "Things Have Changed" won the Oscar for Best Original Song in 2001, which gave Dylan the opportunity to thank the Academy for being "bold enough to give me this award for this song, which obviously is a song that doesn't pussyfoot around or turn a blind eye to human nature."[19] He taped the acceptance speech in Australia, where he was of course on tour, and he would proudly display a replica of the Oscar statuette onstage for years after receiving it.

Two months after accepting the Oscar Dylan was back in the studio to record the album *"Love and Theft."* The quotation marks in the title are as important as the words between them, as Dylan foregrounds his musical borrowing and builds songs largely out of quoted phrases. By this point it was clear that Dylan's love of pre-Elvis American folk and popular music ran deep and wide, but he had never displayed that appreciation in his own compositions as emphatically as he did now. Greg Tate provided as good a list as I've found: "There are blues forms and jazz forms here, gypsy-jazz folk forms, Tin Pan Alley and rockabilly, boxcar rounds, campfire sing-alongs and sea shanty, cowboy songs, madrigals, and various alchemical mixtures as they're needed."[20] Dylan complained that on *Time Out of Mind*, "I couldn't get any of the up-tempo songs that I wanted," but that was not an issue on *"Love and Theft,"* which opens with the rollicking "Tweedle Dee & Tweedle Dum," swings through the jump blues of "Summer Days," shuffles the "Lonesome Day Blues," and gallops its way through the disco-rock of "Honest with Me." His touring band—Larry Campbell on guitar and other stringed instruments, Charlie Sexton on guitar, Tony Garnier on bass, and David Kemper on drums, supplemented by organist Augie Meyers—handles whatever musical style Dylan brings to any given song. Dylan produced the album himself, as he would for the rest of his career, under the alias Jack Frost. Overall the sound is as bright as *Time Out of Mind*'s was dark, but there's no shortage of menace and foreboding on *"Love and Theft."* For instance "Floater (Too Much to Ask)" may sound like a nineteenth-century parlor ballad, but it's a parlor ballad whose singer explicitly warns you not to cross his path again if you want to remain among the living.

The quotation marks might also signal that the phrase "Love and Theft" is itself a quotation from the title of an academic book, Eric Lott's *Love and Theft: Blackface Minstrelsy and the American Working Class*. Lott explored the pervasive cultural influence of minstrelsy in the decades before the Civil War, emphasizing the emulation of Black culture by white performers alongside the overt racism of this bizarre but tenacious cultural phenomenon. Not only were there strong currents of vaudeville and minstrel styles in Dylan's latest songs, but the broader idea of artists stealing what they love (and the proverbial notion of the artist-as-thief) must have appealed to him.

And as it turns out, *"Love and Theft"* relies heavily on quoted material that, aside from the album's title, *doesn't* appear within quotation marks. As he had done throughout his career, Dylan drops allusions to blues and folk songs ("Dust My Broom," "The Cuckoo Bird") and literature (Tweedle Dee and Tweedle Dum from *Through the Looking Glass*; a wonderful quote about repeating the past from *The Great Gatsby*). What's different is the extent to which he pieces together found phrases and his use of source material that no one would have recognized had it not been on a Bob Dylan album and had there not been Internet search engines. A line from "Summer Days," "suckin' the blood out of genius and generosity," also appears, as a condemnation of intemperance, in an obscure speech by Abraham Lincoln from 1842.[21] Several lines from "Floater (Too Much to Ask)" and "Lonesome Day Blues" come from a 1989 book about Japanese gangsters, *Confessions of a Yakuza* by Junichi Saga. In the years immediately following the album's release, writer and musician Scott Warmuth discovered that some songs were essentially a patchwork of disparate lyrical and musical quotations. Odd phrases in "Tweedle Dee & Tweedle Dum," including one about a "multi-thousand-dollar gown," can be found in an old travel guide to New Orleans, and the same song's distinctive musical arrangement is lifted from Johnny &

Jack's 1957 single "Uncle John's Bongos." It was as if the album were an experiment in musical and verbal collage, making something unique and new out of found objects.

The songs' language *sounds* borrowed in most cases and more than a little stagey—but the impression that these speaker/singers are *in character*, repeating things they've heard or read, contributes to the playful, vaudeville effect of *"Love and Theft."* "Floater (Too Much to Ask)" apparently has a single voice—a young man who's in love with his second cousin, who's going fishing, who has some suspicions about the older generation, who's not to be trifled with, and who doesn't know if his grandparents had any dreams or hopes but has buried his own under some tobacco leaves. Dylan is singing all this, but no one would mistake this person for Bob Dylan—we're a long way from *Blood on the Tracks*. And what of the young man Dylan's portraying? He's probably putting on a show for his listener as well, his persona also an assemblage of borrowed lines. "Po' Boy" is essentially a series of old-time stage jokes, sort of like today's dad jokes. "Summer Days" is all bravado and come-on, the patter of a blues singer in top form, even if (as Dylan's voice reveals) he is getting on in years.

But alongside the corny jokes and juke-joint swagger there's a strong current of foreboding and grief. Much of it may have been personal: Dylan's beloved mother Beatty died in early 2000, and (uncharacteristically) he alludes to her passing in "Lonesome Day Blues." In a fateful coincidence the release date of *"Love and Theft"* was September 11, 2001. The apocalyptic strain in Dylan's songwriting can be traced back to "Hard Rain," through "Desolation Row," "All Along the Watchtower," various gospel-era and *Infidels* tracks, "Everything Is Broken"—but, as Greg Tate wrote in the *Village Voice*, "contemporary evidence . . . suggests that the poet of his generation is once again the prophet of his age."[22] A number of lines and entire songs from *"Love and Theft"* reverberated through post-9/11 America. "Mississippi," a song held over from *Time Out of Mind* and re-recorded for the new album, plugs into his longstanding theme of "surviving in a ruthless world"—or perhaps not surviving. He reminds us that our days are numbered, that we're boxed in, no escape, and the sky is on fire. One of Dylan's best songs, "Mississippi" is also, like Matthew Arnold's

"Dover Beach," about pledging your devotion to someone, hoping to bring some meaning to a dark, loveless world.

"Lonesome Day Blues" (another song pieced together from *Confessions of a Yakuza* and other sources) describes ruthless men and recalls others killed in war while conveying a sense of foreboding and a promise of a coming "peace" that doesn't sound very peaceful. (Incidentally Springsteen's 2002 album *The Rising*, which was *deliberately* focused on the 9/11 attacks, begins with a song called "Lonesome Day.") The centerpiece of *"Love and Theft"* has disaster as its refrain: "High Water (For Charley Patton)" recalls "Desolation Row" in its parade of literary and pop culture allusions, while also summoning "Crash on the Levee (Down in the Flood)" in its depiction of desperation and fear as a way of life.

When Dylan returned to the stage in October 2001 he opened his sets with the hopeful Hank Williams song "Wait for the Light to Shine" for the first few weeks, closing with "Blowin' in the Wind." He also began using Aaron Copland's all-American "Hoe-Down" (from the ballet *Rodeo*) as his walk-on music.[23] He maintained a busy road schedule with one of his best bands. Although the Never-Ending Tour has never been a soloist showcase, guitarists Charlie Sexton and Larry Campbell brought energy as well as outstanding chops to the stage, and some of the new songs gave band members a little more opportunity to assert themselves. Some fans were a bit mystified by the new arrangements of classics, which Dylan sang with completely different phrasing than on the original recordings. But for the most part these were crowd-pleasing sets, often highlighted by *"Love and Theft"* songs. The new album repeated *Time Out of Mind*'s critical and commercial success, landing on many "year's-best" lists and cracking the top five on the British and American album charts.

In August 2002 the Never-Ending Tour made a stop at the Newport Folk Festival, marking Dylan's first appearance there since the infamous 1965 electric set. His only nod to the occasion was to walk onstage wearing a fake beard and a long-haired wig under his Stetson, slyly suggesting that he had to sneak in unrecognized. The hijinks continued that fall, when Dylan, amused by a *Buffalo News* article that described him with a series of Dylan clichés, began using the same phrases for a bombastic introduction voiced over the "Hoe-Down" intro each night:

> Ladies and gentlemen, please welcome the poet laureate of rock-n-roll. The voice of the promise of the '60s counterculture. The guy who forced folk into bed with rock. Who donned make-up in the '70s and disappeared into a haze of substance abuse. Who emerged to find Jesus. Who was written off as a has-been by the end of the '80s, and who suddenly shifted gears, releasing some of the strongest music of his career beginning in the late '90s . . . Ladies and gentlemen, Columbia recording artist Bob Dylan.

While still performing over a hundred shows a year in the early 2000s, Dylan recorded songs for tribute CDs and films, notably his own new compositions for the Civil War epic *Gods and Generals* ("Cross the Green Mountain") and *Divine Secrets of the Ya-Ya Sisterhood* ("Waitin' for You," which would become a standard part of his set about a decade later).

Then he had his own movie to do, for which he would not write any new songs: *Masked and Anonymous*, his collaboration with writer-director Larry Charles, best known at the time for his work on the sitcoms *Seinfeld* and *Mad About You*. *Masked and Anonymous* takes place in a nation that resembles the United States, drowning in poverty and homelessness in the aftermath of a violent revolution. The ruthless dictator is on his deathbed, about to be succeeded by an even more ruthless dictator. There isn't much plot, but events revolve around a planned concert to benefit "victims of the revolution." The sole concert performer, because they couldn't get anyone else, is Dylan's character Jack Fate, released from prison for the occasion. The promoter, Uncle Sweetheart (John Goodman), plans to keep the proceeds to pay off his murderous creditors.

Masked and Anonymous is something like the film equivalent of *"Love and Theft"* (in fact the title phrase echoes another academic work on minstrelsy).[24] The landscape is bleak, and everyone is cynical and corrupt. When Fate walks out of his subterranean prison he tells the guard that he "ain't felt free in a long time"; the guard replies, "Keepin' people from bein' free is big business." At one point a very animated animal wrangler played by Val Kilmer explains to Jack Fate that animals are superior to people because "they are just what they are." Human beings on the other hand are duplicitous, "alone with their secrets, masked and anonymous, no one truly knows 'em." But for all its cynicism, it's a fun, sometimes even funny, movie. Larry Charles recalled that "As soon as word went out that Bob Dylan was gonna make a movie, you couldn't stop people from wanting to get involved," and the pleasure for viewers is seeing Goodman, Kilmer, Jeff Bridges, Jessica Lange, Penélope Cruz, Mickey Rourke, Luke Wilson, and others give deliberately histrionic performances in scenes that are often set pieces. The ghost of a blackface minstrel, played by Ed Harris, tells Fate that "the whole world's a stage" (*almost* quoting Shakespeare), and that's certainly true of the world of *Masked and Anonymous*, just as it had been on *"Love and Theft."* The jokes and gags are here too. A Jack Fate cover band is called Simple Twist of Fate. Goodman's and Wilson's characters argue over the meaning of "Drifter's Escape" (from *John Wesley Harding*) in a parody of obsessed Dylan fans. A carnival tent advertises "Man Eating Chicken," only to reveal a man eating a cooked chicken behind the curtain. Maybe you saw that one coming.

In his *New York Times* review Jon Pareles observed that *Masked and Anonymous* "plays like a Dylan song: a shaggy-dog story about power, love, show business, prodigal sons, faith and destiny."[25] And speaking of Dylan songs, the movie's true highlights are Dylan's performances with his band: a tight, bluesy "Down in the Flood" and a blistering "Cold Irons Bound" among them. (He also performs "Dixie" for an onscreen audience of stagehands and actors, including someone dressed as Abraham Lincoln.) His own performances are supplemented on the soundtrack with an eclectic batch of Dylan covers, including Shirley Caesar's inspiring version of "Gotta Serve Somebody," Los Lobos' "On a Night Like This," "My Back Pages" sung in Japanese, and an Italian rap remix of "Like a Rolling Stone."

Dylan's next film project was somewhat briefer but was seen by a few million more people than *Masked and Anonymous*. In 2004

Victoria's Secret aired a thirty-second television commercial titled "Angels in Venice." With "Love Sick" from *Time Out of Mind* as the soundtrack, the ad stars two people who never actually share the screen but stalk the same misty Venetian palazzo: 23-year-old supermodel Adriana Lima, wearing a bra, panties, high heels, and a pair of wings; and 63-year-old Bob Dylan, wearing a black suit with a white tie. He drops a black cowboy hat; she is last seen wearing it, after rubbing it against her thighs. As many observed at the time, it's a strange commercial. Stranger still because Dylan, at a 1965 press conference (discussed in Chapter Six), had been asked, "If you were going to sell out to a commercial interest, which one would it be?" and he jokingly (?) replied, "Ladies garments." Was this a gag with a 39-year pause for the punchline? While it wasn't the first time Dylan's music had been licensed for advertising, it was his first appearance in a TV commercial, and it wouldn't be his last.

Dylan delivered an even bigger surprise that same year in the form of a memoir, *Chronicles, Volume One*. The title suggested a chronological account, but the book is highly impressionistic, built around three separate periods, with huge gaps in between. He spends the most time on his early days in New York City and the experiences that led him there, with other chapters on his attempt to write songs for Archibald MacLeish (leading up to 1970's *New Morning*) and the recording of *Oh Mercy* with Daniel Lanois in New Orleans in 1989. Some of the events and characters are fabricated. For instance, in recounting his couch-surfing days in Greenwich Village he spends several pages describing the apartment and the personalities of his friends Ray Gooch and Chloe Kiel; they may be composites based on people he knew, but they are essentially fictional characters. What eventually got more attention was how much of the book, at the sentence level, was lifted from other sources.

Like *"Love and Theft," Chronicles* is practically a collage of snippets used by other writers, and here too it was Scott Warmuth who led the way in uncovering what Dylan borrowed: sixty or so phrases from the works of Jack London, about a dozen from various old issues of *Time* magazine, several from Tony Horwitz's 1998 book *Confederates in the Attic*, a sprinkling of Hemingway, and so on.[26] Warmuth's mission wasn't to expose Dylan as a plagiarist but to explore the craft (and craftiness) of his strategic use of other texts. According to Warmuth, "Dylan's *Chronicles: Volume One* is a vast palimpsest, with the words of many other writers coming through the text, hundreds and hundreds of times. When you are aware of what the original source material is you find that the subtext often subverts the surface text or adds another meaning to it that you could not be aware of initially."[27] I agree that Dylan's use of other writers' prose is too pervasive to be coincidental or inadvertent and that it is best appreciated as creative intertextuality, an engagement with other texts that generates new levels of potential meaning.

Is it also plagiarism? Not in every instance, but technically yes, in the sense that strands of text, such as "old wolf, gaunt and battle-scarred" (from Jack London) or, in reference to banning nuclear weapons, the phrase "deprive them of . . . highly comforting sense of doom" (*Time*) appear in Dylan's book without quotation marks or attribution. And yet paradoxically the mishmash of quoted phrases creates a distinctive, kinetic style, something that reviewers picked up on even when they weren't aware of what Dylan was doing. Aside from the fact that readers didn't know (and, mostly, still don't know) that he imported a lot of textual fragments, I think that what Dylan does in *Chronicles* is much more collage art than plagiarism. As someone who had to tussle with a self-proclaimed Dylanologist sifting through his trash bins three decades earlier, Dylan must have known that these sources would not go undetected—it wasn't a matter of trying to get away with something. Instead his loving theft is a kind of experiment that raises questions about the meaning of originality, highlighting (by hiding what is sure to be found) the traces of other voices, other texts, in his own. Warmuth puts a bit more edge on his description of Dylan's method: "He charms with his fakery and dares the protesting purist to call him out as a fraud, all the while speaking in a secret language and exhibiting a supreme level of showmanship. It takes tremendous skill and daring to walk that unseen tightrope, and there is nothing faked about that."[28]

While the fabrications and cut-and-paste prose of *Chronicles* allow Dylan to remain masked, the book still offers a wealth of insight, mainly into the music, literature, and art that he embraced, that became part of his self-portrait. In fact, like the album *Self Portrait*, *Chronicles* allows Dylan to portray himself mainly by pointing to his influences and inspirations, from the expected tributes to Guthrie and Seeger to the less-expected shout-outs to Ricky Nelson, Gorgeous George, and Red Grooms. Of course it's also notable for what he *avoids* discussing in any depth: his relationships with women, the gospel phase, his writing process, Albert Grossman, the 1990s. As of this writing we are eagerly anticipating *Chronicles, Volume Two*.

While it took a few years for Warmuth to uncover the extent of the borrowing in *Chronicles*, Dylan's use of *Confessions of a Yakuza* and other sources on *"Love and Theft"* was well established by the time he released his next album, *Modern Times*, in 2006. Within a week of that album's release the *New York Times*'s teasing headline read, "Who's This Guy Dylan Who's Borrowing Lines from Henry Timrod?" Citing Warmuth, the *Times* (and other media outlets) reported that on a few tracks Dylan had appropriated the verses of the "Poet Laureate of the Confederacy," famous in his own time but largely forgotten by 2006. Considering that the Timrod lines are not especially clever or striking ("There is a wisdom that grows up in strife") Dylan probably used them because he liked their stilted, nineteenth-century sonority, or just for the sake of transgressing, doubling down on the game he had played on his last album and memoir. And if he wanted to provoke people he succeeded: "Bob is really a thieving little swine," the *Times* quoted a contributor to a Dylan fan site.[29]

More obvious than importing a few lines from Timrod was the album's central device of rewriting classic blues tunes—"Rollin' and Tumblin'," "Someday Baby," "The Levee's Gonna Break"—while claiming sole songwriter credit. Other titles allude to existing songs: "Workingman's Blues #2" conjures up Merle Haggard's "Working Man Blues" (or, even earlier, King Oliver's 1924 "Workingman Blues"); "When the Deal Goes Down" recalls the traditional country song "Don't Let Your Deal Go Down"; the title "Nettie Moore" alludes to a nineteenth-century minstrel ballad.[30] As much as *"Love and Theft"* was also rooted in historical American popular music, *Modern Times* wears its sources on its album sleeve in the form of song titles. And of course the title *Modern Times* references the 1936 Charlie Chaplin movie, with its hero both accidentally and defiantly out of step with modernity.

Dylan gives us a lot to sift through here. Allusions to old song titles are common in popular music, as are lyrical "floaters" like sleeping in the kitchen with your feet in the hall or having a toothache in your heel. Dylan recontextualizes these lines and, in some cases, titles—"Workingman's Blues #2" is completely different from either of its predecessors. Lines imported from the obscure works of a dead poet were more problematic for some listeners, as were the "new" blues songs with obvious sources. One of the primary defenses of Dylan was that he was engaging in the "folk process," re-using phrases and melodies as he and other performers have done for centuries. Fair enough, to an extent—but claiming sole songwriting credit for "Someday Baby," whose chorus and structure are identical to Muddy Waters's "Trouble No More," is harder to defend, even though Waters drew heavily on earlier songs himself.[31]

Collage, allusion, plagiarism—perhaps it's a little of each, but the set of practices I've been describing had become central to Dylan's work. That said, it's easy to enjoy his work without playing name-that-source or wringing one's hands over what to call it, and *Modern Times* was another strong album. The touring band had evolved, retaining only bassist Tony Garnier; the rest of the new line-up consisted of Stu Kimball and Denny Freeman on guitar, Donnie Herron on various stringed instruments, and George Receli on drums. Their approach was generally more restrained than the *"Love and Theft"* band's, but they had plenty of swing when it was called for. With each album Dylan's voice was getting mellower and richer, without losing the trademark rasp. The combination of toughness and vulnerability in his voice wasn't new, but it was unmistakable and highly effective on songs like "Spirit on the Water," "Nettie Moore," and "Ain't Talkin'." He had also adopted a habit of "upsinging," raising the last note of a line, often against the melody—it was more pronounced in live performance, but the technique was also on display on *Modern Times*'s jump blues tunes.

Modern Times is typically regarded as the third album in a decade-spanning comeback trilogy, in which Dylan returned to older musical styles—mainly antique American pop and blues—and older recording methods. Compared to its two predecessors, the songs on this third installment are less audacious, a little more predictable. Even so, after lulling his listeners into complacency with clichéd or bland lyrics Dylan would throw in some violent, darkly comic line about recruiting an army of orphans or having killed a man back in Paradise. Using fragments of American musical and cultural history, Dylan had pieced together not only compelling new work but another new identity. "Bob Dylan doesn't use the blues anymore—he is the blues," wrote Sean O'Hagan in *The Guardian*'s review of *Modern Times*.[32] No longer trying to sound contemporary—to the point of using elements of old poems and songs like spare parts—Dylan had once again found a way to stake out his own territory and declare his independence.

14
2006–26: Multitude

In May 2019 the University of Tulsa Institute for Bob Dylan Studies hosted its first conference, "The World of Bob Dylan." By this time Dylan had been the subject of innumerable academic books and articles; symposia and college courses had been devoted to his work for years. But this conference was particularly significant for a couple of reasons. It was being held in Tulsa because the George Kaiser Family Foundation, which is based there, had recently purchased Dylan's archives—handwritten lyrics, typescripts, contracts, correspondence, videotapes, and other artifacts including guitars and stage outfits—to establish the Bob Dylan Center in the city's arts district. The conference planted a flag in Tulsa as the center for Dylan research. Another reason was the unprecedented gathering (overflow crowds) of fans and scholars—nearly all the attendees were both of course, but the mixing and blending of approaches to Dylan and the interest in all aspects of his career seemed to inspire everyone who came.[1] Moreover the title of what has become a biennial conference—The *World* of Bob Dylan—reflected the fact that, especially in the twenty-first century, "Dylan" had become something much more multifaceted than a singer and songwriter who occasionally made movies. It wasn't just that Dylan had been "the voice of a generation" once upon a time; he was a gravitational force, a planet around which many cultural moons continue to orbit.

Two films from the mid-2000s demonstrated why Dylan was so attractive while adding to that attraction. The first was Martin Scorsese's 2005 documentary *No Direction Home*, which chronicled

Dylan's career through 1966: his origins in Minnesota, his rise through the Greenwich Village folk music scene, the transition to rock, and the manic, grueling tours leading up to the infamous motorcycle accident. Scorsese's three-and-a-half-hour film featured new and archival interviews with seemingly everyone—Baez, Van Ronk, Suze Rotolo, Allen Ginsberg, Izzy Young, Al Kooper, Bob Johnston, Pete Seeger, Dylan himself—along with rare footage and previously unreleased studio outtakes. It told a familiar story but with details and insights from friends, lovers, and associates that surprised and delighted viewers, and it remains an essential introduction to Dylan's pre-Basement Tapes career.

The other film, Todd Haynes's 2007 fictional feature *I'm Not There*, was less widely acclaimed but perhaps even more illuminating. "Dylan" is not a character—his name is never mentioned—but instead six characters represent various personae associated with him. "I just found [Dylan's] refusal to be fixed as a single self in a single voice as a key to his freedom," Haynes said.[2] Five separate plots are intercut throughout the film, involving a young African American runaway who calls himself Woody Guthrie; Jack Rollins, a 1960s folk singer who becomes an evangelical preacher; Robbie Clark, an

Bob Dylan Center in Tulsa, Oklahoma.

actor who plays Rollins in a film and lives out a *Blood on the Tracks*-inspired marriage and divorce; Jude Quinn, the snarling, cynical pop star straight out of *Dont Look Back* and *Eat the Document*; and Billy the Kid, an outlaw figure who inhabits the world Greil Marcus extrapolated from the Basement Tapes. The sixth Dylan avatar, Arthur Rimbaud, is (as the name suggests) a decadent artist, an interrogation subject who appears briefly and periodically but without any action or plot. The role that got the most attention (and an Oscar nomination) was Jude Quinn, played by Cate Blanchett; her delivery of Dylan's slurry speech and jittery mannerisms, along with Blanchett's cross-dressing, highlighted the subversiveness of Dylan's self-presentation circa 1965. But all the performances—by Marcus Carl Franklin, Christian Bale, Heath Ledger, Richard Gere, and Ben Whishaw as the other Dylanesque characters—were distinctive and compelling. In contrast with *No Direction Home*, which assumes no prior Dylan knowledge, *I'm Not There* caters to the initiated as a tapestry of allusions to his life and career. But it works extremely well as a dramatization of Dylan's various identities and the mythology surrounding each, even incorporating winking allusions to *No Direction Home* as part of that mythology.

Between the release of those two films Dylan took on a new gig as DJ, hosting a satellite radio show called *Theme Time Radio Hour*. The concept was simple, the playlists diverse. The "coffee" episode for instance kicks off with the Ink Spots' "Java Jive" and proceeds through another fourteen selections that include Squeeze's "Black Coffee in Bed" and Lefty Frizzell's "Cigarettes and Coffee Blues"—but not "One More Cup of Coffee (Valley Below)." Dylan explored a hundred themes over three seasons of the show (plus two that were produced later), everything from baseball to Tennessee to birds (two bird episodes!). Dylan's patter included encyclopedic fun facts, personal asides, and corny jokes with deadpan delivery. ("If you think the summer sun is too hot, just remember, at least you don't have to shovel it"; "Lonnie the Cat, he read about the evils of drinking, so he quit reading.") Of course Dylan did not open up about his own career or craft, but he did reveal—if it were not already obvious—his eclectic and fascinating musical taste. He got a lot of help, especially from his friend, writer-producer-record collector Eddie Gorodetsky, but his obviously sincere love of popular music and his sense of humor pervade each episode.

Quirky satellite radio shows, documentaries, and postmodern films might not have reached the masses, but slick TV commercials did. Following the *succès de scandale* of the Victoria's Secret ad Dylan seemed happy to trade on his image with product endorsements. Upon the release of *Modern Times* in 2006 he appeared in a spot for iPod and iTunes singing "Someday Baby." The following year he drove a Cadillac Escalade through a barren Southwestern landscape before delivering the tagline, "What's life without the occasional detour?" He shared the small screen with will.i.am of Black Eyed Peas in a 2009 Pepsi commercial that debuted during the Super Bowl, a remix of "Forever Young" that featured old footage of a young Dylan. Five years later he appeared in another Super Bowl ad, this one a two-minute epic for Chrysler. With "Things Have Changed" playing in the background, he delivers an encomium to American pride beginning with the puzzling question, "Is there anything more American than America?" Meanwhile the video progresses through images of James Dean, Marilyn Monroe, cowboys, and of course Bob Dylan, on its way to a Detroit assembly line and a working-class pool hall. "So let Germany brew your beer," he says, about to close the deal, "let Switzerland make your watch, let Asia assemble your phone . . . WE will build your car." This corporate American exceptionalism was a far cry from the biting irony of "With God on Our Side," but it was an effective ad. He followed it up with a clever 2015 commercial for another American corporate icon, IBM. Their AI bot Watson, upon analyzing Dylan's collected lyrics, declares that his major themes are "time passes, and love fades." Dylan replies, laconically, "That sounds about right."

Dylan was diversifying his portfolio as a visual artist as well. Painting and sketching had been more of a hobby throughout his career, with the occasional album cover and illustrations for 1973's *Writings and Drawings*. In 1994 he published *Drawn Blank*, a book of sketches he had made on the road, to little fanfare. Then in 2007 he had his first museum exhibition at Kunstsammlungen Chemnitz,

Germany, with paintings based on the *Drawn Blank* sketches, and another the following year at Halcyon Gallery in London. He began exhibiting new work regularly: "The Brazil Series" at the National Gallery of Denmark in 2010, "The Asia Series" at the Gagosian Gallery in New York in 2011, "Revisionist Art" at the Gagosian in 2012, "The New Orleans Series" in Milan in 2013, and "Face Value" the same year at London's National Portrait Gallery. More exhibitions followed throughout the 2010s, culminating in 2021's "Bob Dylan: Retrospectrum" at the Frost Art Museum in Miami.

Dylan's twenty-first-century paintings bear little resemblance to the primitivist album covers of *Music from Big Pink* and *Self Portrait*. The style of the 2007 "Drawn Blank Series" exhibition evokes Postimpressionism, and the acrylic works of the following decade look more like the early twentieth-century Realism of John Sloan and Edward Hopper. Reactions were mixed, but in a *New York Times* review of the "Drawn Blank Series" exhibition book Marisha Pessl wrote that Dylan's "brush strokes are like his voice: straightforward, rough, occasionally fragile, but always intent on illustrating the treads of human experience."[3] His style had become more polished and conservative by the time he exhibited "The Beaten Path" in 2016. On that occasion Dylan wrote that "the idea was to create pictures that would not be misinterpreted or misunderstood by me or anybody else," implicitly challenging those who have sought multiple levels of meaning in his song lyrics. He calls his approach "up to the moment realism" and asserts that his paintings "contradict the modern world . . . The purpose is plain, non-experimental or exploratory."[4] The artist Richard Prince, in an essay for the "Retrospectrum" exhibition book, agrees, although it's hard to tell whether his assessment is favorable: "Most of what Dylan pictures is straightforward. There's nothing really to be interpreted or guessed at, and the rendering seems to say, 'I don't want excitement, and I don't want to be exciting.'"[5]

Those descriptions suggest a contrast with Dylan's songwriting, which has always been celebrated for risk-taking and unpredictability. But Dylan's visual art actually shares with his twenty-first century music that defiance of "the modern world"—since the 1990s his recordings have deliberately evoked musical styles older than Dylan himself and recording methods long out of date. As with his music, he was borrowing very directly from other artists—in the case of the "Beaten Path" paintings, film directors and cinematographers. Scott Warmuth, the intrepid Dylan detective, identified nineteen screen shots from a dozen films that Dylan clearly used as models for sketches and paintings. Viewing them alongside their sources makes the paintings a little more interesting: the films tend to be well known (*Touch of Evil*, *Bonnie and Clyde*, *The French Connection*), but the specific scenes are not, and it's intriguing how Dylan alters them, not only by working in a different medium but with small, deliberate alterations to what's depicted in the screen shot. (For the earlier "Revisionist Art" exhibition, Dylan created silkscreens with altered images and text from magazine covers.)

The gamesmanship carries over into Dylan's artist statement for "The Beaten Path," which, like *Chronicles*, is largely a patchwork of phrases pulled from books about art.[6] Dylan used his own previous work—his songs—as inspiration for a series of pencil drawings exhibited under the title "Mondo Scripto": he paired newly handwritten lyrics with images suggested either by individual lines of the song or an overall theme. The drawings are far more detailed and precise than the ones he had done for *Writings and Drawings* decades earlier; some are subtle and evocative, while others are droll: for "Blowin' in the Wind" we get a cemetery scene where a grave marker in the foreground reads "Here lies Joe Fate, Two slugs from .38."

In his visual art Dylan was demonstrating, in his own postmodern way, a principle behind all visual art, as well as music and literature: "originality" is the product of imitation, mutation, and combination. On some level all artists are collage artists, all songs are covers. Nowhere was this principle more on display than in Dylan's other new medium: ironwork. Welding together manufactured metal objects—wrenches, gears, wheels, hooks, chains, tongs, horseshoes, vice grips—he created large, intricate sculptures, often using elongated shafts to frame the arrangement of old tools and spare parts. Dylan's ironworks are more distinctive, more striking, than his paintings, but they also foreground the technique of assemblage, making something new out of old stuff.

Amidst all this new activity Dylan continued touring and making records. On four occasions in the 2000s he devoted legs of the Never-Ending Tour to minor league baseball parks and frequently toured with prominent opening acts including John Mellencamp, Willie Nelson, Mark Knopfler, Wilco, and My Morning Jacket. His band line-up from the mid-2000s through the 2010s was fairly stable, with Tony Garnier on bass, George Receli on drums, Donnie Herron on multiple stringed instruments, Stu Kimball on guitar, and the second guitarist slot filled first by Denny Freeman through 2010 and then (mainly) by Charlie Sexton. Dylan traded his own guitar for a keyboard from 2003 to 2006, and then gave up onstage guitar playing almost entirely in 2012.

In 2006 Dylan called his touring band, which had recently backed him on *Modern Times*, "the best band I've ever been in, I've ever had, man for man . . . I got guys now in my band, they can whip up anything, they surprise even me."[7] Dylan's own performances were somewhat erratic—sometimes great, but not for everyone. While his singing had always been a source of bemusement in some quarters, complaints from ticket-buying fans became more common. It was harder than ever to discern lyrics, and the often-radical re-arrangements of old songs were coupled with the singer's determination not to follow the familiar melody (or sometimes any melody). And of course he had long since abandoned between-song patter. "They say, 'Dylan never talks,'" he acknowledged at the time. "What the hell is there to say! That's not the reason an artist is in front of people."[8] As admirable as Dylan's constant touring was from the perspective of stamina and determination, it also made his latest visit less of an event. He still drew strong crowds, but for many the excitement of getting to see the legendary Bob Dylan was diminished by the fact that he'd probably be back in town next year.

And yet, unlike most of his peers in the rock pantheon, he continued to make albums that were worthy of his reputation, extending the renaissance that had started with *Time Out of Mind*. In 2008 the film director Olivier Dahan, who had no prior connection to Dylan, asked him to write some songs—ten or so—for his next film. Dylan's first reaction, he later recalled, was "Is this guy serious?" But he

Poster for tour of minor league baseball parks, 2004.

decided to do it, partly because he had liked Dahan's previous film *La Vie en Rose*: "I just kind of gave the guy the benefit of the doubt that he knew what he was doing."[9] The film, *My Own Love Song*, would be released in 2010, with Renée Zellweger and Forest Whitaker in leading roles and featuring several Dylan songs, some sung by the actors, as well as some bluesy instrumentals written by Dylan. But by that time the "new" songs had been out for a year on Dylan's 33rd studio album, *Together Through Life*. Dylan again enlisted Grateful Dead lyricist Robert Hunter to collaborate on nine of the album's ten songs, which might explain the lack of hidden quotations from unexpected sources. (And this time he gave Willie Dixon co-writer credit for "My Wife's Home Town," which set new words to Dixon's "I Just Want to Make Love to You," a 1954 hit for Muddy Waters.)

Together Through Life stays in the same musical lane as its predecessors—bluesy, old-fashioned, recorded with the touring band (with Mike Campbell of the Heartbreakers subbing for Denny Freeman on guitar) and produced by "Jack Frost." And yet it sounds like no other Dylan album, thanks almost entirely to Los Lobos' David Hidalgo playing accordion on nearly every track. The accordion flourishes and a few "Latin" rhythm motifs combine with the blues structures to make this, musically, Dylan's "Tex-Mex" album. Douglas Brinkley, in a *Rolling Stone* interview/profile, suggested that the ghost of Dylan's old friend Doug Sahm (of the Sir Douglas Quintet and the Texas Tornadoes) was the guiding spirit of the album, prompting a tribute from Dylan: "Doug was like me, maybe the only figure from that old period of time that I connected with. He was a big soul."[10]

Together Through Life's lyrics are not exactly uplifting—after all, the first two tracks are called "Beyond Here Lies Nothin'" and "Life Is Hard," followed by (Hell Is) "My Wife's Home Town"—but the mood is a bit lighter (maybe it's the accordion?) than on *"Love and Theft"* or *Modern Times*. The corollary, though, is that the songs just kind of roll by, with nothing as poignant or vivid as "Mississippi," "High Water (For Charley Patton)," "Spirit on the Water," or "Ain't Talkin'." The deluxe edition of the CD included a disc of a *Theme Time* show ("Friends and Neighbors"), and in fact Dylan's DJ persona and the voice of *Together Through Life* are pretty consistent: cynical but playful, disgusted but amused, displaying the wit and wisdom of an old man with eclectic taste but whose touchstone is always the blues. The last track, "It's All Good," sarcastically mocks that trite phrase, heard seemingly everywhere at the time. Brinkley may have put it best after spending time with Dylan for his 2009 interview: "Like the dour-faced farmer in Grant Wood's 'American Gothic,' Dylan seems to have the American Songbook in one hand and a raised pitchfork in the other, aimed at rock critics, politicians, Wall Street financiers, back-alley thieves, the World Wide Web—anything that cheapens the spirit of the individual."[11]

Art exhibitions, TV commercials, and a satellite radio show on top of a raft of awards and a recording career nearing its sixth decade . . . by 2009 it would have been fair to ask, what has Bob Dylan *not* done?

The answer, it seems, was a Christmas album, and he would soon check that off the list with *Christmas in the Heart*. The very concept faced the same head scratching and eye rolling that had greeted, for instance, the Victoria's Secret ad, but it was hard to seriously criticize an album whose proceeds were going to Feeding America and other hunger relief organizations. Dylan played the Christmas-album genre straight, with a program that would have made Bing Crosby or Frank Sinatra proud, a half dozen Christian carols ("Hark, the Herald Angels Sing," "The First Noël") mixed with mid-century standards ("Here Comes Santa Claus," "Have Yourself a Merry Little Christmas"). The arrangements and familiar song choices tended to highlight Dylan's vocal limitations, but he did follow the melodies, treating the holiday classics with surprising respect. He sounded most comfortable with "The Christmas Blues" and seemed to have the most fun with "Must Be Santa," an under-the-radar call-and-response song first recorded by Mitch Miller and the Gang in 1960. Dylan used Brave Combo's rollicking 1991 polka arrangement (which he had played on *Theme Time*) as his template and starred in a hilarious video, sporting his long-haired wig and smoking a cigar at a festive Christmas party where singing and dancing abound, uninterrupted by a frantic chase and brawl that rages through the house.

As the touring continued Dylan showed up in some unexpected places over the next few years. In July 2009, hours before a ballpark show in Lakewood, New Jersey, he went for a walk in nearby Long Branch and was picked up and questioned by a police officer, who had received a call about a suspicious, shabbily dressed man out in the rain, peering into a house with a for-sale sign out front. Dylan, who had an abiding interest in the old homes of his rock-star peers, might have been looking for the house where Springsteen had written "Born to Run," but that probably wouldn't have made any difference to the 24-year-old cop who thought the man was delusional when he told her his name was Bob Dylan but couldn't produce any identification. The suspect didn't seem to mind; she drove him back to his tour bus, where someone produced a passport, and it was on with the show—but the incident was picked up by news outlets and websites, prompting amusement at the famous man going unrecognized thanks to his own eccentricity. In an equally amusing (but clearly staged) surprise, the following year he would pop up in Las Vegas on the popular reality TV show *Pawn Stars* to sign a recently purchased copy of *Self Portrait*.

Some observers were less amused by another unexpected appearance—Dylan's visit to China in April 2011 as part of an Asian tour. *New York Times* columnist Maureen Dowd, for one, claimed Dylan had broken "creative new ground in selling out" by giving Chinese authorities a setlist in advance and not using the occasion to protest the government's human rights abuses.[12] In fact Dylan's setlists in Beijing and Shanghai were consistent with later sets in the tour, and no one who had been following his career would still expect him to sing protest songs *anywhere*. Surprisingly Dylan cared enough to issue a statement, not defending his decision to play in China but asserting that "If there were any songs, verses or lines censored, nobody ever told me about it and we played all the songs that we intended to play."[13]

Between the fall 2011 and late spring 2012 tours Dylan and the band recorded another album of new material, and, although it seemed almost impossible, he pushed his songwriting even further into the darkness of the human heart, the tragedy of existence and the glory of folk and blues traditions. The jaunty old-time swing of the opener, "Duquesne Whistle," is a decoy—*Tempest* is a tough, brooding album. Musically Dylan was still living in a place where guitars are plugged in but rock and roll is just a rumor. The band chugs along gamely through songs that, with a couple of exceptions, avoid choruses and bridges—a dozen verses, maybe two dozen, no solos. After the first two songs Dylan declaims more than sings, with a new emphasis on threats and violence, proclaiming that he pays in blood—but not his own. Often the violence is linked to sex and desire. The story "Tin Angel" tells may be the oldest folk tale there is: a man's wife runs off with another man, so he hunts the lovers down, confronts them, and all three end up dead. In "Scarlet Town" he sketches out a Desolation Row-like setting for "Barbara Allen," a ballad that dates back at least to the seventeenth century—in which Sweet William dies after being snubbed by the beautiful woman he loves.

Indeed there is something primal in the way *Tempest* returns to uncomplicated expressions of love, pain, and loss. It ends with a tribute to Dylan's old friend and rival John Lennon, mournfully riffing on Lennon's own lyrics. That song is preceded by the epic title track, the 14-minute, 45-verse story of the *Titanic*'s sinking. The *Titanic*'s fate was a staple of early twentieth-century folk songs, a modern tragedy that tells an eternal story of hubris, greed, violence, and an inscrutable God. Like "Tin Angel" and a few other songs on *Tempest*, it's longer than it needs to be, but it's a perfect demonstration of Dylan's devotion to tradition. He doesn't have to begin the song with "Come gather 'round, people" for you to sense the prophecy, to understand that the sinking of this colossal "unsinkable" ship—full of people who will fight tooth and nail for a place in a lifeboat when the time comes—has a certain symbolic weight. Throughout the song he refers repeatedly to a "watchman" for whom the *Titanic*'s sinking is only a dream. Because he doesn't believe it himself, the watchman—it's hard not to think of that earlier impending-disaster song about a watchtower—doesn't warn anyone until it's too late.

But the most indelible song on *Tempest* may be "Early Roman Kings," which Dylan has played more than five hundred times since November 2012. Here too he uses a specific motif to evoke a type known to every place and time: the gangster, the kingpin, the rock star, the men who ignore the law and civilized norms, who get ballads written about them, who get (and discard) women that honest, peaceful men only dream about. Their number includes Muddy Waters, whose "Mannish Boy" provides the song's musical template and, one can only assume, Bob Dylan. If you look at any of the three photographs of Dylan that accompany *Tempest* you can see the modern-day "Early Roman King" pose, eyes either behind shades, in shadow as he stares down at us, or squinting menacingly as he puffs a cigar, flanked by his unsmiling band. Dylan had long since stopped greeting audiences or talking between songs, or even bowing to acknowledge applause, instead standing with his legs slightly apart, hands on his hips, staring straight back at the adoring crowd.

Tempest gave Dylan another hit with the critics, and it sold well enough to land at number three on the British and American album charts. With its weighty themes and epic-length songs it had the feel of a "major" album, possibly a final statement (like *Time Out of Mind*, fifteen years and five albums before). As was often the case, Dylan was slow to promote the new material onstage, but eventually *Tempest* would dominate his setlists in the mid- to late 2010s.

Now in his seventies, he remained a vital, evolving songwriter and performer even as he continued to collect lifetime achievement awards. In 2012 Barack Obama awarded him the Presidential Medal of Freedom in a White House ceremony alongside (among others) Toni Morrison, John Glenn, and Madeleine Albright. Even Dylan seemed impressed by the Medal of Freedom—in an interview that summer with Mikal Gilmore he said that he turned down more awards than he picked up but that this one was "an incredible honor . . . I mean, who wouldn't want to get a letter from the White House?"

He had a few choice words for the naysayers though. In the same interview he lashed out at those who questioned his uncredited use of other writers:

> And as far as Henry Timrod is concerned, have you even heard of him? Who's been reading him lately? . . . And if you think it's so easy to quote him and it can help your work, do it yourself and see how far you can get. Wussies and pussies complain about that stuff. It's an old thing—it's part of the tradition. It goes way back. These are the same people that tried to pin the name Judas on me. Judas, the most hated name in human history! If you think you've been called a bad name, try to work your way out from under that.

He takes the position that all songwriters borrow whatever they like and that only he gets singled out, held to a different standard. As for his critics, "All those evil motherfuckers can rot in hell."[14]

It was one of the strangest interviews of the hundreds Dylan has done over the course of his career. Dylan presented Gilmore with a copy of the book *Hell's Angel: The Life and Times of Sonny Barger and the Hell's Angels Motorcycle Club*. He had Gilmore read aloud a passage about the tragic death of a Hell's Angel named Bobby Zimmerman in

1964 and then claimed that he (Dylan) had been "transfigured." What exactly that meant for Dylan never really became clear, but he insisted that the other Bobby Zimmerman's motorcycle accident and his own two years later were somehow linked, and that "when you ask some of your questions, you're asking them to a person who's long dead. You're asking them to a person that doesn't exist." Bob Dylan does exist ("You're talking to him") and has experienced transfiguration, which allows him "to crawl out from under the chaos and fly above it. That's how I can still do what I do and write the songs I sing and just keep on moving."[15] Assuming he was serious, he seemed to be saying that Bob Dylan was not just a stage name adopted by Robert Zimmerman, but that at some point (1964? 1966?) he had been "transfigured" from Zimmerman to Dylan, an artist with superhuman powers.

But for the next few years he would not be using those powers to write new songs. The endless touring continued, but in the studio Dylan devoted his next three releases to jazz and pop standards from the 1940s and '50s, focusing on songs associated with Frank Sinatra: *Shadows in the Night* (2015), *Fallen Angels* (2016), and the triple-disc appropriately titled *Triplicate* (2017). Following Willie Nelson's *Stardust* in 1978, albums of pop standards from roughly the second quarter of the twentieth century performed by rock, country, and contemporary pop singers had become commonplace: a highly selective list includes Linda Ronstadt, Carly Simon, Boz Scaggs, Cyndi Lauper, Merle Haggard, Diana Ross, Brian Wilson, and Paul McCartney; Rod Stewart virtually reinvented himself with five "Great American Songbook" volumes between 2002 and 2010. So on the face of it exploring the world of Irving Berlin, Hoagy Carmichael, Harold Arlen, and Johnny Mercer was not a brazen move—it had almost become a cliché by 2015. Dylan had dabbled in the "songbook" as far back as 1987, performing the song "Soon" at a Gershwin Gala; *Theme Time Radio Hour* and *Christmas in the Heart* offered further evidence of his affection for the pop music of his childhood. And yet this still seemed like an odd move for the ultimate singer-songwriter, the guy who had once claimed to have put an end to Tin Pan Alley.

And then what about that voice? "I'm a Fool to Want You," "Some Enchanted Evening," "Skylark"—these were songs meant to showcase the voice as a musical instrument, and Dylan's instrument, always a point of contention between fans and detractors, was, at age 74, more whiskey-soaked, smoke-stained, and weather-beaten than ever, which might be the whole point of these albums. The vocals are not pretty; he wavers, strains for notes, and while his timbre is smooth here compared to, say, *Tempest*, it's still a bit creaky. And yet Dylan understands these songs and sings them with affection. Especially when the lyrics involve looking back with regret, as on *Triplicate*'s "September of My Years" or "Once Upon a Time," the aged voice is effective, as it had been for Dylan's friend Johnny Cash on his late recordings. And unlike many younger singers who take on these classics, Dylan never tries to show off or upstage the song. Similarly the arrangements of his touring band—guitar, steel guitar, bass and drums, supplemented on *Triplicate* by a small horn section—are sensitive and respectful. These are not the records to introduce a newcomer to the pop standards of Sinatra's prime or to Bob Dylan's voice, but for those who already have an affinity for both they make a lot of sense.

Dylan made headlines again in 2016 when, after two decades of nominations and rumors, he was awarded the Nobel Prize in Literature. Predictably many of those headlines were followed by discussion of whether Dylan was an appropriate choice. Throughout his career Dylan had been the focus of debates over whether song lyrics were poetry, always with the implicit understanding of a value judgment—are song lyrics *good enough* to be considered poetry? Even as they declared their admiration for Dylan some commentators bristled at the Nobel committee's elevation or inclusion of songwriting into the loftier category of "literature," a realm where words move readers without the benefit of musical accompaniment. Anna North wrote in the *New York Times* that Dylan "is great because he is a great musician, and when the Nobel committee gives the literature prize to a musician, it misses the opportunity to honor a *writer*" (my italics).[16] Others argued that as a rock star, Dylan was already rich, famous, and widely honored; a respected but not-so-famous poet or novelist could use the recognition more—a fair point, but "need" had never been a criterion for the prize. The bottom line I think was the recognition that song lyrics didn't have to read like poetry on the silent page in order to be literature. Journalist and critic David Hajdu expressed the larger significance of the award: "It's literature, but it's music, it's performance, it's art, it's also highly commercial. The old categories of high and low art, they've been collapsing for a long time, but this is it being made official."[17]

Further controversy surrounded Dylan's reaction to being awarded the Nobel: for two weeks he ignored the announcement and the Nobel committee altogether. He broke his silence when the reporter Edna Gundersen, who had a scheduled interview with Dylan about his latest art exhibition, asked if he planned to attend the award ceremony. "Absolutely," he said, quickly qualifying, "if it's at all possible." In true Dylan fashion he offered no explanation for his silence, but he seemed pleased by the honor, which came with a check for 8 million Swedish kronor (about $900,000).[18]

Dylan did not attend the ceremony that December; his friend Patti Smith accepted for him and sang "A Hard Rain's A-Gonna Fall" at the event. He sent a gracious banquet speech that was read by the U.S. ambassador to Sweden, in which he made an apt comparison between his songs and Shakespeare's plays as literature. He imagined that Shakespeare never gave a thought to whether his plays were literature: "When he was writing *Hamlet*, I'm sure he was thinking about a lot of different things: 'Who're the right actors for these roles?' 'How should this be staged?' 'Do I really want to set this in Denmark?' . . . 'Where am I going to get a human skull?' I would bet that the farthest thing from Shakespeare's mind was the question 'Is this *literature*?'" Similarly he had professional questions of his own to sort out: "'Who are the best musicians for these songs?' 'Am I recording in the right studio?' 'Is this song in the right key?' Some things never change, even in 400 years . . . Not once have I ever had the time to ask myself, 'Are my songs *literature*?'" He concluded by thanking the Nobel committee "for taking the time to consider that very question, and, ultimately, for providing such a wonderful answer."[19]

The committee required a longer Nobel Lecture, which Dylan dutifully recorded and submitted within the six-month deadline. He padded this speech with a discussion of three works "that have stuck with me ever since I read them all the way back in grammar school":

Moby-Dick, *All Quiet on the Western Front*, and *The Odyssey*. Taking up about two-thirds of the lecture, this portion reads like the cut-and-paste high school book report that it basically is, down to a little assistance from SparkNotes.[20] On a more heartfelt note, early in the speech he described the "folk process" of absorbing and repurposing material from the blues and other traditional music, in part justifying his own practice but, more importantly, explaining how he came to be a Nobel laureate: "By listening to all the early folk artists and singing the songs yourself, you pick up the vernacular. You internalize it. You sing it in the ragtime blues, work songs, Georgia sea shanties, Appalachian ballads and cowboy songs. You hear all the finer points, and you learn the details . . . I could make it all connect and move with the current of the day."[21]

Dylan submitted the lecture and picked up the Nobel Prize in Stockholm that April; fittingly he also played two shows at the Stockholm Waterfront, kicking off a six-week European itinerary. He would play 84 concerts over the next eight months, concluding with a five-night stand at New York's Beacon Theater. (He would do the same multi-night engagement there at the end of his 2018 and 2019 tours.) His sets now included about a half dozen of his own classics, four or five standards from the "Sinatra albums," and eight or nine songs from the previous twenty years, heaviest on *Tempest*. He seemed prepared to continue performing as long as he was physically able, but by 2019 it had been seven years since he had released an album of new songs, and that last one had a ring of finality to it. Meanwhile he seemed to be getting his affairs in order, or at least cashing in on his legacy in new, more lucrative ways. In addition to selling his archives to the Kaiser Family Foundation in 2016 he would sell his publishing to Universal Music for over $300 million in 2020 and his recording masters to Sony for an estimated $200 million the following year. In 2018 he partnered with liquor entrepreneur Marc Bushala to create a boutique whiskey brand under the evocative name Heaven's Door and revived *Theme Time Radio Hour* for a celebratory "whiskey" episode two years later.

The COVID-19 pandemic finally took Dylan off the road for all of 2020 (41 shows in Japan and North America were cancelled) and most of 2021. The Never-Ending Tour (which, to be fair, was never Dylan's name for it) had finally ended. But on March 27, 2020, just as lockdowns were becoming the new reality for most of the world, Dylan issued a single track, the seventeen-minute, spoken-word "Murder Most Foul." It wasn't a complete stylistic departure, but "Murder Most Foul" felt different from anything he had done before—solemn, with a musical backing that included two pianos and a bowed bass. Dylan preached on the text of John F. Kennedy's assassination, which had occurred just as his career was taking off in 1963. (He makes it clear that he did not believe Lee Harvey Oswald acted alone.) He had spent over fifty years insisting he was *not* the voice of a generation, but that's exactly the kind of the role he takes on here. The assassination is often seen as the galvanizing event for the American 1960s consciousness, and that's how Dylan treats it. He calls on the legendary DJ Wolfman Jack to play one artist after another, naming and alluding to dozens of songs. His selections are not confined the 1960s, as he includes older jazz musicians like Thelonious Monk and Bud Powell, as well as later rock bands like the Eagles and Queen. Nor are they confined to music, as he calls out silent film stars and famous gangsters. Dylan the collage artist/DJ seems to be designing an alternate *Sgt. Pepper* album cover as a recording rather than a visual image. The catalogs are rhymed free association, providing a sense of community and inspiration against the corruption and conspiracy surrounding JFK's killing. The timing of the release suggested a parallel: the world seemed to be coming apart, the future radically uncertain in March 2020, but the artists on Dylan's playlist—not to mention Dylan himself—might help get us through it.

"Murder Most Foul" was followed in April by "I Contain Multitudes" and then in May "False Prophet," before the full *Rough and Rowdy Ways* album was released in June. The title "I Contain Multitudes" alludes to Walt Whitman's lyric-epic "Song of Myself": "Do I contradict myself?/ Very well then I contradict myself,/ (I am large, I contain multitudes.)" At first "Multitudes" comes across as an abbreviated "Murder Most Foul," but the voice is indeed more Whitmanseque—the insistent "I" is ostensibly Dylan but also (as with Whitman) a unifying spirit associated with America but not exclusively American (not exclusive at all—that's the whole point). And yet, unlike Whitman, Dylan fixates on rhyme, as he has throughout his career. It seems to be the glue that holds together the contradictions and multitudes on this song and "Murder Most Foul."

Rough and Rowdy Ways retains much of the orneriness and world-weary scorn of its predecessors, but those notes are balanced with appreciation (mostly for artistic creation) and a calmer reflectiveness. There's also a little more humor, as in "My Own Version of You," when the singer is brainstorming the qualities of the Frankenstein's monster he'll create (for instance a piano style that combines Leon Russell, Liberace, and John the Apostle). The subject of the dirge-like "Black Rider" seems to be a personification of death (one of the Four Horsemen of the Apocalypse?)—but this is a Death who can be cajoled and even threatened.

Even more than *Time Out of Mind, Rough and Rowdy Ways* contemplates life's end and what that end means. On "Goodbye Jimmy Reed" there's no doubt that the blues is his religion as he seeks to follow Reed's footsteps. Similarly "Mother of Muses" is a prayer in which eternal life is the domain of music. "Crossing the Rubicon" also suggests the crossing into an afterlife. And in the meditative "Key West (Philosopher Pirate)" the singer alternately reflects on his past life and the attractions of his new home, a place of immortality. But even here, in the "paradise" of Key West, he's seeking out music, tuning in to a pirate radio station with a long-distance dedication.

For the third time since 1997 Dylan had made an album with a distinct air of finality about it, although that's the kind of claim he would scoff at—and perhaps rightly so, because he obviously wasn't retiring with *Rough and Rowdy Ways*. In July 2021, still off the road due to the pandemic, he released the concert film *Shadow Kingdom: The Early Songs of Bob Dylan* through a livestreaming platform. The film reflects Dylan's late-career aesthetic—shot in black and white, set primarily in an imaginary nightclub that seems frozen in a film-noir past. Director Alma Har'el creates a surreal, stagey atmosphere that vaguely recalls Dylan's 1964 performance on the Canadian public television show *Quest* (see Chapter Four). Audience members (or rather, actors playing audience members) sit around smoking cigarettes and listening without much reaction—except when Dylan and the band play "Watching the River Flow," which elicits dancing and applause. Musician-actors mime the pre-recorded tracks on bass, guitar, and accordion; in the only gesture to the present day, they wear COVID masks, while Dylan and the audience do not. Sixty years into his career the subtitle, "The Early Songs of Bob Dylan," could mean almost anything, but he performs nothing earlier than 1965's "It's All Over Now, Baby Blue" (which closes the set) and only one song later than 1974's "Forever Young"—"What Was It You Wanted" from 1989. Dylan was in good voice, demonstrating that he could still carry tunes as needed, and the new, mostly unplugged arrangements, played by a drummerless pick-up band that included Doug Lacy on accordion, T-Bone Burnett on guitar, and Don Was on upright bass, reinterpreted a dozen well-known but not-quite-greatest hits.

Dylan's other pandemic project was his book *The Philosophy of Modern Song*, published in November 2022. The title points to Poe's "The Philosophy of Composition," in which he describes (unreliably) how he wrote "The Raven," but Dylan's book is not about process, least of all his own. *The Philosophy of Modern Song* is an appreciation, a tribute to 66 pop recordings—not explicitly a companion to *Theme Time*, but very much in the same vein. Most chapters consist of an impressionistic section followed by a more sober reflection that often includes information about the songwriter or performer but just as often veers off into amusing tangents concerning technology, house keys, or songs about fools. Dylan may not be cutting and pasting, but the collage aesthetic still prevails. There is a stitched-together, second-hand feel to his sentences, but a unique, lively voice emerges through overwrought, arcane phrases. What we hear throughout the book is Dylan's exuberance, an enduring excitement for records he loves: "This is the sound that made America great" (Sonny Burgess's "Feel So Good"); "This song melts everything down, browns it up and deep-fries it—it'll milk the cow till it gives blood" (Uncle Dave Macon's "Keep My Skillet Good and Greasy").[22] The selections span about eight decades, but not surprisingly Dylan spends more time in the 1950s, his teenage years, than anywhere else—and not just early rock and roll but country and pop hits like "There Stands the Glass,"

"El Paso," "You Don't Know Me," "My Prayer," "It's All in the Game," even "Volare."

The Philosophy of Modern Song is less about songwriting than about performance—or it might be more accurate to say that Dylan refuses to separate the two, true to his Nobel speech. The exhilaration that he exhibits throughout the book comes from perfect marriages of song, singer, and arrangement, and most of the time, those arrangements are spare: "If Hank [Williams] was to sing ['Your Cheatin' Heart'] and you had somebody like Joe Satriani playing answer licks to the vocal, like they do in a lot of blues bands, it just wouldn't work and would be a waste of a great song." He writes that the music of blues singer-guitarist Jimmy Reed "is about space. About air being moved around the room . . . You put him with Jimmie Rodgers and Thelonious Monk, two other musicians whose work never sounds crowded no matter how many players are there."[23] Space, simplicity, freedom: those are the principles Dylan returns to throughout the book.

Between his return to the live stage in November 2021 and the end of 2025 Dylan performed 334 shows in 20 countries, with another 27 scheduled through May 1, 2026. Naming the tour for his most recent album—not his usual practice—made sense: while he has never performed "Murder Most Foul" onstage he typically included all other nine songs from *Rough and Rowdy Ways* in the nightly setlist. That list was fairly static through April 2024, opening shows with "Watching the River Flow," closing with "Every Grain of Sand," and mixing in a handful of other familiar older songs and one nightly cover (for a while he was inserting a different Grateful Dead song every night). The show pleased hard-core Dylan fans, who marveled at his continued vitality, his commitment to his new material, and the frequent re-arrangements of the songs—changing tempos, riffs, sometimes melodies. (Reviews of virtually every performance can be found on Ray Padgett's Substack *Flagging Down the Double E's*.) The band—anchored by bassist Tony Garnier, who has been playing behind Dylan for 35 years—also featured Bob Britt and Doug Lancio on guitar, Donnie Herron (through April 2024) on steel guitar and other instruments, and a succession of drummers, at one point Jim Keltner, whose work with Dylan goes back to the early 1970s. Dylan leads them from behind his piano, and it's clear that they have to watch him closely for unexpected musical cues. That became even more the case over the summer of 2024, when Dylan headlined the Outlaw Music Festival, which also featured Willie Nelson, John Mellencamp, Billy Strings, and Robert Plant and Alison Krauss. He ditched the setlist he'd been playing for over two years, reviving several crowd-pleasers ("Highway 61 Revisited," "Things Have Changed," "Simple Twist of Fate") and throwing in multiple covers every night. He returned to the Outlaw Festival with similarly unpredictable setlists in 2025.

Standing behind an upright or baby grand piano, Dylan at 84 is still a mesmerizing performer. For all the changes he's experienced and inspired, the commitment he brings to the stage is perhaps the one constant in his career. That commitment has carried over to his twenty-first-century studio albums as well: probably the best move he ever made as a recording artist was to become "Jack Frost," the producer who insisted on getting that live-performance sound. From his manic, Little Richard-inspired performances at Hibbing High to playing unbidden at house parties in Minneapolis; to Greenwich Village open-mic nights, the Newport festivals, and the riotous shows that followed; Tour '74 and the Rolling Thunder Revue, to the gospel tours and the Never-Ending Tour . . . performing for an audience has been Dylan's creative lifeblood. He may not smile or chat much, and he certainly isn't going to bow, but he is fully engaged and fully alive. Onstage he embodies the artistic freedom and control that he has sought throughout his career.

Bob Dylan is undeniably the greatest songwriter of his time, with 40 studio albums (and many more compilations and live albums), three books of prose, numerous art exhibitions, a research center and museum devoted to his work, and a Nobel Prize on top of dozens of other awards and honors. But he is essentially a performer, and as a performer his true home is the road. And what better symbol could there be for a restless, ever-changing artist? His partly fabricated "My Life in a Stolen Moment"—the story of a hard travelin' runaway—remained true in spirit long after he presented it in 1963, at the dawn of his career. Sixty years later, in *The Philosophy of Modern Song*, Dylan wrote about the life of a touring musician in his chapter on Willie Nelson's "On the Road Again": "The thing about being on the road is that you're not bogged down by anything. Not even bad news. You give pleasure to other people and you keep your grief to yourself."[24] Somewhere in between, at the age of 45, he was already being asked how long he could continue to tour. He was not even halfway through his career in 1986 when he replied, "I'll be doing this for as long as I'm around. And all the people I admired, they've all done it all the way to the end, too. It's all I do."[25] A rolling stone gathers no moss.

REFERENCES

1 Jonathan Cott, ed., *Bob Dylan: The Essential Interviews* (New York, 2006), p. 370.

1 1941–60: Origins

1 Bob Dylan, *Writings and Drawings* (New York, 1973), pp. 49–51.
2 Dave Van Ronk with Elijah Wald, *The Mayor of MacDougal Street: A Memoir* (Cambridge, MA, 2005), p. 162.
3 Clinton Heylin, *The Double Life of Bob Dylan*, vol. I: *1941–1966: A Restless, Hungry Feeling* (New York, 2021), p. 155.
4 Anthony Scaduto, *Bob Dylan: An Intimate Biography* (New York, 1971), pp. 4–5.
5 Dave Engel, *Just Like Bob Zimmerman's Blues: Dylan in Minnesota* (Amherst, WI, 1997), p. 55.
6 "Bob Dylan: Not Like a Rolling Stone Interview," *Spin*, www.spin.com, December 1985.
7 Engel, *Just Like Bob Zimmerman's Blues*, p. 74.
8 Howard Sounes, *Down the Highway: The Life of Bob Dylan* (New York, 2001), p. 21; Clinton Heylin, *Bob Dylan: Behind the Shades Revisited* (New York, 2001), p. 9.
9 Edward S. Shapiro, *We Are Many: Reflections on American Jewish History and Identity* (Syracuse, NY, 2005), pp. 30–49; Hasia R. Diner, *The Jews of the United States, 1654 to 2000* (Berkeley, CA, 2004), pp. 259–61.
10 Kurt Loder, "Interview for *Rolling Stone*, 1984," in *Bob Dylan: The Essential Interviews*, ed. Jonathan Cott (New York, 2006), p. 312.
11 Bob Dylan, *Chronicles, Volume One* (New York, 2004), p. 28.
12 Bill Flanagan, "Q&A," www.bobdylan.com/news/qa-with-bill-flanagan, March 22, 2017.
13 Sounes, *Down the Highway*, p. 27.
14 Michael Gray, *The Bob Dylan Encyclopedia* (New York and London, 2008), p. 423.
15 Ibid., p. 425.
16 Bob Dylan, "Nobel Lecture," www.nobelprize.org, June 4, 2017.

17 Dylan, *Chronicles*, p. 44.
18 Louie Kemp, *Dylan & Me: Fifty Years of Adventures* (Los Angeles, CA, 2019), p. 6.
19 Heylin, *Double Life of Bob Dylan*, vol. I, p. 51–2.
20 Kemp, *Dylan & Me*, p. 25.
21 Gray, *The Bob Dylan Encyclopedia*, p. 377.
22 Ibid., p. 21. Dylan, Kegan and Rutman's rendition of "Let the Good Times Roll" can be heard on the Bootleg Series vol. XVIII: *Through the Open Window, 1956–1963* (Sony Music, 2025).
23 Anthony Scaduto, *The Dylan Tapes: Friends, Players, & Lovers Talkin' Early Bob Dylan*, ed. Stephanie Trudeau (Minneapolis, MN, 2022), p. 16.
24 Ibid., p. 14.
25 Toby Thompson, *Positively Main Street: Bob Dylan's Minnesota* (1971; repr. Minneapolis, MN, 2008), p. 72.
26 Sounes, *Down the Highway*, p. 41.
27 Dylan, *Chronicles*, pp. 79–80.
28 Ibid., pp. 78–9.
29 Scaduto, *Dylan Tapes*, p. 217.
30 Sounes, *Down the Highway*, p. 37; David Hajdu, *Positively 4th Street: The Lives and Times of Joan Baez, Bob Dylan, Mimi Baez Fariña and Richard Fariña* (New York, 2001), p. 69.
31 Douglas Brinkley, "Inside Bob Dylan's Lost Interviews and Unseen Letters," *Rolling Stone*, www.rollingstone.com, October 21, 2020.
32 Heylin, *Behind the Shades Revisited*, pp. 36, 38.
33 Gray, *The Bob Dylan Encyclopedia*, pp. 598–9.
34 Dylan, *Chronicles*, p. 44.
35 Van Ronk, *Mayor of MacDougal Street*, p. 47.
36 Scaduto, *Dylan Tapes*, pp. 27–8.
37 Ibid., p. 42.
38 Scaduto, *An Intimate Biography*, p. 43.
39 Sounes, *Down the Highway*, p. 61.
40 Dylan, *Chronicles*, p. 245.
41 Ibid., pp. 244, 245.
42 Sounes, *Down the Highway*, p. 65.
43 Dylan, *Chronicles*, pp. 248, 250.
44 Ibid., p. 251.
45 Clinton Heylin, *Bob Dylan: The Recording Sessions* (New York, 1995). The "Karen Wallace Tape," consisting of about sixteen minutes excerpted from the full recording, is widely bootlegged. This version, recorded onto a cassette from external speakers, was made by Ms. Wallace in an effort to sell the original reel-to-reel tape. Dylan was recorded on at least two other occasions in 1960.
46 Sounes, *Down the Highway*, p. 68.

2 1961–62: Becoming

1 Anthony Scaduto, *The Dylan Tapes: Friends, Players, & Lovers Talkin' Early Bob Dylan*, ed. Stephanie Trudeau (Minneapolis, MN, 2022), pp. 49–50.
2 Howard Sounes, *Down the Highway: The Life of Bob Dylan* (New York, 2001), p. 21; Clinton Heylin, *Bob Dylan: Behind the Shades Revisited* (New York, 2001), pp. 70–71. Dylan also performed on an amateur recording while in Madison, which can be heard on the Bootleg Series vol. XVIII: *Through the Open Window* (Sony Music, 2025). As Clinton Heylin notes, it contradicts Jennifer Warren's assessment of Dylan's abilities and others who found his style unremarkable at this stage of his development (Heylin, *The Double Life of Bob Dylan*, vol. I: *1941–1966: A Restless, Hungry Feeling* (New York, 2021), p. 74).
3 Heylin, *Behind the Shades Revisited*, p. 58.
4 Bob Dylan, *Chronicles, Volume One* (New York, 2004), p. 9.
5 Heylin, *Behind the Shades Revisited*, p. 58.
6 Andrea Cossu, *It Ain't Me, Babe: Bob Dylan and the Performance of Authenticity* (Boulder, CO, 2012), pp. 8–18.
7 John Hughes, *Invisible Now: Bob Dylan in the 1960s* (London, 2013), p. 25.
8 Ibid., p. 26.
9 Daniel Mark Epstein, *The Ballad of Bob Dylan: A Portrait* (New York, 2011), p. 92.
10 Sounes, *Down the Highway*, pp. 76–7.
11 Scaduto, *Dylan Tapes*, p. 59.
12 Ibid., p. 122; Epstein, *Ballad of Bob Dylan*, pp. 71–4.
13 Scaduto, *Dylan Tapes*, p. 117.
14 Greil Marcus, *Folk Music: A Bob Dylan Biography in Seven Songs* (New Haven, CT, 2022), p. 184.
15 Dave Van Ronk with Elijah Wald, *The Mayor of MacDougal Street: A Memoir* (Cambridge, MA, 2005), pp. 155–6.
16 Dylan, *Chronicles*, p. 16.
17 Ibid., p. 15.
18 Ibid., p. 261.
19 Van Ronk, *Mayor of MacDougall Street*, p. 164.
20 Anthony Scaduto, *Bob Dylan: An Intimate Biography* (New York, 1971), p. 64.
21 Heylin, *Double Life of Bob Dylan*, vol. I, p. 26.
22 Ibid., p. 40.
23 David Hajdu, *Positively 4th Street: The Lives and Times of Joan Baez, Bob Dylan, Mimi Baez Fariña and Richard Fariña* (New York, 2001), p. 75.
24 Van Ronk, *Mayor of MacDougall Street*, p. 162.
25 Scaduto, *Dylan Tapes*, p. 311.
26 Suze Rotolo, *A Freewheelin' Time: A Memoir of Greenwich Village in the Sixties* (New York, 2008), p. 91.
27 Dylan, *Chronicles*, p. 71.

28 Scaduto, *Dylan Tapes*, pp. 296–7.
29 Rotolo, *A Freewheelin' Time*, p. 92.
30 Dylan, *Chronicles*, p. 265.
31 Heylin, *Double Life of Bob Dylan*, vol. I, p. 129.
32 Dylan, *Chronicles*, p. 269.
33 Heylin, *Double Life of Bob Dylan*, vol. I, p. 86.
34 Robert Shelton, "20-Year-Old Singer Is Bright New Face at Gerde's Club," *New York Times*, www.nytimes.com, September 29, 1961.
35 Heylin, *Behind the Shades Revisited*, pp. 76–7.
36 Paul Williams, *Bob Dylan, Performing Artist: The Early Years, 1960–1973* (Novato, CA, and Lancaster, PA, 1990), p. 37.
37 Marcus, *Folk Music*, pp. 34–5; interview from *No Direction Home*, dir. Martin Scorsese (2005; Capitol Home Video, 2016).
38 Heylin, *Double Life of Bob Dylan*, vol. I, p. 86.
39 Rotolo, *A Freewheelin' Time*, p. 97.
40 Marcus, *Folk Music*, p. 42.
41 Heylin, *Behind the Shades Revisited*, p. 94. See also Michael Gray, *The Bob Dylan Encyclopedia* (New York, 2008), p. 62.
42 Bob Dylan, "MusiCares Person of the Year Speech," *Los Angeles Times*, www.latimes.com, February 7, 2015.
43 Marcus, *Folk Music*, p. 52.
44 Dylan, *Chronicles*, p. 4.
45 Hajdu, *Positively 4th Street*, p. 95.
46 Scaduto, *Dylan Tapes*, p. 102.
47 Van Ronk, *Mayor of MacDougal Street*, p. 167.
48 Sounes, *Down the Highway*, p. 103.
49 Rotolo, *A Freewheelin' Time*, p. 295.
50 Colin Escott, "The Leeds and Witmark Demos," the text of the booklet for the Bootleg Series vol. IX: *The Witmark Demos, 1962–1964* (Sony Music, 2010); Heylin, *Behind the Shades Revisited*, p. 95.
51 Joan Baez, *And A Voice to Sing With: A Memoir* (New York, 1987), pp. 83–4.
52 "Folk Singing: Sibyl with Guitar," *Time*, www.time.com/archive, November 23, 1962.
53 Jonathan Cott, ed., *Bob Dylan: The Essential Interviews* (New York, 2006), p. 7.

3 1962–63: Awakening

1 Bob Dylan, *Chronicles, Volume One* (New York, 2004), pp. 283–4.
2 Suze Rotolo, *A Freewheelin' Time: A Memoir of Greenwich Village in the Sixties* (New York, 2008), p. 184.
3 Clinton Heylin, *Bob Dylan: Behind the Shades Revisited* (New York, 2001), p. 100.
4 Tudor Jones, *Bob Dylan and the British Sixties: A Cultural History* (Oxford, 2019), p. 15.
5 Ibid., p. 16.
6 Ibid., pp. 12–15.
7 Heylin, *Behind the Shades Revisited*, pp. 108–10.

8 See David Hajdu's *Positively 4th Street: The Lives and Times of Joan Baez, Bob Dylan, Mimi Baez Fariña and Richard Fariña* (New York, 2001), especially pp. 187–91.
9 Rotolo, *A Freewheelin' Time*, pp. 197, 199.
10 Columbia had already pressed a small run of *The Freewheelin'* with the original track listing, which was reissued on vinyl by Columbia/Legacy for Record Store Day/Black Friday in 2025. See Clinton Heylin, *Bob Dylan: The Recording Sessions, 1960–1994* (New York, 1995), p. 18; and Clinton Heylin, *The Double Life of Bob Dylan*, vol. I: *1941–1966: A Restless, Hungry Feeling* (New York, 2021), pp. 145–8, 177–9, 197–8.
11 Rotolo, *A Freewheelin' Time*, p. 217.
12 Paul Williams, *Bob Dylan, Performing Artist: The Early Years, 1960–1973* (Lancaster, PA, 1991), p. 73.
13 Howard Sounes, *Down the Highway: The Life of Bob Dylan* (New York, 2001), p. 131; Heylin, *The Double Life of Bob Dylan*, vol. I, pp. 205–7.
14 Edwin Miller, "Bob Dylan," *Seventeen*, September 1962, p. 117.
15 Hajdu, *Positively 4th Street*, pp. 145–8.
16 Ibid., p. 166.
17 Ibid., p. 158.
18 Bob Dylan, "For Dave Glover," 1963, retrieved from www.tumblr.com/seanhowe, accessed June 1, 2023.
19 Mike Marqusee, *Wicked Messenger: Bob Dylan and the 1960s* (New York, 2005), p. 81.
20 See Will Kaufman, "The Civil Rights Movement," in *The World of Bob Dylan*, ed. Sean Latham (Cambridge, 2021), pp. 239–50, and specifically his discussion of "Only a Pawn," p. 246.
21 Heylin, *Behind the Shades Revisited*, p. 125.
22 Hajdu, *Positively 4th Street*, p. 183.
23 Rotolo, *A Freewheelin' Time*, pp. 255–7.
24 Ian Nagoski, "'To Show that All's Equal': The Devoted Life and Lonesome Death of Hattie Carroll," *Folklife Magazine*, https://folklife.si.edu, February 9, 2023.
25 See Marqusee, *Wicked Messenger*, pp. 86–9.
26 Heylin, *Bob Dylan: The Recording Sessions*, p. 26; Cameron Crowe, Liner Notes, *Biograph* (Columbia Records, 1985).
27 "'I Am My Words,'" *Newsweek*, www.newsweek.com, November 4, 1963.
28 Robert Shelton, *No Direction Home: The Life and Music of Bob Dylan* (New York, 1986), p. 193.
29 Heylin, *Behind the Shades Revisited*, p. 143.
30 Rotolo, *A Freewheelin' Time*, p. 261.
31 Anthony Scaduto, *Bob Dylan: An Intimate Biography* (New York, 1971), p. 160.
32 Ibid., p. 160. On Dylan's verse response to Kennedy's assassination, see Heylin, *The Double Life of Bob Dylan*, vol. I, p. 234.
33 Marqusee, *Wicked Messenger*, p. 94.
34 Shelton, pp. 200–201.
35 Ibid., pp. 201–2.

4 1964: Transformation

1 "A Letter from Bob Dylan," *Broadside*, 38, https://singout.org/broadside, January 20, 1964.
2 Suze Rotolo, *A Freewheelin' Time: A Memoir of Greenwich Village in the Sixties* (New York, 2008), p. 285.
3 Anthony Scaduto, *Bob Dylan: An Intimate Biography* (New York, 1971), p. 166.
4 Howard Sounes, *Down the Highway: The Life of Bob Dylan* (New York, 2001), p. 146.
5 Victor Maymudes and Jacob Maymudes, *Another Side of Bob Dylan* (New York, 2014), pp. 74–5; Robert Shelton, *No Direction Home: The Life and Music of Bob Dylan* (New York, 1986), pp. 242–3; Clinton Heylin, *The Double Life of Bob Dylan*, vol. I: *1941–1966: A Restless, Hungry Feeling* (New York, 2021), p. 245.
6 Shelton, *No Direction Home*, pp. 244–7; Maymudes, *Another Side of Bob Dylan*, pp. 77–9.
7 Maymudes, *Another Side of Bob Dylan*, p. 77.
8 Sounes, *Down the Highway*, p. 152. See also Heylin, *The Double Life of Bob Dylan*, vol. I, p. 249.
9 Bob Dylan, *Chronicles, Volume One* (New York, 2004), p. 48.
10 "A Letter from Johnny Cash," *Broadside*, 41, https://singout.org/broadside, March 1964.
11 Johnny Cash to Bob Dylan, personal correspondence, March 1964. Bob Dylan Archive, Box 1, added to collection 2017.
12 Sean Wilentz, *Bob Dylan in America* (New York, 2010), p. 69.
13 Rotolo, *A Freewheelin' Time*, p. 274.
14 Ibid., pp. 276–7.
15 Shelton, *No Direction Home*, p. 255.
16 Maymudes, *Another Side of Bob Dylan*, p. 90.
17 Nat Hentoff, "The Crackin', Shakin', Breakin' Sounds," *New Yorker* (October 24, 1964), in Jonathan Cott, ed., *Bob Dylan: The Essential Interviews* (New York, 2006), p. 16.
18 Paul Williams, *Bob Dylan, Performing Artist: The Early Years, 1960–1973* (Lancaster, PA, 1991), p. 110.
19 Mike Marqusee, *Wicked Messenger: Bob Dylan and the 1960s* (New York, 2005), p. 111.
20 Ibid., p. 100.
21 Sleeve notes to *Biograph*; Michael Gray, *The Bob Dylan Encyclopedia* (New York, 2008), p. 401; Rotolo, p. 127; Heylin, *The Double Life of Bob Dylan*, vol. I, p. 253; "Julien's Auctions Celebrates Bob Dylan, Rock Journalist Al Aronowitz with Record-Breaking Sale," www.juliensauctions.com, January 25, 2025.
22 Shelton, *No Direction Home*, pp. 260–61.
23 *The Other Side of the Mirror*, dir. Murray Lerner (Sony, 2007).
24 Irwin Silber, "An Open Letter to Bob Dylan," *Sing Out!*, November 1964, available at www.edlis.org, accessed July 3, 2023.

25 Dave Van Ronk with Elijah Wald, *The Mayor of MacDougal Street: A Memoir* (Cambridge, MA, 2005), p. 217.
26 Heylin, *The Double Life of Bob Dylan*, vol. I, p. 265.
27 Sounes, *Down the Highway*, p. 162.
28 Maymudes, *Another Side of Bob Dylan*, p. 108.
29 Wilentz, *Bob Dylan in America*, p. 96.
30 John Rothchild, "A Discordant Dylan: 'I Don't Want to Know Anything,'" *Yale Daily News* (November 17, 1964), p. 1.
31 Daniel Kramer, *Bob Dylan: A Year and a Day* (Cologne, 2018), pp. 10, 13, 66.

5 1965: Electricity

1 Bob Dylan, *Writings and Drawings by Bob Dylan* (New York, 1973), pp. 118–19.
2 Clinton Heylin, *The Double Life of Bob Dylan*, vol. I: *1941–1966: A Restless, Hungry Feeling* (New York, 2021), p. 299.
3 Elijah Wald, *Dylan Goes Electric! Newport, Seeger, Dylan, and the Night that Split the Sixties* (New York, 2015), pp. 187, 197.
4 David Hajdu, *Positively 4th Street: The Lives and Times of Joan Baez, Bob Dylan, Mimi Baez Fariña and Richard Fariña* (New York, 2001), p. 233.
5 Daniel Kramer, *Bob Dylan: A Year and a Day* (Cologne, 2018), p. 118.
6 Mark Polizzotti, *Highway 61 Revisited*, 33⅓ Series (New York, 2006), p. 20.
7 Peter Doggett, *There's a Riot Going On: Revolutionaries, Rock Stars, and the Rise and Fall of the '60s* (New York, 2007), p. 26.
8 Hajdu, *Positively 4th Street*, p. 248.
9 Kramer, *A Year and a Day*, p. 132.
10 Hajdu, *Positively 4th Street*, p. 239.
11 Ibid.
12 The apostrophe was deliberately left out of "Don't" in the film's title.
13 Marianne Faithfull with David Dalton, *Faithfull: An Autobiography* (1994; repr. New York, 2000), p. 41.
14 Notably absent from the film are the Beatles, who were among Dylan's hotel visitors in London.
15 Hajdu, *Positively 4th Street*, pp. 251–2.
16 Ibid., p. 253.
17 See Heylin, *The Double Life of Bob Dylan*, vol. I, pp. 312–38.
18 Wald, *Dylan Goes Electric!*, pp. 187–8.
19 Television Press Conference, KQED San Francisco, in *Bob Dylan: The Essential Interviews*, ed. Jonathan Cott (New York, 2017), p. 67.
20 Wald, *Dylan Goes Electric!*, p. 181.
21 Polizzotti, *Highway 61 Revisited*, p. 32.
22 "Feb 20, 1966—Bob Dylan: Martin Bronstein Interview, Montreal (Audio)," Born to Listen blog, https://alldylan.com, accessed August 20, 2023.
23 Polizzotti, *Highway 61 Revisited*, quoting a 1966 *Saturday Evening Post* article by Jules Siegel, p. 33.

24 *No Direction Home: Bob Dylan*, dir. Martin Scorsese (2005; Capitol Home Video, 2016).
25 Shaun Considine, "The Hit We Almost Missed," *New York Times*, www.nytimes.com, December 3, 2004.
26 After "Maggie's Farm" Kooper replaced Arnold on bass, and Barry Goldberg took over on organ for the second and third songs.
27 Wald, *Dylan Goes Electric!*, p. 256.
28 Ibid., p. 259.
29 Ibid.
30 Douglas Brinkley, "Inside Bob Dylan's Lost Interviews and Unseen Letters," *Rolling Stone*, www.rollingstone.com, October 21, 2020.
31 Wald, *Dylan Goes Electric!*, p. 283.
32 Interview with Jann Wenner in *Rolling Stone*, November 29, 1969, in Cott, ed., *Bob Dylan: The Essential Interviews*, p. 151.
33 Polizzotti, *Highway 61 Revisited*, p. 74.
34 Bob Dylan Archive, Series 1, Subseries 1 (2), Box 34, Folder 05.
35 Polizzotti, *Highway 61 Revisited*, pp. 134–5.
36 Faithfull, *Faithfull: An Autobiography*, p. 40.
37 Robbie Robertson, *Testimony* (New York, 2016), p. 171.
38 Ibid.
39 Ibid., p. 173.
40 Joe Jackson, "On This Day in 1971: Joni Mitchell Releases Blue," *Hot Press*, www.hotpress.com, June 22, 2020.
41 Anthony Scaduto, *The Dylan Tapes: Friends, Players, & Lovers Talkin' Early Bob Dylan*, ed. Stephanie Trudeau (Minneapolis, MN, 2022), p. 324.

6 1965–66: Acceleration

1 Andy Gill, *Bob Dylan: The Stories Behind the Songs, 1962–1969* (London, 2011), p. 145.
2 Howard Sounes, *Down the Highway: The Life of Bob Dylan* (New York, 2001), p. 195.
3 Ibid., pp. 194–7.
4 Jonathan Cott, ed., *Bob Dylan: The Essential Interviews* (New York, 2006), pp. 65–86. The quotations are not consecutive questions; they are excerpted from the press conference transcript.
5 Ibid., pp. 104–6. See Clinton Heylin, *Behind the Shades Revisited* (New York, 2001), pp. 229–30, for Hentoff's account of the "interview."
6 Sounes, *Down the Highway*, p. 193; Cott, ed., *The Essential Interviews*, p. 62.
7 Heylin, *Behind the Shades Revisited*, p. 236.
8 Sean Wilentz, *Bob Dylan in America* (New York, 2010), p. 112.
9 Ibid., p. 116; Daryl Sanders, *That Thin, Wild Mercury Sound: Dylan, Nashville, and the Making of "Blonde on Blonde"* (Chicago, IL, 2018), p. 76.
10 Cott, ed., *The Essential Interviews*, p. 223.
11 Sanders, *Mercury*, pp. 116–17.
12 Heylin, *Behind the Shades Revisited*, p. 241.

13 Gill, *Stories Behind the Songs*, p. 137.
14 Ibid.; Sounes, *Down the Highway*, pp. 203–4; Sanders, *Mercury*, pp. 158–64. Sounes quotes Wayne Moss and Henry Strzelecki describing "Leprechaun cocktails" as well as marijuana. Wilentz casts doubt on their accounts, citing counter-testimony from Charlie McCoy and Al Kooper. In any event the musicians must not have gotten terribly wasted, since "Rainy Day Women #12 & 35" was only the first tune to be recorded in a session that would also yield master takes of "Obviously 5 Believers" and "I Want You."
15 Quoted in Sanders, *Mercury*, pp. 95–8.
16 Gill, *Stories Behind the Songs*, pp. 146–8; Sanders, *Mercury*, pp. 51–2, 153; Michael Gray, *The Bob Dylan Encyclopedia* (New York, 2006), p. 613.
17 Paul Williams, *Bob Dylan, Performing Artist: The Early Years, 1960–1973* (Lancaster, PA, 1991), pp. 190–91.
18 Gill, *Stories Behind the Songs*, p. 139.
19 The Rolling Stones paid homage to this line by draping jewels and binoculars on the donkey who adorns the cover of their 1970 live album *Get Yer Ya-Ya's Out*.
20 Gill, *Stories Behind the Songs*, p. 140.
21 Greil Marcus, *Bob Dylan by Greil Marcus: Writings 1968–2010* (New York, 2010), p. 377.
22 Williams, *Bob Dylan, Performing Artist*, p. 188; Robert Shelton, *No Direction Home: The Life and Music of Bob Dylan* (New York, 1986), p. 325.
23 Christopher Ricks, *Dylan's Vision of Sin* (New York and London, 2003), pp. 97–108.
24 Sanders, *Mercury*, p. 177.
25 Suze Rotolo, *A Freewheelin' Time: A Memoir of Greenwich Village in the Sixties* (New York, 2008), pp. 233–4; Sanders, *Mercury*, p. 179.
26 Williams, *Bob Dylan, Performing Artist*, p. 206.
27 Quoted in Clinton Heylin, *The Double Life of Bob Dylan*, vol. I: *1941–1966: A Restless, Hungry Feeling* (New York, 2021), p. 436.
28 C. P. Lee, *Like the Night: Bob Dylan and the Road to the Manchester Free Trade Hall* (London, 1998), p. 130.
29 Ibid., p. 100.
30 Sounes, *Down the Highway*, p. 213; Lee, *Like the Night*, p. 152.
31 Video of this moment is featured in Martin Scorsese, dir., *No Direction Home: Bob Dylan* (2005; Capitol Home Video, 2016).
32 Heylin, *The Double Life of Bob Dylan*, vol. I, p. 446.
33 Lee, *Like the Night*, p. 116, quoting from an article in *Melody Maker*. See also Ray Padgett, "I Wanna Get Out of Here as Fast as You Wanna Get Out of Here," *Flagging Down the Double E's*, www.flaggingdown.com, May 20, 2020.
34 Heylin, *The Double Life of Bob Dylan*, vol. I, pp. 442–3; Sounes, *Down the Highway*, p. 213. Heylin identifies the shouter of "Judas" and the man on camera as Keith Butler. Sounes also identifies Keith Butler as the "Judas" heckler.
35 Jann Wenner, "Lennon Remembers, Part 2," *Rolling Stone*, www.rollingstone.com, February 4, 1971.

36 Heylin, *The Double Life of Bob Dylan*, vol. I, pp. 428, 432–3.
37 Williams, *Bob Dylan, Performing Artist*, p. 171. For a more appreciative description of *Tarantula*, see Amanda Petrusich, "Reflections on *Tarantula*," in *Bob Dylan: Mixing Up the Medicine*, ed. Mark Davidson and Parker Fishel (New York, 2023), pp. 180–81.
38 Williams, *Bob Dylan, Performing Artist*, p. 215; Shelton, *No Direction Home*, p. 374; Davidson and Fishel, eds, *Mixing Up the Medicine*, p. 195.
39 Shelton, *No Direction Home*, p. 374.
40 Cott, ed., *The Essential Interviews*, pp. 387–8; Sounes, *Down the Highway*, pp. 217–19. For helpful overviews of conflicting accounts, see Sid Griffin, *Million Dollar Bash: Bob Dylan, the Band, and the Basement Tapes* (London, 2014), pp. 33–45; and Fred Bals, "Crawling from the Wreckage: Bob Dylan and His Motorpsycho Nitemare," *Medium*, https://fredbals.medium.com, January 26, 2019.
41 Shelton, *No Direction Home*, p. 375.
42 Bob Dylan, *Chronicles, Volume One* (New York, 2004), p. 114.

7 1967–68: Withdrawal

1 Devon Powers, *Writing the Record: The Village Voice and the Birth of Rock Criticism* (Amherst, MA, 2013), p. 14.
2 Ibid., pp. 14–17.
3 Daniel Mark Epstein, *The Ballad of Bob Dylan: A Portrait* (New York, 2011), p. 216.
4 Clinton Heylin, *Behind the Shades Revisited* (New York, 2001), p. 285.
5 Sid Griffin, *Million Dollar Bash: Bob Dylan, The Band and the Basement Tapes* (London, 2014), p. 48.
6 Bob Dylan, *Chronicles, Volume One* (New York, 2004), pp. 114–15.
7 Michael Iachetta, "Scarred Bob Dylan Is Comin' Back," *New York Daily News* (May 8, 1967), p. 3.
8 Heylin, *Behind the Shades Revisited*, pp. 282–3.
9 Griffin, *Million Dollar Bash*, p. 83.
10 Jann Wenner, interview for *Rolling Stone*, November 29, 1969, in Jonathan Cott, ed., *Bob Dylan: The Essential Interviews* (New York, 2017), p. 161.
11 Griffin, *Million Dollar Bash*, p. 128.
12 Ibid., p. 121.
13 Greil Marcus, *The Old, Weird America: The World of Bob Dylan's Basement Tapes* (1997; repr. New York, 2011), p. 79.
14 Paul Williams, *Bob Dylan, Performing Artist: The Early Years, 1960–1973* (Lancaster, PA, 1991), p. 225.
15 Ibid., p. 235; Griffin, *Million Dollar Bash*, pp. 169–74.
16 Oliver Trager, *Keys to the Rain: The Definitive Bob Dylan Encyclopedia* (New York, 2004), pp. 505–6; Robbie Robertson, *Testimony* (New York, 2016), p. 275.
17 Cameron Crowe, inner sleeve notes, *Biograph* (Columbia Records, 1985).
18 Andrew McCarron, *Light Come Shining: The Transformations of Bob Dylan* (New York, 2017), p. 65.

19 Mike Marqusee, *Wicked Messenger: Bob Dylan and the 1960s* (New York, 2005), p. 238; McCarron, *Light Come Shining*, p. 240.
20 For a full list of Basement Tapes cover versions, see Griffin, *Million Dollar Bash*, pp. 304–16.
21 Clinton Heylin, *Bootleg! The Rise & Fall of the Secret Recording Industry* (London, 2003), pp. 32–54.
22 Williams, *Bob Dylan, Performing Artist*, p. 222.
23 Rob Bowman, Liner Notes, *The Band: A Musical History* (Capitol Records, 2005), p. 27.
24 Levon Helm and Stephen Davis, *This Wheel's on Fire: Levon Helm and the Story of the Band* (Chicago, IL, 2000), p. 156; Bowman, Liner Notes, p. 27.
25 Dylan, *Chronicles*, p. 117.
26 Griffin, *Million Dollar Bash*, p. 131.
27 Ibid., p. 283.
28 Anthony Scaduto, *The Dylan Tapes*, ed. by Stephanie Trudeau (Minneapolis, MN, 2022), p. 395.
29 Robertson, *Testimony*, p. 295.
30 Richard Goldstein, "Dylan: Nothing Is Revealed," *Village Voice*, February 1, 1968, p. 1.
31 Cott, ed., *The Essential Interviews*, p. 247.
32 Williams, *Bob Dylan: Performing Artist*, p. 247.
33 Helm and Davis, *This Wheel's On Fire*, p. 159; Howard Sounes, *Down the Highway: The Life of Bob Dylan* (New York, 2001), p. 229.
34 Al Aronowitz, "The Woodstock Papers of Al Aronowitz," in Derek Barker, ed., *ISIS: A Bob Dylan Anthology* (London, 2004), pp. 152–3.
35 Hubert Saal, "Dylan Is Back," *Newsweek* (February 26, 1968), pp. 92–3.
36 Cott, *The Essential Interviews*, p. 131.
37 Ibid.
38 Dylan, *Chronicles*, p. 108.
39 Sounes, *Down the Highway*, p. 235.

8 1969–71: Reinvention

1 Bob Dylan Archive, Series IV: Notebooks, Box 01, Folder 09.
2 Clinton Heylin, *Bob Dylan: Behind the Shades Revisited* (London, 2001), p. 295.
3 Douglas Brinkley, "Inside Bob Dylan's Lost Interviews and Unseen Letters," *Rolling Stone*, www.rollingstone.com, October 21, 2021; Clinton Heylin, *Bob Dylan: The Recording Sessions, 1960–1994* (New York, 1995), p. 74; Howard Sounes, *Down the Highway: The Life of Bob Dylan* (New York, 2001), p. 237. Brinkley excerpts an unpublished interview with Tony Glover, March 18, 1971. A transcript of the interview was auctioned in 2019. "Lay Lady Lay" was also supposedly the song Dylan intended to contribute to the film *Midnight Cowboy* but was late in submitting it.
4 Mark Davidson and Parker Fishel, *Bob Dylan: Mixing Up the Medicine* (New York, 2023), pp. 225–7.
5 Heylin, *Behind the Shades Revisited*, p. 295.

6 Colin Escott, "The Leeds and Witmark Demos," the text of the booklet for the Bootleg Series vol. IX: *The Witmark Demos, 1962–1964* (Sony Music, 2010), p. 27.
7 Cameron Crowe, inner sleeve notes, *Biograph* (Columbia Records, 1985).
8 Dylan's often-cited claim to have killed Tin Pan Alley comes from an interview with Cameron Crowe for the *Biograph* companion book: "They were good song writers but the world they knew and the world I knew were totally different. Most of all the songs, though, being recorded came from there [the Brill Building, which was the successor to Tin Pan Alley], I guess because most singers didn't write their own. They didn't even think about it. Anyway, Tin Pan Alley is gone. I put an end to it. People can write their own songs now" (p. 11).
9 Robert Shelton, *No Direction Home: The Life and Music of Bob Dylan* (New York, 1986), p. 399.
10 Ibid.
11 Bob Dylan Archive, Series X: Correspondence, Box 37, F11 as reproduced in Davidson and Fishel, *Mixing Up the Medicine*, p. 221.
12 Brinkley, "Inside Bob Dylan's Lost Interviews."
13 Dayton Duncan and Ken Burns, *Country Music: An Illustrated History* (New York, 2019), p. 326.
14 Sounes, *Down the Highway*, p. 242.
15 Ibid., p. 247; Heylin, *Behind the Shades Revisited*, pp. 304–5.
16 Sounes, *Down the Highway*, p. 248.
17 Ibid., pp. 250–51.
18 Al Aronowitz, "The Isle of Wight Papers of Al Aronowitz," in Derek Barker, ed., *ISIS: A Bob Dylan Anthology* (London, 2004), p. 166.
19 Shelton, *No Direction Home*, p. 408; Aronowitz, "Isle of Wight Papers," p. 167.
20 Aronowitz, "Isle of Wight Papers," pp. 169–73.
21 Shelton, *No Direction Home*, p. 408.
22 Interview with Kurt Loder, in Jonathan Cott, ed., *The Essential Interviews* (New York, 2006), p. 320.
23 Shelton, *No Direction Home*, pp. 410–12, 420–21; Heylin, *Behind the Shades Revisited*, pp. 325–6; David Kinney, *The Dylanologists: Adventures in the Land of Bob* (New York, 2014), pp. 58–61.
24 Greil Marcus, *Bob Dylan by Greil Marcus: Writings 1968–2010* (New York, 2010), pp. 12, 20.
25 Shelton, *No Direction Home*, p. 419.
26 Interview with Kurt Loder, in Cott, ed., *The Essential Interviews*, p. 320.
27 Marcus, *Bob Dylan by Greil Marcus*, p. 10.
28 Sounes, *Down the Highway*, p. 259.
29 Cott, ed., *The Essential Interviews*, p. 113.
30 Shelton, *No Direction Home*, p. 417.
31 Bob Dylan, *Chronicles, Volume One* (New York, 2004), p. 133.
32 Ibid., p. 125.
33 Shelton, *No Direction Home*, p. 419.
34 Clinton Heylin, *A Life in Stolen Moments: Bob Dylan, Day by Day, 1941–1995* (London, 1996), pp. 125–33.

35 Robert Christgau, "The Answer, My Friends, Is Still Blowin' in the Wind," *New York Times* (June 27, 1971), Section BR, p. 3.
36 Heylin, *Bob Dylan: The Recording Sessions*, p. 90.
37 The letter is reproduced in Davidson and Fishel, *Mixing Up the Medicine*, p. 236.
38 Sean Wilentz, *Bob Dylan in America* (New York, 2010), p. 79.

9 1972–74: Resurgence

1 Clinton Heylin, *Bob Dylan, A Life in Stolen Moments Day by Day: 1941–1995* (Taunton, MA, 1996).
2 Howard Sounes, *Down the Highway: The Life of Bob Dylan* (New York, 2001), p. 268.
3 Paul Seydor, *The Authentic Death & Contentious Afterlife of Pat Garrett & Billy the Kid: The Untold Story of Peckinpah's Last Western Film* (Evanston, IL, 2015), p. 349.
4 Clinton Heylin, *Bob Dylan: Behind the Shades Revisited* (New York, 2001), p. 341.
5 Ibid., p. 346.
6 Sounes, *Down the Highway*, pp. 271–2.
7 Quoted in Cameron Crowe, *Biograph* companion book (Columbia Records, 1985), p. 21.
8 Ibid.
9 Ibid.
10 Sounes, *Down the Highway*, pp. 277–8.
11 Albert Goldman, "What Sings Doesn't Always Read," *New York Times Book Review* (September 30, 1973), p. 42.
12 Clive James, Review of *Writings and Drawings* by Bob Dylan, *The Guardian*, www.theguardian.com, July 26, 1973.
13 Ronald Brownstein, *Rock Me on the Water: 1974, The Year Los Angeles Transformed Movies, Music, Television, and Politics* (New York, 2021), p. 118; Heylin, *Behind the Shades Revisited*, pp. 352–3.
14 Jackson Browne grew up in California but had been based in New York in the late 1960s.
15 Levon Helm and Stephen Davis, *This Wheel's on Fire: Levon Helm and the Story of the Band* (Chicago, IL, 2000), p. 238.
16 Mark Davidson and Parker Fishel, *Bob Dylan: Mixing Up the Medicine* (New York, 2023), p. 283.
17 Bob Dylan Archive, Series 1, Subseries 1 (8): 1974, Box 89, Folder 4.
18 Heylin, *Behind the Shades Revisited*, p. 356: Robbie Robertson, *Testimony* (New York, 2016), p. 426. Heylin reports that the tape box for the Planet Waves masters listed the song as "Dirge for Martha," which is also the title Robbie Robertson uses when he refers to it.
19 Heylin, *Bob Dylan: The Recording Sessions, 1960–1994* (New York, 1995), p. 98.
20 Davidson and Fishel, *Mixing Up the Medicine*, pp. 280–81; Mary Wharton, dir., *Jimmy Carter: Rock and Roll President* (Greenwich Entertainment, 2020).

21 Helm and Davis, *This Wheel's On Fire*, p. 242.
22 Daniel Mark Epstein, *The Ballad of Bob Dylan: A Portrait* (New York, 2011), p. 191; Paul Williams, *Bob Dylan: Performing Artist: 1974–1986, The Middle Years* (1992; London, 2004), p. 7.
23 Heylin, *Behind the Shades Revisited*, p. 361.
24 Helm and Davis, *This Wheel's On Fire*, pp. 241–2.
25 Larry "Ratso" Sloman, *On the Road with Bob Dylan* (1978; London, 2002), p. 451; Crowe, *Biograph* companion book, p. 22.
26 Sloman, *On the Road*, p. 452.
27 Heylin, *Behind the Shades Revisited*, p. 378; Clinton Heylin, *The Double Life of Bob Dylan*, vol. II: *1966–2021: Far Away From Myself* (London, 2023), p. 204.
28 Pete Oppel, "Enter the 'Tambourine Man'," *Dallas Morning News* (November 22, 1978), p. 19A.
29 Ibid.
30 Quoted in Andy Gill and Kevin Odegard, *A Simple Twist of Fate: Bob Dylan and the Making of "Blood on the Tracks"* (Cambridge, MA, 2004), p. 38.
31 Ibid., p. 39.
32 See Sam Sussman, "The Silent Type: On (Possibly) Being Bob Dylan's Son," *Harper's* (May 2021), pp. 43–7. Sussman's memoir is primarily a tribute to his mother, who had a relationship with Dylan in 1974. Sussman does not claim to be Dylan's son but speculates on the possibility. In 2025 he published an autobiographical novel, *Boy from the North Country*, that further develops this scenario. Ellen Bernstein's affair with Dylan is well established; see for instance Heylin, *Behind the Shades Revisited*, pp. 371–81.
33 A facsimile of the red notebook is included in the companion book *Bob Dylan: Stories in the Press (Photographs, Writings and Memorabilia)*, pp. 39–65, part of the Bootleg Series vol. XIV: *More Blood, More Tracks* (Sony Music, 2018).
34 Sloman, *On the Road*, p. 296.
35 "Mary Travers and Friend," KNX-FM, www.youtube.com, April 20, 1975.
36 The New York sessions can be heard on the Bootleg Series vol. XIV: *More Blood, More Tracks*, where they span five-and-a-half discs, supplemented by the five tracks re-recorded in Minneapolis.
37 Gill and Odegard, *A Simple Twist of Fate*, p. 64.
38 Ibid., p. 92.
39 Heylin, *Double Life of Bob Dylan*, vol. II, p. 231.
40 See the reproduction of the notebook in *Stories in the Press*, p. 53; "Simple Twist of Fate (June/July 1981)," dylyricus—Bob Dylan Lyric Variations from Original Versions of His Songs, https://dylyricus.com, accessed February 20, 2024.
41 The places referenced in the final verse are all associated with Bernstein, who had lived in Honolulu, was working in San Francisco when she met Dylan, and was born in Ashtabula, Ohio.
42 Sean Wilentz, *Bob Dylan in America* (New York, 2010), p. 139; Gill and Odegard, *Simple Twist of Fate*, p. 155.
43 Reproduced in *Stories in the Press*, p. 102.

10 1975–78: Revelation

1 Craig McGregor, "'Tomorrow Is Another Day': Two Encounters with Bob Dylan," reprinted in *The Mammoth Book of Bob Dylan*, ed. Sean Egan (Philadelphia, PA, and London, 2011), p. 275.
2 Two different Oppenheim paintings are featured on variant back covers of *Blood on the Tracks*.
3 Clinton Heylin, *The Double Life of Bob Dylan*, vol. II: *1966–2021: Far Away From Myself* (London, 2023), p. 235.
4 Ray Padgett, *Pledging My Time: Conversations with Bob Dylan Band Members* (Burlington, VT, 2023), p. 114.
5 Heylin, *Double Life of Bob Dylan*, vol. II, p. 258.
6 Jacques Levy Interview, Prism Films Archive, www.youtube.com, May 2004.
7 Clinton Heylin, *Behind the Shades Revisited* (New York, 2001), p. 404.
8 Philippe Margotin and Jean-Michel Guesdon, *Bob Dylan: All the Songs* (New York, 2015), p. 436.
9 Pete Hamill, "Bright Lives, Big City," *New York Times* (January 2, 2005), Section 4, p. 9.
10 Dave Herman, "Dylan London Interview July 1981" (recorded July 2, 1981), www.youtube.com.
11 Wesley Stace, companion book to Bob Dylan, *The Rolling Thunder Revue* box set (Sony Music, 2018), p. 9.
12 Jacques Levy Interview, Prism Films Archive.
13 Sean Wilentz, *Bob Dylan in America* (New York, 2010), p. 164.
14 Howard Sounes, *Down the Highway: The Life of Bob Dylan* (New York, 2001), p. 290.
15 Larry "Ratso" Sloman, *On the Road with Bob Dylan* (1978; London, 2002), p. 19.
16 Ibid., pp. 136–7; Stace, companion book to *The Rolling Thunder Revue*, p. 15; Davidson and Fishel, *Mixing Up the Medicine*, p. 317.
17 Wilentz, *Bob Dylan in America*, pp. 162–3; Sloman, *On the Road*, pp. 198–9.
18 Stace, companion book to *The Rolling Thunder Revue*, p. 24.
19 Ibid.
20 Clinton Heylin, *Bob Dylan, A Life in Stolen Moments Day by Day: 1941–1995* (Taunton, MA, 1996), pp. 162–3; Stace, companion book to *The Rolling Thunder Revue*, pp. 19–28.
21 Joan Baez, *And a Voice to Sing With* (New York, 1987), p. 239.
22 Heylin, *Double Life of Bob Dylan*, vol. II, p. 298.
23 Sloman, *On the Road*, pp. 394–5. Sloman, who takes credit for setting up the photograph, claimed that they couldn't find actual prison bars at the prison.
24 Chet Flippo, "Hurricane's Night: Dylan, Baez, Others Bring Thunder to the Garden," *Rolling Stone*, www.rollingstone.com, January 15, 1976.
25 Sloman, *On the Road*, pp. 406–8; Flippo, "Hurricane's Night."
26 Lucian Truscott, "When Dylan Practiced Downstairs from My Loft," Lucian Truscott Newsletter, https://luciantruscott.substack.com, May 24, 2021, originally published in the *Village Voice* (2016).

27 Padgett, *Pledging My Time*, p. 45.
28 Sounes, *Down the Highway*, p. 299.
29 Heylin, *A Life in Stolen Moments*, pp. 176–7.
30 Padgett, *Pledging My Time*, p. 160.
31 Heylin, *Double Life of Bob Dylan*, vol. II, p. 278.
32 Heylin, *Behind the Shades Revisited*, p. 447.
33 Sounes, *Down the Highway*, p. 303.
34 Ibid., p. 306.
35 Levon Helm and Stephen Davis, *This Wheel's on Fire: Levon Helm and the Story of the Band* (Chicago, IL, 2000), pp. 258, 266.
36 Ibid., pp. 258–66; see also Louie Kemp, *Dylan & Me: 50 Years of Adventures* (Los Angeles, CA, 2019), pp. 145–7.
37 Sounes, *Down the Highway*, pp. 312–13.
38 Heylin, *Behind the Shades Revisited*, p. 456.
39 Heylin, *Double Life of Bob Dylan*, vol. II, p. 305; Padgett, *Pledging My Time*, p. 161.
40 Greil Marcus, *Bob Dylan by Greil Marcus* (New York, 2010), pp. 90–91.
41 Michael Gray, *The Bob Dylan Encyclopedia* (New York, 2006), p. 654.
42 Michael Gray, *Song and Dance Man III: The Art of Bob Dylan* (London and New York, 2004), p. 190.
43 Sean Egan, "*Hard Rain/Street-Legal*," in *The Mammoth Book of Bob Dylan*, ed. Sean Egan (London, 2011), p. 299.
44 Heylin, *Double Life of Bob Dylan*, vol. II, p. 304.
45 Pete Oppel, "Mixed Reaction Puzzles Dylan," *Dallas Morning News* (November 18, 1978), p. F1.
46 Pete Oppel, "Blocking Out the Past, Looking to the Future," *Dallas Morning News* (November 23, 1978), p. A58.
47 Craig McGregor "'Tomorrow Is Another Day': Two Encounters with Bob Dylan," in *The Mammoth Book of Bob Dylan*, ed. Egan, p. 268.
48 Jonathan Cott, ed., *Bob Dylan: The Essential Interviews* (New York, 2006), p. 248.
49 McGregor, "'Tomorrow Is Another Day,'" p. 277.

11 1978–84: Conversion

1 In 1978 the Who released *Who Are You?*, which combined the energy and aggression that had made them a touchstone for the punks with the bombast, heavy use of synthesizers, and ponderousness that punks rejected. Much of the album is a meditation on the music scene and the situation the band then found themselves in.
2 Andrew McCarron, *Light Come Shining: The Transformations of Bob Dylan* (New York, 2017), p. 79.
3 Robert Hilburn, "Dylan: 'I Learned that Jesus Is Real and I Wanted That,'" *Los Angeles Times* (1980), repr. in Benjamin Hedin, ed., *Studio A: The Bob Dylan Reader* (New York and London, 2004), p. 148; Clinton Heylin, *Trouble in Mind: Bob Dylan's Gospel Years, What Really Happened* (New York, 2017), p. 16.
4 Hilburn, "I Learned that Jesus Is Real," p. 151.

5 Heylin, *Trouble in Mind*, p. 44.
6 Ibid.
7 Jann S. Wenner, review of *Slow Train Coming*, *Rolling Stone*, www.rollingstone.com, September 20, 1979.
8 Greil Marcus, "Amazing Chutzpah," *New West* (September 24, 1979), repr. in Greil Marcus, *Bob Dylan by Greil Marcus* (New York, 2010), p. 95.
9 Ray Padgett, *Pledging My Time: Conversations with Bob Dylan Band Members* (Burlington, VT, 2023), p. 93.
10 Heylin, *Trouble in Mind*, pp. 76, 78–9.
11 Ibid., p. 85.
12 Ibid., p. 103; Clinton Heylin, ed., *Saved!: The Gospel Speeches of Bob Dylan* (Madras and New York, 1990), p. 103.
13 Heylin, *Trouble in Mind*, p. 153.
14 Ibid., p. 128.
15 David Browne, "Clydie King, Unsung Backup Singer for Ray Charles and Bob Dylan, Dead at 75," *Rolling Stone*, www.rollingstone.com, January 10, 2019.
16 Hilburn, "I Learned that Jesus Is Real," p. 153.
17 Paul Williams, *Bob Dylan, Performing Artist: The Middle Years, 1974–1986* (1992; London, 2004), p. 185.
18 William Blake, "Auguries of Innocence" [1863], available at Poetry Foundation, www.poetryfoundation.org, accessed October 18, 2024.
19 Williams, *Bob Dylan, Performing Artist, 1974–1986*, p. 188; Cameron Crowe, *Biograph* companion book (Columbia Records, 1985).
20 Williams, *Bob Dylan, Performing Artist, 1974–1986*, p. 189.
21 Clinton Heylin, *The Double Life of Bob Dylan*, vol. II: *1966–2021: Far Away From Myself* (London, 2023), p. 400.
22 Heylin, *Double Life of Bob Dylan*, vol. II, p. 405.
23 Lester Bangs, "Love or Confusion?" in *Studio A: The Bob Dylan Reader*, ed. Benjamin Hedin (New York and London, 2004), p. 157.
24 Clinton Heylin, *Bob Dylan, A Life in Stolen Moments Day by Day: 1941–1995* (Taunton, MA, 1996), p. 236.
25 Howard Sounes, *Down the Highway: The Life of Bob Dylan* (New York, 2001), p. 351.
26 Terry Gans, *Surviving in a Ruthless World: Bob Dylan's Voyage to Infidels* (Falmouth, 2020), pp. 19–20.
27 Heylin, *A Life in Stolen Moments*, p. 239.
28 Bob Dylan, *Chronicles, Volume One* (New York, 2004), p. 288.
29 Gans, *Surviving in a Ruthless World*, p. 49.
30 Ibid., p. 138.
31 Ibid., p. 137.
32 Robert Hayden, *Collected Poems* (New York and London, 2013), p. 32.
33 Sean Wilentz, *Bob Dylan in America* (New York, 2010), pp. 172–6, 188–90; Michael Gray, *Song and Dance Man III: The Art of Bob Dylan* (London and New York, 2004), pp. 517–23.
34 Gray, *Song and Dance Man III*, p. 518.
35 Gans, *Surviving in a Ruthless World*, p. 46.

36 Gray, *Song and Dance Man III*, p. 529.
37 Gans, *Surviving in a Ruthless World*, pp. 232–5.
38 Padgett, *Pledging My Time*, p. 249.
39 Mailgram from David Letterman, Bob Dylan Archive, Gaylord Box 19.

12 1984–92: Restoration

1 *The Greatest Night in Pop*, dir. Bao Nguyen (Netflix, 2024).
2 Howard Sounes, *Down the Highway: The Life of Bob Dylan* (New York, 2001), p. 366.
3 Andrew Muir, *Razor's Edge: Bob Dylan and the Never-Ending Tour* (London, 2001), pp. 14–16.
4 Bob Dylan, *Chronicles, Volume One* (New York, 2004), p. 148.
5 Michael Gray, *Song and Dance Man III: The Art of Bob Dylan* (London and New York, 2004), pp. 552–3, 556; Larry Fyffe, "Movies and the Post Modern Technique: Tight Connection to My Heart," Untold Dylan (blog), http://bob-dylan.org.uk, July 24, 2018; Nathaniel Williams, "Fact Check: Did Dylan Quote Star Trek?" http://nathanielwms.com (blog), October 24, 2021.
6 Clinton Heylin, *The Double Life of Bob Dylan*, vol. II: *1966–2021: Far Away From Myself* (London, 2023), p. 471.
7 "When the Night Comes Falling" provided the album's only other music video, a relatively straightforward black-and-white performance clip directed by Eddie Arno and Markus Innocenti.
8 Heylin, *Double Life of Bob Dylan*, vol. II, p. 466.
9 Damien Love, companion book to the Bootleg Series vol. XVI: *Springtime in New York* (Sony Music, 2021), p. 55. Love interviewed Arthur Baker for the notes.
10 Interview with Mikal Gilmore, in *Bob Dylan: The Essential Interviews*, ed. Jonathan Cott (New York, 2006), p. 362.
11 The Queens of Rhythm line-up for Australia and Japan was Quebec, Marrow, Debra Byrd, and Elisecia Wright. See the website "Maggie's Farm," www.maggiesfarm.eu, accessed August 8, 2024.
12 Ray Padgett, *Pledging My Time: Conversations with Bob Dylan Band Members* (Burlington, VT, 2023), pp. 274, 275.
13 Cott, ed., *The Essential Interviews*, p. 345.
14 Sounes, *Down the Highway*, p. 381.
15 Heylin, *Double Life of Bob Dylan*, vol. II, pp. 459, 476.
16 Sounes, *Down the Highway*, p. 391.
17 Ibid., p. 379.
18 Padgett, *Pledging My Time*, pp. 95–6.
19 Muir, *Razor's Edge*, p. 22.
20 Dylan, *Chronicles, Volume One*, p. 154.
21 Michael Gray, *The Bob Dylan Encyclopedia* (New York, 2006), pp. 174–5.
22 Padgett, *Pledging My Time*, pp. 318–19.
23 Dylan, *Chronicles, Volume One*, p. 179.
24 Ibid., p. 181.

25 Andrew McCarron, *Light Come Shining: The Transformations of Bob Dylan* (New York, 2017), pp. 126–7.
26 Stephen Holden, "Recordings: A 'New Dylan' Crosses Paths with the Old," *New York Times* (October 1, 1989), Section 2, p. 29; Anthony DeCurtis, Review of *Oh Mercy*, *Rolling Stone*, www.rollingstone.com (September 21, 1989).
27 Bruce Springsteen, "The Rock and Roll Hall of Fame Speech," in *Studio A: The Bob Dylan Reader*, ed. Benjamin Hedin (New York, 2004), p. 203.
28 Martin Grossman, "Bob Dylan's Grammy Speech 1991," Expecting Rain, www.expectingrain.com, August 10, 1998.
29 In addition to the Bootleg Series Sony has released box sets containing all available live performances from the 1966 tour, the first Rolling Thunder tour and the 1974 tour with the Band.
30 Cott, ed., *The Essential Interviews*, pp. 395, 413.
31 Sounes, *Down the Highway*, pp. 3–8.

13 1993–2006: Renewal

1 Jonathan Cott, ed., *Bob Dylan: The Essential Interviews* (New York, 2017), p. 446.
2 Ibid., p. 416.
3 Howard Sounes, *Down the Highway: The Life of Bob Dylan* (New York, 2001), p. 408.
4 Victor Maymudes and Jacob Maymudes, *Another Side of Bob Dylan* (New York, 2014), pp. 249–50.
5 Sounes, *Down the Highway*, p. 411.
6 Ibid., p. 423.
7 Maymudes, *Another Side*, pp. 268–70; Sounes, *Down the Highway*, pp. 421–3.
8 *The Simpsons* also used the "Steel Wheelchair" joke in a 1995 episode predicting that the Stones would still be touring in 2010.
9 Daniel Lanois, *Soul Mining: A Musical Life* (New York, 2010), p. 150.
10 Ibid., p. 165.
11 Cott, ed., *Bob Dylan: The Essential Interviews*, p. 418.
12 Sounes, *Down the Highway*, p. 420.
13 Note from Frank Sinatra, May 30, 1997, Bob Dylan Archive, Gaylord Box 19.
14 Cott, ed., *Bob Dylan: The Essential Interviews*, p. 441.
15 Ray Padgett, *Pledging My Time: Conversations with Bob Dylan Band Members* (Burlington, VT, 2023), p. 366.
16 Note from Raquel Welch, February 29, 1998, Bob Dylan Archive, Gaylord Box 19.
17 Ann Powers, "Gender and Sexuality: Bob Dylan's Body," in *The World of Bob Dylan*, ed. Sean Latham (Cambridge, 2021), p. 374.
18 Note from Paul Simon, January 2011, Bob Dylan Archive, Gaylord Box 19. The song is titled "Love and Blindness."
19 "Still on the Road: 2001 Australian Tour," About Bob—Olof's Files, http://bobserve.com, accessed October 18, 2024.

20 Greg Tate, "Intelligence Report," in *Studio A: The Bob Dylan Reader* (New York, 2004), p. 277.
21 Sean Wilentz, *Bob Dylan in America* (New York, 2010), p. 269.
22 Tate, "Intelligence Report," p. 275.
23 For a discussion of Dylan's connections to Copland, see Wilentz, *Bob Dylan in America*, pp. 17–46.
24 Dale Cockrell, *Demons of Disorder: Early Blackface Minstrels and Their World* (Cambridge, 1997), p. 122. See also Sean Wilentz's discussion of *Masked and Anonymous* in *Bob Dylan and America*, pp. 288–94.
25 Jon Pareles, "Film: Bob Dylan Plays Bob Dylan, Whoever That Is," *New York Times* (July 27, 2003), Section 2, p. 7.
26 See various articles on Scott Warmuth's blog, Goon Talk, http://swarmuth.blogspot.com. A good place to start is the post listing the correspondences between Jack London's works and *Chronicles*, "Dylan Dossier: The Jack London File," May 9, 2011.
27 Scott Warmuth, "Bob Dylan, the Mermaid, and the Hemingway Code," Goon Talk, http://swarmuth.blogspot.com, August 16, 2012.
28 Scott Warmuth, "Bob Dylan and the Matter of TIME," Goon Talk, http://swarmuth.blogspot.com, May 16, 2011.
29 Motoko Rich, "Who's This Guy Dylan Who's Borrowing Lines from Henry Timrod?" *New York Times*, www.nytimes.com, September 14, 2006.
30 Wilentz, *Bob Dylan in America*, pp. 314–15.
31 For a fuller discussion of these issues in *Modern Times*, see Wilentz, *Bob Dylan in America*, pp. 305–19.
32 Sean O'Hagan, Review of *Modern Times*, *The Guardian*, www.theguardian.com, September 16, 2006.

14 2006–26: Multitude

1 See Kevin Dettmar, "All Along the Ivory Tower," *The Chronicle of Higher Education*, www.chronicle.com, July 11, 2019.
2 Robert Sullivan, "This Is Not a Bob Dylan Movie," *New York Times Magazine*, www.nytimes.com, October 7, 2007.
3 Marisha Pessl, "When I Paint My Masterpiece," *New York Times*, www.nytimes.com, June 1, 2008.
4 Bob Dylan, "The Beaten Path," in *Bob Dylan: Retrospectrum*, ed. Shai Baitel (Milan, 2022), pp. 95–6.
5 Richard Prince, "There Goes My Hero," in *Bob Dylan: Retrospectrum*, ed. Baitel, p. 80.
6 Scott Warmuth, "Bob Dylan's 'The Beaten Path': Selling the Brooklyn Bridge," Goon Talk blog, http://swarmuth.blogspot.com, December 25, 2016.
7 Jonathan Lethem, "The Genius and Modern Times of Bob Dylan," *Rolling Stone*, www.rollingstone.com, September 7, 2006.
8 Ibid.
9 Douglas Brinkley, "Bob Dylan's Late-Era, Old-Style American Individualism," *Rolling Stone*, www.rollingstone.com, May 14, 2009.

10 Ibid.
11 Ibid.
12 Maureen Dowd, "Blowin' in the Idiot Wind," *New York Times*, www.nytimes.com, April 9, 2011.
13 Bob Dylan, "To My Fans and Followers," www.bobdylan.com, May 13, 2011.
14 Mikal Gilmore, "Bob Dylan Unleashed," *Rolling Stone*, www.rollingstone.com, Sept 27, 2012.
15 Ibid.
16 Anna North, "Why Bob Dylan Shouldn't Have Gotten a Nobel," *New York Times*, www.nytimes.com, October 13, 2016.
17 Ben Sisario, Alexandra Alter, and Sewell Chan, "Bob Dylan Wins Nobel Prize, Redefining Boundaries of Literature," *New York Times*, www.nytimes.com, October 13, 2016.
18 Edna Gundersen, "World Exclusive: Bob Dylan—I'll Be at the Nobel Prize Ceremony . . . If I Can," *Daily Telegraph*, www.telegraph.co.uk, October 29, 2016.
19 Bob Dylan, "Banquet Speech," The Nobel Prize, www.nobelprize.org, 2016.
20 Andrea Pitzer, "The Freewheelin' Bob Dylan," *Slate*, https://slate.com, June 13, 2017.
21 Bob Dylan, "Nobel Lecture," The Nobel Prize, www.nobelprize.org, 2016.
22 Bob Dylan, *The Philosophy of Modern Song* (New York, 2022), pp. 224, 240.
23 Ibid., pp. 165, 260.
24 Ibid., p. 92.
25 Clinton Heylin, *The Double Life of Bob Dylan*, vol. II: *1966–2021: Far Away from Myself* (London, 2023), p. 748.

SELECTED BIBLIOGRAPHY

Cott, Jonathan, ed., *Bob Dylan: The Essential Interviews* (New York, 2017)
Davidson, Mark, and Parker Fishel, *Bob Dylan: Mixing Up the Medicine* (New York, 2023)
Dettmar, Kevin J. H., ed., *The Cambridge Companion to Bob Dylan* (Cambridge and New York, 2009)
Dylan, Bob, *Chronicles, Volume One* (New York, 2004)
—, *The Lyrics, 1961–2012* (New York, 2016)
—, *The Philosophy of Modern Song* (New York, 2022)
Epstein, Daniel Mark, *The Ballad of Bob Dylan: A Portrait* (New York, 2011)
Gill, Andy, and Kevin Odegard, *A Simple Twist of Fate: Bob Dylan and the Making of "Blood on the Tracks"* (Cambridge, MA, 2004)
Gray, Michael, *Song and Dance Man III: The Art of Bob Dylan* (London, 2004)
Griffin, Sid, *Million Dollar Bash: Bob Dylan, The Band, and the Basement Tapes* (London, 2014)
Hajdu, David, *Positively 4th Street: The Lives and Times of Joan Baez, Bob Dylan, Mimi Baez Fariña and Richard Fariña* (New York, 2001)
Hedin, Benjamin, ed., *Studio A: The Bob Dylan Reader* (New York, 2004)
Heylin, Clinton, *Bob Dylan: Behind the Shades Revisited* (New York, 2001)
—, *The Double Life of Bob Dylan*, vol. I: *1941–1966: A Restless, Hungry Feeling* (New York, 2021)
—, *The Double Life of Bob Dylan*, vol. II: *1966–2021: Far Away from Myself* (London, 2023)
—, *Trouble in Mind: Bob Dylan's Gospel Years, What Really Happened* (New York, 2017)
Kinney, David, *The Dylanologists: Adventures in the Land of Bob* (New York, 2014)
Latham, Sean, ed., *The World of Bob Dylan* (Cambridge and New York, 2021)
McCarron, Andrew, *Light Come Shining: The Transformations of Bob Dylan* (New York, 2017)
Marcus, Greil, *Folk Music: A Bob Dylan Biography in Seven Songs* (New Haven, CT, and London, 2022)

—, *The Old, Weird America: The World of Bob Dylan's Basement Tapes* (New York, 2011)
Marqusee, Mike, *Wicked Messenger: Bob Dylan and the 1960s* (New York, 2005)
Padgett, Ray, *Pledging My Time: Conversations with Dylan Band Members* (Burlington, VT, 2023)
Rotolo, Suze, *A Freewheelin' Time: A Memoir of Greenwich Village in the Sixties* (New York, 2008)
Scaduto, Anthony, *The Dylan Tapes: Friends, Players, & Lovers Talkin' Early Bob Dylan*, ed. Stephanie Trudeau (Minneapolis, MN, 2022)
Shelton, Robert, *No Direction Home: The Life and Music of Bob Dylan* (New York, 1986)
Sounes, Howard, *Down the Highway: The Life of Bob Dylan* (New York, 2001)
Van Ronk, Dave, with Elijah Wald, *The Mayor of MacDougal Street* (Boston, MA, 2013)
Wald, Elijah, *Dylan Goes Electric!: Newport, Seeger, Dylan, and the Night That Split the Sixties* (New York, 2015)
Wilentz, Sean, *Bob Dylan in America* (New York, 2010)
Williams, Paul, *Bob Dylan, Performing Artist: The Early Years 1960–1973* (London and New York, 1994)
—, *Bob Dylan, Performing Artist: The Middle Years, 1974–1986* (London and New York, 2004)
—, *Bob Dylan, Performing Artist: Mind Out of Time, 1986–1990 and Beyond* (London and New York, 2005)

ACKNOWLEDGMENTS

This book originated with a course I taught at the College of Charleston in 2018 called "Bob Dylan and the American Dream," so my first thanks go to the students in that class who shared their enthusiasm and ideas while patiently helping me get a handle on Dylan's long, complex career. Two other students, Meg Carroll and Brandon Eichelberg, worked with me on independent projects and helped me understand Dylan better.

I received generous support from the College of Charleston—specifically the Department of English, the School of Humanities and Social Sciences, and the Office of Academic Affairs. They made it possible to complete this book.

Mark Davidson and Stephanie Stewart at the Bob Dylan Archive were extremely helpful and patient during and after my research visit to Tulsa. Rowland Scherman, Heinrich Klaffs, and the estates of Douglas Gilbert and Peter Simon generously granted permission to use their photographs, and I'd also like to thank the staff members at the University of Massachusetts-Amherst Special Collections, Grand Valley State University's Lemmen Library & Archives, and the Richland Library (Columbia, SC) for their help with images and permissions.

There are so many Dylan scholars, biographers, and fans whose work I've drawn from and been inspired by that I can't list them all here, but I owe a great debt to the people whose names appear and reappear in the endnotes and whose books have piled up all over my house, as well as the podcasters and bloggers whose wonderful obsession knows no limits. Thanks too to Sean Latham and the staff of the Tulsa Institute for Bob Dylan Studies for organizing the World of Bob Dylan conferences since 2019, which have been an inspiration throughout my work on this project.

I'm grateful to Kirk Curnutt for helping me get this project started and to Vivian Constantinopoulos and Robert Sharman at Reaktion Books for seeing it through. My friends Bill Russell, Tony Varallo, and Ellen Clair Lamb generously commented on and helped edit the manuscript. Other friends and colleagues offered helpful suggestions and lots of moral support, especially Jerry Kennedy, Phil Jos, Joe Kelly, Susan Farrell, Julia Eichelberger, and Phil Nel. Roy Hutchinson was always up for another Dylan concert; he read the manuscript and kept the conversation going.

Finally I want to thank my family—my brothers and sisters for bringing all those early Dylan records back home and getting me hooked at a young age, and my wife Nancy and son Alex for their love and encouragement every step of the way.

PHOTO ACKNOWLEDGMENTS

The author and publishers wish to express their thanks to the sources listed below for illustrative material and/or permission to reproduce it:

Alamy: pp. 23 (Archivio GBB), 125 (Dale Smith), 134 (TT News Agency), 138 (TT News Agency), 143 (TT News Agency), 174 (PA Images), 177 (Mike Walker), 189 (Keystone Press), 266 (John Atashian), 269 (ColourNews); Flickr: p. 262 (photo Heinrich Klaffs, reproduced with permission); Lemmen Library and Archives, Grand Valley State University, Allendale, MI: pp. 92 and 104 (with permission of the Estate of Douglas Gilbert); Library of Congress, Prints and Photographs Division, Washington, DC: p. 29; Scott Peeples: pp. 303, 309; The State Newspaper Photograph Archive, Richland Library, Columbia, SC: p. 235; Topfoto: pp. 140 (Fonds France-Soir/BHVP/Roger-Viollet), 247 (Christian Rose/Roger-Viollet), 281 (Christian Rose/Roger-Viollet); University of Massachusetts Amherst Libraries, Special Collections and University Archives: pp. 63, 67 (with permission of Rowland Scherman), 90, 202 and 220 (with permission of the Estate of Peter Simon).

INDEX

Page numbers in *italics* refer to illustrations